Violence Elsewhere 2

Studies in German Literature, Linguistics, and Culture

Violence Elsewhere 2

Imagining Distant Violence
in Germany since 2001

Edited by
Clare Bielby and Mererid Puw Davies

CAMDEN HOUSE
Rochester, New York

First published 2024 by Camden House

Camden House is an imprint of Boydell & Brewer Inc.
668 Mt. Hope Avenue, Rochester, NY 14620, USA
and of Boydell & Brewer Limited
PO Box 9, Woodbridge, Suffolk IP12 3DF, UK
www.boydellandbrewer.com

ISBN-13: 978-1-64014-137-7

Library of Congress Cataloging-in-Publication Data
CIP data is available from the Library of Congress.

The publisher has no responsibility for the continued existence
or accuracy of URLs for external or third-party internet websites
referred to in this book, and does not guarantee that any content
on such websites is, or will remain, accurate or appropriate

Contents

Illustrations

Acknowledgments

THIS COLLECTED VOLUME of essays is the second of two to emerge from a research project titled "Violence Elsewhere: Imagining Violence outside Germany since 1945," which we co-led from the Centre for Women's Studies (CWS) at the University of York and the School of European Languages, Cultures and Society-Centre for Multidisciplinary Intercultural Inquiry (SELCS-CMII) at University College London (UCL).

Neither the project, nor this volume showcasing some of its work, could have come into being without generous funding from 2018 to 2021 from the Deutscher Akademischer Austauchdienst /German Academic Exchange Service through its "Promoting German Studies" program. We thank the German Academic Exchange Service very warmly, and Katie James, in particular, for her collegial support throughout the project's lifetime.

At the University of York, we wish to acknowledge material and administrative support from CWS, the Department of English and Related Literature, and from the Professional Services teams at the Humanities Research Centre and Research Grants Operations. At UCL, we express our thanks to the Institute for Advanced Studies for hosting and supporting our events, and the Professional Services team at SELCS-CMII for its support.

We are also grateful to our colleagues at York and UCL more broadly for their continued interest in, and support in many practical and moral forms for, the work of the "Violence Elsewhere" project and this publication.

We are indebted to all at Camden House, and most especially Jim Walker, for his wise guidance and editorial counsel throughout the development and publication of this volume. We wish also to acknowledge the anonymous peer reviewers who advised on the manuscript.

Especially warm thanks are due to the Core Group of scholars who animated and sustained "Violence Elsewhere," as well as the publication of this book: Katharina Karcher, Susanne C. Knittel, Birga Meyer, Katherine Stone, and Lizzie Stewart.

In particular, we would like to highlight the many contributions of the project's two coordinators, Francesca Lewis and Kathrin Wunderlich.

They not only furthered its research in key ways through discussions and events but also conceptualized, designed, developed, and maintained its online presence in the form of its website, blog, bibliography, and other resources. We also thank Sarah Colvin for her support early on in the project's development.

In addition, we are grateful to Francesca Lewis for the project artwork from which the design of the cover of this and its companion volume evolved.

We also wish here to thank the authors of the chapters in this volume for their gracious and patient collaboration.

We are pleased to acknowledge kind permission from Suhrkamp Verlag to cite from Durs Grünbein's poems in chapter 5.

Finally, we wish to express our appreciation to the scholars, artists, and activists who participated in the "Violence Elsewhere" project at various times and in many ways: at its events and seminars, in discussions of many kinds beyond them, and in the development of this volume. We are grateful for all their work and ideas, which enriched and deepened it.

Clare Bielby and Mererid Puw Davies
April 2024

Introduction

Clare Bielby and Mererid Puw Davies

THE COVER IMAGE OF THIS BOOK shows a cloudy sky, its heavy, ominous air accentuated by a colored wash.[1] A companion volume, *Violence Elsewhere 1: Imagining Distant Violence in Germany 1945–2001* (2024), likewise a collection by a group of scholars in German, historical, and cultural studies, features the same photograph.[2] This choice of image reflects on some of the complexities of our theme; namely, constructions, in and around German culture, of violence that takes place in distant or imagined times and places.[3] Selecting an image for a book cover is never straightforward. This task comes with particular challenges, however, for a volume on "violence elsewhere": a concept that brings together two notions that are ambiguous, politically fraught, and elude representation in distinctive ways.

How to represent violence, for example, in ways that do not sensationalize, fetishize, or reify the very idea of it? How to depict it at all, even in just some of its multiple paradoxical meanings and dimensions? At one level, violence can be understood in a self-evident sense as a class of physical acts that do bodily harm to other people in immediate ways and that are carried out by an identifiable human actor, or actors, with intention to do that harm.[4] Such an understanding can raise key and familiar

---

1   Thanks to Francesca Lewis, who originated the idea of an ominous sky to visually capture the concept of violence elsewhere.

2   Clare Bielby and Mererid Puw Davies, eds., *Violence Elsewhere 1: Imagining Distant Violence in Germany 1945–2001* (Rochester, NY: Camden House, 2024).

3   Both volumes developed from a research project titled "Violence Elsewhere: Imagining Violence outside Germany since 1945." Based at University College London (UCL) and the University of York and funded by the Deutscher Akademischer Austauschdienst/German Academic Exchange Service, the project ran from 2018 to 2021. For further details, including the project team and events, see the project website, https://sites.google.com/york.ac.uk/violence-elsewhere/home.

4   Johan Galtung's well-known elaboration of "structural violence" provides a helpful overview of what does and does not count as violence in popular perceptions. Johan Galtung, "Violence, Peace, and Peace Research," *Journal of Peace*

questions for representation that remain resonant. Yet at a different level, these books on violence elsewhere at times work toward more expansive interpretations of violence, which may seem to demand different, novel images. In so doing, they draw attention also to less conventional and sometimes more innovative ways of reflecting on or engaging with violence in an array of aesthetic and discursive modes.

As for the "elsewhere": How to represent a concept whose "invocation," as scholar Lizzie Stewart argues in this volume, "functions to make a 'somewhere' 'nowhere'—unknown, unknowable"? In other words, Stewart poses the conundrum of how to represent elsewhere in ways that do not "other" or, sometimes, "Orientalize,"[5] in ways that move us beyond binary constructions of "here" and "elsewhere," "self" and "other," and allow us to account for what the postcolonial feminist filmmaker and theorist Trinh T. Minh-ha, cited by Stewart, has termed the "elsewhere within here."[6]

Our cover images of clouds seek to respond to such reflections by resisting reductive images of violence and elsewhere. Instead, they invite more expansive critical contemplation. For example, dark clouds dominate the image, suggesting an oppressive quality often associated with violence. Yet the top left-hand quarter of the photograph is different. The cover image thereby evokes the threatening, destructive qualities we commonly link to violence, while also leaving space for potentially more complex associations.[7]

At the same time, the (implied) constant drift of clouds from one part of the sky to another, their amorphous, evanescent nature, underlines the impossibility of separating neatly and definitively between one interpretation of violence and another, or one space on earth and another. Nonetheless, elsewhere is evoked through the idea of the sky itself, a space rich in symbolism and broader connotative meaning in German culture and beyond.[8] That concept tends to imply a perspective from a particular

---

Research 6, no. 3 (1969): 167–91. On the significance of temporality to understandings of violence, see Rob Nixon, *Slow Violence and the Environmentalism of the Poor* (Cambridge, MA: Harvard University Press, 2011).

5   Edward W. Said, *Orientalism*, rev. ed. (London: Penguin, 2003).

6   Trinh T. Minh-ha, *elsewhere, within here: immigration, refugeeism, and the boundary event* (New York: Routledge, 2011).

7   Cf., for example, Bielby's analysis of West German terrorist Inge Viett's autobiography, which suggests that imagining "violent agency elsewhere" offered Viett "significant points of identification in the re/construction of her militant subjectivity." Clare Bielby, "Narrating Violent Agency Elsewhere in Inge Viett's *Nie war ich furchtloser* (Never Was I More Fearless)," in Bielby and Davies, *Violence Elsewhere 1*, 149–73, here 171.

8   See, for example, Jennifer Zahrt, "The Celestial Imaginary in Weimar Cinema," in *Sky and Symbol: Proceedings of the Ninth Annual Sophia*

vantage point: the surface of the earth. As such, the clouds thematize a contemporary preoccupation that comes to the fore in the present volume: that of thinking about the world not only as a place of human activity but as a larger space embedded in deeper time.

The work of these twin volumes looks, then, to problematize not only apparently straightforward ideas about violence but also what is conventionally considered to be "here" and "elsewhere." Furthermore, their concerns include the politics of representation, and as such they contribute to a longstanding debate in German cultural history about figuring violence.[9] German histories of violence and war, particularly those of the twentieth century, have cast shadows over the immediate postwar years, as well as those since 1990 and of the new century. Those shadows have rendered the discussion, representation, and imagining of violence painful, fragmentary, or sometimes even apparently impossible. Thus, making sense of, or at times even identifying the significance of violence in and for the postwar German states, including unified Germany of the twenty-first century, becomes challenging.

Yet the essays in *Violence Elsewhere 1* demonstrate that critical analysis of constructions of violence elsewhere is a productive way to approach this challenge. That collection identifies violence elsewhere as a "significant trope in German culture of the postwar period."[10] Violence elsewhere, the volume suggests, "has offered a stage where violence could become imaginable and representable for what could loosely be termed the German imaginary." And since constructions of violence elsewhere are, inter alia, "simultaneously images of Germany itself," they "reveal something about otherwise submerged or deeply encoded meanings and functions of violence in German cultures."[11] Critical engagement with ideas of violence elsewhere, then, can yield nuanced understandings of violence in its many forms, providing insight into how that violence has resonated through time and, in turn, facilitating broader reflection on the complex ways in which violence, history, culture, community, and identity are entangled.

This introduction has the following objectives, as it sets the scene for our second volume on violence elsewhere, this time with a focus on the period since 2001. First, it outlines some insights from its predecessor volume and some of the questions for further study it broached. Second,

Centre Conference, 2011, ed. Nicholas Campion and Liz Green (Ceredigion, Wales: Sophia Centre Press, 2013), 229–55.

9   Cf., for example, *Lyrik nach Auschwitz? Adorno und die Dichter*, ed. Petra Kiedaisch (Stuttgart: Reclam, 1995).

10   Bielby and Davies, "Introduction," in Bielby and Davies, *Violence Elsewhere 1*, 1–17, here 15.

11   Bielby and Davies, "Introduction," 1.

it presents the chapters of the present volume. Third, it indicates ways in which these new studies break ground in inquiry into violence elsewhere in Germany. Fourth, and in conclusion, we highlight the scope for future work on violence elsewhere in German culture, inclusively imagined, and beyond.

* * *

Engaging critically with a range of emblematic texts and cultural and political moments, *Violence Elsewhere 1* explores eight case studies from the years 1945 to 2001 in the Federal Republic of Germany (FRG), the German Democratic Republic (GDR), and, after 1990, unified Germany. The year 2001 as end point (and starting point for the present volume) reflects the common perception that the events of September 11, 2001, marked a critical shift in understandings of global violence: a complex perception to which we return below. Exploring works of literature, film, and life writing, as well as other kinds of discourse, the authors of *Violence Elsewhere 1* draw on perspectives from literary, cultural, film, visual, and gender studies as they develop and elaborate theoretical approaches to the topic of violence elsewhere.

Certain thematic clusters and concentrations emerge in that volume. A critical mass of chapters on the GDR and the FRG prior to unification most obviously reflects the fact that Germany was divided for most of the period under consideration. This focus may also suggest, however, that violence elsewhere during the Cold War era "had particular, compelling contours related to awareness of a paradoxically German elsewhere that had been generated violently and was both foreign and proximate."[12] An emphasis, too, on constructions of violence taking place in countries of the Global South, or the "Third World" as it tended to be known at the time in Europe and beyond, also materializes in our first volume. Chapters consider depictions of violence taking place, for instance, in Vietnam, Cambodia, the USA, or Latin America. That stress reflects, among other things, the significance of the often-violent decolonizing processes occurring during this period and the postcolonial politics associated with them.

Inevitably too, German history plays a key part in the preoccupations of *Violence Elsewhere 1*. It explores works, for example, that frame the "other" Germany as elsewhere; in addition, a significant recurring concern in the texts under consideration is the extreme violence of Germany's own recent past. Nonetheless, while the past thus features in the volume, contributors approach the notion of elsewhere for the most part in a geographical sense. At the same time, *Violence Elsewhere 1* holds open the prospect of complicating such an understanding of "elsewhere." Its introduction argues that the multilayered relationship between "here"

---

12   Bielby and Davies, "Introduction," 11.

and "elsewhere" in Germany is illuminated, for example, by the work of historian Quinn Slobodian on the internationalist protest movement of the 1960s in West Germany. Published a few years previously, Slobodian's study was an important reading in the development of our inquiry.[13] It shows that far from being a movement only originated and populated by (West) Germans taking action in support of oppressed peoples in the decolonizing world, activists from the "Third World" itself played a key part—not least in instigating it. This account challenges some traditional European narratives about Western subjects acting on behalf of power-less people in the Global South and hence, too, the idea that "here" and "there" are entirely separate. It invites serious engagement not only with the ways in which "elsewhere" can be imagined from a German point of view but also with the agency and perspectives of subjects associated with that "elsewhere" and how these factors can change perceptions of all such positionalities.

The opening chapter of *Violence Elsewhere 1*, by Katherine Stone, memorably puts forward a theorization of "narrative elsewhering" as a literary strategy.[14] Following Stone's lead, the volume's introduction defines "elsewhering" as "the deflection of disturbing preoccupations onto different, more distant spaces and agents [as a way to make] them speakable"—as a central "discursive mode of the times."[15] This inter-pretation of elsewhere/"elsewhering" demonstrates the complexity and paradoxical character of such processes by underlining the impossibility of distinguishing neatly between "here" and "elsewhere" and recognizes that they are mutually interdependent, intertwined in complex ways. Such perspectives open up consideration of the complicated positions of Germany and its inhabitants in relation to a wider world in ways that undermine reductive conceptualizations of identity. The implications for who and what can be considered to be in some way "of Germany," and so proper subject matter for German studies, are significant. Indeed, they call for wider, more capacious understandings of the discipline itself.[16]

In the volume's closing chapter, Katharina Karcher and Evelien Geerts challenge received ideas about historical periodization, complicating the notion of the terrorist attacks of September 11, 2001, in the USA as a moment that altered perceptions of political violence (and other forms

---

13   Quinn Slobodian, *Foreign Front: Third World Politics in Sixties West Germany* (Durham, NC: Duke University Press, 2012).

14   Katherine Stone, "Projecting Violence Elsewhere: Remembering Conflict-Related Sexual Violence in Cold War Germany," in Bielby and Davies, *Violence Elsewhere 1*, 18–37.

15   Bielby and Davies, "Introduction," 14, 15.

16   See also Rebecca Braun and Benedict Schofield, eds., *Transnational German Studies* (Liverpool: Liverpool University Press, 2020).

of violence too) worldwide.[17] As noted above, this idea was central to our initial conceptualization of these two volumes on violence elsewhere, the first considering the period from 1945 to 2001, and the second the years that came after. Karcher and Geerts point out, however, that the murders committed by the far-right underground Nationalsozialistischer Untergrund (NSU) in Germany spanned a long period, which began before September 11, 2001, and ended only much later. They also argue how memory of the September 11 attacks, functioning discursively as "9/11," paradoxically contributed to the perpetuation of certain notions of violence in Germany, rather than to their transformation. As such, the authors propose that there are complex continuities in the years leading up to and beyond 2001; call into question conventional periodization; and complicate ideas of temporality itself.

* * *

The chapters collected in the present volume do new work in reflecting on "violence elsewhere" in Germany, not least in the sense that they address the years after 2001. Arranged as they are in chronological order, they sketch a short—if also, inevitably, partial and provisional—cultural history in Germany of thinking about violence elsewhere from 2001 on. Yet at the same time, it is our hope that, to use the imagery evoked by Stewart's study of Argentinian-Armenian, Berlin-based artist Silvina Der Meguerditchian's textile works, readers may also follow the book's multiple threads through complex, perhaps less predictable patterns. Such an approach can resonate with the critique of exclusive reliance on conventional historical periodizations offered in *Violence Elsewhere 1* by Karcher and Geerts.

The volume's opening chapter, by Marie Kolkenbrock, provides a philosophical perspective on violence elsewhere from which to consider the chapters that follow. As Kolkenbrock notes, the notion of violence elsewhere calls to mind a longstanding debate among philosophers, psychologists, and others on the ethics of distant suffering, and she analyzes contributions to it by Peter Singer, Michael Slote, Martha Nussbaum, Paul Bloom, and Hannah Arendt, among others. This discussion considers why humans seem often to respond more powerfully to the suffering of people who are near to them, rather than to the travails of those far away. Kolkenbrock proposes, however, that distant suffering tends to function as a "phantasmatic scene," as Judith Butler puts it, which allows

---

17   Katharina Karcher and Evelien Geerts, "Problematizing Political Violence in the Federal Republic of Germany: A Hauntological Analysis of the NSU Terror and a Hyper-Exceptionalized '9/11,'" in Bielby and Davies, *Violence Elsewhere 1*, 174–95.

the ethical subject to adopt a posture of seemingly uninvolved, impartial detachment.

As Kolkenbrock argues, with this debate, "philosophical ethics may contribute to an understanding of the ways violence elsewhere, as a specific form of distant suffering, is interpreted and represented in wider cultural contexts." More specifically, she links this theme to the project of understanding questions in Germany of violence elsewhere in recent times, reflecting on its relevance for both 1960s traditions of activism and their omissions with regard to "Third-World" subjects, as discussed, for instance, by Slobodian; and responses in Germany to the Black Lives Matter movement in the US in 2020.

In chapter 2, Kathrin Wunderlich examines public discourse, perceptions of life writing, and literary fiction about the German military engagement in Afghanistan that followed the September 11 attacks.[18] After the post–Second World War decades in which neither Germany had fought abroad, this deployment was groundbreaking and controversial. Indeed, for some observers it seemed to represent, in Wunderlich's words, "the Federal Republic's loss of (military) innocence." This chapter's exploration of a wide-ranging set of works and discourses highlights what the experience of engagement in Afghanistan meant for Germany: a changed foreign policy, changed language, and a changed self-image. As Wunderlich demonstrates, even though the contours of Afghanistan itself remain schematic in the writings under discussion, they are eloquent about Germany itself.

The chapter draws attention to how the commitment of German troops in Afghanistan was originally framed by politicians as a peace mission and only later described as a war: a painful linguistic evolution that constituted the gradual return of a long-disused lexis of war in public discourse. Another cultural revival is the publication of military life writing that had long been out of the public eye in postwar Germany; for instance, communications home from personnel in the field and military memoirs. A further renewed genre is the war novel; for example, Norbert Scheuer's *Die Sprache der Vögel* (2015; *The Language of Birds*, 2018); a work that, Wunderlich argues, recalls Erich Maria Remarque's classic First World War novel *Im Westen nichts Neues* (1929; *All Quiet on the Western Front*, 1929). As such, Scheuer's text references older military self-images that are apparently unrelated to the more recent, atrocious Nazi past. Wunderlich spotlights, too, ways in which depictions of fighting and violence in Afghanistan tend to be marginalized and evaded in recent war literature and so concludes that German military violence

18   Chapter 2 explores texts and discourses that emerged between 2001 and 2021. It is the first in our volume's chronologically ordered sequence because the earliest sources it considers date from 2001.

elsewhere apparently remains a fraught theme in the shadow of the mid-twentieth century.

The volume's third chapter, by Susanne C. Knittel and Sofia Forchieri, takes a critical theoretical approach to the contemporary German genre of the *Generationenroman*, or multigenerational family novel. The *Generationenroman* typically traces the experiences of several generations of one family across time and space to narrate long, complex, and multidimensional personal and political histories. Analyzing one example of the genre, *Usambara* (2007) by Christof Hamann, Knittel and Forchieri show how it links up, through one family's stories, a series of extremely violent phenomena taking place (apparently) at a distance, past or present: colonialism in Africa, the Holocaust, and ecological crisis.

The novel depicts a present-day German protagonist who takes part in a run on Kilimanjaro in Tanzania to raise money for conservation of its glaciers, an ironic project given the negative impact of tourism and climate change on the mountain's habitats. It also tells of the protagonist's great-grandfather, who, according to family lore, discovered and brought to Europe the popular African violet, or "Usambaraveilchen." The protagonist chooses to idealize that development and to downplay other, more evidently violent aspects of the German colonial project in East Africa, while a further strand of the novel addresses the enthusiastic participation of another ancestor in Nazism.

Knittel and Forchieri argue that given the complex, entangled histories of complicity and implication across Hamann's novel, which resist separation into discrete categories, the text ultimately suggests that "there can be no 'elsewhere'" when it comes to modern forms of violence, including environmental violence. Moreover, using their analysis of *Usambara* as a case study in a wider project of exploring the difficulties of simultaneously representing different orders of extreme violence across a range of historical times and places, the authors highlight the affordances of this particular genre, the *Generationenroman*, as a literary scaling device for thinking about different forms of violence.

In chapter 4, Joanne Leal continues investigation of the legacy of September 11, 2001, on the one hand; and on the other, of the potential of contemporary German novels to engage with violence elsewhere. She analyzes representations of Islamic terrorists in two novels by German-Iraqi writer Sherko Fatah, *Das dunkle Schiff* (2008; *The Dark Ship*, 2021) and *Der letzte Ort* (The Last Place, 2014). These two works link modern-day Germany and Iraq through young male protagonists who variously encounter, suffer, commit, witness, and are implicated in violence. In *Das dunkle Schiff*, a young Iraqi Kurdish man, who is impacted by extreme violence, flees to Berlin from his involvement in a fundamentalist terrorist group in Iraq. Unable to make meaningful connections and a new life, however, he is ultimately drawn back into that sphere in Germany itself.

In *Der letzte Ort*, a white German man, a researcher from the former GDR, is kidnapped by terrorists while on a visit to Iraq around 2004, after the US invasion. His translator, a local man, is kidnapped too, and the novel switches between both men's perspectives as they tell each other their stories in captivity. Ultimately, they escape: the German to likely rescue by US forces, the Iraqi to an uncertain fate.

Fatah's two novels, like Hamann's, switch between different settings, in this case Germany and Iraq. They consider connections between different instances and experiences of violence in both countries and how they shape subjective positions, ideas of self and other, and notions of community. Leal argues that while the Islamic terrorist is often an underdeveloped figure in European and North American literature, Fatah's two novels offer more complex representations. She also considers the role of storytelling in numerous senses in the novels as a possible means of generating dialogue and empathy, both between their characters and for readers. While this process is, for Fatah's characters, at best fragile and ambiguous, for his readers it might hold out prospects for new perceptions of self and other, and of German identity, in the post-9/11 world.

Nicola Thomas's chapter 5 broaches both a different literary genre and a different elsewhere. It analyzes Durs Grünbein's cycle of poems *Cyrano oder Die Rückkehr vom Mond* (Cyrano; or, The Return from the Moon, 2014), a collection that references the early science fiction of French author Cyrano de Bergerac (1619–55), who wrote about a successful journey to—and return from—the moon. Thomas notes that the elegiac tone of Grünbein's poems can be inserted into a tradition of intellectual skepticism about the Space Race and related, potentially destructive technology that is associated with cultural traditions originating in the German-speaking world in the later twentieth century and exemplified by Günther Anders and Arendt. At the same time, Thomas thematizes the difficulty, and limitations, of attempts at isolating a specific tradition linked to German(-language) thought in the context of planetary crisis.

Thomas argues that Grünbein's poems offer opportunities to reflect on contemporary, "slow" environmental violence on a planetary scale, in which it is difficult to distinguish between here and elsewhere in conventional ways, and between perpetrators, agents, and victims too. In a related way, she suggests, the poems can be read as a critique of the epistemic violence inherent in certain Eurocentric traditions of thinking about the world, as highlighted by postcolonial thinkers like Gayatri Chakravorty Spivak. Thus, this chapter considers what *Cyrano oder Die Rückkehr vom Mond* might tell us, after the end of the triumphant era of space travel between the 1950s and 1980s, about the complexities of imagining the world in its entirety. It makes a case, too, for the value of thinking about extraterrestrial space as an approach to conceptualizing both violence and elsewhere in the context of the Anthropocene, which seems urgently to demand new understandings of both. Simultaneously, Thomas foregrounds the particular qualities of poetic language for enhancing "humankind's ability to imagine violence on a planetary scale." The subtle, complex language of poetry, she argues, "offers a space to reflect on the instability of positionality and comprehension, undermining subject/object binaries and the illusions of objectivity they generate."

In the sixth chapter, Stewart turns to a further art form: Der Meguerditchian's combination of installation and live performance at the Gorki Theatre in Berlin, which commemorates the Armenian genocide of 1915–17. Stewart examines this work's potential for understanding violence elsewhere—or, rather, for calling into question the very idea of elsewhere as a meaningful term, erasing as it does, in its nonspecificity, the reality of other locations, and "[positioning] it as outside of comprehension." With reference to such theorists as Alyosxa Tudor, Stewart argues also that the agency involved in positing an elsewhere means that power relations are at work too.

The work in question, *Verstrickungen* (*Entanglements*, 2013, 2014, and 2015), blends visual images, textiles, speech, movement, and the artist's interaction with an audience. It uses archival photographs of Ottoman Armenians, held together by crocheted threads, to evoke dense interconnections between Armenian and German pasts. Thus, Der Meguerditchian's work shows that the here and there, and the past and present, prove always to be connected. That entanglement calls into question, moreover, the apparently simple division of Berlin's inhabitants into people with "migrant backgrounds" and those without such backgrounds. The chapter thus sees modern Berlin as the site of multiple, overlapping, transnational histories of violence that, like Der Meguerditchian's threads, are legible in terms of Minh-ha's "elsewhere, within here."

Frauke Matthes focuses on a different location in contemporary Germany in chapter 7: the apparently provincial sphere of Clemens Meyer's short-story collection *Die stillen Trabanten* (The Silent Satellites, 2017; in English as *Dark Satellites*, 2020). In particular, she discusses the story "Glasscherben im Objekt 95" ("Broken Glass in Unit 95"), a narrative that, as heralded by the volume's title, is set in the margins of a satellite town of a city in East Germany, in or around 2015. In this space, "East Germany's communist past meets its capitalist as well as postmigrant present," and present-day violence erupts. A German security guard patrols night shifts at a site, "Objekt 95," which is near a building accommodating refugees. He glimpses a woman at the accommodation who reminds him of a different one, whom he had met there twenty years previously. That woman encountered so long ago had come from the former Soviet Union and was likely displaced owing to conflict in that region after 1990. Soon after the protagonist sees the second woman in the present day, the residents of the hostel are transferred to a different location due to a racist attack.

If, at first sight, Meyer's text seems to address events in a single, tightly circumscribed space, Matthes shows that it also draws attention to global-local relationships. Important in her analysis too are the nature and significance of peripheral, liminal areas in geographic, and indeed other, senses, and ways in which these ambiguous zones articulate with apparently more easily defined notions of here and elsewhere. The past is a key "elsewhere" here as well, for the story blends distant and recent memories of various kinds.

Matthes takes forward the discussion of textual form established earlier on in this volume as she comments on the specific potential of the short story for underscoring the interconnectedness of violence here and elsewhere. Moreover, she identifies the short story as a genre that emerges from Anglo-American traditions. As such, its generic legacies hook hyperlocal contexts into a mobile transnational literature, which both calls on ideas of elsewhere and calls them into question.

In chapter 8, Francesca Lewis introduces a feature film, *Suspiria* (2018). This multilingual horror movie was made in Italy and Germany by Italian director Luca Guadagnino, with an international cast and crew, and screened internationally. With this choice of material, the chapter expands understandings of what kind of work(s) might be considered to be "of Germany" in a transnational industry and age. *Suspiria* is set in a West Berlin dance school in 1977, the time of the "Deutscher Herbst," or German Autumn, when the actions of the urban terrorist group the Rote Armee Fraktion (Red Army Faction) reached a notorious and tragic crisis. While the film references that historical moment, it is primarily concerned with a young woman dancer who joins the school and the supernatural events that follow, for the academy proves to be run by murderous coven of witches. The plot also follows the attempts of an elderly psychoanalyst, Klemperer, to understand these mysteries, and gradually, his personal history of suffering and loss in the National Socialist era is uncovered.

Violence takes place within the dance school and outside it; and in the past as it does in the present. Lewis reads these instances of violence in light of Karen Barad's feminist new materialist philosophy and its critiques of conventional ideas of time. She argues that *Suspiria* does not reconstruct narratives about German history, either from the 1930s and 1940s or the 1970s, as much as it challenges the limitations of thinking about that history in terms of conventional temporality. Instead, this conspicuously nonrealist film makes "Germany's complex history of violence, guilt, perpetration, and trauma tangible, visceral, felt, and embodied." The understanding of violence that emerges, Lewis concludes, is "never elsewhere, or elsewhen, but always here—always embodied, always collective, and always bound up with others."

In the ninth and final chapter, Priscilla Layne opens up discussion of a further literary genre, Black feminist speculative fiction, with reference to Ghanaian-British-German author Sharon Dodua Otoo's acclaimed novel *Adas Raum* (Ada's Room, 2021; in English as *Ada's Realm*, 2023). In four interconnected narrative strands, this text engages with extremely violent transnational histories and their aftermaths in and around fifteenth-century West Africa (the location of present-day Ghana), Victorian London, the Nazi concentration camp Dora-Mittelbau in Germany, and the Ghana, London, and Berlin of today. In each narrative, that violence is experienced or witnessed by one of four young women protagonists, all called Ada. These characters are accompanied through their lives by a mysterious being who takes the form of a series of silent objects that witness and narrate the women's troubles sympathetically and shed light on the metaphysics of Otoo's speculative universe.

Layne reads Otoo's novel as an example of feminist Black German Afrofuturism that is brought into productive conversation with the philosophical insights of object-oriented ontology, or "Triple O." Triple O reimagines the place, meaning, and significance both of humans and of objects in the world. It can, therefore, interrogate the limitations of traditional concepts of both. In so doing, it chimes with the work of writers like Otoo, which reimagines and foregrounds with political intent the traditionally excluded positions of Black subjectivities, women, and motherhood. Layne suggests, too, that from a world riven with violence, *Adas Raum* explores the idea of a restorative justice and a shared futurity for men and women, thinking derived from Black feminist thought and practice and an ethics of care.

* * *

The present volume primarily brings together works from Germany produced by artists and writers from a highly diverse range of backgrounds. There is a strong emphasis on international or transnational voices and currents in theory and criticism, notably including postcolonial theorists. In this way, these studies, for all their variety, mirror something of the "many non-opposing worlds—all located in the very same place" of which Minh-ha writes in a text cited by Stewart,[19] and the complexities and multiplicities of German cultures and identities in the twenty-first century.

There was a stress in *Violence Elsewhere 1* on direct physical, "political violence,"[20] and here that focus is maintained. Chapters like Wunderlich's

---

19   Minh-ha, *elsewhere*, 2. See also Stewart's chapter in this volume.

20   On the problematics of constructions of "political violence," see Bielby, "Gendering the Perpetrator; Gendering Perpetrator Studies," in *The Routledge International Handbook of Perpetrator Studies*, ed. Susanne C. Knittel and

and Leal's draw in texts about physical political violence, albeit of very different types, as they consider aftermaths of 9/11. Matthes focuses on a story involving a different kind of direct, physical violence—namely, a racist attack in (near-)contemporary Germany, against the backdrop of political conflict—while Stewart considers artistic responses to historical genocide, and Layne, a panoply of directly physical violent events through time in *Adas Raum*, many of which are political in the conventional sense. Other chapters widen understandings of violence. Striking, for instance, is the discussion of environmental, "slow," and epistemic violence in the chapters by Knittel and Forchieri and Thomas, which work toward more planetary perspectives.

In terms of conceptualizing elsewhere, there is significant emphasis here, as in the previous volume, on geographic locations outside Germany, including Afghanistan, Iraq, Tanzania, West Africa and Ghana, Argentina, Turkey, the loci of the Armenian diaspora, France, the former Soviet Union, the US, and the UK. These sites reflect certain dominant events and themes in world affairs after 2001: for example, the impact of post-9/11 wars in Afghanistan and Iraq, or the Black Lives Matter movement in the US. In keeping with debates of the twenty-first century in Germany, too, a particular interest emerges here in modern German literature that examines legacies of colonial violence in Africa in the chapters by Knittel and Forchieri and Layne. Thus, work on violence elsewhere continues to develop with shifting times and historical currents.

An especially marked feature of this collection as a whole is its authors' vivid interest in works and theoretical approaches that critique or break down binary notions of here and elsewhere, thereby foregrounding Minh-ha's idea of nonopposing yet colocated worlds and the perpetual presence at many levels of "elsewhere, within here." Of course, as Otoo's novel *Adas Raum* or Hamann's *Usambara* remind us with their long historical views, it is not the case that relationships between here and elsewhere were necessarily simpler in the past, or that borders were less complex or fragile than they are today. The studies collected here, however, might suggest, first, that in a world that is more intensively interconnected in some respects than before, the limitations of the here-elsewhere binary are illuminated in new ways. Second, and in an evidently related manner, they might imply that the works of numerous contemporary artists, theorists, and others have the potential to complicate such binaries and that that complication is central to the work of contemporary cultural studies in general. Hence, it is key for German studies in particular too.

Zachary J. Goldberg (London: Routledge, 2020), 155–68, here 164. Stone's chapter in *Violence Elsewhere 1* also seeks to problematize conventional constructions of "political violence" through drawing attention to sexual abuse in war (and postwar) contexts. Stone, "Projecting Violence Elsewhere."

Elsewheres that are not geographical or spatial come to the fore in this volume also. Extraterrestrial space is thematized here by Thomas as a perspective, however limited, from which to observe a planet in crisis; a further elsewhere in her study is the science-fictional space of premodern space travel. Fantasy is central to Lewis's chapter on *Suspiria* as well, and its interest in magical spaces as prompts for a diffractive reading that undoes standard notions of time and, indeed, space. And *Adas Raum*, discussed by Layne, mobilizes speculative fiction as a way of troubling conventional European narratives about history and subjectivity.

What is perhaps most noticeable across the volume is emphasis on the ways in which the elsewhere of the past—or "elsewhen," as Lewis puts it—resonates in the present. A number of the essays consider, to a greater or lesser extent, the reverberations of Nazi-era violence in recent works. In different ways, Knittel and Forchieri, Lewis, and Layne all focus on texts that explicitly thematize the legacy of that past in the present, with Lewis, echoing Karcher and Geerts, complicating ideas of temporality itself. More subtle repercussions are detected by other authors; for example, Wunderlich, where she links the tendency to avoid direct representations of German military violence in Afghanistan in recent writing to the baleful memory of National Socialism.

Other, more diverse instances of past violence prove to disrupt the present as well: the commemoration of the Armenian genocide in Berlin, colonialism in Africa, the German Autumn, and the long-lasting impact of conflict in the former Soviet Union after 1990 as it is witnessed by Meyer's East German protagonist, as highlighted by Matthes. Other, more surprising pasts surface too, such as Cyrano's early Enlightenment, in which, according to Thomas, paradoxically some seeds of contemporary epistemic violence were sown. Thus, past violence is multilayered and complex, and memories of it are often "multidirectional," to use Michael Rothberg's influential term.[21]

A remarkable feature in the studies collected here is a shared interest in works that not only reflect explicitly on the relationship of past and present in some way but actively mobilize narrative strategies that juxtapose accounts of past and recent or present times, just as they shuttle strikingly between different locations. Examples include Hamann's *Usambara*, Meyer's "Glasscherben im Objekt 95," Grünbein's *Cyrano oder Die Rückkehr vom Mond*, Der Meguerditchian's *Verstrickungen*, Guadagnino's *Suspiria*, and Otoo's *Adas Raum*. This observation of literary and artistic technique, in turn, draws attention to another major theme hallmarking this collection of essays; namely, discussion of genre and form. The chapters consider a wide array of textual and artistic forms,

21   Michael Rothberg, *Multidirectional Memory: Remembering the Holocaust in the Age of Decolonization* (Stanford, CA: Stanford University Press, 2009).

from life writing to memoir, novel, short story, and poetry, to film, visual, textile, and performance art. And what is noticeably consistent between them is the explicit reflection on their specific affordances—to use a central contemporary term foregrounded by Knittel and Forchieri—for conveying something about violence elsewhere, albeit not necessarily in realist or figurative ways.[22] These individual debates about form, in turn, amount to an extended, sustained reflection not only on the many things that violence elsewhere is and can mean today but also on how expressive form can shape and account for it.

* * *

In sum, contributions to this volume cover a range of remarkable works and perspectives that cast light on important facets of violence elsewhere. In doing so, they point, also, to fields of potential future work. For example, a central focus of our previous volume, *Violence Elsewhere 1*, was the gendering of representations of violence elsewhere—an emphasis bound up with the prominence of gender in discourses of violence but also those of place, home, nation, and "elsewhere." Future study in this field could make more of this connection, as well as focusing further, as Stone's chapter on literature about conflict-related sexual violence against women and girls in *Violence Elsewhere 1* does,[23] on forms of violence that are themselves more explicitly gendered. Other examples beyond such misogynistic violence could include homophobic or transphobic violence, among many other forms. Such discussion offers intersections with other current conceptualizations of violence; it is striking, for example, that in passing, Rob Nixon discusses the "slow" violence of domestic abuse in his elaboration of that concept.[24] Picking up the feminist new materialist and posthuman approaches employed by Lewis and Stewart in this volume, future work on violence elsewhere could make fruitful use of such thought.[25]

Such more nuanced approaches to violence could connect to a further widening of the range of cultural producers under discussion. The present volume has considered works by writers and artists from a variety of backgrounds; future work interested in exploring feminist and queer perspectives could offer more sustained, productive focus on the cultural production of women and nonbinary artists and writers.

---

22 This strand is evident, too, in the previous volume of essays, with an emphasis on narrative form in Stone's chapter and a cluster of chapters on (post-) Brechtian theory and practice and on often polemical, often visual modernism.

23 Stone, "Projecting Violence Elsewhere."

24 Nixon, *Slow Violence*, 16.

25 On posthuman approaches to perpetration, see Jonathan Luke Austin, "Posthumanism and Perpetrators," in Knittel and Goldberg, *Routledge International Handbook of Perpetrator Studies*, 169–80.

The present volume has employed an expansive interpretation of violence, with a clear interest in the subject of environmental "slow" violence, a theme that without doubt demands urgent further inquiry. The volume also indicates that further consideration of epistemic violence and its history would reward study. At the same time, such work would need to remain alert to the dangers of widening its focus on violence in ways that might risk blurring or obscuring important historical detail or specificities, and so inadvertently "washing away ... violence, its histories, and its traces."[26] That is to say, we remain mindful of the risks in stretching the idea of violence so far that it becomes conceptually weakened. Therefore, as we move to the close of these reflections, we ask whether it is possible simultaneously to hold open different ideas on the limits of violence, if the notion of "violence elsewhere" is to remain eloquent. Can we, on one hand, insist on retaining some sort of emphasis on physical harm or destruction as essential in understanding violence while, on the other hand, recognizing that such a definition always remains open to critical contestation?

As noted above, a striking feature of this volume is the way in which, within some of its discussions, polar notions of here and elsewhere are critiqued, with emphasis on what we have been terming, with Minh-ha, the "elsewhere, within here." In many ways this circumstance is not surprising in a study that considers the period since 2001, a period that has seen new and prolific links made around the world; for instance, as people move and knowledge is transmitted in novel ways. Applying the conceptual tool of the "elsewhere, within here" to the violence of earlier moments of history could be a productive line of inquiry for future study. Meaningful, too, could be comparative study of violence and "the elsewhere within here" in different glocal contexts; for example, manifestations of violence "elsewhere within here" in many loci across the world, alongside those in Berlin or Germany.

Finally, this volume has underscored the importance of analyzing discursive and artistic form for an understanding of violence elsewhere and how it can be imagined, conveyed, and codified. Its chapters have focused, in the main, on individual works, or groups of works in a range of genres, from philosophy to life writing to prose fiction to poetry. Taken together, then, they offer a comparative study of different kinds of expression and what they do. It seems to us that this kind of study is an avenue to further work that would move beyond these often relatively classical textual and cultural genres to take account of further popular forms and media. In

---

26   Yael Navaro et al., "Introduction: Reverberations of Violence across Time and Space," in *Reverberations: Violence across Time and Space,* ed. Yael Navaro et al. (Philadelphia: University of Pennsylvania Press, 2021), 1–29, here 6. See also Stewart's chapter in the present volume.

particular, examination of the online world would seem to be a highly significant area for sustained future consideration. This kind of inquiry is urgent, not only because of the accelerated ubiquity and reach of the internet and social media but also because of the novel ways it relates to violence and creates new ideas of elsewhere.

1: "Violence Elsewhere" and the Phantasmatic Scene of "Distant Suffering": Intersections of Emotional and Spatial Distance

Marie Kolkenbrock

"VIOLENCE ELSEWHERE," write Clare Bielby and Mererid Puw Davies, "has offered a stage where violence could become imaginable and representable for what could loosely be termed the German imaginary."[1] This definition calls to mind a conversation between German journalist Mohamed Amjahid, US German studies scholar Priscilla Layne, and German writer Max Czollek, which formed part of a conversation series titled "Radical Diversity" at the Goethe-Institut USA in Washington, DC, in the summer of 2020.[2] Amjahid described his ambivalent feelings at a Black Lives Matter protest in Berlin following the murder of George Floyd in the US in the same year. While he was glad about the high turnout of the event, he said, he could not help but wonder where all those people had been after the fatal racist shootings in the German town of Hanau only a few months earlier.[3] Both Amjahid's example and the premise of the "Violence Elsewhere" project suggest that at least in some cases, geographical distance may elicit a greater readiness to engage with violence at an emotional, ethical, and political level—arguably because it can make it easier for individuals to disregard their own subject position and its

---

1   Clare Bielby and Mererid Puw Davies, "Introduction," in *Violence Elsewhere 1: Imagining Distant Violence in Germany 1945–2001*, ed. Clare Bielby and Mererid Puw Davies (Rochester, NY: Camden House, 2024), 1–17, here 1.

2   "Radical Diversity: Los Angeles," Goethe-Institut USA, Washington, DC. Recorded August 26, 2020, published September 4, 2020, https://www.youtube.com/watch?v=JUAwi2tv3i0.

3   On February 19, 2020, a right-wing extremist fatally shot nine young people in Hanau: Gökhan Gültekin, Sedat Gürbüz, Said Nesar Hashemi, Mercedes Kierpacz, Hamza Kurtović, Vili Viorel Păun, Fatih Saraçoğlu, Ferhat Unvar, and Kaloyan Velkov. See the websites of Initiative 19. Februar Hanau, accessed January 4, 2023, https://19feb-hanau.org; and Bildungsinitiative Ferhat Unvar, accessed January 4, 2023, https://www.bildungsinitiative-ferhatunvar.de.

possible entanglement with the violence taking place. Geographical distance becomes, then, emotionally safe distance.

This chapter explores the conceptual connection between emotional and geographical distance in philosophical debates concerned with the ethics of distant suffering. Violence elsewhere, I argue, is a specific form of distant suffering, which is itself a recurring "phantasmatic scene" in Western philosophical debates around ethical responsibility. A phantasmatic scene, writes Judith Butler in *The Force of Nonviolence* (2020), is formed by an "interplay of socially shared, or communicable, unconscious and conscious fantasies" that provide a "structuring psychic modality, by which reality is invariably interpreted."[4] "Fantasy" here also retains the Freudian elements of centering the subject as protagonist and the function of a wish-fulfillment. Thus, by creating a phantasmatic scene of suffering at a distance, philosophical ethics may contribute to an understanding of the ways violence elsewhere, as a specific form of distant suffering, is interpreted and represented in wider cultural contexts. A phantasmatic scene, like a theatrical scene, includes a constellation of characters, one of whom holds the position of the identificatory protagonist. Moreover, in keeping with the theatrical metaphor, a phantasmatic scene entails a certain "stage setting" within which the characters hold certain positions that are separated by certain distances. A critical analysis of the phantasmatic scene of distant suffering, of its protagonists, character constellations, and structuring relations of proximity and distance, provides fundamental insights for understanding the cultural fantasies and wish fulfillments that are at work in narratives of violence elsewhere.

With reference to the work of literary scholar Arlene A. Teraoka on the topos of the so-called Third World in the works of German post-Second World War leftist writers, Bielby and Davies explain that German "representations of violence elsewhere are simultaneously images of Germany itself."[5] "If discourse about others is self-referential," I too want to ask, with Teraoka, What function does the conceptualization of distant suffering serve for the construction of "self" in the philosophical texts I discuss in this chapter?[6] And what kind of "self" that is "here," and not "distant" or "elsewhere," is being constructed in this way? While in this chapter I focus on twentieth- and twenty-first-century texts that can be broadly located within the fields of "Western political philosophy and philosophical ethics" that lie mostly outside the German-language

---

4   Judith Butler, *The Force of Nonviolence: An Ethico-Political Bind* (London: Verso, 2020), 35.

5   Bielby and Davies, "Introduction," 2.

6   Arlene A. Teraoka, *East, West, and Others: The Third World in Postwar German Literature* (Lincoln: University of Nebraska Press, 1996), 1.

context, these questions retain a crucial and perhaps particular urgency in constructions of German national identity today.

As the analysis of some texts in Teraoka's study suggests, solidarity with victims of violence elsewhere can take a form of overproximity: engagement with the so-called Third World provided some postwar German writers with a way to imagine a German identity "liberated from [its] fascist past" via an identification with an unspecified oppressed other.[7] I will return to these questions and tentatively reflect on the connection of this more specific German context to the phantasmatic scene of distant suffering at the end of this chapter. At the same time, if the overproximity of identification and projection is undoubtedly problematic, my focus in this chapter lies on what could be called the opposite side of the same coin: not overproximity but an idealized notion of detachment that lies at the root of the phantasmatic scene of distant suffering.

An innovative and crucial aspect of Bielby and Davies's conceptualization of "Violence Elsewhere" is, in my view, the way it runs contrary to the conventional focus of the philosophical debates around morality and geographical distance, as the selected examples discussed in this chapter will suggest. These examples tend to be primarily concerned with people's indifference, ignorance, and inaction in the face of distant suffering: When things are happening far away from us, so the argument goes, we tend to care less about them. Of course, one can easily think of many examples that support this observation. COVID-19—about which the world only started caring when it was no longer just China's problem—and the reluctance of Western governments to waive patent rights for the vaccines against it belong to the more recent examples that illustrate this truth.

Although the COVID-19 pandemic in some ways highlighted a certain "reversibility of proximity and distance" ("elsewhere" can be "here," and vice versa, within a few months or even weeks), this heightened sense of interdependency and shared physical vulnerability has so far not engendered lasting forms of global solidarity and care.[8] At the time of writing, too, the UK government had recently introduced fundamental changes to the country's asylum system via its controversial "Nationality and Borders Act," which was passed on April 28, 2022. This new set of policies will likely prevent the rescue of people who, seeking refuge from violence elsewhere, are drowning in the English Channel: intentionally refusing to provide safe routes into the UK, and criminalizing those who will attempt to enter the country regardless, will make the journey even

---

7   Teraoka, *East, West, and Others,* 169; see also 165.

8   Judith Butler, *Notes toward a Performative Theory of Assembly* (Cambridge, MA: Harvard University Press, 2015), 120. Butler uses this formulation in a different context.

more perilous.[9] These examples also show the complex and at times contradictory layers of violence elsewhere. The new legislation is an attempt at keeping distant suffering distant, denying the political responsibility that the recognition of proximity—migrants requesting entry at the borders—could entail.

Inquiries into ways of creating a sense of ethical responsibility for distant strangers therefore remains an important ethical and political task, and it is not my intention in this chapter to dismiss concerns about the human capacity for caring at a distance per se. Where the philosophical approaches I discuss in this chapter aim to overcome an ethics of proximity that does not go beyond a "parochial, communitarian, exclusionary" form of care, as Butler writes, they offer important interventions at both philosophical and political levels.[10] While, however, a narrow ethical concern only for those in immediate emotional, social, or geographical proximity is obviously problematic, an ethical concern predominantly focused on those suffering at a distance entails dangers too. If, as Butler points out, "I am only bound to those who suffer at a distance, and never those who are close to me, then I evacuate my situation in an effort to secure the distance that allows me to entertain ethical feeling and even myself to be ethical."[11] This evacuation of one's own situation must be understood as an expression of solidarity with the suffering of distant others for whom one feels compassion but no responsibility, which replaces an engagement with the violence at one's doorstep. The exclusive focus on suffering at a distance can therefore help obfuscate one's own entangled role within such violent structures and secures one's own position as ethical. Such an evacuation, I will propose, implicitly exists in the phantasmatic scene of suffering at a distance developed in the philosophical ethics that I will analyze in this chapter. Amjahid's comment on antiracist protests in Germany could hint that they might entail an element of this very kind of evacuation. This chapter will seek to explore how such theorizing can illuminate the phenomenon of violence elsewhere, also and particularly in the German context. At the same time, the discussion of the theoretical texts in this chapter shows that the questions arising from the exploration of violence elsewhere have a wider cultural currency outside Germany.

9   For more background on the bill, see, e.g., "Amnesty International UK: Nationality & Borders Bill; The Truth behind the Claims," Amnesty International, last modified September 22, 2022, https://www.amnesty.org.uk/nationality-borders-bill-truth-behind-claims.

10   Butler, *Notes toward a Performative Theory*, 104.

11   Butler, *Notes toward a Performative Theory*, 104.

Overcoming Distance for Moral Refinement

One of the most crucial interventions in the twentieth-century philosophical discussion about ethical responses and responsibilities to suffering at a distance is the 1972 article "Famine, Affluence, and Morality" by
the eminent and controversial Peter Singer.[12] The essay has since been
reprinted in over fifty anthologies with titles such as *Western Philosophy: An
Anthology, Ethical Theory: An Anthology*, or *Moral Philosophy: A Reader*.[13]
These contexts demonstrate that it is considered one of the key texts in
modern Western philosophical ethics. Singer refuses "to take proximity
and distance into account" when considering moral obligations. Using
the by now often-cited scenario of a child drowning in a shallow pond
nearby versus a child suffering from famine in a country far away, Singer
argues that the moral obligations to help are the same in both cases.[14]
He concludes that while physical nearness might make it more *likely* that
people assist a person in peril, for example, when a child is drowning right
in front of them, moral obligations do not depend on proximity. If it is
within our capabilities, we ought to help someone whether we are close
to them or not. In this way, spending money on things beyond the bare
necessities instead of donating to people in peril elsewhere is as morally
wrong as walking by the drowning child so as not to get one's clothes
muddy. While the general premise that any person's life should be considered worth saving or preserving irrespective of their location on the globe
will certainly form the basis of most ethical approaches and religious systems, Singer's conceptualization of an individual's ethical responsibility to
distant strangers does appear to be a paradigm shift. As Amia Srinivasan
has noted, Singer's approach to moral responsibility is so radical that it
would require "us to overhaul our daily lives in ways unimaginable to
most."[15]

---

12   Peter Singer, "Famine, Affluence, and Morality," *Philosophy and Public
Affairs* 1, no. 3 (Spring 1972): 229–43, here 232.

13   John Cottingham, ed., *Western Philosophy: An Anthology* (Cambridge, MA:
Blackwell, 1996); Russ Shafer-Landau, ed., *Ethical Theory: An Anthology* (Mal-
den, MA: Blackwell, 2007); Louis P. Pojman, ed., *Moral Philosophy: A Reader*
(Indianapolis: Hackett, 2003). See also Singer's own preface to the book version
of his essay: *Famine, Affluence, and Morality* (Oxford: Oxford University Press,
2016), xii.

14   See Singer, "Famine, Affluence, and Morality," 231, as well as Singer,
"The Drowning Child and the Expanding Circle," *Internationalist* (April 1997),
https://web.archive.org/web/20200106211128/https://www.utilitarian.net/
singer/by/199704--.htm.

15   Amia Srinivasan, "Stop the Robot Apocalypse," *London Review of Books*
37, no. 18 (September 24, 2015), https://www.lrb.co.uk/the-paper/v37/n18/
amia-srinivasan/stop-the-robot-apocalypse.

In practice, most individuals, and more importantly, most large organizations and nation-states, do not tend to comply with the obligation Singer articulates. A reason for this general reluctance to accept Singer's understanding of moral responsibility can arguably be found in the way geographical distance tends to be linked to emotional distance: several thinkers have considered the role that the human capacity for empathy, compassion, or pity may play in the context of ethical responsibility and distant suffering. Moral philosopher Michael Slote, for example, has proposed that we need an ethics of care that is based on the enhancement of empathy for distant strangers. Slote's approach relativizes Singer's claim somewhat, as he argues that people intuitively do have a greater ethical obligation to suffering that is immediate. He concedes, however, that this necessary ethical consideration of immediacy is linked to the thus far limited scope of human empathy. The moral obligation of humanity at large is therefore to widen that scope of empathy as much as possible, to increase the human capacity of empathy through training and education, which then ought to lead to more ethical and just decision-making at both individual and social-political levels:

> If we (as individuals, as societies, as a species) haven't in fact made our best efforts to stimulate and educate our empathic capacities for concern for people we don't know, then we presumably don't know how far those capacities can or eventually will take us; and although I suspect (and have tentatively said) that those developed capacities wouldn't lead us to sacrifice our own welfare (and that of our family and friends) on behalf of distant others to *anything like the extent* that Singer ... *et al.* regard as obligatory, I also believe that (more) fully developed empathic concern for others would lead to *greater personal sacrifices* than most of us now make.[16]

Here, then, the stimulation of empathy is promoted to bridge or overcome interpersonal distance in the emotional as well as geographical, and arguably also social, senses of the word. Slote concedes that there are social biases—for example, regarding gender, race, or class—that may impede empathic concern or cause an unjust distribution of it. He does not accept this existence of bias as an argument against an ethics of empathy, however: "I don't think a moral philosophy that appeals to empathy is in any grave danger of justifying unjustifiable distinctions."[17] Slote's hope is, therefore, that an ethics of empathy would actively work against such empathetic biases.

---

16 Michael Slote, *The Ethics of Care and Empathy* (Oxford: Routledge, 2007), 33 (italics in original).

17 Slote, *Ethics of Care and Empathy*, 35.

A similar hope can be found in Martha Nussbaum's project for the cultivation of political emotions, where she argues that the conscious cultivation of certain emotions—and the containment of others—should be seen as an essential tool for societies to achieve both stability and justice.[18] For this undertaking to be successful, societies need to find solutions for the problem that emotions are "'eudaimonistic,' meaning that they appraise the world from the person's own viewpoint and the viewpoint, therefore, of that person's evolving conception of a worthwhile life."[19] On this view, it depends heavily on a person's individual perspective which incidents or situations stimulate deep emotions in them; and that perspective in turn tends to be limited by emotional and geographical distance:

> We grieve for people we care about, not for total strangers. We fear damages that threaten ourselves and those we care about, not earthquakes on Mars. Eudaimonism is not egoism: we may hold that other people have intrinsic value. But the ones who will stir deep emotions in us are the ones to whom we are somehow connected through our imagining of a valuable life, what I shall henceforth call our "circle of concern." If distant people and abstract principles are to get a grip on our emotions, therefore, these emotions must somehow position them within our circle of concern, creating a sense of "our" life in which these people and events matter as parts of our "us," our own flourishing.[20]

Nussbaum hopes that collective symbols, rituals, and culture can bring about such movement. Societies that strive for justice, she argues, must "build stable structures that expand compassion broadly, but, eudaimonism tells us, this will require creating a bridge between our current concerns and a broader circle of concerns that is still recognizable as 'us' and 'ours.'"[21] Rituals and spectacles (such as theatrical tragedy) that stimulate cultivation of compassion, which she understands as a "painful emotion directed at the serious suffering of another creature or creatures," could, then, according to Nussbaum, function as such bridges.[22] Nussbaum distinguishes her concept of compassion explicitly from empathy, which she understands as a more calculated understanding of a suffering other's situation. By contrast, compassion is seen as an

---

18   Martha Nussbaum, *Political Emotions: Why Love Matters for Justice* (Cambridge, MA: Belknap Press of Harvard University Press, 2013).
19   Nussbaum, *Political Emotions*, 11.
20   Nussbaum, *Political Emotions*, 11.
21   Nussbaum, *Political Emotions*, 145.
22   Nussbaum, *Political Emotions*, 142.

"outgrowth of empathy."[23] Despite these (to some extent above all terminological) differences, Slote's and Nussbaum's agendas are comparable in the sense that they articulate a similar goal: to bring distant suffering emotionally closer by stimulating feelings of co-suffering to stabilize ethical "response-ability."[24]

This hope that empathy, sympathy, compassion, and pity (understood as the imagination of another's pain or co-suffering) could be made useful as ethical categories has a long philosophical tradition full of proponents and critics. As Katja Haustein's brief summary of the history of pity and the related concepts that surround it (which are not always neatly terminologically separated) shows, these debates are far from being resolved.[25] Those who argue for the ethical usefulness of the human capacity to imagine another's pain appear to understand co-suffering as a practice that may bridge interpersonal separation and help overcome egotism; for instance, Jean-Jacques Rousseau, Gotthold Ephraim Lessing, and Arthur Schopenhauer. According to Schopenhauer, for example, compassion (or *Mitleid*) "demolishes the separation between 'you' and 'I.'"[26] Nussbaum's and Slote's approaches to compassion and empathy, respectively, can therefore be regarded within this tradition of thought that regards the cultivation of emotional proximity to a suffering other as an ethical practice that enables the subject to feel and act ethically.

If emotional connection and closeness are therefore seen as ethical motivators, then the ability to widen one's scope of emotional care appears as a particularly high achievement of moral refinement for both individuals and societies at large. In this way, the phantasmatic scene of suffering at a distance may entail an ethical subject who (emotionally) cares about someone suffering far away and may therefore be able to consider themselves as particularly ethical. As such, it has an ideological function because it enables postures of ethical refinement and "decency" without an interrogation of the subject's or society's own embeddedness

---

23 Nussbaum, *Political Emotions*, 144.

24 I am borrowing the term "response-ability" from Donna Haraway, who highlights the dual meaning of "responsibility" as both obligation and (emotional) capability of responding ethically. Donna Haraway, *Staying with the Trouble: Making Kin in the Chthulucene* (Durham, NC: Duke University Press, 2016), 2.

25 Katja Haustein, "'J'ai mal à l'autre': Barthes on Pity," *L'Esprit créateur* 55, no. 4 (Winter 2015): 131–47, here 132–33.

26 Haustein, "'J'ai mal à l'autre,'" 136. Haustein cites Arthur Schopenhauer, "Zur Ethik," in Schopenhauer, *Sämtliche Werke in fünf Bänden*, ed. Wolfgang von Löhneysen, 5 vols., (Frankfurt am Main: Suhrkamp, 1986), 5:242 (§110). For a variation on this text, see Schopenhauer, "Die beiden Grundprobleme der Ethik," in *Sämtliche Werke in fünf Bänden*, 3:763.

in structures of violence and oppression.[27] Examples of "Violence Elsewhere" may then provide a specific version of distant suffering, where such moral refinement can be cultivated and performed.

Against such approaches that emphasize the importance of empathy and compassion in moral matters, the psychologist Paul Bloom has claimed that such a widening of our empathetic scope is psychologically unrealistic. In his popular book *Against Empathy: The Case for Rational Compassion* (2016), he argues that our ability to feel empathy for other people depends to a large extent on how geographically, socially, and emotionally close we are to them:

> Although we might intellectually believe that the suffering of our neighbor is just as awful as the suffering of someone living in another country, it is far easier to empathize with those close to us, those who are similar to us, and those we see as more attractive or vulnerable or less scary.[28]

In other words, empathy reflects racist, sexist, nationalist, speciesist biases, among others. While this argument appears still to be very much in line with Slote's and Nussbaum's observations, Bloom does not share their optimism that there is anything one could actively do to widen the human scope of emotional concern in any politically sustainable way. He does not deny that perceptions of difference are culturally contingent and can change over time. He insists, however, that the specific feeling of empathy will always be too reliant in some ways on proximity and sameness. Even if it is possible to momentarily extend one's empathetic concern to someone or one specific group at a distance, this will always be a limited operation, as empathy has a form of tunnel vision: "Indeed, you cannot empathize with more than one or two people at the same time."[29] This formulation is perhaps misleading, because Bloom's own examples show that it is very much possible to empathize with whole groups of people: among other things, he mentions the empathy that was expressed by the public with the families of victims of a school shooting.

Bloom's point is, however, that humans are incapable of really feeling empathy for more than one or two causes at once, and that this position may have unjust political consequences. It is hard to deny, for example, that the empathy stimulated by media coverage focusing public attention on one incident of human suffering may come at the expense of others.

---

27 Nussbaum in particular frequently uses the notion of a "decent society," an ideal of a society "worth aspiring to and sustaining." Nussbaum, *Political Emotions*, 19.

28 Paul Bloom, *Against Empathy: The Case for Rational Compassion* (London: Penguin, 2016), 33.

29 Bloom, *Against Empathy*, 33.

Of course, one could argue, like Slote and Nussbaum, that the problem is not empathy itself but simply biased cultural conceptions of similarity and difference. Bloom, however, insists that while we are intellectually capable of *grasping* that all suffering deserves empathy, we are not able to *feel* it. Therefore, the goal of increasing empathy is, from Bloom's perspective as a psychologist, unrealistic. He surmises quite persuasively that empathy should therefore not inform anyone's ethics and politics. For these, Bloom argues, a more emotionally distanced approach is needed. Against the ethics of empathy, he makes a case for what he calls in the subtitle of his book "rational compassion": "Much better," he writes, is "drawing on a more distanced compassion and kindness."[30] Emotional distance is therefore introduced here as an ideal for ethical decision-making, precisely in order to widen the ethical scope beyond the proximity bias of empathy. Or, in other words, instead of trying to feel closer to distant strangers—or anyone one might not feel able to emotionally care about— Bloom suggests that cultivating emotional distance is necessary to care for them effectively and fairly.

Not surprisingly, perhaps, Bloom expresses an interest in Singer and the social and philosophical movement of Effective Altruism (EA), which, following Singer, is based on the idea that people in wealthy countries have the moral obligation to donate large sums to save as many lives overseas as possible.[31] The movement originally started in the form of two charities: Giving What We Can was founded by the philosophers William McAskill and Toby Ord as well as the then physician-in-training Bernadette Young in Oxford in 2009. Members pledge to give at least 10 percent of their income to selected charities that have been deemed by the organization as effective.[32] In 2011, McAskill also cofounded the non-profit 80,000 Hours, which refers to the length of an average career.[33] In the same year, the Oxford-based Centre for Effective Altruism was formed as an umbrella for both organizations. Since then, the Centre has incubated more charities, hosted several conferences, and published academic research as well as popular outputs.[34] Like Bloom, the EA movement puts a strong emphasis on rationalist decision-making, suggesting

30 Bloom, *Against Empathy*, 39.

31 See Bloom, *Against Empathy*, 102–5.

32 See Giving What We Can, accessed August 1, 2022, https://www.givingwhatwecan.org. I would like to thank Mererid Puw Davies for pointing out that this suggestion harks back to Christian tradition, 10 percent being literally a "tithe" (tenth), formerly taken to support the church and clergy.

33 See 80,000 Hours, accessed August 1, 2022, https://80000hours.org.

34 See "History," Centre for Effective Altruism, accessed August 1, 2022, https://www.centreforeffectivealtruism.org/history.

the use of "evidence and reason in order to find the most promising causes to work on."[35]

The principles of EA are surrounded by controversy: critics have challenged the fact that the approach seems to shift responsibility from politics to individuals; raised concerns that the movement is ultimately a form of elitist philanthropy; or problematized the overvaluation of measurable impact.[36] Interestingly in the context of this chapter, American writer Larissa MacFarquhar has described EA as the "drone program of altruism," referring to the ideal of emotional distance it ascribes to "doing good" in the right way. EA requires one to "act upon people at such a distance they become abstractions," which MacFarquhar likens to the detached brutality of drone warfare. It is this abstraction, she writes, that makes the approach off-putting to many.[37] Note that geographical and emotional distance become entangled here: arguably, the problematic distance MacFarquhar observes as part of the EA approach is less related to the fact that EA encourages people to (also) help geographically distant strangers than to its exhortation that people override their intuitive emotional responses to immediate urgency and consider whether their help could go farther elsewhere. MacFarquhar argues that "to many people, to suppress emotional connection to make way for a more rational altruism is to crush their moral roots."[38] In other words, the emotional distance required to follow EA principles may, according to MacFarquhar, prevent people from feeling any ethical motivation in the first place.

According to Bloom, however, MacFarquhar's line of thinking would arguably be one of the detrimental effects of an ethics based on empathy, because it may let emotional proximity guide our decisions on who deserves our care or help. Bloom follows Singer's ethical dictum that distance *should* not matter for morality; but as a psychologist, he is interested

---

35 See Effective Altruism, accessed May 25, 2023, https://www. effectivealtruism.org. See also William MacAskill, *Doing Good Better: Effective Altruism and a Radical New Way to Make a Difference* (New York: Avery, 2015).

36 See for example, Srinivasan, "Stop the Robot Apocalypse"; Paul Gomberg, "The Fallacy of Philanthropy," *Canadian Journal of Philosophy* 32, no. 1 (March 2002): 29–66; Mathew Snow, "Against Charity," *Jacobin*, August 25, 2015, https://www.jacobinmag.com/2015/08/peter-singer-charity-effective-altruism/. Some of these criticisms have in turn been rejected by the EA movement as "myths and misconceptions." See, for example, Ben Chugg, "Don't We Need Political Action Rather than Charity?," Giving What We Can, April 21, 2021, https://www.givingwhatwecan.org/post/2021/04/dont-we-need-political-action-rather-than-charity/.

37 Larissa MacFarquhar, "Response to Effective Altruism," *Boston Review*, July 1, 2015, https://bostonreview.net/forum_response/response-larissa-macfarquhar/.

38 MacFarquhar, "Response to Effective Altruism."

in explaining why it nevertheless *does* matter to most people in their every-day ethical decision-making. So, while all four writers I have discussed so far—Singer, Slote, Nussbaum, and Bloom—are concerned with creating ethical responses to distant suffering, their approaches differ: Slote's ethics of care and empathy and Nussbaum's project of civic compassion aim at bringing distant strangers emotionally closer, while both Singer and Bloom propagate the cultivation of distance as a kind of universalist "detachment from one's own cultural affiliations" to cancel out the intuitive bias of empathic proximity.[39]

Cultivating Distance for Rational Compassion

As the discussion above indicates, there exists a lack of terminological clarity regarding the definitory separation between the related concepts of empathy, sympathy, pity, and compassion. Bloom's understanding of empathy as an identificatory co-suffering could be specified, as he says himself, through the distinction between cognitive and emotional empathy. The former merely recognizes someone else's emotion, whereas the latter means that one individual experiences the same emotions as another person.[40] This distinction seems to have been originally made by psychologist Paul Ekman.[41] Bloom's critique is therefore mainly directed at emotional empathy, as it appears, just like Schopenhauer's conception of *Mitleid*, to do away with the interpersonal distance that separates the subject from the other in pain. His idea of "rational compassion" could then perhaps best be described as a combination of cognitive empathy and a third type of empathy; that is to say, "compassionate empathy," which, according to Ekman, refers to the willingness to help a suffering other.[42] Crucially, Ekman too highlights that cognitive empathy is a prerequisite for compassionate empathy, but emotional empathy is not. Against critics like MacFarquhar, the ideas of psychologists Bloom and Ekman therefore seem to resonate with Singer's position that empathy understood as a form of emotional identification is not necessary for, and in Bloom's argument is even detrimental to, ethical action.

Bloom's criticism of empathy as ethical motivator is that, above all, it tends to make the people acting on their empathy feel good about themselves, as it lets them identify as a caring, warm, generally good person,

---

39 Amanda Anderson, *The Power of Distance: Cosmopolitanism and the Cultivation of Detachment* (Princeton, NJ: Princeton University Press, 2001), 63.

40 Bloom, *Against Empathy*, 17.

41 Paul Ekman, *Emotions Revealed: Understanding Faces and Feelings* (London: Phoenix, 2003), 180.

42 Ekman, *Emotions Revealed*, 180. See also Haustein, "'J'ai mal à l'autre,'" 132.

while possibly yielding less effective or even harmful results.[43] It seems indisputable that an informed and possibly unbiased approach is crucial when considering ethical questions, at an individual or political level. What interests me for the purposes of this chapter is how Bloom's concept of rational compassion offers an ideal of both emotional and physical distance. Arguably, this ideal also informs the psycho-social aspects of ethical "response-ability" at a distance that play a role in the workings of "Violence Elsewhere": emotional detachment, as a form of cultivated distance (Bloom suggests to "take a step back"), is here seen as a marker of rationality and impartiality.[44] This oppositional juxtaposition of emotionality and reason has its roots in the philosophy of the Enlightenment and has since then informed many critiques of co-suffering long before Bloom: "In the man who lives by the guidance of reason," writes Baruch Spinoza, for example, "pity is in itself bad and disadvantageous."[45]

This subordination of emotion to reason has long been critically analyzed by feminist and critical race theorists. One of the most rigorous critical analyses of these politics of emotion has been provided by Sara Ahmed. The primacy of reason over emotions is, as Ahmed writes, "bound up with the securing of social hierarchy," in which expressions of strong emotions are associated with stereotypes of femininity and of racialized groups.[46] Being personally and emotionally affected is, then, interpreted as a lack of objectivity and of critical distance. This lack of distance in turn allegedly leads to a limited ability to form valid moral judgments. The Kantian separation of emotion and morality establishes, Ahmed argues, those social hierarchies "which allow women and racial others to be seen as less moral, as less capable of making judgments: it is such others, of course, who are often presented as being 'swayed by their emotions.'"[47] Bloom is certainly right to criticize the "feel-good narratives" that an empathy- or emotionality-based approach to ethics may create. At the same time, I want to argue here that reason-focused approaches like Bloom's own concept of rational compassion offer a similarly comfortable identificatory position. If an ethics of empathy, like Slote's, may implicitly entail the judgment that a deeply felt emotional response to someone else's suffering as the motivation to providing help is an attribute of a "good person," Bloom's "rational compassion" invokes the superior

43 Bloom, *Against Empathy*, 101.

44 Bloom, *Against Empathy*, 101.

45 Baruch Spinoza, *Ethics. Treatise on the Emendation of the Intellect and Selected Letters*, ed. Seymur Feldman, trans. Samuel Shirley (Indianapolis: Hackett, 1992), 50, 181. I take this quotation from Haustein, "'J'ai mal à l'autre,'" 133.

46 Sara Ahmed, *The Cultural Politics of Emotion* (2004; Edinburgh: Edinburgh University Press, 2014), 3.

47 Ahmed, *Cultural Politics of Emotion*, 195.

position of the detached, unswayable, rational—implicitly conceptualized as male—subject in the tradition of the Enlightenment. His idea of distance, in the concept of "distanced compassion," creates a Kantian impression of neutrality, of an intellectual detachment that enables objective judgments, as opposed to the biased spotlight of empathy that favors certain individuals or groups over others. These judgments are then supposed to inform Bloom's concept of "distant compassion": the individual responds here to distant suffering not based on emotions but on a possibly objective evaluation. This ideal of distance uncritically reproduces the Kantian ideal of detachment and in this way runs the risk of also reestablishing the same social hierarchies. As such, it provides readers with the same comfortable identificatory subject position of impartiality and superiority.

Several decades before Bloom, political philosopher Hannah Arendt articulated a similar ideal of cultivated distance in politics in her seminal book *On Revolution* (1963). According to Arendt, politics needs distance and should avoid any kind of identificatory co-suffering. Arendt's critique of compassion corresponds here to Bloom's problematization of empathy:

> Compassion, by its very nature, cannot be touched off by the suffering of a whole class or people, or, least of all, mankind as a whole. It cannot reach out farther than one person and still remain what it is supposed to be, co-suffering. Its strength hinges on the strength of passion itself, which, in contrast to reason, can comprehend only the particular, but has no notion of the general and no capacity for generalization.[48]

Notably, for Arendt, compassion is characterized by a distinct lack of distance and resembles the element of co-suffering in emotional empathy: "compassion abolishes the distance, the worldly space between men where political matters ... are located."[49] By contrast, "pity" means "to be sorry without being touched in the flesh," and is thus perhaps comparable to cognitive empathy.[50] As such, pity is for Arendt a "perversion of compassion" that may, by dint of its sentimental distance, reach farther than compassion and therefore enter politics but runs the risk of being enjoyed for its own sake.[51] A politics of pity, Arendt writes, depends on the existence of suffering and therefore may be invested in its continued existence.[52] The real alternative to compassion is therefore not a politics of pity, but

48   Hannah Arendt, *On Revolution* (London: Penguin, 1963), 85.
49   Arendt, *On Revolution*, 86.
50   Arendt, *On Revolution*, 85.
51   Arendt, *On Revolution*, 87.
52   Arendt, *On Revolution*, 89.

"solidarity," a principle that enables "men" to establish "dispassionately a community of interest with the oppressed and exploited."[53]

Like Bloom with his critique of the proximity bias of empathy, Arendt dismisses what she calls compassion. Because it necessarily entails emotional investment, it cannot reach further than the individual case. Bloom's concept of "rational compassion" would perhaps be dismissed by Arendt as a politics of pity. With her principle of solidarity, however, she puts a very similar emphasis on the separation of rationality and emotion. For Arendt, the supposed lack of emotionality involved in solidarity appears to count as evidence for its rational and therefore objective quality. Emotional distance—or "dispassionateness," in Arendt's words— is therefore presented as a necessary condition for a political approach to suffering that is based on rationality. Arendt invokes here, therefore, the same dichotomy of emotionality and reason as the tradition of the Enlightenment. Another aspect in Arendt's passage is insightful, however, because it also reveals something that is only implicit in Bloom's book. Note the use of the passive voice in Arendt's language, which entirely removes the positionality and subjectivity of the oppressor: on one side, there is the vague group of the "oppressed" (by whom?) and on the other, we seem to have "men," the universalist, unmarked, and "neutral" position that seems to be the target group of address in Arendt's writing here. Solidarity is enacted by those who find themselves, as it were, lucky to not be suffering, while their possible complicity with or implication in those structures of oppression is not mentioned, let alone explored. In this way Arendt creates a subject position that combines emotional distance ("dispassionately") with a position of uninvolved distance.

It is undoubtedly easier to maintain this sense of distance when one is also separated by geographical distance from suffering taking place elsewhere. An ethical and political focus on violence elsewhere is therefore more likely to allow the subject to present themselves as rationally detached and therefore ethically superior. In this way, the phantasmatic scene of distant suffering, and "violence elsewhere" as a specific variation of this scene that provides a "stage" for imaginable and representable violence, offer two—in themselves perhaps conflicting—invitations to identify with a protagonist position of moral superiority. As I have shown in the first section of this chapter, the notion of "caring at a distance" carries within itself the narrative of moral refinement through the cultivation of emotions that is supposed to overcome distance. In this second section, I have focused on the ideal of cultivated emotional distance as a stance of moral superiority. Bloom's concept of "rational compassion," while putting a strong emphasis on rational detachment, manages nevertheless to

---

53 Arendt, *On Revolution*, 86.

offer both invitations by combining rationality with compassion (as a feeling for, and not with, the suffering other).

One can argue that there is nothing wrong with such a concept of rational compassion, in the same way that there is nothing wrong with the strong turnout at the Black Lives Matter protest in Berlin that Amjahid witnessed. In both cases, however, there emerges a sense of lack, of something crucial that is missing: "Where were all these people after Hanau?" asks Amjahid, with good reason. One answer may lie in the very concept of "distanced compassion": in response to Nussbaum's ideal of political compassion, briefly discussed in the previous section, Srinivasan has argued that compassion is not a useful concept in the political context. Even though Nussbaum's hope is that compassion could be cultivated to *overcome* distance, it does, Srinivasan points out, quite the opposite: "Compassion is," in fact, "too distancing, representing the suffering as not having anything to do with our own actions or position."[54] Srinivasan's criticism reveals the tacit function of many ideals of cultivated distance: it seemingly removes the subject from the entangled messes of violence, oppression, and power.

In other words, the use of compassion as universal ethico-political category tends to automatically center the subject position of the uninvolved spectator who is not implicated in whatever injustice, violence, or suffering that is seen as the cause for compassion in the first place. And as convincing as Bloom's critique of the proximity bias of empathy is, his alternative proposal of distanced compassion also uncritically reproduces the illusion of a neutral position that seems to lie completely outside of any victim-perpetrator dynamic. On the face of it, "distance" has here the function of countering biases. This detachment, however, also creates a conveniently "safe distance" from suffering, violence, and injustice by conceptualizing the ethical subject as an uninvolved spectator.

Accordingly, Bloom's book does not address questions of asymmetric power structures, positionality, complicity, or implication. Besides moral refinement and superior ethical judgment, distant suffering and "violence elsewhere" therefore offer another rather comfortable subject position: that of innocence. Arguably, this is why a case of violence elsewhere, such as racist police brutality in the United States, can engender more widespread "rational compassion" in Germany than a racist terrorist attack in the German central state of Hessen, for the latter would require a confrontation and deeper engagement with institutionally and culturally embedded structures of racism within Germany itself.

---

54   Amia Srinivasan, "The Political Limits of Compassion," in *Political Emotions: Towards a Decent Public Sphere*, ed. Thom Brooks (London: Palgrave, 2022), 99–114, here 104.

Standing By and Stepping Back:
Two Interrelated Idealized Myths of Distance

Despite the differing approaches of all the thinkers so far discussed in this chapter, they all create a phantasmatic scene of distant suffering that implicitly centers the uninvolved spectator as protagonist. I have argued that this is the case in Bloom's book with its focus on rational, distanced compassion, and in Arendt's principle of dispassionate solidarity. Singer does discuss the fact that nations in the Global North tend to carry direct and indirect responsibility for many forms of suffering happening in the Global South, and he also addresses different forms of individual and collective complicity.[55] His signature scenario of a child drowning in a shallow pond, however, does not consider the ethical subject as being initially involved or complicit in the victim's peril. Rather, it is the classic scenario of the uninvolved bystander and a discussion of the moral obligations that emerge from that position. Slote creates in the cited passage a universally shared "we" that consists of mostly detached bystanders who could be made to care more for others suffering at a distance but who do not seem to have to grapple with the ways they might be complicit in such suffering. Nussbaum draws connections between the moral citizen and the spectator of theatrical tragedy, thereby explicitly constituting the ethical subject as compassionate spectator.[56]

This commonality between the thinkers in question is not accidental but, rather, has similar intellectual roots to the ideal of critical emotional distance and rationality. As Luc Boltanski has shown in his book *Distant Suffering: Morality, Media and Politics* (1999), the ethical subject who is confronted with an other's suffering has been conceptualized, since the political philosophy of the eighteenth century, as an uninvolved spectator. Boltanski offers a helpful account of the intellectual history of this spectator figure, which in turn also plays an integral role in his own development of what he calls a politics of pity: Adam Smith, in *The Theory of Moral Sentiments* (1759), appears here as the most systematic and rigorous architect of the figure of the "uninvolved spectator observing a suffering unfortunate."[57] In order for Smith's theory to work, Boltanski explains, it is "absolutely necessary" that the spectator "be defined as someone *uninvolved*," as Smith's interest lies in exploring the "fundamental

---

55 Peter Singer, *Practical Ethics* (Cambridge: Cambridge University Press, 1979); e.g., 165, 210, 229–30, 237. See also Luc Boltanski, *Distant Suffering: Morality, Media and Politics*, trans. Graham Burchell (Cambridge: Cambridge University Press, 1999), 16–17.

56 See the informative passage on the conceptual intersections between the moral subject as a spectator and the theater as a metaphor for social life in Boltanski, *Distant Suffering*, 24–27.

57 Boltanski, *Distant Suffering*, 35.

political question" of possibilities of agreement and communication between "unequally *affected* or unequally *concerned* persons."[58]

At the same time, Boltanski, following Smith, asserts that speaking of atrocities "with the same kind of detachment and precision one would use to speak of a system of economic regulation" is immoral in its own way. Therefore, a language of complete objectivity is not appropriate for a discursive engagement with distant suffering. Boltanski argues that while detachment and impartiality are crucial requirements for the role of the spectator, it is nevertheless necessary to develop an "emotive style," which both guarantees the factual objectivity of an impartial spectator and the ethical responsiveness and commitment that may inspire others to act.[59] To this end, spectators must not simply observe the distant suffering but must detach themselves from this observing position and report the feelings they experience when confronted with the suffering. The affectedness of the spectator, however, is explicitly not one of empathy in the sense of co-suffering and identification but a more distanced form of sympathy that is simply the presupposition for human morality.[60] This type of second-order observation, Boltanski argues, enables the ethical subject to fulfill the demands of both objective factuality and subjective affectedness. The latter is necessary for individual ethical commitment to facilitate change. Despite the spectator's own emotional affectedness and introspective self-involvement in their report of suffering, "he" [*sic*, i.e., the spectator] is therefore a figure of "purity," in the sense that "he [*sic*] is completely independent of the scene he views."[61]

Michael Rothberg's book *The Implicated Subject: Beyond Victims and Perpetrators* (2019), however, has offered a generative critique of this tradition of the "'caring' but detached bystander."[62] Rothberg writes that discourses about injustice tend to invoke the three neatly separated figures of victims, perpetrators, and bystanders. He argues persuasively that while this third position is important because it goes beyond the perpetrator/victim dichotomy, the innocent, uninvolved bystander is, in most cases, an idealized myth.[63] Against this myth, Rothberg then introduces his own

---

58 Boltanski, *Distant Suffering*, 36 (italics in original).
59 Boltanski, *Distant Suffering*, 41.
60 Boltanski, *Distant Suffering*, 37.
61 Boltanski, *Distant Suffering*, 27.
62 Michael Rothberg, *The Implicated Subject: Beyond Victims and Perpetrators* (Stanford, CA: Stanford University Press, 2019), 33.
63 Rothberg, *The Implicated Subject*, 202. Another category, frequently invoked particularly in the context of German Nazism, is that of the "Mitläufer" (passive follower). While certainly not a term that designates ethical superiority, it nevertheless provides a "mantle of relative innocence in the face of forces presented as beyond their [the followers'] control or understanding," according to Jonas Bach and Benjamin Nienass, "Introduction: Innocence and the Politics of

category of the implicated subject: "A theory of implication," he writes, takes into account "the fact that—except for some fantasized ultimate victim or resistance fighter—most subjects find themselves enmeshed in histories and structures of violence they may not realize they inhabit or prop up.... Analysis of implication refuses a moralization of politics by remaining skeptical of assertions of purity."[64] Rothberg's theory of the implicated subject has highlighted, then, that "unaffected" does, in fact, not automatically equal "uninvolved."

The disruptive potential of Rothberg's critique becomes clear when one considers how much the figure of the uninvolved spectator has dominated the discourses of political philosophy and how influential this subject position remains in political debates today. Boltanski emphasizes that the modern conception of the public sphere "presupposes the existence of a detached, casual observer who can survey the peculiarities of society in a way that the geographer, cartographer or painter inspired by the cartographic ideal surveys the peculiarities of a landscape."[65] Boltanski argues that while Smith's original setting of this scene is primarily concerned with a face-to-face encounter between the spectator and the unfortunate, it can nevertheless serve as a "modelling of moral relationships between persons when the political order incorporates a reference to pity."[66] Boltanski's reasoning is crucial for the discussion of "violence elsewhere." By basing their theory on the neat separation between the spectator and the "unfortunate," thinkers concerned with the ethics of suffering since Smith have set the phantasmatic scene of suffering at a distance, starring the uninvolved bystander as a safe, identificatory protagonist, a figure of purity and innocence. Boltanski's own analysis both complicates and upholds this separation at the same time. For example, he makes clear that Smith's positions of spectator and unfortunate in the public sphere are not fixed identities but, rather, functions or roles within a particular constellation of suffering: "The same person may be sufferer and spectator in turn."[67] He also acknowledges that distant spectators, as members of wealthy nations, may be called accomplices and beneficiaries in the exploitation of members of distant nations, which causes the

---

Memory," *German Politics and Society* 39, no. 1 (2021): 1–14, here 5. I believe that Rothberg's category of the bystander does imply both the superior neutral observer and the morally deficient, yet still relatively innocent, passive follower. Rothberg's suggestion to complicate these categories through the concept of implication effectively avoids the relativization inherent in the idea of the "Mitläufer."

64 Rothberg, *The Implicated Subject*, 49.
65 Boltanski, *Distant Suffering*, 29.
66 Boltanski, *Distant Suffering*, 37.
67 Boltanski, *Distant Suffering*, 39.

members of the latter nations to suffer.[68] He dismisses such forms of collective responsibility, however, for the development of his own politics of pity, the exploration of which would exceed the scope this chapter.

The necessary distance between spectator and unfortunate is even easier to maintain when both subject positions are additionally separated through geographical distance. As we have seen through the selective assembly of paradigmatic examples in this chapter, the idealized myth of the bystander continues to be implicitly and repeatedly reproduced in the philosophical approaches to distant suffering: the phantasmatic scene of distant suffering and of "violence elsewhere" as a specific variation of this scene precisely provide the position of such distanced spectatorship. And this subject position of the uninvolved bystander appears to be inextricably linked to yet another idealized myth of the same philosophical tradition; that is to say, the ideal of emotional distance as a marker of neutrality, objectivity, and intellectual inquiry. "Standing by" and "stepping back" are therefore two interrelated ideals of cultivated distance that play an integral part in the way suffering at a distance is constructed as a phantasmatic scene by many philosophical thinkers.

The intersection between these two idealized myths of distance in the phantasmatic scene of distant suffering is not surprising. They both belong to the "old saws of Western philosophy," as Donna Haraway has put it—in particular, to the idea of "bounded individualism."[69] The figure of the uninvolved, detached, neutral bystander is an offspring of "the primary and founding figure of the human," who is not only unequivocally masculine but also, conveniently, from the start an independent, self-sufficient adult, as Butler has argued.[70] Both Haraway and Butler problematize this figure of independent, detached individualism as a social-cultural fiction that props up anthropocentric, androcentric, and Western-centric narratives. In the context of "violence elsewhere," I think it is worth making this point explicit: the figure of the uninvolved but caring bystander is above all a figure of innocence. But it is also connected to the figure of the superior, detached observer; that is to say, to the constructs of ideological impartiality and objectivity. The notion of suffering at a distance operates, then, as a phantasmatic scene in which the caring, uninvolved bystander holds the role of the protagonist. This scene implicitly provides the fulfillment of two ego-driven desires: a position of both innocence and superiority.

Moreover, if ethical response-ability is primarily conceptualized through distant suffering, this conception has more problematic effects than just offering a comfortable subject position of neutrality and

---

68 Boltanski, *Distant Suffering*, 16–17.
69 Haraway, *Staying with the Trouble*, 30.
70 Butler, *The Force of Nonviolence*, 37.

innocence. It also excludes those with ties and proximities to the suffering from participating in the discourse around it. Boltanski's insistence on distance to suffering as essential for a politics of pity makes this exclusionary aspect explicit:

> It is inherent in a politics of pity to deal with suffering from the standpoint of distance since it must rely upon the massification of a collection of unfortunates who are not there in person. For when they come together in person to invade the space of those more fortunate than they and with the desire to mix with them, to live in the same places and to share the same objects, then they no longer appear as unfortunates and, as Hannah Arendt says, are transformed into "*les enragés*."[71]

The idea of suffering that deserves pity but not a right to active participation seems to take the etymological roots of "emotionality" as "passivity" literally: Ahmed points out that emotionality—that is, being moved by the passions—comes from the Latin *passio*, suffering.[72] A suffering other who encroaches on the fortunate's space and who is actively and emotionally making demands is no longer seen to be unfortunate and, one may deduce, apparently no longer deserving of care. A politics of pity that is defined in such ways therefore can never function as a form of solidarity within one's own societal structures. It is exclusively directed at suffering others whose distance to the ethical subject (supposedly) secures that subject's position of impartiality and innocence.

Additionally, the figure of the spectator does not only create an assumption of purity at the individual level but seems to imply a homogeneous group of spectators looking at the suffering from a distance. In her famous essay *Regarding the Pain of Others*, Susan Sontag has both critiqued and analyzed the use of "we" that seems to crop up so easily in the discourse of distant suffering: "No 'we' should be taken for granted," she writes in the beginning, "when the subject is other people's pain."[73] At the end of her essay, Sontag herself slips into that "we," but here she makes its homogenizing function fully transparent. Writing about photographs of victims of war, she speaks about "us" as the spectators of these images: "Why should they [the depicted victims] seek our gaze? What would they have to say to us? 'We'—this 'we' is everyone who has never experienced anything like what they went through—don't understand. We truly can't imagine what it was like."[74] Sontag's focus lies on the spe-

---

71   Boltanski, *Distant Suffering*, 13.
72   Ahmed, *Cultural Politics of Emotion*, 4.
73   Susan Sontag, *Regarding the Pain of Others* (London: Penguin, 2003), 6.
74   Sontag, *Regarding the Pain of Others*, 113.

cific function of images that bring distant suffering affectively closer and on the ethical implications this new proximity might carry.

A differentiated engagement with the topic of distant suffering and media images lies beyond the scope of this chapter and has been discussed by thinkers like Boltanski and Butler.[75] My interest here lies in Sontag's delineation of the "we," which, I believe, may give productive impulses for the discussion of "violence elsewhere," perhaps also specifically in the German-language context. If "we" always designates a distance to suffering, it creates the illusion of a homogenous community of spectators. The phantasmatic scene of distant suffering therefore relies not only on a "massification of a collection of unfortunates," as Boltanski puts it, but also on a generalization of "fortunate spectators."[76] As such, this phantasmatic scene relies on the notion of what the literary scholar Jessica Berman has termed the assumption of a "shared conception of 'we.'"[77] This assumption becomes problematic, Berman explains, when it fails to account for "the metaphysics that make such a 'we' possible."[78] In other words, this shared conception of "we" tends to assume a neutral universality without considering the different positionalities, perspectives, and power imbalances that may structure such a "we."

This tendency is reflected quite literally in the writing discussed above in the frequent use of the word "we" in the subject position: Bloom, Slote, and Nussbaum are prone to this rhetorical move that implicitly creates the sense of a both universal and homogenous group of subjects. In the context of suffering at a distance, this "we" stands homogenously apart from those who suffer, which simplifies and obscures the complex ways different positionalities may imply different entanglements with such suffering.

Distant Suffering and the "Shared We" in the German Context

This problematization of a "shared we" and its "metaphysics" has a distinctive significance in the German context. As the author Deniz Utlu writes in his important essay of 2018, "Empathische Solidarität: Gegenwartsbewältigung als Emanzipation" (Empathetic Solidarity: Coming to Terms with the Present as Emancipation), the German dominant culture suffers from an "unbewältigten nationalistischen

75 See, for example, Boltanski, *Distant Suffering*; Butler, *Notes toward a Performative Theory*, 102–4, 120–21.

76 Boltanski, *Distant Suffering*, 13.

77 Jessica Berman, *Modernist Fiction: Cosmopolitanism and the Politics of Community* (Cambridge: Cambridge University Press, 2001), 12.

78 Berman, *Modernist Fiction*, 12.

Pathologie" (unresolved nationalist pathology) that is rooted in a paradoxical construction of its national identity. The dominant cultural narrative that defines German identity is inextricably linked to the idea of *Vergangenheitsbewältigung*.[79] The common English translation of this term as "coming to terms with the past" appears to lose the complicated elements of "mastering" and "overcoming" that are inherent in the German original term. The term seems to suggest that the German nation has now worked through its past as perpetrators and is now defined by this process and its supposed result: an "open" society.

But how can a society really be open if its national identity is defined by the task of having come to terms with its Nazi past? Utlu asks, How can immigrants and their descendants, people who do not share family histories implicated in the "Third Reich" and the Shoah, become part of a nation that defines its identity precisely by the overcoming of that past?[80] Moreover, a society whose self-image is based on the necessary assumption that it sees itself as "open" is incapable of investigating and showing accountability for its own prevailing racist and discriminatory structures: "Eine Gesellschaft wie die deutsche, die sich von anderen durch Offenheit abgrenzen möchte, kann den eigenen Rassismus nicht leicht eingestehen, weil dies ihre Identitätskonstruktion destabilisieren würde" (For a society that wishes to distinguish itself from others through openness, as the German society does, it is difficult to acknowledge its own racism because this would destabilize the construction of its identity).[81]

Here, the phantasmatic scene of distant suffering that appears with great frequency in North American and European philosophical discourses on the ethics of suffering makes a convenient identificatory offer whose reliance on the purity of the spectator chimes well with the wish in German dominant culture to sever all ties to the former role as perpetrator. For an ethical response-ability that avoids the evacuation of one's own situation as described by Butler, however, a different, critical interrogation of one's subject position is required: "A clear understanding of one's own implication in multileveled conditions of violence and injustice is not a sufficient condition for social change, but it may be a necessary step for the creation of alliances among differently situated subjects," writes Rothberg.[82] Utlu makes a case for such an alliance when he discusses the emancipatory potential of Turkish-Jewish solidarities in Germany that could create new forms of belonging that are not geared

---

79   Deniz Utlu, "Empathische Solidarität: Gegenwartsbewältigung als Emanzipation," *Jalta: Positionen zur jüdischen Gegenwart* 4, no. 2 (2018): 65–72, here 65. Unless otherwise stated, translations are the author's own.

80   Utlu, "Empathische Solidarität," 65.

81   Utlu, "Empathische Solidarität," 68.

82   Rothberg, *The Implicated Subject*, 33.

to the recognition practices of German dominant culture.[83] Crucially, the concept Utlu proposes for this alliance, empathetic solidarity, drawing upon the work of sociologist Uwe Schimank, overcomes the simplistic dichotomy of emotion, on the one hand, and reason, on the other: empathy for the other group's position overcomes the particular strategic interests of one's own group. Through this process of empathetic understanding, a common goal is reached that is ultimately a better result for all. Utlu highlights that in the case of empathetic solidarity between two marginalized groups, the common goal goes beyond the strategic aims of each individual group and produces a reorientation of both groups away from the dominant culture.[84]

Utlu's essay is only one of a number of important intellectual contributions that in recent years have critically interrogated the constructions of a "shared we" in German culture. Other selected examples are Czollek's books *Desintegriert Euch!* (Disintegrate Yourselves!, 2018) and *Gegenwartsbewältigung* (Coming to Terms with the Present, 2020); the anthology *Eure Heimat ist unser Alptraum* (Your Home Country Is Our Nightmare, 2020), edited by Fatma Aydemir and Hengameh Yaghoobifarah; Asal Dardan's *Betrachtungen einer Barbarin* (Reflections of a [Female] Barbarian, 2021); or the unscripted Instagram live conversation between the artist Moshtari Hilal and the political geographer Sinthujan Varatharajah, in which they coined the term "Menschen mit Nazihintergrund" (people with a Nazi background).[85]

Hilal's and Varatharajah's term "people with a Nazi background" is supposed to serve as a countercategory to the expression "Menschen mit Migrationshintergrund" (people with a migration background) to mark the group of Germans who usually reserve the right to mark others and the privilege to exist as the unmarked, universal norm. Moreover, it is meant to highlight the material continuities of Nazi heritage and, indeed, concrete inheritance that allow some Germans still to benefit from the appropriation of Jewish property during Nazi rule.[86] Hilal's

---

83   Utlu, "Empathische Solidarität," 72.

84   See Utlu, "Empathische Solidarität," 71.

85   See Max Czollek, *Desintegriert Euch!* (Munich: Hanser, 2018); Max Czollek, *Gegenwartsbewältigung* (Munich: Hanser: 2020); Fatma Aydemir and Hengameh Yaghoobifarah, eds., *Eure Heimat ist unser Alptraum* (Berlin: Ullstein, 2019); Asal Dardan, *Betrachtungen einer Barbarin* (Hamburg: Hoffmann und Kampe, 2021); Moshtari Hilal and Sinthujan Varatharajah, "Nazierbe," Instagram Live, February 15, 2021, https://www.instagram.com/tv/CLU2dZiqv MG/?igshid=YmMyMTA2M2Y=.

86   See the interview with both thinkers in *ze.tt*, the youth magazine of *Zeit Online*, March 19, 2021, https://www.zeit.de/zett/politik/2021-03/ ns-familiengeschichte-instagram-diskussion-nazihintergrund-moshtari-hilal-sinthujan-varatharajah#comments.

and Varatharajah's notion was picked up by none other than Rothberg in an op-ed in the *Berliner Zeitung* that later appeared in English in the *Los Angeles Review of Books*. Praising Hilal's and Varatharajah's important contribution to the German memory discourse, he concluded,

> The notion of "people with a Nazi background" produces discomfort. Yet it also provides an opportunity to address the paradoxes at the heart of German society: the need to acknowledge both the particular and universal dimensions of historical responsibility. What we need—in Germany and elsewhere—is a differentiated solidarity that constructs commonality across the recognition of differences.[87]

This acknowledgment could also invite critical engagement with the way the phantasmatic scenes of distant suffering and "violence elsewhere" have served, and continue to serve, in constructions of white German innocence.

While an appropriately deep engagement with this question lies beyond the scope of this chapter, work on "violence elsewhere" can give some indication as to which directions such an exploration could take. An example could be the internationalism of the German left in the 1960s and 1970s, which has often been criticized as a self-reflexive projection: identification with oppressed oppositions in faraway countries, so the argument goes, helped German leftists to distance themselves from their parents' positionality as former Nazi perpetrators by siding with the not necessarily further specified "oppressed Other."[88]

At the same time, the real efforts of internationalist collaboration in the West German student movement should not be reduced to mere "projections" of the German psyche, as historian Quinn Slobodian convincingly argues. Doing so means denying the important activist presence of actual individuals and groups in or from the Global South in West German leftist circles and discourses: "The perverse legacy of [Edward] Said's Orientalism has been that modern European historians pay attention to 'the East' primarily as a mirror with which to see the West more clearly."[89] This does not mean, of course, that the critical analysis of Western-centric projection narratives is no longer necessary. Rather, Slobodian suggests that historical research needs to look beyond those

---

87 Michael Rothberg, "'People with a Nazi Background': Race, Memory, and Responsibility," *Los Angeles Review of Books*, May 2, 2021, https://lareviewofbooks. org/article/people-with-a-nazi-background-race-memory-and-responsibility.

88 Teraoka, *East, West, and Others*, 165. See also Bielby and Davies, "Introduction."

89 Quinn Slobodian, *Foreign Front: Third World Politics in Sixties West Germany* (Durham, NC: Duke University Press, 2012), 11. See also Bielby and Davies, "Introduction."

narratives and make sure they do not occlude transnational "embodied collaborations" as well as the agency and intellectual influence of political actors from the Global South in so-called Western protest movements.[90] The overproximity of identification and self-projection may have played a problematic role in the affective solidarities of white German leftists with oppressed minorities in what was then known as the "Third World." It appears to me, however, that the retrospective framing of such solidarities also can turn them into narratives that follow the logic of the phantasmatic scene of distant suffering that I have analyzed here.

One of the chapters in Slobodian's study is concerned with the memory of June 2, 1967, the day German student Benno Ohnesorg was killed in West Berlin by police during student protests against the state visit of the Iranian shah. Against the conventional historical narratives of this incident as the inner-German political moment that provided the zero hour for the West German "1968," Slobodian highlights the transnational quality of these protests. It was the Iranian student organization Confederation of Iranian Students, National Union, who organized the protests, while the leadership of the Socialist German Students Union was initially reluctant to get involved. The fact that the demonstrations on June 2 turned out to be an "impressive showing of solidarity with a group of Iranian dissidents" did therefore not emerge out of thin air but was mostly due to the impressive educational and mobilization efforts by the members of that very group.[91] Moreover, Bahman Nirumand's book *Persien: Modell eines Entwicklungslandes* (Persia: Model of a Developing Country, 1967), which criticized the Iranian regime, was circulated and read widely in leftist student circles.[92] In the historical narratives, however, as Slobodian notes critically, the central role of these Iranian activists has become marginalized.[93]

In her excellent article "68, ein deutsches Unschuldsmoment" (68, A Moment of German Innocence), the literary critic and Iranian studies scholar Maryam Aras analyzes this systematic neglect of both the participation and the leading role of Iranian students in the German memory culture of June 2, 1967.[94] Aras highlights the construction of a "shared we" of the white German students protesting against the shah and his so-called *Jubelperser* (a goon squad hired by the shah) in the dominant

90 Slobodian, *Foreign Front*, 13.
91 Slobodian, *Foreign Front*, 101.
92 Mererid Puw Davies, *Writing and the West German Protest Movements: Textual Liberation* (London: imlr books, 2016), 70–71.
93 Slobodian, *Foreign Front*, 13.
94 Maryam Aras, "68, ein deutsches Unschuldsmoment," *Collateral: Online Journal for Cross-Cultural Close Reading* 70 (June 2021), http://collateral-journal.com/index.php?collision=70&fbclid=IwAR2k7Yr3fWmzlnxIl8mkztxbHx k9d3Keur5NUPZ1IUCt9IXNLpd8_g9zfyg.

cultural memory of this historical moment. This "shared we," writes Aras, was necessary for the liberating moment of "1968" that emancipated that generation of German students from the Nazi past of their parents:

> Mit 68 hatte man sich von den Nazi-Eltern und -Professoren eman-zipiert. Geschichte wurde selbst in die Hand genommen. Und irgendwie—auch wenn das niemand so sagen würde—wurde man damit selbst zu besseren Menschen. Moralisch überlegen; 68, ein deutsches Unschuldsmoment.[95]

> [With 68, one emancipated oneself from one's Nazi parents. History was taken into one's own hands. And somehow—even though no one would put it this way—one became a better person for it. Morally superior; 68, a moment of German innocence.]

As I have argued in the previous sections of this chapter, both moral superiority and innocence are crucial elements in the phantasmatic scene of distant suffering. It appears that the dominant narratives of "1968" fail to acknowledge the June 2, 1967, protests as a "transnational" event, as Slobodian calls it. And, as Aras rightly summarizes, they fail to recognize the history of the Iranian left in Germany as a part of *German* history. Instead, June 2, 1967, as the initiating event of the "1968" era, is turned into the narrative of white German students that tended to the oppression of Iranian activists as a phantasmatic scene of distant suffering. Acknowledging the role of Iranian activists as an active part of this German history would complicate the construction of the emancipatory "shared we" and therefore of the elements of ethical superiority and innocence.

It is this false sense of distance that arguably still informs some of the dominant notions of white German innocence today. For instance, I do not believe that Amjahid's example of the antiracist protests in present-day Germany—or, rather, their apparent inconsistency as mentioned at the beginning of this chapter—suggests that for the white German majority, the solidarity they demonstrate with victims of police violence in the US is one of identification. Rather, there seems to exist a tendency to excessive distance in this solidarity, which allows some white Germans to position themselves as antiracist without critically questioning the image of Germany as a postfascist society in which institutional racism is no longer a problem. The identificatory position of the uninvolved bystander provided by the phantasmatic scene of distant suffering allows for precisely such uncritical position-taking. Of course, this interpretation does not account for the multiple positionalities within the group of white

---

95   Aras, "68, ein deutsches Unschuldsmoment."

Germans supporting the Black Lives Matter movement. It merely offers another aspect to Amjahid's observation that the support for protests against racist violence seems to be disproportionately stronger when that violence is perceived to be happening elsewhere.

As the author of this chapter, I am writing from the positionality of a German "with a Nazi background," whose late parents played an active part in the "1968" student movement. Critics like Slobodian and Aras convincingly point to the existence of exclusionary, patriarchal, and white hegemonial practices that allowed "1968" to become the moment of German innocence that still prevails in the dominant public discourses about German identity today. Although "1968" itself is arguably a construct that glosses over the diversity of viewpoints, submovements, and positionalities within this movement, I and many other Germans are therefore not only implicated in the violence of Nazi Germany but also in these problematic aspects of the narratives that surround "1968." If confronting "socially sanctioned denial and ignorance and unconscious and conscious investments in privilege and hierarchy"[96] is one of the responsibilities that emerge from implication, then the understanding and critical interrogation of phantasmatic scenes that facilitate and conceal such forms of investment and denial appears like a necessary, albeit not sufficient, component of such confrontations. I hope to have shown in this chapter that "violence elsewhere" can function as a specific variant of distant suffering that operates as one of those phantasmatic scenes.

96 Rothberg, *The Implicated Subject*, 203.

2: War of Words/Words of War: The "Normalization" of War in the Context of Germany's War in Afghanistan (2001–21)

Kathrin Wunderlich

IN 2011, CHRISTIAN RUCK, a member of the German parliament for the Christian Democratic Union, stated that "Afghanistan hat Deutschland verändert" (Afghanistan has changed Germany).[1] Ruck thus suggested that Afghanistan, the country, had been reduced to a signifier for a war that lastingly transformed Germany. Yet, more than a decade after Ruck made this assertion, the exact nature of this transformation remains difficult to ascertain. In the first instance, the transformative nature of the War in Afghanistan can be located in a series of superlatives and "firsts."[2] The military engagement of the Federal Republic of Germany (FRG) in Afghanistan lasted from December 2001 until June 2021, rendering it one of the longest missions in the history of the Bundeswehr, the armed forces of Germany.[3] The Bundeswehr was founded by the West German government in 1955 and absorbed the East German Nationale

---

1   Cited in Michael Daxner, "Heimatdiskurs—ein deutsches Problem?," in *Heimatdiskurs: Wie die Auslandseinsätze der Bundeswehr Deutschland verändern*, ed. Michael Daxner and Hannah Neumann (Bielefeld: transcript, 2012), 15–68, here 56. Unless otherwise indicated, all English translations of German quotations are mine.

2   The term "War in Afghanistan" as it is used here refers to the successive military interventions by United Nations (UN) and North Atlantic Treaty Organisation (NATO) forces in Afghanistan, which lasted from October 2001 until August 2021. The term will be capitalized throughout to reflect its status as a proper noun both in German and in the Afghan dialects Dari and Pashto.

3   Discounting the evacuation mission in 2021, the Bundeswehr was involved in four separate missions in Afghanistan: "Operation Enduring Freedom" (OEF), "International Security Assistance Force" (ISAF), "United Nations Assistance Mission in Afghanistan" (UNAMA) and "Resolute Support." Only the Bundeswehr's involvement in Kosovo, which began in 1999 and, at the time of writing in mid-2024, is ongoing, lasted longer than the military engagement in Afghanistan.

Volksarmee (NVA [National People's Army]) in 1990 in the aftermath of unification. In Afghanistan, more than 150,000 German men and women were deployed as part of the most expensive and deadly mission the Bundeswehr has undertaken to date. Afghanistan also marks the first time since World War II that a German soldier died in battle, the first use of German heavy artillery in combat, and the first military offensive in the Bundeswehr's history.[4] For some, the War in Afghanistan furthermore represents the Federal Republic's loss of (military) innocence; a perspective that highlights both the uncounted civilian victims of the Bundeswehr's actions and frames the country's increasingly militarized foreign policy as part of its coming-of-age process.[5]

Germany's participation in the War in Afghanistan can be considered part of the "normalization" of its foreign policy after unification.[6] After decades of pursuing a largely civilian foreign policy that excluded the use of military force beyond the country's borders, the 1990s saw a gradual remilitarization of German foreign policy that culminated in the participation in air strikes against Serbian targets during the Kosovo War in 1999.[7] The decision to participate in the United States' military response to 9/11 constituted a new level in the process of "normalization." In the aftermath of 9/11, the FRG aimed to articulate a new "normalized" understanding of its foreign policy based on combatting terrorism at its point of origin and confirming its status as a "normal" ally; that is, a country that acted like its peers.[8] In addition to these political "normalizations," the FRG's participation in the War in Afghanistan engendered a significant sense of historical "normalization," as it marked the first time

4   Richard Manner, "Die Bundeswehr in Afghanistan—Eine Chronik von 2001–2010," Bundeswehr.de, accessed June 23, 2022, https://www.bundeswehr.de/de/aktuelles/schwerpunkte/abzug-afghanistan/bundeswehr-afghanistan-2001-2010.

5   Daxner, "Heimatdiskurs," 56; Ralf Beste et al., "Abmarsch in die Realität," *Der Spiegel*, November 11, 2001, https://www.spiegel.de/politik/abmarsch-in-die-realitaet-a-605b894c-0002-0001-0000-000020660098.

6   Quotation marks have been used to indicate that the meanings of this concept and related terms are ambiguous and contested. The scope of this chapter does not allow for an in-depth examination of "normalization." For an introduction to Germany's foreign policy "normalization," see Philip H. Gordon, "Berlin's Difficulties: The Normalization of German Foreign Policy," *Orbis* 38, no. 2 (1994): 225–42.

7   Thomas U. Berger, "A Perfectly Normal Abnormality: German Foreign Policy after Kosovo and Afghanistan," *Japanese Journal of Political Science* 3, no. 2 (2002): 173–93, here 175.

8   Kai Oppermann, "Der 11. September 2001 und die Normalisierung der deutschen Außenpolitik," in *Zeitenwende 9/11? Eine transatlantische Bilanz*, ed. Till Karmann et al. (Opladen: Verlag Barbara Budrich, 2016), 115–42, here 118–19, 130.

that the German parliamentary debates about a military intervention did not invoke the legacy of National Socialism to legitimate or delegitimate the Bundeswehr's involvement.[9] As a result, the military engagement in Afghanistan has been termed the FRG's first "Krieg ohne Hitler" (war without Hitler).[10]

Many of these apparent "normalizations" and "firsts" simultane-ously represent returns: for instance, the return to a state where German military foreign policy was not primarily determined by the legacy of National Socialism but by apparent self-interest in defending Germany against potential future terrorist attacks; the return to war in the form of offensive military action; and the return to a lexis of war. War returned to German political rhetoric, which initially rejected the label "Krieg" (war) but, in 2010, after almost a decade, conceded that the Bundeswehr involvement in Afghanistan indeed resembled a war. The lexis of war also returned to the German vocabulary via a number of terms, like "Front" (front), "Gefallene" (the fallen; that is, soldiers who died in the context of their deployment), and "Feldpost" (war letters), which, like "war" itself, had previously been consigned largely to the German past.

The aim of this chapter is to trace the return of "war" to the political lexis of the Federal Republic and its literary sphere and to determine the extent to which these returns can be conceptualized as "normalizations." The chapter is divided into three parts. The first provides an outline of Germany's involvement in the War in Afghanistan and traces the return of the lexis of "war" in the public realm. The second considers the return of nonfictional war writing in the form of anthologized war letters and military memoirs. The third part turns to Norbert Scheuer's novel *Die Sprache der Vögel* (2016; *The Language of Birds*, 2018).[11] This work par-adigmatically represents the return of fictional war writing to the German-language literary realm, and the chapter proposes a reading of the text based on its intertextual relationship with Erich Maria Remarque's *Im*

9   Wilhelm Knelangen, "Die deutsche Reaktion auf 9/11: Eine 'neue' Politik der Terrorismusbekämpfung?," in Karmann et al., *Zeitenwende 9/11?*, 87–114, here 112. By contrast, political debates about military interventions in the Bos-nian War and the Kosovo War made frequent references to the National Socialist past. See Michael Schwab-Trapp, *Kriegsdiskurse: Die politische Kultur des Krieges im Wandel 1991–1999* (Opladen: Leske & Budrich, 2002).

10   Stefan Reinecke, "Krieg ohne Hitler," *taz*, November 8, 2001, https://taz.de/!1142096/; Maja Zehfuss, *Wounds of Memory: The Politics of War in Germany* (Cambridge: Cambridge University Press, 2007), 7.

11   Norbert Scheuer, *Die Sprache der Vögel* (Munich: Fischer Taschenbuch, 2016). Subsequent references to this source will be indicated in the text and footnotes by the abbreviation *SDV* and page numbers. The novel is translated by Stephen Brown as *The Language of Birds* (London: Haus, 2018), unpaginated eBook, which is the source of the English translations of quotations used here.

Westen nichts Neues (1997 [first published 1929]; *All Quiet on the Western Front*, 2005).[12] In light of the absence of any references to the legacy of National Socialism in Scheuer's text, the novel's intertextual dialogue with Remarque is read as a return to a form of war writing that is untainted by this legacy and thus echoes the historical "normalization" inherent in the FRG's "first war without Hitler." To conclude, this chapter then draws on the returns in language and literature to reflect on what these apparent "normalizations" of war can tell us about the FRG's contemporary relationship to, and role in, violence elsewhere.

Germany's War in Afghanistan: The Return to War

In the immediate aftermath of the terrorist attacks on September 11, 2001, the UN Security Council passed a resolution declaring terrorism to be a threat to global peace and international security and affirmed the right of member states to individual or collective self-defense in line with Article 51 of the UN Charter.[13] At the same time, for the first time in its history NATO invoked Article 5, which considers an attack on one NATO member an attack against all NATO countries, thereby calling upon its members to support the United States in its fight against terrorism.[14] US president George W. Bush presented the Taliban, a reactionary Islamic movement that controlled the majority of Afghanistan at the time, with an ultimatum, demanding that they hand over members of al-Qaeda, including its leader, Osama bin Laden, who was suspected of orchestrating the 9/11 attacks and was believed to be in Afghanistan. After the Taliban refused to comply with these demands, the United States and Great Britain, under the banner of "Operation Enduring Freedom" (OEF), commenced aerial attacks against suspected terrorist targets on October 7, 2001, and were able, with the help of the Afghan Northern Alliance, to defeat the Taliban by mid-November of that year.[15]

The Federal Republic joined OEF in November 2001 and participated in the subsequent International Security Assistance Force (ISAF)

---

12   Erich Maria Remarque, *Im Westen nichts Neues* (1929; Cologne: Kiepenheuer & Witsch, 1997). Subsequent references to this source will be indicated by the abbreviation *IW* and page numbers. The English translation cited is *All Quiet on the Western Front*, trans. Brian Murdoch (London: Vintage, 2005).

13   Klaus Brummer and Stefan Fröhlich, "Einleitung: Zehn Jahre Deutschland in Afghanistan," ed. Klaus Brummer and Stefan Fröhlich, *Sonderheft der Zeitschrift für Außen- und Sicherheitspolitik: Zehn Jahre Deutschland in Afghanistan* 3 (2011): 3–30, here 7.

14   Brummer and Fröhlich, "Einleitung," 8.

15   Margit Reiter and Helga Embacher, "Einleitung," in *Europa und der 11. September 2001*, ed. Margit Reiter and Helga Embacher (Vienna: Böhlau, 2011), 7–23, here 8.

for Afghanistan, assembled by the UN, which specified as its primary objective the support of the interim Afghan government by maintaining security in and around the Afghan capital, Kabul.[16] Initially, German political discourse surrounding the OEF and ISAF mandates categorically rejected the designator "war" for either mission. Despite German involvement in OEF, during the parliamentary debates about this mission it was rhetorically delineated as a US combat operation, whereas ISAF was categorized emphatically as a peacekeeping effort. A clear distinction between "war" and German involvement in Afghanistan was established,[17] to the extent that the Bundeswehr mission was expressly labeled a "Friedensmission" (peace mission) and the Bundeswehr contingent designated to be deployed in this context summarily dubbed "Friedenstruppe" (peace troops).[18]

The rejection and avoidance of the label "war" for the Bundeswehr's engagement in Afghanistan within German political discourse continued for almost a decade. From the late 2000s onward, however, political rhetoric evolved as the conditions for the Bundeswehr in Afghanistan deteriorated. According to Robert Clifford Mann, who was deployed in Afghanistan twice during his ten-year career, Germany's involvement in the War in Afghanistan up to 2011 can be divided into three phases: "Helferzeit" (helper period) from 2002 to 2006, "Opferzeit" (victim period) from 2007 to 2009, and "Kämpferzeit" (warrior period) from 2010 to 2011.[19] The first phase saw NATO take over control of ISAF from the UN and the expansion of the mission to the whole of Afghanistan. Germany assumed responsibility for the northern provinces, which were considered relatively calm and stable.[20] Photographs and film footage from this period taken by news agencies often show Bundeswehr soldiers

16 Brummer and Fröhlich, "Einleitung," 10–11.

17 Semjon Borchert and Martin Wengeler, "Friedensmission, kriegsähnliche Zustände oder Krieg? Öffentliche Sprachreflexion im Zusammenhang mit dem Einsatz der Bundeswehr in Afghanistan," in *Sprachvariation und Sprachreflexion in interkulturellen Kontexten*, ed. Corinna Peschel and Kerstin Runschke (Frankfurt am Main: Peter Lang, 2015), 263–82, here 268.

18 See Deutscher Bundestag, "Plenarprotokoll 14/210," December 22, 2001, https://dserver.bundestag.de/btp/14/14210.pdf.

19 Robert Clifford Mann, "German Warriors," in *Deutschland in Afghanistan*, ed. Michael Daxner (Oldenburg: BIS-Verlag, 2014), 139–53, here 145. The remaining ten years of the war remain uncategorized by Clifford Mann, who blends autobiography, sociology, and military analysis in his writing about the Bundeswehr.

20 Thomas Wiegold, "Der Bundeswehreinsatz in Afghanistan," Bundeszentrale für politische Bildung, December 15, 2016, https://www.bpb.de/themen/militaer/deutsche-verteidigungspolitik/238332/der-bundeswehreinsatz-in-afghanistan/.

traveling in open, unarmored vehicles, often without helmets.[21] Dirk Meyer-Schumann, a Bundeswehr soldier who suffers from post-traumatic stress disorder since his deployment in Afghanistan in 2003, stated that early on, German soldiers were discouraged—presumably by their superiors—from wearing helmets so as to not appear too bellicose.[22] While British and American troops were engaged in active combat in the southern regions of Afghanistan, the Bundeswehr's assignments focused mainly on providing security and reconstruction efforts.[23] From 2006 onward, however, during what Clifford Mann refers to as the "victim period," targeted attacks on German troops increased.[24] Confronted with rising casualty numbers and, according to Clifford Mann, unprepared in terms of equipment and "Mindset," the Bundeswehr was increasingly forced to travel in armored vehicles and to withdraw to its fortified camps.[25]

The "victim period" came to an end in 2009, when the Bundeswehr began to take an increasingly offensive approach in Afghanistan. In July 2009, the Ministry of Defense updated the Bundeswehr's "Taschenkarte" (pocket card). This classified dossier, a multipage document that specifies the "rules of engagement" and is carried by all Bundeswehr soldiers during their deployments, was altered to permit a more offensive use of weapons.[26] German soldiers were now allowed to shoot not only to defend themselves but also to prevent potential attacks,[27] leading to what Clifford Mann refers to as the Bundeswehr's "warrior period."[28]

21 See, for example, Wiegold, "Der Bundeswehreinsatz in Afghanistan."

22 "Wenn die Seele krankt," *Nachtcafé*, Südwestrundfunk (SWR), March 11, 2022, https://www.ardmediathek.de/video/nachtcafe/wenn-die-seele-krankt-oder-talk/swr/Y3JpZDovL3N3ci5kZS9hZXgvbzE2Mjc0NDY.

23 Clifford Mann, "German Warriors," 146.

24 It is not always clear who attacked the German troops. While the media generally identifies the Taliban as the Bundeswehr's main opponent in Afghanistan, Clifford Mann refrains from giving a precise source of the attacks, 147–48, while Johannes Clair states unequivocally that he and his colleagues frequently knew neither who attacked them nor why. Johannes Clair, *Vier Tage im November: Mein Kampfeinsatz in Afghanistan* (Berlin: Ullstein, 2012), 163, 196.

25 Clifford Mann, "German Warriors," 147.

26 Michael Schmidt, "Bundeswehr darf in Afghanistan schneller schießen," *Die Zeit*, July 27, 2009, https://www.zeit.de/online/2009/31/afghanistan-taschenkarte-bundeswehr-jung.

27 Schmidt, "Bundeswehr darf in Afghanistan."

28 Clifford Mann, "German Warriors," 148–49. Neither the operation itself nor its historically charged name, which is reminiscent of "Blitzkrieg" (rapidly advancing warfare) and the "Blitz," a common descriptor for the German aerial bombing campaigns against the United Kingdom during World War II, received much attention in Germany at the time. See "Unser Krieg—Kampfeinsatz in Afghanistan," Zweites Deutsches

The warrior period saw the first use of heavy artillery in the history of the Bundeswehr.[29] German soldiers with support from other ISAF and Afghan troops engaged in offensive combat missions with the aim of recapturing territory from returning Taliban forces. "Operation Halmazag" (the name was chosen by the participating Afghan military forces and is frequently translated as "Blitz" [lightning] in German), which took place in November 2010, marked the first such operation and the first German military offensive since World War II.[30]

It was also during this period, on September 4, 2009, that German Colonel Georg Klein ordered the aerial bombardment of two hijacked fuel trucks stuck in a riverbank near Kunduz, an action that led to the deaths of an estimated 142 persons, the majority of them civilians.[31] Klein's actions constituted "by far, the most aggressive and in its consequences most deadly operational decision for which a German soldier had been responsible since the end of the Second World War."[32] The newsmagazine *Der Spiegel* called it the bloodiest German military operation since World War II and referred to the incident as a "Kriegsverbreche[n]" (war crime).[33] The sentiment circulated widely in the media that Germany, a country that had for decades considered "Nie Wieder Krieg" (Never Again War) to be among its foundational doctrines and prided itself on its humanitarian approach in Afghanistan, had lost its "innocence" in Kunduz.[34] The evolution of the Bundeswehr in Afghanistan, from a force that eschewed the use of helmets for fear of appearing too hostile to one that engaged in full-scale offensive military battle using heavy artillery, illustrates the gradual "normalization" of Germany's War in Afghanistan. That process was reflected in the political rhetoric as well.

With the transformation of ISAF from a security and reconstruction effort into an increasingly offensive combat mission, political discourse around it adapted. Under Angela Merkel's chancellorship, politicians abandoned the term "Friedensmission" (peacekeeping mission) in

---

Fernsehen (ZDF), October 8, 2013, https://www.fernsehserien.de/zdfzeit/folgen/55-unser-krieg-1-kampfeinsatz-afghanistan-538803.

29   "Bundeswehr setzt erstmals schwere Artillerie ein," *Hamburger Abendblatt*, July 12, 2010, https://www.abendblatt.de/politik/ausland/article107820690/Bundeswehr-setzt-erstmals-schwere-Artillerie-ein.html.

30   Manner, "Die Bundeswehr in Afghanistan."

31   Timo Noetzel, "The German Politics of War: Kunduz and the War in Afghanistan," *International Affairs* 87, no. 2 (2011): 397–417, here 397.

32   Noetzel, "German Politics of War," 397.

33   Ulrike Demmer et al., "Ein deutsches Verbrechen," *Der Spiegel* (October 6, 2016), https://www.spiegel.de/spiegel/kunduz-bombardement-ein-deutsches-verbrechen-a-1115445.html.

34   Demmer et al., "Ein deutsches Verbrechen"; Daxner, "Heimatdiskurs," 56.

favor of terms like "Stabilisierungseinsatz" (stabilization deployment) and "Kriseneinsatz" (crisis intervention effort).[35] In the aftermath of Kunduz, the newly appointed minister of defense, Karl-Theodor zu Guttenberg of the Christian Social Union, was the first member of the German government to acknowledge that the Bundeswehr's military engagement in Afghanistan resembled a war. He conceded that the situation in Afghanistan amounted to "kriegsähnliche Zustände" (warlike conditions) but maintained that according to international law, it did not constitute a war, as the conflict was not fought between nation-states.[36]

In 2010, the government officially categorized the situation in Afghanistan as "bewaffneter Konflikt" (armed conflict), which essentially equated it with a civil war, and equipped Bundeswehr soldiers with additional legal protections in events involving the use of lethal force.[37] While this legal framework was upheld, it was rhetorically softened. Guttenberg, for example, described the conditions in Afghanistan "umgangssprachlich als Krieg" (as war in the colloquial sense).[38] Chancellor Merkel similarly maintained the distinction between the legal and the colloquial understanding of the situation:

> Dass die meisten Soldatinnen und Soldaten das, was sie in Afghanistan täglich erleben, Bürgerkrieg oder einfach nur Krieg nennen, das verstehe ich gut. Wer täglich fürchten muss, in einen Hinterhalt zu geraten oder unter gezieltes Feuer zu kommen, der denkt nicht in juristischen Begrifflichkeiten. Wer so etwas erlebt, der fürchtet vielmehr, dass derjenige, der völkerrechtlich korrekt vom nicht internationalen bewaffneten Konflikt spricht, die Situation zu verharmlosen versucht.[39]

> [I understand very well that most soldiers refer to what they experience every day in Afghanistan as a civil war or simply as war. Those who must fear an ambush or being fired at every day do not think in legal concepts. Those who experience such things fear instead that the person who speaks of noninternational armed conflict in line with international law is trying to downplay the situation.]

35 Borchert and Wengeler, "Friedensmission," 270.
36 Borchert and Wengeler, "Friedensmission," 270–71.
37 Hauke Friedrichs, "Der Krieg um die Worte geht zu Ende," *Die Zeit*, February 10, 2010, https://www.zeit.de/politik/deutschland/2010-02/westerwelle-steinmeier-afghanistan/komplettansicht.
38 Borchert and Wengeler, "Friedensmission," 273.
39 Klaus Brummer, "Überzeugungen und Handeln in der Außenpolitik: Der Operational Code von Angela Merkel und Deutschlands Afghanistanpolitik," ed. Klaus Brummer and Stefan Fröhlich, *Sonderheft der Zeitschrift für Außen- und Sicherheitspolitik:Zehn Jahre Deutschland in Afghanistan* 3 (2011): 143–69, here 152.

Merkel's statement is both an illustration of the continued avoidance of the term "war" and a concession to the reality of the Bundeswehr soldiers in Afghanistan and to the German press, which had increasingly employed the word "war" since 2008 and critiqued the government's reluctance to do the same.[40] When Merkel, in December 2010, during a troop visit in Afghanistan, used the term "war" even more explicitly to refer to the Bundeswehr's circumstances in Afghanistan, she generated headlines that affirmed the return of "Krieg" (war) to the German political lexicon.[41] In this context, linguists Semjon Borchert and Martin Wengeler, who have chronicled and analyzed the evolution of terms used to refer to the Bundeswehr's Afghanistan mission, diagnose a "merkwürdige 'Rehabilitierung'" (curious "rehabilitation") of the word "Krieg."[42]

"War" was not the only term to undergo such a rehabilitation. The political scientists Daniel Jacobi, Gunther Hellmann, and Sebastian Nieke note a similar reacceptance of terms like "Kameraden" (comrades) and "Ehre" (honor) into German political and public discourse.[43] Furthermore, they observe, from 2008 onward, a linguistic shift from "getötet" (killed) to "gefallen" (fallen) as a descriptor for soldiers who died during their deployment to Afghanistan.[44] In contrast to the rehabilitation of the term "Krieg," however, this linguistic shift or return to a term that would have last been used during World War II did not provoke a public debate and was even welcomed in certain sections of the German

40   Borchert and Wengeler, "Friedensmission," 270; Some publications used the term "Krieg" from the beginning, see Daniel Jacobi, Gunther Hellmann, and Sebastian Nieke, "Deutschlands Verteidigung am Hindukusch: Ein Fall misslingender Sicherheitskommunikation," *Sonderheft der Zeitschrift für Außen- und Sicherheitspolitik. Zehn Jahre Deutschland in Afghanistan* 3 (2011): 171–96, here 181; Beste et al., "Abmarsch in die Realität."

41   "Merkel nennt Afghanistan-Einsatz 'Krieg,'" *Der Spiegel*, December 18, 2010,   https://www.spiegel.de/politik/ausland/blitzbesuch-der-kanzlerin-merkel-nennt-afghanistan-einsatz-krieg-a-735432.html;   Stephan   Stickelmann and Annamaria Sigrist, "Merkel Spricht von 'Krieg' in Afghanistan," *Deutsche Welle*, December 20, 2010, https://www.dw.com/de/merkel-spricht-von-krieg-in-afghanistan/a-6354840; Hauke Zepelin, "Angela Merkel erklärt den Krieg," *Financial Times Deutschland*, December 20, 2010, Factiva, https://global-factiva-com.proxy.jbs.cam.ac.uk/du/article.aspx/?accessionno=FTD000002010 1220e6ck0000u&fcpil=en&napc=S&sa_from=&cat=a.

42   Borchert and Wengeler, "Friedensmission," 279.

43   Jacobi, Hellmann, and Nieke, "Deutschlands Verteidigung am Hindukusch," 183. The term "Kamerad" does not translate straightforwardly into English. In German it is increasingly used as a synonym for Bundeswehr soldiers but, when used by soldiers, can also denote a colleague and the comradeship that constitutes one of the foundational principles of the German Bundeswehr.

44   Jacobi, Hellmann, and Nieke, "Deutschlands Verteidigung am Hindukusch," 183.

media.[45] Thus the "normalization" of war in the context of Afghanistan could be seen to extend into the realm of language.[46]

The Return of War Writing

The War in Afghanistan also precipitated the return of German-language war writing. In the realm of nonfiction, war writing returned in a variety of formats, such as war letters and military memoirs. A notable example emerges in the form of a collection of letters written by Bundeswehr soldiers while in Afghanistan, which was published by the *Süddeutsche Zeitung Magazin* in December 2009.[47] Journalists Marc Baumann, Mauritius Much, Bastian Obermayer, Martin Langeder, and Franziska Storz, who compiled more than one hundred letters against the express wishes of the Bundeswehr and the Ministry of Defense, were awarded the prestigious Henri Nannen Prize for journalism, sponsored by the Gruner + Jahr media corporation, in 2010.[48] In her award speech, the literary critic and author Elke Heidenreich praised the letters, stating, "Diese Feldpost vermittelt ein authentisches Gefühl dafür, wie die Deutschen in den Krieg und der Krieg zu den Deutschen kam. Eine ferne Front ist plötzlich ganz nah" (These war letters convey an authentic sense of how the Germans got into war and how war got to the Germans. A distant front is suddenly very close).[49] The following year, the collection was expanded and published as an anthology titled *Feldpost: Briefe Deutscher*

---

45 Jacobi, Hellmann, and Nieke, "Deutschlands Verteidigung am Hindukusch," 183–84.

46 The "normalization" of war in the realm of language is furthermore documented by the fact that in the context of the War in Afghanistan, the practice of naming battles returned. The so-called *Karfreitagsgefecht* (Good Friday Battle), which took place on Good Friday, April 2, 2010, near Isa Khel, exemplifies this. For further details, see Deutscher Bundestag, "Der Afghanistan-Einsatz 2001–2021: Eine sicherheitspolitische Chronologie" (Wissenschaftliche Dienste, January 20, 2022), 124, https://www.bundestag.de/resource/blob/881198/27fd4f 597e1d4ee43350aafffc6f9d8c/WD-2-062-21-pdf-data.pdf.

47 Originally published as "Die Weihnachtspost der deutschen Soldaten in Afghanistan," the collection has been retitled "Gestern Abend mit einem komischen Gefühl meine Ausrüstung fertig gemacht," *Süddeutsche Zeitung Magazin*, December 22, 2009, https://sz-magazin.sueddeutsche.de/leben-und-gesellschaft/gestern-abend-mit-einem-komischen-gefuehl-meine-ausruestung-fertig-gemacht-76914.

48 Marc Baumann et al., eds., *Feldpost: Briefe Deutscher Soldaten aus Afghanistan* (Reinbek bei Hamburg: Rowohlt, 2011), 10–14.

49 In Jens Ebert, "Ein Gefallen für die Bundeswehr," in *Attitudes to War: Literatur und Film von Shakespeare bis Afghanistan*, ed. Claudia Glunz and Thomas F. Schneider (Göttingen: V&R unipress, 2012), 139–42, here 140.

Soldaten aus Afghanistan (War Letters: Letters by German Soldiers from Afghanistan).[50] In their introduction to the volume, the editors declare:

> Es gibt wieder Feldpost aus einem Krieg mit deutscher Beteiligung, es gibt wieder deutsche Briefe von einer Front. Wieder. Viele Jahrzehnte stand der Begriff Feldpost für etwas aus der Vergangenheit, das in staubigen Kisten auf Großmutters Speicher lag und das ungemein anrührte, weil in jedem Brief ausgesprochen oder unausgesprochen mitschwang, dass diese Zeilen das Letzte sein könnten, was man voneinander hört.
>
> Der Krieg der Deutschen ist ein anderer, die Angst der Soldaten und die der Daheimgebliebenen bleibt die gleiche: Dass es kein Wiedersehen gibt.[51]

> [Once again, Germans are sending letters home from a war they're in; once again, German letters are coming home from a war front. Again. For many decades the term "war letters" stood for something from the past that lay in dusty boxes in grandmother's attic and was immensely touching because every letter resonated with the said or unsaid sentiment that these lines could be the last thing one person heard from another.
>
> This is a different German war, yet the fear of the soldiers and those who stayed at home remains the same: That there will be no reunion.]

While these words do not quite amount to a celebration of the return of German war letters, they are apparently devoid of any regret regarding their existence. The literary historian Jens Ebert, who has extensively researched the history of "Feldpost," notes that the term, like "Front" (front) and "Gefallene" (fallen soldiers), belongs to a period of German history that he had believed to be firmly in the past:

> Feldpost war bislang ein Begriff, der einem vergangenen, vermeintlich abgeschlossenen und zudem beschämenden Teil der deutschen Geschichte zugerechnet wurde. Das *Nie wieder Krieg* nach 1945 schloss ein, dass nie wieder Feldpost geschrieben werden müsste.[52]

---

50 The editors refer to them as letters; these are, however, short, out-of-context excerpts from letters, emails, and text messages, followed by the author's name—many of them fictitious to protect the soldiers' anonymity—and the year in which the message was written. See also Ebert, "Ein Gefallen für die Bundeswehr," 141.

51 Baumann et al., *Feldpost*, 9.

52 Ebert, "Ein Gefallen für die Bundeswehr," 139.

[Until recently, "war letters" was a term that was attributed to a supposedly closed, and moreover, shameful part of German history. The dictum *Never Again War* after 1945 also meant that war letters would never again have to be written.]

The editors of *Feldpost* appear to ignore the historical dimension of the term they have revitalized. The memory of those who last wrote war letters, including those German soldiers who witnessed or committed atrocities all over Europe, is supplanted here by the nostalgic image of their letters gathering dust in grandmother's attic. The memory of World War II and its consequences is here only present in its negation: "Der Krieg der Deutschen ist ein anderer" (This is a different German war).[53] With this sentence, the editors appear intent on divorcing their volume from Germany's twentieth-century military legacy.

But their choice of title, *Feldpost*, which is expanded in the table of contents to "Feldpost—Briefe von der Front" (War Letters—Letters from the Front), evokes the image of an anachronistic war. It conjures impressions of a war fought on a battlefield, with clearly drawn battle lines and clear distinctions between soldiers and the civilian population—none of which was the case in Afghanistan. The volume's cover design, which displays the title in a rugged and uneven font that looks as though it was produced by a battered old typewriter and imitates the look of an old-fashioned envelope, seems to signal the return of a historical type of war correspondence. This design appears entirely anachronistic, given that—while some soldiers certainly did write letters on paper—they also had access to email and sent text messages home. The positive reception of *Feldpost* by reviewers not only conveys the successful rehabilitation of terms like "Feldpost" and "Front" but also signals a pronounced interest in soldiers' perspectives on the War in Afghanistan.[54]

The growing interest in the soldiers' perspectives is furthermore illustrated by the number of military memoirs that were published about Afghanistan from the late 2000s onward.[55] These memoirs represent a

---

53   Baumann et al., *Feldpost*, 9.

54   For examples of positive reviews, see Andreas Rosenfelder, "Wie deutsche Soldaten Afghanistan erleben," *Die Welt*, February 8, 2011, https://www.welt.de/kultur/literarischewelt/article12471991/Wie-deutsche-Soldaten-Afghanistan-erleben.html; Andreas Niesmann, "Post aus dem Kriegsgebiet," *Der Spiegel* (February 19, 2011), https://www.spiegel.de/politik/deutschland/briefe-deutscher-soldaten-post-aus-dem-kriegsgebiet-a-745092.html.

55   See, for example, Achim Wohlgethan, *Endstation Kabul: Als deutscher Soldat in Afghanistan—ein Insiderbericht* (Berlin: Econ, 2008); Achim Wohlgethan, *Operation Kundus: Mein zweiter Einsatz in Afghanisation* (Berlin: Econ, 2009); Heike Groos, *Ein schöner Tag zum Sterben: Als Bundeswehrärztin in Afghanistan* (Frankfurt am Main: S. Fischer, 2009); Andreas Timmermann-Levanas, *Die*

novelty, in the sense that the genre had previously been practically non-existent in the Federal Republic.[56] There is no comparable body of work about Kosovo or any of the other missions the Bundeswehr had engaged in since the 1990s.[57] These texts thus constitute the first accounts by German soldiers that relate their experiences in war since World War II.[58] The memoirs, like *Feldpost*, represent the return and a rehabilitation of a form of writing that, to paraphrase Andrew Plowman, is deeply enmeshed with Adolf Hitler's military, the apologetics of Wehrmacht officers after the war, and the attempted revision and construction of a useable World War II past.[59] Plowman, who is among the few scholars who have critically engaged with contemporary German military memoirs so far, argues that some of the recent memoirs represent a "partial 'normalization' of the figure of the soldier and of the military memoir as a literary form."[60] While Plowman considers the resurgence of the genre "striking," he also notes that in terms of content, recent German military memoirs resemble less those of Wehrmacht officers or older writings about the Bundeswehr and more those written by soldiers from other NATO countries.[61] Furthermore, Plowman argues that the memoirs' publication by mainstream rather than specialist military publishers suggests a certain demand for these texts.[62]

The success of Johannes Clair's memoir, *Vier Tage im November: Mein Kampfeinsatz in Afghanistan* (Four Days in November: My Combat Deployment in Afghanistan, 2012),[63] seems further to confirm Plowman's assessment. The memoir reached the *Spiegel* bestseller list and is currently in its eighth edition.[64] Clair stated publicly that rather

---

reden—Wir sterben: Wie unsere Soldaten zu Opfern der deutschen Politik werden (Frankfurt am Main: Campus, 2010); Robert Sedlatzek-Müller, *Soldatenglück: Mein Leben nach dem Überleben* (Hamburg: Edel, 2012).

56 Andrew Plowman, "The Return of the Military Memoir: The Bundeswehr Deployment to Afghanistan and the Re-Emergence of a Literary Form," *Modern Languages Open* 1 (2020): 1–19, here 2. For an examination of military memoirs written by members of the NVA, some of which were published after unification, see Tom Smith, *Comrades in Arms: Military Masculinities in East German Culture* (New York: Berghahn, 2020).

57 Peter Goebel's volume constitutes a rare exception. Peter Goebel, ed., *Von Kambodscha bis Kosovo: Auslandseinsätze der Bundeswehr seit Ende des Kalten Krieges* (Frankfurt am Main: Report, 2000).

58 Plowman, "The Return," 2.

59 Plowman, "The Return," 1, 4, 7.

60 Plowman, "The Return," 16.

61 Plowman, "The Return," 8.

62 Plowman, "The Return," 1, 2.

63 Subsequent references to this source will be indicated in the text and footnotes by the abbreviation *VT* and page numbers.

64 Henning Sußebach calls into question the public success of Clair's memoir. While Sußebach acknowledges the bestseller status of the work, which sold

than writing the text of his own accord, he was approached by his publisher, who, keen to fill a gap in its existing catalog, was interested in the account of a rank-and-file soldier who was in Afghanistan during the Bundeswehr's offensive period.[65] This aspect of the memoir is advertised in its title, which also refers to the four-day-long "Operation Halmazag," in which Clair had participated in November 2010. Only the first and last chapter of the memoir are dedicated to that offensive, however. The remainder of the text chronicles Clair's journey from volunteering for the Afghanistan mission to his arrival, routine tasks, and combat experiences. What stands out is Clair's openness about his emotions, which range from desiring revenge for his colleagues who were killed during the so-called Karfreitagsgefecht (Good Friday Battle; *VT*, 29, 101), to fear after being trapped in an ambush (*VT*, 208–38), to elation and euphoria during combat scenarios (*VT*, 191, 195, 403, 406). After the successful completion of "Operation Halmazag," for example, Clair records an incredible "Hochgefühl …, das uns wie ein Rausch erfasst hatte" (*VT*, 406; a sense of elation …, that seized us like intoxication). With equal frankness, he describes the moments before he is about to shoot another person:

> Gleich würde ich abdrücken. Konnte ihm mit einem Schuss das Leben wegnehmen. Nur ein Druck mit dem Finger, dem so große Macht innewohnte. Alles, was er jemals getan hatte, alles, was er noch tun könnte, wäre vorbei. Es war der vierte Tag im November, als ich abdrückte. (*VT*, 403)

> [In a moment, I would pull the trigger. Could take away his life with one shot. Just one press of the finger that holds so much power. Everything he had ever done, everything he could still do, would be over. It was the fourth day in November when I pulled the trigger.]

While the reader never learns whether Clair killed anyone, his memoir illustrates the return of narratives by German soldiers who had engaged in lethal combat. *Vier Tage im November*, like other military memoirs and the collection of soldiers' letters, furthermore illustrates, through its language and style, the rehabilitation of the lexis of war. And while the writing

---

more than twenty-five thousand copies, he claims that only soldiers read the text, which, he notes, did not receive a single review in any major German newspaper. Henning Sußebach, "Krieg im Frieden," *Die Zeit*, March 20, 2014, https://www.zeit.de/2014/13/bundeswehr-veteranen-afghanistan.

65   Clair made this statement as part of a lecture he gave about his deployment to Afghanistan, a recording of which he subsequently uploaded to his YouTube channel: "2015: Ehemaliger Fallschirmjäger über Afghanistan und Kampfeinsatz—Klartext #1," accessed November 8, 2023, https://www.youtube.com/watch?v=SjfuyKMgI7s.

about Afghanistan by soldiers, including Clair's, is not entirely uncritical of the war, the "striking" return of these kinds of texts signifies the "normalization" of war in the domain of German-language nonfiction.

The Return of War Writing in German-Language Fiction

In addition to war letters and military memoirs, Germany's participation in the War in Afghanistan also prompted the return of fictional German-language war writing. For the first time in the history of the FRG, a corpus of literary texts about a war with Bundeswehr involvement emerged, many of which were written from the perspective of soldiers at war or of those who had returned from war. The existence of this corpus of texts further affirms the "normalization" of war in the German cultural sphere. The return of contemporary fictional war writing is illustrated, for example, by Ingo Niermann and Alexander Wallasch's novel *Deutscher Sohn* (German Son, 2010) and Dirk Kurbjuweit's *Kriegsbraut* (War Bride, 2011).[66]

Among this new crop of German-language war writing that emerged from the late 2000s onward, Scheuer's *Die Sprache der Vögel* stands out as one of the more "self-consciously literary" engagements with the war.[67] The novel received generally favorable reviews and was shortlisted for the Leipzig Book Fair Prize in 2015.[68] Scheuer's text consists of 120

66　Additional examples include Timo Hemmann's novel *Und weil die Stunde kommt* (Leipzig: Engelsdorfer Verlag, 2007); Stephan Waldscheidt's short narrative "Fünf Tage im Bernstein," *Am Erker: Zeitschrift für Literatur* (2007), 41–53; Wolfgang Schorlau's thriller *Brennende Kälte: Denglers vierter Fall* (Cologne: Kiepenheuer & Witsch, 2008); and Dea Loher's play *Land ohne Worte*, in Loher, *Das letzte Feuer: Land ohne Worte* (Frankfurt am Main: Verlag der Autoren, 2008). On these texts, see Kai Köhler, "Frieden, Nation, Kultur: Ambivalenzen in deutschsprachigen Werken zum Krieg in Afghanistan," in *Kriegsdiskurse in Literatur und Medien nach 1989*, ed. Carsten Gansel and Heinrich Kaulen (Göttingen: V&R unipress, 2011), 275–96.

67　Andrew Plowman, "Afghanistan, Soldiers' Experiences and Literary Invention in Dirk Kurbjuweit's *Kriegsbraut* (2011) and Norbert Scheuer's *Die Sprache der Vögel* (2015)," *Oxford German Studies* 47, no. 4 (2018): 523–40, here 525.

68　Sandra Kegel, "Der Krieg am Hindukusch aus der Vogelperspektive," *Frankfurter Allgemeine Zeitung*, April 4, 2015, https://www.faz.net/aktuell/feuilleton/buecher/norbert-scheuers-neuer-roman-der-krieg-am-hindukusch-aus-der-vogelperspektive-13461815.html; Sebastian Hammelehle, "Das deutsche Unglück wird am Hindukusch bekämpft," *Der Spiegel* (March 9, 2015), https://www.spiegel.de/kultur/literatur/norbert-scheuers-sprache-der-voegel-ueber-afghanistan-einsatz-a-1021249.html; Katharina Granzin, "Nicht eine, sondern viele Welten," *taz*, March 10, 2015, https://taz.de/!213613/.

short chapters, the majority of which are taken up by a journal written by the protagonist, Paul Arimond, during his deployment in Afghanistan. The continuity of this journal is consistently interrupted by chapters that alternate between Paul's childhood recollections; excerpts from another journal, attributed to Paul's ancestor Ambrosius, which details his eighteenth-century travels in the Hindu Kush region; and third-person narratives that revolve around Paul's ex-girlfriend Theresa and his former teacher Helena. Based in Paul's small hometown Kall in the Eifel region, Helena also emerges as the recipient of Paul's loose-leafed notes (*SDV*, 32), which she organizes and reconstructs into his journal (*SDV*, 179), rendering her an implied editor of the journal.

Paul joined the Bundeswehr as a medic (*SDV*, 11) and volunteered to be sent to Afghanistan after he caused a car accident that left his best friend permanently injured (*SDV*, 165–66). Paul's journal begins with his arrival in Afghanistan on April 14, 2003, and details his everyday life, which takes place in an unnamed Bundeswehr camp where he works, interacts with fellow soldiers, and feels increasingly trapped, a feeling that is barely alleviated by occasional missions that take him beyond the camp's heavily guarded and fortified walls. As a narrator, Paul appears less concerned with the war and his tasks as a medic and more focused on the local bird population, which he avidly observes and catalogs, and which takes up considerably more space in his journal than everything else that goes on around him. As a result, contemporary Afghanistan remains something of a blank space in Scheuer's novel. The war is depicted as a frequent obstacle to Paul's bird-watching and provides a consistent backdrop that grows more dangerous and threatening as the text advances. Paul's ornithological obsession is so extensive that it gets him into trouble with his superiors and leaves him increasingly socially isolated. His personal crisis intensifies when he learns that the friend he injured prior to enlisting has suddenly died (*SDV*, 224). Seemingly driven to insanity, Paul escapes the Bundeswehr camp (*SDV*, 225–26) and roams the Afghan countryside for months, until an American military unit picks him up as a suspected insurgent and returns him to the Germans (*SDV*, 227).

The details of what happened to Paul after he left the camp are no longer part of his journal but are reconstructed by Helena (*SDV*, 227). This reconstruction is supplemented by a news report, attributed to the Deutsche Presse Agentur (dpa; German Press Agency), dated June 9, 2004, reporting a suspected suicide attack on a bus filled with German soldiers on their way home, which leads the reader to believe that Paul, likely a passenger on the bus, was killed just hours before he was due to fly back to Germany (*SDV*, 229).[69] The article in the novel is fictitious,

---

69 The fact that Paul survived the attack but was severely injured and is now confined to a wheelchair is revealed in Scheuer's subsequent novel, *Am Grund*

but an attack on a Bundeswehr bus on its way to the airport did take place on June 7, 2003.[70] Scheuer has merely pushed the date of the attack back by one year to fit with his novel's timeline.

This blending of fact into fiction is paradigmatic for the whole text. In the same way that the novel is a montage of different narrators and perspectives, Paul's journal is a montage of approximately thirteen years of war in Afghanistan, which condenses real events, persons, anecdotes, and observations into a work of fiction that covers Paul's one-year deployment to Afghanistan from 2003 to 2004. In some cases, the origins of Scheuer's characters and the events depicted remain identifiable. The protagonist, for example, is based at least in part on the American soldier Jonathan Trouern-Trend, who was stationed with a medical support battalion in Iraq and published his war journal *Birding Babylon* in 2006.[71] Another influence was Frank Joisten, a Bundeswehr officer who was deployed to Afghanistan three times and, unlike Paul, was allowed to indulge in his love for ornithology.[72] Additional characters are also based on real Bundeswehr soldiers. Paul's roommate Sergej appears to have been modeled on Sergej Motz, who was the first German soldier to die in combat since World War II.[73] The fictional and the real Sergej are connected by the fact that their fathers had already fought a war in Afghanistan in the 1980s as members of the Soviet Army (*SDV*, 59).[74] Another example is an unnamed character in Paul's journal who commits suicide (*SDV*, 101); the details recall the story of Oliver Preß, who died at Camp Marmal in Mazar-i-Sharif in 2013 of a suspected self-inflicted gunshot wound.[75] Even the anecdote Paul hears from a fellow soldier about children who act as human scarecrows on the fields of Afghanistan is based in reality (*SDV*, 194); a similar observation can be found in Clair's

---

des Universums (Munich: C. S. Beck, 2017). Monika Wolting, *Der neue Kriegsroman: Repräsentationen des Afghanistankriegs in der deutschen Gegenwartsliteratur* (Heidelberg: Universitätsverlag Winter, 2019), 30–31.

70 "The incident marked the first time German soldiers have been attacked since they were first deployed in Afghanistan in January 2002." Deutsche Welle, "4 Germans Killed in Kabul Suicide Bombing," June 7, 2003, https://www.dw.com/en/4-germans-killed-in-kabul-suicide-bombing/a-888028.

71 Trouern-Trend's military memoir is listed in the bibliography of *Die Sprache der Vögel*, 237: Jonathan Trouern-Trend, *Birding Babylon: A Soldier's Journal from Iraq* (San Francisco: Sierra Club Books, 2006).

72 Joisten is mentioned in the novel's acknowledgments, 231–32.

73 Lars Gaede, "Das ist Krieg, Sergej, Krieg!," *taz*, October 2, 2010, https://taz.de/!377809/.

74 Gaede, "Das ist Krieg, Sergej, Krieg!"

75 Matthias Gebauer, "Bundeswehr rätselt über Tod eines Soldaten," *Spiegel Ausland* (June 12, 2013), https://www.spiegel.de/politik/ausland/tod-eines-bundeswehr-soldaten-in-masar-i-scharif-wirft-fragen-auf-a-905383.html.

military memoir (*VT*, 252).[76] The blending of fact into fiction in this process of montage allows Scheuer to compress the chronology of the German War in Afghanistan, which, over the course of years, grew more dangerous and more offensive, into the much shorter timeline of Paul's deployment.

Beyond that, Scheuer's method fulfills an additional function. The factual elements of his novel invest it with authenticity. According to Elisabeth Krimmer, authenticity emerges as the "gold standard of war writing."[77] Indeed, there is a long tradition of writing about war that elevates "the status of truth in relation to that of art."[78] For his study of accounts of World War I, *Témoins—Witnesses* (1929), Jean Norton Cru analyzed over three hundred fictional and nonfictional representations of the war, only twenty-nine of which met his standard for faithful witnessing.[79] That similar standards are still applied to war writing today is evidenced by the covers of military memoirs about Afghanistan.[80] Almost every single one shows the author, usually in uniform, which serves to authenticate their experience and authorizes their account as that of a witness.

Scheuer, who has never been to Afghanistan, is not a witness, yet his montage of fact and fiction strives for a sense of authenticity nonetheless. He not only includes a range of characters based on real soldiers and events that took place during the Bundeswehr mission in Afghanistan but supports the narrative with a glossary of terms (*SDV*, 234), an extensive bibliography (*SDV*, 236–38), and acknowledgments that verify and legitimate his sources (*SDV*, 231–33).[81] Scheuer even appends a note that invokes poetic license for a single error he believes he made, when he placed a Dead Sea sparrow in a location in Afghanistan where this bird has never, in fact, been observed (*SDV*, 235).[82] By authenticating

---

76 Clair's memoir is also listed in the bibliography of *Die Sprache der Vögel*, 236.

77 Elisabeth Krimmer, *The Representation of War in German Literature: From 1800 to the Present* (Cambridge: Cambridge University Press, 2010), 5.

78 Michael Minden, "The First World War and Its Aftermath in the German Novel," in *The Cambridge Companion to the Modern German Novel*, ed. Graham Bartram (Cambridge: Cambridge University Press, 2004), 138–51, here 140.

79 See Jay Winter, *Remembering War: The Great War between Memory and History in the Twentieth Century* (New Haven, CT: Yale University Press, 2006), 249.

80 For a discussion of the relevance of authenticity in contemporary war writing, see also Plowman, "Afghanistan," 526–28.

81 Plowman, "Afghanistan," 527; Stephanie Willeke, *Grenzfall Krieg: Zur Darstellung der neuen Kriege nach 9/11 in der deutschsprachigen Gegenwartsliteratur* (Bielefeld: transcript, 2018), 131.

82 This is by no means the only factual error in the novel. Scheuer's process of condensing thirteen years of war into a single year has resulted in a number of

his novel in this manner, Scheuer situates himself in a literary tradition of war writing that insists on authenticity, and he thus places his text in an intertextual dialogue with his literary predecessors.[83]

Among Scheuer's predecessors, Remarque stands out. Remarque, who experienced World War I firsthand, published his fictional war memoir *Im Westen nichts Neues* in 1929. He later described the text as a "collection of the best stories that I told and that my friends told as we sat over drinks and relived the war."[84] Remarque's text, which is perhaps the paradigmatic modern German war novel, is thus constructed using the same technique of montage that Scheuer, who lacked firsthand experience, uses in his narrativization of the War in Afghanistan. The first edition of Remarque's novel features on its cover the following words by Walter von Mole: "Remarques Buch ist das Denkmal unseres unbekannten Soldaten von allen Toten geschrieben" (Remarque's book is the memorial for our Unknown Soldier, written by all the dead).[85] Scheuer's inclusion of fictionalized versions of Sergej Motz and Oliver Preß similarly renders his novel a memorial to the Bundeswehr soldiers who died in Afghanistan.

Beyond that, Remarque's and Scheuer's texts evidence a number of additional similarities. The protagonists have the same first name, Paul. Both texts use the format of the journal, with which their authors convey an immediacy of the narrated experience. The novels furthermore have similar endings. Scheuer abandons his existing narrators to append a fictional news article reporting what the reader may suspect is Paul's death, just before he was due to fly home (*SDV*, 229). Remarque discontinues his otherwise consistent first-person narration to conclude with a brief epilogue, written in the third person, that conveys that the protagonist died in October 1918, mere weeks before the armistice (*IW*, 263). The fact that both texts drop their original narrators and convey the deaths through third-person narration and a news report highlights

---

inaccuracies. For example, the text refers to the Bundeswehr Camp Marmal in Mazar-i-Sharif (*SDV*, 204), which was not opened until 2006; and to an "Ehrenhain" (honor grove) in the Bundeswehr camp in Kunduz (*SDV*, 216), which was not created until 2007.

83   Given the prominence of birds and their observation in the text, many critics have focused on this aspect of the novel and pointed out its intertextual link to texts like Robert Musil's "Die Amsel" (1928), Ernst Toller's *Das Schwalbenbuch* (1924), and Marcel Beyer's *Kaltenburg* (2008). See Kegel, "Der Krieg am Hindukusch aus der Vogelperspektive"; Wolting, *Der neue Kriegsroman*, 28–29; Ursula Hennigfeld, "Im Krieg Federn lassen: Vogel-Metaphern in zeitgenössischen Kriegsromanen (Khadra, Scheuer, Surminski, Rothmann)," *Romanische Studien Beihefte* 4 (2018): 199–219, here 215–18.

84   Remarque, cited in Minden, "The First World War," 148.

85   Peter Bekes, *Erich Maria Remarque: Im Westen nichts neues*, Oldenbourg Interpretationen, vol. 90 (Munich: R. Oldenbourg, 1998), 7.

the protagonists' loss of agency in war, while their deaths in such close proximity to the end of their respective wars invest their dying with a sense of futility.

In addition to these similarities, Scheuer's novel echoes, in parts, Remarque's narrative style, especially with regard to descriptions of injury and death, as the following excerpts illustrate:

> Wir sehen Menschen leben, denen der Schädel fehlt; wir sehen Soldaten laufen, denen beide Füße weggefetzt sind; sie stolpern auf den splitternden Stümpfen bis zum nächsten Loch; ein Gefreiter kriecht zwei Kilometer weit auf den Händen und schleppt die zerschmetterten Knie hinter sich her; ein anderer geht zur Verbandsstelle, und über seine festhaltenden Hände quellen die Därme. (*IW*, 126)

> [We see men go on living with the top of their skulls missing; we see soldiers go on running when both their feet have been shot away— they stumble on their splintering stumps to the next shell hole. One lance-corporal crawls for a full half-mile on his hands, dragging his legs behind him, with both knees shattered. Another man makes it to a dressing station with his guts spilling out over his hands as he holds them in.][86]

> Die Explosion hat ihm die Kleider vom Leib gerissen, ihn in zwei Hälften zerfetzt, seine Eingeweide verteilen sich um ihn, ein Bein hängt über seine Schulter. (*SDV*, 102)

> [The explosion has torn the clothes from his body, blasted him into two halves, his bowels scattered around him, one leg hangs over his shoulder.][87]

> Plötzlich halte ich warme Gedärme in der Hand. Ich drücke sie zurück in den Bauchraum, wische mir die Hände ab und notiere auf einem Block die Verletzungen....] (*SDV*, 165)

> [Suddenly I am holding warm intestines in my hands. I push them back into the abdomen, wipe my hands and note down the injuries on a pad....][88]

86 Remarque, *All Quiet on the Western Front*, 97.
87 Scheuer, *The Language of Birds*, n.pag.
88 Scheuer, *The Language of Birds*, n.p.

Confronted with these quotations, taken out of their context, a reader might struggle to identify which passages were written by Remarque and which by Scheuer. In both texts, the protagonist narrators convey injury and death in a cold, detached, and matter-of-fact manner. The passages are graphic, descriptive, and designed to convey detail and information, but each remains apparently devoid of emotion. This detachment from the events described is emphasized further as both narrators move on from these descriptions without further qualification or pause for reflection. Such descriptive yet detached representations of injury and death are characteristic for World War I narratives. Similar passages can also be found in Ernst Jünger's *In Stahlgewittern* (Storms of Steel, 1920), for example.[89] In texts about World War I, these passages convey the omnipresence and mundanity of injury and death and how familiar soldiers were with such sights after years of fighting. In *Die Sprache der Vögel*, by contrast, the protagonist's factual narration of injury and death reflects his overall detachment from the war and constitutes another parallel with Remarque's text.

Although significant differences between *Im Westen nichts Neues* and *Die Sprache der Vögel* remain, Remarque's fictional memoir can be considered a crucial intertext for Scheuer's novel. The parallels between the two texts suggest furthermore that Scheuer's novel signifies a return to a form of war writing that predated World War II. Combined with the fact that Scheuer's text contains no references to World War II or its military legacy, this circumstance suggests that *Die Sprache der Vögel* can be read as a return to a scenario where war writing remains untainted by the legacy of National Socialism.[90] Scheuer's novel thus does not merely omit references to World War II. In addition, the text elides the legacy of National Socialism by seamlessly connecting to a form of war writing that existed before elements of the German language emerged as contaminated, before certain literary traditions, forms, and styles were delegitimated by those who used them to relativize their own guilt, and before soldier narratives disappeared from the German literary landscape. By modeling Paul's war journal on Remarque's fictional memoir and omitting any reference to World War II, Scheuer conveys not only that that war's legacy has no relevance for the FRG's War in Afghanistan but also that this legacy no longer constitutes a touchstone for writing about war in Germany.

89 See Ernst Jünger, *In Stahlgewittern: Historisch-kritische Ausgabe*, vol. 1: *Die gedruckten Fassungen unter Berücksichtigung der Korrekturbücher*, ed. Helmuth Kiesel (Stuttgart: Klett-Cotta, 2013), 67.

90 By contrast, in the subsequent novel *Winterbienen* (Munich: C. H. Beck, 2019), which details the memories of one of Paul's ancestors, Scheuer engages extensively with World War II and National Socialism.

Remarque's *Im Westen nichts Neues* as well as Jünger's *In Stahlgewittern* are notably absent from Scheuer's extensive bibliography, which lists *Feldpost: Briefe Deutscher Soldaten aus Afghanistan*, Clair's *Vier Tage im November*, and a number of additional military memoirs as well as texts by Jacques Derrida, Michel Foucault, and Immanuel Kant. Yet the link *Die Sprache der Vögel* establishes between writing about Afghanistan and war writing about World War I appears nonetheless to circulate in the German public consciousness. In her review of Scheuer's novel, Iris Radisch compared its protagonist to Ernst Jünger.[91] George Tenner's Afghanistan novel *Jenseits von Deutschland* (Beyond Germany, 2011) advertises its link to Remarque in the blurb: "Dieser Anti-Kriegsroman gewährt im Stil von Erich Maria Remarques 'Im Westen nichts Neues' einen Einblick in das Seelenleben von Soldaten, die an einem bewaffneten Auslandseinsatz teilnehmen" (In the style of Erich Maria Remarque's *All Quiet on the Western Front*, this antiwar novel offers insight into the inner lives of soldiers who participate in an armed deployment abroad).[92] The literary critic Henning Sußebach invokes Remarque in his discussion of Clair, and Clair's publisher marketed *Vier Tage im November* as "'Im Westen nichts Neues' für das 21. Jahrhundert" (*All Quiet on the Western Front* for the twenty-first century).[93] The frequent recourse to World War I texts apparent here suggests that German-language literature lacks more recent, legitimate examples of war writing to which to compare or on which to model representations of the War in Afghanistan.

The recurring references to Remarque and his novel, moreover, may be owed to the fact that *Im Westen nichts Neues* is frequently read as an antiwar novel. The implicit and explicit references in *Die Sprache der Vögel* to Remarque's novel may thus be designed to convey that the contemporary text is equally opposed to, or at least critical of, the War in Afghanistan. Such a reading of Scheuer's and the other contemporary texts mentioned here, however, is somewhat undercut by Evelyn Cobley's compelling demonstration that a plethora of World War I texts, including Remarque's, constitute contradictory sites of inscription that are frequently rendered ideologically complicit in the object of their apparent critique by their choice of narrative form and style.[94] At the most basic level, the literary links between writing about World War I and texts about the War in Afghanistan thus merely proclaim the return of

91   Iris Radisch, "Naturkunde des Soldaten," *Die Zeit*, March 12, 2015, https://www.zeit.de/2015/11/norbert-scheuer-afghanistan-kriegsliteratur.

92   George Tenner, *Jenseits von Deutschland* (Oldenburg: Schardt, 2011).

93   Sußebach, "Krieg im Frieden."

94   Further discussion of this topos exceeds the scope of this chapter; see Evelyn Cobley, *Representing War: Form and Ideology in First World War Narratives* (Toronto: University of Toronto Press, 1993).

German-language war writing. Moreover, like Scheuer's text, they illustrate the disappearance of the primary influence of the legacy of World War II within the literary and public consciousness and a return to a memory of war that is untainted by it.

Concluding Thoughts

Afghanistan changed Germany, or, rather, Germany changed itself in the context of the War in Afghanistan. The return *to* war both in action and language as well as the return of German-language war writing are testament to this change. While the War in Afghanistan catalyzed these returns and the "normalization" of German foreign policy, Afghanistan the country remained a rather blank space for the German imagination, a backdrop against which these changes took place. This impression of Afghanistan as a somewhat generic and to a certain extent interchangeable elsewhere is reinforced by the texts discussed in this chapter, none of which engage with the country, its people, and culture beyond their function as the location for the Bundeswehr's deployment.

In this context it is also worth noting how many literary texts simply elide the War in Afghanistan and with it the FRG's engagement in violence elsewhere. A number of German novels that are considered part of the German literary response to the 9/11 terrorist attacks devote considerable space to the Iraq War, which took place from 2003 until 2011 without active German participation, but neglect Afghanistan. For example, Thomas Lehr's novel *September: Fata Morgana* (September: Mirage, 2010), which can be read as a critique of the Iraq War, is set in part in Iraq and features a number of Iraqi characters but only contains three scant references to Afghanistan. In Thomas Hettche's *Woraus wir gemacht sind* (What We Are Made Of, 2006), the War in Afghanistan appears on two pages, while the build-up to the Iraq War acts as the novel's constant background noise. Similarly, in Katharina Hacker's *Die Habenichtse* (The Have-Nots, 2006), which is set after 9/11 but before the Iraq War (which is nonetheless omnipresent in the text), the War in Afghanistan is mentioned only once and only in the past perfect: "Es hatte den Afghanistan-Krieg gegeben, es gab zerstörte Häuser, verbrannte Menschen, hastig beerdigte Tote und in unwegsamen Bergen weiter Taliban- oder Al-Qaida Kämpfer" (The Afghanistan War had occurred, there were destroyed houses, burnt people, the hastily buried dead and in impassable mountains there were still Taliban or al-Qaeda fighters).[95] None of these novels makes any reference to the Bundeswehr or its involvement in the War in Afghanistan. While these authors clearly do not shy away from

---

95   Katharina Hacker, *Die Habenichtse* (Frankfurt am Main: Suhrkamp, 2007), 93.

addressing violence beyond Germany's borders, their lack of engagement with Afghanistan suggests a certain reluctance to confront the notion of violence elsewhere in cases where German soldiers are active participants in and recipients of violence.

Even the texts that explicitly focus on Afghanistan tend to focus on the mundane rather than the violent aspects of war. Scheuer's *Die Sprache der Vögel*, with its focus on ornithology, paradigmatically illustrates this point. While the novel depicts both Clifford Mann's "helper" and "victim" periods in its condensed chronology of the war, it omits any representation of the "warrior period." Moreover, by rendering his main character, Paul, a medic, who, by virtue of his duties, is confronted with the effects of violence but does not have to engage in violence himself, Scheuer appears intent on foreclosing the potential for his protagonist to hurt or kill another human being. In fact, none of the texts about Afghanistan discussed in this chapter depict a German soldier killing another person. Even Clair's memoir, which sees him contemplating the act of killing another person, remains ambiguous regarding the outcome of the shot he took. Clair's ambiguity and the texts' omission of representations of lethal action can perhaps be attributed to the fact that the image of German soldiers killing others is still deeply entangled with the memory of National Socialism.

Moreover, the reluctance to represent the reality of lethal violence perpetrated by German soldiers in fictional and nonfictional engagements with the War in Afghanistan suggests that in the German imagination violence elsewhere in the form of war is not entirely "normalized." In this respect, German war writing about Afghanistan reflects political discourse, which only reluctantly adopted the term "war" for the Bundeswehr mission but readily returned to the term "Gefallene." While Afghanistan may have been labeled Germany's "first war without Hitler" and evolved over time into an offensive combat scenario, it appears as though the Germans still need to come to terms with their "new" role as perpetrators of violence elsewhere.

3: There Is No "Elsewhere": Scales of Complicity and Implication in the Contemporary German Family Novel

Susanne C. Knittel and Sofía Forchieri[1]

Introduction

SINCE THE LATE 1990s, there has been a remarkable boom in multi-generational family novels, or *Generationenromane*, in the German-speaking world. In texts such as Monika Maron's *Pawels Briefe* (1999; *Pavel's Letters*, 2002), Manfred Gebert's *Welwitschia Mirabilis* (2008), Verena Boos's *Blutorangen* (Blood Oranges, 2015), and Nino Haratischwili's *Das achte Leben (für Brilka)* (2014; *The Eighth Life [for Brilka]*, 2019), the often semiautobiographical narrators confront the entanglements of their parents, grandparents, and great-grandparents in the violent histories of the past century and beyond. As such, these novels are emblematic of what literary critic Sigrid Weigel has called the "Ära des Generationendiskurses" (era of generational discourse),[2] in which the category of generation assumes a central place in the cultural, public, and scholarly understanding of the experience of history, and intergenerational conflict and transgenerational transmission provide an analytic lens through which to understand historical developments.[3]

The era of generational discourse has been marked by the rise to prominence of concepts such as postmemory and transgenerational trauma.[4] What these concepts help to articulate is how histories of violence

1   We would like to thank Kári Driscoll for his invaluable advice and input during the conceptualization of this chapter.
2   Sigrid Weigel, *Genea-Logik: Generation, Tradition und Evolution zwischen Kultur- und Naturwissenschaften* (Munich: Fink, 2006), 87.
3   See Ulrike Jureit, "Generationengeschichte als Beziehungsgeschichte: Über einen Mechanismus der sozialen Verortung," in *Der Generationenroman*, ed. Helmut Grugger and Johann Holzner (Berlin: De Gruyter, 2021), 18–32.
4   Marianne Hirsch, "The Generation of Postmemory," *Poetics Today* 29, no. 1 (2008): 103–28; Gabriele Schwab, *Haunting Legacies: Violent Histories and Transgenerational Trauma* (New York: Columbia University Press, 2010); Stef Craps, *Postcolonial Witnessing: Trauma out of Bounds* (Basingstoke, UK: Palgrave

live on and are transmitted across generations, often indirectly, covertly, or in the form of silences and taboos. These histories may be geographically and temporally distant, but they pervade the family memory, and it can be difficult for the heirs to that memory to understand how they are connected to this "violence elsewhere." It is this difficulty that provides one central narrative impetus for the contemporary Generationenroman. A salient characteristic of these novels is their metahistorical dimension.[5] Incorporating material traces of the familial archive such as photos, diaries, letters, and inherited objects, these novels not only reconstruct a family history but also reflect on the complex role of mediation and remediation in the process of remembering and forgetting and on questions of representation and representability, the relationship between history and memory, and truth and fiction.[6]

Two recent developments in historiography and cultural memory studies in Germany and beyond provide an important context for understanding the rise of the Generationenroman: on the one hand, there is the turn to microhistory and small-scale explorations of the direct and indirect ways in which ordinary people become involved in violent regimes.[7] Rather than focusing exclusively on perpetrators and victims, this microhistorical approach examines more ambiguous categories such as the bystander and the *Mitläufer* (follower) and questions of complicity and implication.[8]

Macmillan, 2013); Lucy Bond and Stef Craps, *Trauma* (Abingdon, UK: Routledge, 2020).

5   Friederike Eigler, *Gedächtnis und Geschichte in Generationenromanen seit der Wende* (Berlin: Erich Schmidt, 2005), 61.

6   See Helmut Grugger, "Zum Begriff des Generationenromans," in Grugger and Holzner, *Der Generationenroman*, 3–17; Daniel Fulda and Stephan Jaeger, eds., *Romanhaftes Erzählen von Geschichte: Vergegenwärtigte Vergangenheiten im beginnenden 21. Jahrhundert* (Berlin: De Gruyter, 2019); Matteo Galli and Simone Costagli, "Chronotopoi: Vom Familienroman zum Generationenroman," in *Deutsche Familienromane*, ed. Matteo Galli and Simone Costagli (Paderborn: Fink, 2010), 7–20.

7   See, for example, Mary Fulbrook, *Dissonant Lives: Generations and Violence through the German Dictatorships* (Oxford: Oxford University Press, 2011); Mary Fulbrook, *A Small Town near Auschwitz: Ordinary Nazis and the Holocaust* (Oxford: Oxford University Press, 2012); Claire Zalc and Tal Bruttmann, eds., *Microhistories of the Holocaust* (New York: Berghahn, 2016); Geraldien von Frijtag Drabbe Künzel and Valeria Galimi, eds., "Microcosms of the Holocaust: Exploring New Venues into Small-Scale Research of the Holocaust," special issue, *Journal of Genocide Research* 21, no. 3 (2019): 335–41.

8   See, for example, Frank Bajohr, "Neuere Täterforschung," in *Nationalsozialistische Täterschaften: Nachwirkungen in Gesellschaft und Familie*, ed. Oliver von Wrochem (Berlin: Metropol, 2016), 19–31; Christina Morina and Krijn Thijs, eds., *Probing the Limits of Categorization: The Bystander in Holocaust*

On the other hand, and conversely, there is also a turn to macrohistorical and large-scale frameworks that conceive of history and memory in relational or "multidirectional" terms.[9] Such an approach emphasizes not only the empirical connections between different histories of violence but also how the memories of those different histories interact with and both facilitate and obstruct each other. Thus, for example, Michael Rothberg has shown how the memories of colonialism and the Holocaust have reinforced each other since the end of World War II; that is, how Holocaust representation continues to inform the representation of other genocides and forms of mass violence and vice versa.[10] More recently, this approach has rekindled debates about the comparability of different histories of violence and about the place and significance of colonialism in German history and memory.[11]

The Generationenroman occupies a pivotal position at the intersection of these micro- and macrohistorical approaches to the German past. As a genre that negotiates the relationship between individual and collective history and memory, it can be regarded as what literary scholar Mark McGurl has termed a "scaling device."[12] Because of its transgenerational scope and palimpsestic nature, the Generationenroman is able to shuttle between scales—micro and macro, individual and national or transnational—and thereby place different, seemingly unrelated histories of violence side by side without equating them or eliding the differences.

History (New York: Berghahn, 2018); Debarati Sanyal, *Memory and Complicity: Migrations of Holocaust Remembrance* (New York: Fordham University Press, 2015); Michael Rothberg, *The Implicated Subject: Beyond Victims and Perpetrators* (Stanford, CA: Stanford University Press, 2019).

9   Jürgen Zimmerer, *Von Windhuk nach Auschwitz? Beiträge zum Verhältnis von Kolonialismus und Holocaust* (Münster: Lit, 2011); Kristin Kopp, *Germany's Wild East: Constructing Poland as Colonial Space* (Ann Arbor: University of Michigan Press, 2012); Michael Rothberg, *Multidirectional Memory: Remembering the Holocaust in the Age of Decolonization* (Stanford, CA: Stanford University Press, 2009).

10   Rothberg, *Multidirectional Memory*. See also Angi Buettner, *Holocaust Images and Picturing Catastrophe: The Cultural Politics of Seeing* (Farnham, UK: Ashgate, 2011); Rebecca Jinks, *Representing Genocide: The Holocaust as Paradigm?* (London: Bloomsbury, 2016).

11   Jürgen Zimmerer and Michael Rothberg, "Enttabuisiert den Vergleich!," *Zeit Online*, April 4, 2021, https://www.zeit.de/2021/14/erinnerungskultur-gedenken-pluralisieren-holocaust-vergleich-globalisierung-geschichte; Saul Friedländer, Norbert Frei, Sibylle Steinbacher, and Dan Diner, *Ein Verbrechen ohne Namen: Anmerkungen zum Streit über den Holocaust* (Munich: C. H. Beck, 2022).

12   Mark McGurl, "Critical Response II—'Neither Indeed Could I Forebear Smiling at My Self': A Reply to Wai Chee Dimock," *Critical Inquiry* 39, no. 3 (2013): 632–38, here 634.

As such, it has become a crucial cultural location for working through Germany's violent pasts and for negotiating uncomfortable questions surrounding guilt, complicity, and responsibility.[13] By revisiting the past through the prism of a single family, these novels make visible the continuities between the past and the present and explore how individuals can be implicated in different structures of violence across different temporal and geographic scales. These structures of violence often stretch beyond Germany's borders, are situated elsewhere (geographically or historically), and operate over extended and complex temporalities. Moreover, the forms of implication pertaining to them cannot be easily tracked or explained in terms of causal relations or individual agency. As we will show, imagining the complexities and indirectness of implication in such forms of violence thus requires careful scaling procedures in order to render understandable the relationships between individual and collective agency and large-scale systems of violence.

Existing scholarship has shown compellingly how a wide range of recent Generationenromane negotiate the relationship between individual and collective memory and deal with the complex question of responsibility.[14] Yet there is one scale of violence and implication that has so far gone largely unnoticed; namely, the ecological scale of environmental devastation. This is somewhat surprising, given that nature and the environment play a significant role in many of these novels, which moreover bring the issue of environmental devastation, implicitly or explicitly, into connection with the colonial and genocidal histories they tackle. Many of these recent Generationenromane, such as, for example, Stefan Wackwitz's *Ein unsichtbares Land* (2003; *An Invisible Country*, 2005), Christof Hamann's *Usambara* (2007), or Amanda Lasker-Berlin's *Iva atmet* (Iva Breathes, 2021), feature an uncanny proliferation of nonhuman presences that haunt the texts, often in the form of inherited material traces of violence against the natural world: taxidermied animals, animal skins, and other hunting trophies, but also exotic trees and plants. This nonhuman dimension points to a third important context for the rise of the Generationenroman, beyond the micro- and the macro-historical turns; namely, the public and scientific discourse on climate change, species extinction, and the Anthropocene.

---

13   See Eigler, *Gedächtnis und Geschichte*; Jureit, "Generationengeschichte als Beziehungsgeschichte."

14   See, for example, Eigler, *Gedächtnis und Geschichte*; Anne Fuchs, *Phantoms of War in Contemporary German Literature, Films and Discourse: The Politics of Memory* (Basingstoke, UK: Palgrave Macmillan, 2008); Dirk Göttsche, *Remembering Africa: The Rediscovery of Colonialism in Contemporary German Literature* (Rochester, NY: Camden House, 2013).

To the extent that these nonhuman presences have been addressed by existing scholarship, they have typically been read allegorically (as referring to the return of the repressed), or else as a mere thematic backdrop to the plot.[15] Such interpretations are plausible enough and in many cases even implied by the texts themselves, but they also serve to reframe these legacies of environmental violence in terms of individual psychology and national memory, thus recentering the human and drawing attention away from the ecological scale. What would happen if we read these nonhuman presences not as symbols of violence against humans or as mere backgrounds for the unfolding human story but as embodiments of violence against the natural world that is an inextricable part of the histories of colonialism and genocide? In this chapter, we explore how paying attention to the ecological dimension of these novels invites us to reframe our understanding of complicity and implication in violence that stretches across temporal and geographical scales.

In the first part of this chapter, we develop a model for scaling complicity and implication in literary analysis. In order to do so, we draw on recent theorizations of complicity and implication in memory studies and postcolonial studies[16] and bring them into conversation with theories of scale framing and scale reading developed in the field of ecocriticism. In the second part, we analyze one of the above-mentioned novels, Christof Hamann's *Usambara*, which combines an engagement with the entangled histories and legacies of German colonialism and the Holocaust with a reflection on the question of transgenerational implication in ecological violence. In our reading, we will show that the pervasive nonhuman presence in this novel cannot be read merely as a symbol of violence against humans or as a background for the unfolding human story. Rather, it can and indeed must be seen as the embodiment of violence against the natural world that is an inextricable part of the histories of colonialism and genocide that the novel tackles. From this perspective, the questions of complicity and implication become even more complex, because the nonhuman dimension inscribes German colonialism and the Holocaust within the ecological framework of climate change and extinction, without downplaying or relativizing the human dimension. Once the ecological dimension is factored in, "there is no distant place"[17] that could be said to be unaffected by our individual and collective agency. Hence, when it comes to the question of violence on these scales, there can be no "elsewhere."

---

15   See, for example, Eigler, *Gedächtnis und Geschichte*; Göttsche, *Remembering Africa*; Fuchs, *Phantoms of War*.

16   See also Marie Kolkenbrock's chapter in this volume.

17   Bruno Latour, "Agency at the Time of the Anthropocene," *New Literary History* 45, no. 1 (2014): 1–18, here 2.

Scaling Complicity and Implication

In *Complicities: Ethics and Law for a Collective Age*, legal scholar Christopher Kutz calls attention to the darker consequences of our increasingly interconnected world. "Try as we might to live well," he notes, "we find ourselves connected to harms and wrongs, albeit by relations that fall outside the paradigm of individual, intentional wrongdoing."[18] This observation is followed by a sobering diagnosis regarding the effectiveness of our critical frameworks to grasp these indirect, often unconscious and unintentional relations to violence and harm. Traditional legal and philosophical framings of responsibility and accountability, Kutz argues, cannot even begin to address the complexity of our involvements. Focused as they are on individual, deliberate, and discrete acts of wrongdoing, they offer limited resources for understanding how large-scale processes of violence such as genocide or long-term structures of violence such as colonialism unfold. When it comes to thinking about agency and responsibility in current global problems such as climate change, systemic racism, or neocolonial exploitation, conventional legal-philosophical conceptions of responsibility turn out to be even less useful.

Since the early 2000s, scholars from a range of fields—including memory studies, political philosophy, and comparative literature—have mobilized complicity as an analytical tool for addressing this problem. Moving beyond the legal definition of complicity as conscious and deliberate cooperation in a crime, they work with a more expansive definition of the term as "the state of being complex or involved,"[19] which in turn evokes the etymological meaning of "complicity" as interlacement, intertwinement, or "folded-together-ness."[20] In doing so, they draw on the philosophical reflections on complicity, guilt, and responsibility that took place after World War II and the Holocaust, led by thinkers such as Hannah Arendt, Karl Jaspers, and Theodor W. Adorno. But while these early discussions framed the issue of complicity "as an evil to be opposed," the new wave of complicity critique approaches it as an inescapable state of entanglement to be "managed, negotiated, contained, and controlled."[21]

In his influential book *Complicities: The Intellectual and Apartheid*, literary scholar Mark Sanders argues that complicity is not about

18 Christopher Kutz, *Complicity: Ethics and Law for a Collective Age* (Cambridge: Cambridge University Press, 2000), 1.

19 *Oxford English Dictionary*, s.v. "complicity, *n.*" www.oed.com/view/Entry/37715.

20 Mark Sanders, *Complicities: The Intellectual and Apartheid* (Durham, NC: Duke University Press, 2002), 5.

21 Naomi Mandel, "Toward a New Complicity for New Media," *Comparative Literature Studies* 56, no. 4 (2019): 693–710, here 696.

"accusing or excusing" but, rather, about striving to understand and ethically respond to our fundamental state of entanglement with the human and nonhuman other.[22] Put differently, complicity is a critical tool for thinking about our positionality in a "continuum of foldedness."[23] For this very reason, according to Sanders, an "actively assumed complicity"[24] is the precondition for any act of solidarity and resistance. Literature has a crucial role to play in the process of acknowledging and responding to complicity, for it "can reveal an opening to responsibility."[25] Building on Sanders's work, cultural memory scholar Debarati Sanyal approaches complicity as "a catalyst for ethical and political action,"[26] exploring how literature and the arts can open up new patterns of remembrance by revealing how seemingly disparate histories of violence are connected and alerting us to our "entanglement with distant others and ongoing histories of violence and loss."[27]

Most recently, Rothberg has offered important conceptual tools for distinguishing between synchronic (present-day) and diachronic (historical) forms of involvement in violence. Rothberg favors the term "implication" over "complicity," since, as he theorizes, it describes *indirect* forms of participation in both historical legacies and contemporary structures of violence and oppression.[28] Synchronic or structural implication concerns the position individuals occupy in present structures of violence and inequality, themselves often the result of violent events in the past. Diachronic or genealogical implication illuminates the positions of those who are imbricated, as descendants, in histories of perpetration, thus complementing Marianne Hirsch's concept of postmemory and her work on the intergenerational dynamics on the victims' side.[29] Artistic works, in Rothberg's account, can make these two forms of implication "tangible and perceptible"[30] by deploying formal strategies such as direct modes of address, reversals, and displacements.

What unites these recent approaches to complex involvement in large-scale violence is, first, their attempt to describe scalar relations between the individual and phenomena that exist in realms different—and vaster—than our own, such as genocide and state violence, colonialism and its

---

22   Sanders, *Complicities*, x.
23   Sanders, *Complicities*, 11.
24   Sanders, *Complicities*, 5.
25   Sanders, *Complicities*, 17.
26   Sanyal, *Memory and Complicity*, 13.
27   Sanyal, *Memory and Complicity*, 267.
28   Rothberg, *The Implicated Subject*, 13.
29   Susanne C. Knittel and Sofía Forchieri, "Navigating Implication: An Interview with Michael Rothberg," *Journal of Perpetrator Research* 3, no. 1 (2020): 6–19, here 13.
30   Rothberg, *The Implicated Subject*, 199.

enduring effects, or ecological destruction; and, second, their emphasis on the potential of works of art to render these scalar relations understandable by creatively bridging the gap between individual agency and broader structures and histories of violence. Questions of scale and scalar representation are in this sense central to, yet surprisingly absent from, recent thinking on complicity and implication.[31] One of the aims of this chapter is to address this gap by working with scale as a crucial concept and practice for making individual and collective involvement in large-scale forms of violence more amenable to understanding.

The word "scale," as media philosopher Joanna Zylinska reminds us, comes from the Latin *scala*, meaning "ladder," and is "a practical and conceptual device that allows us to climb up and down various spatio-temporal dimensions in order to see things from different viewpoints."[32] Understood in this way, scale is as much a verb as it is a noun, as much an exercise as it is an instrument. Its main task, though, is to represent or project relational arrangements between phenomena that exist at different, and often incommensurable, scales. In recent years, discussions of scale have taken center stage in the field of ecocriticism. The present ecological crisis "has destabilized traditional understandings of human scale"[33] and disrupted our conception of individual agency. The notion of the Anthropocene, which refers to a geological epoch in which human impact on the planet has become massive and often devastating, gives expression to the puzzling predicament that human agency has been revealed to have an influence on phenomena that are "immensely vaster than we are."[34] The Anthropocene thus articulates "a problem of scale"[35] that entails both epistemological and representational challenges.

Complex, abstract, and incremental processes such as ecological devastation, environmental pollution, or species extinction—all forms of what

31   Other important recent critical theorizations of complicity beyond those already mentioned include Jade Schiff, *Burdens of Political Responsibility: Narrative and the Cultivation of Responsiveness* (New York: Cambridge University Press, 2014); Adam Kelly and Will Norman, eds., "Complicity in Post-1945 Literature: Theory, Aesthetics, Politics," special issue, *Comparative Literature Studies* 56, no. 4 (2019): 673–92; Mihaela Mihai, *Political Memory and the Aesthetics of Care: The Art of Complicity and Resistance* (Stanford, CA: Stanford University Press, 2022).

32   Joanna Zylinska, *Minimal Ethics for the Anthropocene* (Ann Arbor, MI: Open Humanities Press, 2014), 26.

33   Michael Tavel Clarke and David Wittenberg, "Introduction," in *Scale in Literature and Culture*, ed. Michael Tavel Clarke and David Wittenberg (Cham, Switzerland: Palgrave Macmillan, 2017): 1–32, here 7.

34   Bruno Latour, "Anti-Zoom," in Clarke and Wittenberg, *Scale in Literature*, 93–101, here 93.

35   Latour, "Anti-Zoom," 93.

literary scholar Rob Nixon calls "slow violence"—"overspill clear boundaries in time and space" and play out on a planetary scale.[36] Rendering these phenomena and the ways in which they are shaped by human agency understandable and representable requires careful scaling procedures that can "shift between, connect, and make sense of multiple, interconnected dimensions."[37] In ecocritical debates, scaling is often thought about in relation to the question of representation and is therefore conceptualized, as Roman Bartosch has argued, either as a practice of writing or as a practice of reading.[38]

On the one hand, indeed, scholars such as McGurl and Wai Chee Dimock focus on scaling as a textual performance. Dimock calls attention to the potential of certain artworks to give visual and narrative shape to "the otherwise abstract and disembodied concept of scale,"[39] but also to relations across scales. McGurl, for his part, explores the capacity of certain literary genres to act "as scaling device[s], scaling up and down as needed"[40] to mediate between the vast and the small. Literary genres, following McGurl, can, in other words, enable textual performances of compression and expansion that give comprehensible form to the relations between human beings and "the inhumanly large and long."[41] Yet it is important to emphasize that while such scaling procedures may "offer the *impression*"[42] that it is possible to zoom smoothly in and out between scales, this is, in fact, a specific "zoom effect" produced by the representational apparatus (think: Google Earth), which disregards the incommensurability of different scales, or what Derek Woods calls "scale variance."[43]

---

36 Rob Nixon, *Slow Violence and the Environmentalism of the Poor* (Cambridge, MA: Harvard University Press, 2011), 10.

37 Stacy Alaimo, "When the Newt Shut off the Lights: Scale, Practice, Politics," in *Teaching Climate Change in the Humanities*, ed. Stephen Siperstein, Shane Hall, and Stephanie LeMenager (London: Routledge, 2017), 31–36, here 31.

38 See Roman Bartosch, "Scale, Climate Change, and the Pedagogic Potential of Literature: Scaling (in) the Work of Barbara Kingsolver and T. C. Boyle," *Open Library of Humanities* 4, no. 2 (2018): 1–21.

39 Wai Chee Dimock, "Low Epic," *Critical Inquiry* 39, no. 3 (2013): 614–31, here 617.

40 McGurl, "Critical Response II," 634.

41 Mark McGurl, "The Posthuman Comedy," *Critical Inquiry* 38, no. 3 (2012): 533–53, here 549.

42 Latour, "Anti-Zoom," 94; Latour's emphasis.

43 Derek Woods, "Scale Variance and the Concept of Matter," in *The Politics of New Materialism: History, Philosophy, Science*, ed. Sarah Ellenzweig and John H. Zammito (London: Routledge, 2017), 200–224.

On the other hand, Timothy Clark focuses on scaling as a readerly enterprise aimed at taking into account multiple different scales at the same time in the process of interpreting a literary text. In *Ecocriticism on the Edge*, Clark distinguishes between three spatiotemporal scales at which a given text can be read and interpreted. First, the individual, psychological scale, where the reader focuses on the thoughts and actions of the individual characters and the relationships and conflicts between them. Second, the (trans)national, (multi)generational, and historical scale, at which one usually takes into account "a 'historical period' of some kind."[44] Third, the planetary scale, which moves beyond the usual scope of literary analysis to consider a geological and environmental history that unfolds over a time frame of millions of years.

Clark takes issue with the way traditional modes of interpretation tend to privilege the first or second scale and thus "miniaturize" environmental concerns as symbols or metaphors for psychological, social, and historical phenomena.[45] He proposes an alternative reading practice that consists of approaching "the same literary text through a series of increasingly broad spatial and temporal scales, one after the other."[46] Importantly, the aim of this reading practice is not to abolish or relativize the first or the second scale in favor of the third. Indeed, Clark specifically warns against taking the third scale as an absolute or "final frame of reference"[47] merely by virtue of its largeness. Rather, he advocates multiscalar reading as a way of "enriching, singularizing and yet also creatively deranging the text by embedding it in multiple and even contradictory frames at the same time."[48]

The goal of this form of readerly experimentation is twofold. First, to make visible how certain readings at one scale—together with the assumptions that sustain them—are recast or even fall apart at another scale. For instance, phenomena that pertain to the third scale, such as climate change, can "derange" established frameworks for thinking about cause and effect, action and agency, and meaning making. The second goal is to show the "hidden costs"[49] of monoscalar readings and how, for example, traditional modes of interpretation that privilege the first and second scales may perpetuate and thus render us complicit in forms of epistemic violence that only become visible at the third scale. As noted above, it is possible and even plausible to read the nonhuman presences

---

44 Timothy Clark, *Ecocriticism on the Edge: The Anthropocene as a Threshold Concept* (London: Bloomsbury, 2015), 100.
45 Clark, *Ecocriticism on the Edge*, 75–80.
46 Clark, *Ecocriticism on the Edge*, 97.
47 Clark, *Ecocriticism on the Edge*, 108.
48 Clark, *Ecocriticism on the Edge*, 108.
49 Clark, *Ecocriticism on the Edge*, 147.

in these Generationenromane as symbols for human concerns, but to do so is to obscure the more-than-human dimension of the violent histories depicted. Scale reading can thus help to trouble the self-evidence of established, anthropocentric hermeneutic frameworks.

With this in mind, let us now turn to Hamann's *Usambara*. In our reading we combine attention to the text's own scaling operations with a resolve to co-scale with the text; that is, to engage with it at the individual, the (trans)national, and the ecological scales. The aim of this multiscalar reading is to detect how *Usambara* renders visible the complex relations that link individual and collective human agency to violent phenomena that exist in increasingly larger scalar realms such as fascism, colonialism, and environmental violence.

Violets Elsewhere

Hamann's *Usambara* is a work of historical metafiction that draws on documentary materials to construct a narrative that intermingles real events with fictitious characters and episodes. Its protagonist is the fictional Fritz Binder, a middle-aged postman from Wuppertal. Fritz is obsessed with his great-grandfather, Leonhard Hagebucher, who, according to family lore, was part of the first German expedition to the top of Mount Kilimanjaro in East Africa in October 1889 and, so he claimed, the true yet unsung discoverer of the "Usambaraveilchen" (African violet, *Saintpaulia ionantha*).[50] The romanticized stories of Hagebucher's adventures in Africa have been transmitted from generation to generation to Fritz, who, in turn, seizes every opportunity to retell these stories to others. A small inheritance from his mother eventually enables Fritz to follow in his great-grandfather's footsteps by signing up for the "Kilimanjaro Benefit Run," a sponsored race to the summit aimed at raising money for the melting glaciers of Kilimanjaro.

The novel follows two alternating narrative strands that cross-map the great-grandfather's historical expedition up Mount Kilimanjaro in 1888–89 with the benefit run in 2006. The first strand, apparently told by a third-person (heterodiegetic) narrator, is set in the distant colonial past, three generations before the present of the narration, and offers a highly sanitized account of Hagebucher's time in East Africa, which coincided with the so-called *Araberaufstand* (Arab uprising) against the German East Africa Company in 1888. The uprising lasted for two years, and its brutal suppression led ultimately to the founding of the colony of German East Africa. This aspect of the history and the bloody violence

50 Christof Hamann, *Usambara* (Göttingen: Steidl, 2007). Further references to this novel will be given parenthetically in the text. All translations are our own.

associated with it are conspicuously absent from the narrator's account.[51] This strand of the narrative revolves around Hagebucher's supposed discovery of the Usambaraveilchen while participating in the expedition, led by geographer Hans Meyer and alpinist Ludwig Purtscheller, to the top of Mount Kilimanjaro. This expedition actually took place, but without the fictional Hagebucher; Meyer and Purtscheller are historical figures, and Hamann draws on their accounts of the ascent. According to Hagebucher, they wanted to take all the credit for the successful climb, which explains why his name was erased from the historical record of the expedition, and which also meant that his discovery of the violet went unrecognized.

The second narrative strand takes place in the present day and is told by Fritz in the first person. The reader follows him as he becomes romantically involved with Camilla, his mother's former nurse; begins to train for the Benefit Run; and, having traveled to Tanzania, ultimately fails to reach the summit owing to a bout of altitude sickness. The novel's two narrative voices initially appear to be distinct; and throughout the course of the prologue and the first three chapters, the two narrative strands alternate and are kept separate by means of blank lines and asterisks. While Hagebucher's story progresses chronologically, Fritz's features often dizzying leaps in time and space, bouncing from the Benefit Run to the months of preparation that precede it, but also to scenes from his childhood and teenage years.

The juxtaposition of different temporalities, in Hamann's hands, becomes a productive tool for exploring complex scalar relations and unexpected connections between disparate times and places. To start with, it produces a fragmented yet rich picture of how individual members of the family become implicated—at different points in time and in varying ways—in vast and long-running (trans)national histories of violence. In this map of cross-scalar complicitous entanglements, Hagebucher emerges (contrary to the family legend) as a *Mitläufer* and beneficiary of German colonial violence and exploitation. The novel leaves ambiguous whether Hagebucher's claim to have discovered the African violet is true (within the fiction of the novel) or whether he was ever even in Africa. Hence, it is unclear whether he actively took part in what was an explicit act of colonial land appropriation that laid claim to Kilimanjaro as part of Imperial Germany.[52] What is clear, however, is that Hagebucher

51 For a concise history of the uprising, see Steven Fabian, "Locating the Local in the Coastal Rebellion of 1888–1890," *Journal of Eastern African Studies* 7, no. 3 (2013): 432–49.

52 For more on the colonial history of Mount Kilimanjaro, see Christof Hamann and Alexander Honold, *Kilimandscharo: Die deutsche Geschichte eines afrikanischen Berges* (Berlin: Wagenbach, 2011).

profited financially from the German colonial endeavor insofar as he later built his fortune by growing and selling exotic African flowers such as the Usambaraveilchen.[53]

The question of Hagebucher's status as a "Mitläufer"—a term that corresponds roughly to the English "fellow traveler," or, more literally, "fellow runner"—haunts the narrative, which consistently plays on the polysemy of the verb "laufen" (to run): Fritz attributes his great-grandfather's thirst for adventure to a medical condition, restless leg syndrome, which, he claims, runs in the family (10). This diagnosis allows Fritz to cast his great-grandfather as an apolitical and romantic dreamer, whose only motivation for going to Africa was to move his legs and chase his flower (85). As a participant in the Benefit Run, Fritz becomes a literal Mitläufer, in the sense of someone who "runs alongside" or "with" others, while his relentless and uncritical endorsement of his great-grandfather's self-aggrandizing stories also renders him complicit in perpetuating an exculpatory narrative of German colonialism. Furthermore, over the course of the novel, the reader comes to see Fritz as what one might call a "Wegläufer," someone who "runs away" from the ugly truth of his genealogical implication in Germany's violent past. When one of his fellow runners remarks that restless leg syndrome is common in runners, Fritz replies, "Kann sein, aber bei uns in der Familie ist es keine Krankheit. Es ist eine Frage des Gedächtnisses" (That may be, but in our family it's not an illness. It is a question of memory, 188).

The family narrative that he has inherited, readers soon discover, not only hides the brutal reality of the German colonial occupation in East Africa but also functions as a screen memory that covers up the troubling history of the protagonist's grandfather, August Ködling, an avid Nazi who as early as 1932 would parade around in his uniform day and night. Ködling is almost completely screened out from the family history as someone who, according to his daughter, Fritz's mother, "hat nicht zu uns gepasst" (wasn't one of us, 207). The family story even implies that Hagebucher had a hand in Ködling's fatal accident during a hike in the mountains. And yet, in the family photo, the supposed victim and perpetrator are standing "ganz nah beieinander" (very close, 148). Even Fritz himself wonders why, despite Hagebucher's supposed aversion to National Socialism, he welcomed Ködling into the family with open arms (199). Gradually, the official family memory of Hagebucher as a stubborn yet silent opposer of Nazism begins to seem doubtful even to Fritz.

Fritz's failure to acknowledge his family's complicity in German colonialism and National Socialism finds expression in a form of repetition

53 Göttsche, *Remembering Africa*, 404.

compulsion[54] that only entangles him further in the past he is running away from. While Fritz tries to make sense of his great-grandfather's legacy, he inadvertently invokes the buried history of National Socialism: "Ich fülle die Lücken auf. Reime mir das alles zusammen. Mein Kilimandscharo. Mein Kampf. Na und?" (I fill in the blanks. I piece it all together. My Kilimanjaro. My struggle. So what?, 213). *His* struggle is to reach the summit and emulate his great-grandfather, but the phrase "mein Kampf," of course, alludes to Adolf Hitler's infamous 1925 antisemitic manifesto—a connotation that implicitly, but also literally, juxtaposes colonialism and National Socialism.

Read on the second scale, the novel presents the Kilimanjaro Benefit Run as a "neocolonial variation of colonial travels,"[55] where latent colonial and racist practices still shape the interaction between tourists and locals. Hamann thus clearly brings to the fore what Ann Laura Stoler describes as the "duress" of colonial histories: that is, the "tenacious presence" of "colonial constraints and imperial dispositions" in the present.[56] The resonances and continuities between the colonial past and the neocolonial present are reinforced by the successive and incrementally anarchic changes to the narrative structure toward the end of the novel. When Fritz arrives in Tanzania in chapter 5, readers learn that what appeared to be two isolated narrative strands uttered by two different narrators are in fact nested narratives with one and the same narrator; namely, Fritz. More precisely, we discover that it is Fritz who has been narrating the story of his great-grandfather all along, and that what we have been reading is a composite version of the many different iterations of the same story he has been telling repeatedly to different audiences: first, presumably, to Camilla and, later, to his fellow runners. In chapters 6 and 7, which recount the Benefit Run and Fritz's collapse because of altitude sickness, these different diegetic levels also collapse, and the two storylines begin to merge thematically and syntactically. Scenes from Hagebucher's expedition meld into Fritz's own account of his ascent of Kilimanjaro, at the same time as sentences starting in one narrative strand are cut short, only to resume in the other strand, thus yoking together both storylines. In this way, *Usambara* performatively enacts the entanglement of past and present, underscoring that colonial history "is past but not over."[57] By

---

54 See Priscilla Layne, "The Collective Responsibility of Colonialism: Postcolonial Fantasies in Christof Hamann's *Usambara* (2007)," in *After the Imperialist Imagination: Two Decades of Research on Global Germany and Its Legacies,* ed. Sara Pugach, David Pizzo, and Adam Blackler (Oxford: Peter Lang, 2020), 297–316, here 304.

55 Göttsche, *Remembering Africa,* 298.

56 Ann Laura Stoler, *Duress: Imperial Durabilities in Our Times* (Durham, NC: Duke University Press, 2016), 4.

57 Stoler, *Duress,* 25.

participating in the run, Fritz contributes to perpetuating this history and therefore becomes both diachronically and synchronically implicated in colonial violence and its aftermath.

Crucially, this is not an insight spelled out by the narrator himself. The narrative voice in *Usambara* is, in fact, characterized by a radical inability to come to terms with uncomfortable questions of complicity and responsibility.[58] The map of intergenerational implication in *Usambara* materializes rather as an effect of the play of juxtapositions in the text and requires an active reader who can order the juxtaposed fragments into a meaningful whole, even if that often entails reading against the grain of Fritz's narration.[59]

Two important structural elements in *Usambara* serve to cast doubt on the narrator's reliability. The first is the presence of Camilla, who functions as a critical conscience in the novel, tirelessly questioning the stories passed down to Fritz—from their portrayal of Hagebucher as a noble character driven exclusively by romantic love and scientific curiosity (85), to their absolute erasure of colonial violence (100), and to their latent racism (85). The second is the text's metafictionality. Throughout the novel, the narrator frequently introduces self-reflexive comments that draw attention to the constructedness of the narrative he weaves and reweaves "um Urgroßvater wieder auf den Weg zu bringen" (in order to get great-grandfather moving again, 166). Often, these interventions explicitly spotlight the narrator's own inaccuracies, slips, and failings: his unscrupulous filling in of the gaps (213) and fiddling with the truth (82), his use of what he calls "Effekthascherei" (gimmickry, 100) to make the story more exciting, or his habit of changing the story's ending to impress his audience (135). These metafictional reflections cast doubt on his reliability as a narrator and therefore compel readers to work actively with the text—behind the narrator's back, as it were—to tease out the past and present forms of complicity and implication in violence that Fritz refuses to address in his narrative.

Existing scholarship on *Usambara* has contributed to disentangling different layers of complicity and implication that crisscross the first and

58 See Axel Dunker, "'Es ist eine Frage des Gedächtnisses': Relektüren historischer und literarischer Texte in Christof Hamanns Roman *Usambara*," in *Literarische Entdeckungsreisen: Vorfahren, Nachfahrten, Revisionen*, ed. Hansjörg Bay and Wolfgang Struck (Cologne: Böhlau, 2012), 157–71; Daniela Gretz, "Expeditionen ins 'i/Innere Afrika/s': Zur Reziprozität von existenzieller Fremdheitserfahrung und kultureller Fremderfahrung in Afrika-Romanen der deutschsprachigen Gegenwartsliteratur," in *Literatur als Wagnis/Literature as a Risk: Dfg-Symposium 2011*, ed. Georg Braungart, Monika Schmitz-Emans, Achim Geisenhanslüke, and Christine Lubkoll (Berlin: De Gruyter, 2013), 702–23; Göttsche, *Remembering Africa*; Layne, "The Collective Responsibility."

59 See Dunker, "'Eine Frage des Gedächtnisses,'" 171.

second scales by examining how members of the Hagebucher family are involved in the Holocaust, colonialism, and their legacies.[60] None of these approaches, however, has pursued the question of complicity and implication on the third scale, despite the powerful textual cues in the novel that would seem to invite such a reading: vibrant nonhuman presences such as the melting glaciers of Kilimanjaro or the Usambaraveilchen itself are central to the novel's plot and yet have mostly been overlooked as mere backgrounds or props to Fritz's family history. Closely attending to these nonhuman presences, we argue, offers a way of taking part in *Usambara*'s up- and downscaling efforts and of coproducing, through that shuttling movement, a projection of relationality and implication that extends to the planetary scale.

Glaciers are emblematic of slow processes that extend over vast geological time periods, and the glaciers atop Mount Kilimanjaro likely formed some eleven thousand years ago; but their entry into Western history can be pinpointed to October 1889, when the Meyer expedition reached the Kibo summit, one of the three volcanic cones of Kilimanjaro. The "discovery" of the glaciers was a momentous event from both a scientific and a political point of view. On the one hand, it put an end to the skepticism of scientific authorities at the time about the capacity of glacial ice to withstand the equatorial temperatures around Kilimanjaro. On the other hand, it served to legitimize an act of colonial land appropriation. Fritz retells the heroic moment when Meyer reached the summit and planted the German flag to lay claim to the peak, uttering the words: "Mit dem Recht des ersten Besteigers … taufe ich diese bisher unbekannte, namenlose Spitze des Kibo, den höchsten Punkt afrikanischer und deutscher Erde, Meyerspitze" (By the right of the first person to reach the summit … I christen this hitherto unknown, unnamed peak of Mount Kibo, the highest point on African and German soil, Meyer Peak, 248).[61] This act constitutes an example of what performance scholar Diana Taylor calls a "scenario of discovery": a key instance of colonialist discourse by which "the self-proclaimed discoverers" stake a claim to the land and the human and nonhuman beings that inhabit it by enacting specific rituals meant to legitimize the transfer.[62] The "scenario of discovery" is, moreover, a per-

---

60 See Dunker, "'Eine Frage des Gedächtnisses'"; Gretz, "Expeditionen ins 'i/Innere Afrika/s'"; Göttsche, *Remembering Africa*; Layne, "The Collective Responsibility."

61 See Hans Meyer, *Ostafrikanische Gletscherfahrten: Forschungsreisen im Kilimandscharo-Gebiet* (Leipzig: Duncker & Humblot, 1890); cf. Christof Hamann, "Ruinieren, Verketten, Verformen: Zum Umgang mit Materialien beim Schreiben," in *Ins Fremde Schreiben*, ed. Christof Hamann and Alexander Honold (Göttingen: Wallstein, 2009), 313–22, here 315.

62 Diana Taylor, *The Archive and the Repertoire: Performing Cultural Memory in the Americas* (Durham, NC: Duke University Press, 2003), 56.

formance of mastery that establishes a hierarchical relationship between "the discoverer" and "the discovered" and, as decolonial critic Julietta Singh argues, allows "particular *material* actions" such as indiscriminate exploitation, control, or consumption.[63]

Indeed, Meyer's successful ascent of Kilimanjaro paved the way for agricultural exploitation and the zealous search for raw materials and new settlement areas in and around the Kilimanjaro region.[64] As the creeks, ridges, streams, lakes, craters, glaciers, and peaks scattered across the Kilimanjaro area were successively "discovered," named, scientifically classified, and cartographically represented, they became German colonial possessions and resources. The native inhabitants fared no better. They, too, were regarded as natural resources, "ebenso wie Mineralschätze, Pflanzen und Tiere" (just like mineral deposits, plants, and animals).[65]

The history of colonial exploitation that followed the German "conquest" of Kilimanjaro remains an ellipsis in the novel. Fritz's return to Africa nearly twelve decades after Meyer's expedition, however, allows Hamann to recall this history by way of an examination of its material effects. The Kilimanjaro glaciers play a key role in this endeavor. By juxtaposing Hagebucher's and Fritz's scaling of Kilimanjaro, *Usambara* creates a powerful contrast between the imposing state of the glaciers in 1889 and their dire condition a little more than a century later. Fritz imagines Hagebucher's sense of awe at the sublime spectacle of the ice as he nears the summit (226), its unique way of reflecting the sunlight (232), its loud cracking and groaning (233). But when he himself arrives at the same point more than a hundred years later, Fritz is greeted by an absence: "So stelle ich es mir auf dem Mond vor. Trostlos. Hässlich. Eine Geröllhalde" (225; This is how I picture the surface of the moon. Desolate. Ugly. A sea of debris). The text jumps back and forth between these two ascents, collapsing on a narrative level the temporal distance between them, in order to highlight the stark contrast in the vista that greets Hagebucher and Fritz. As they each scale the mountain, the scale of the present-day devastation of the Kilimanjaro glaciers becomes clear to the reader. In a gesture of refusal to face this devastation as well as his own failure to reach the top, Fritz removes his glasses, preferring to imagine his great-grandfather's glorious summitting instead (230).

The two ascents bookend a particularly disastrous century in the much longer history of the Kilimanjaro glaciers: almost 85 percent of the glacier cover that used to crown Mount Kilimanjaro disappeared between 1912 and 2007 owing to rising temperatures, droughts, and pollution

---

63   Julietta Singh, *Unthinking Mastery: Dehumanism and Decolonial Entanglements* (Durham, NC: Duke University Press, 2018), 17.

64   Hamann and Honold, *Kilimandscharo*, 117.

65   Hamann and Honold, *Kilimandscharo*, 99. Our translation.

related to overtourism.[66] This environmental disaster, ironically, is the motivation for the Kilimanjaro Benefit Run: an event that is supposed to raise money for conservation efforts but that at the same time sustains the same tourism industry that attracts fifty thousand hikers to the slopes of Kilimanjaro every year. Tellingly, neither Fritz nor the other runners seem to care much about the retreating glaciers, or for that matter, their own implication in that process. None of them, and certainly not Fritz, seems to be willing to acknowledge that flying en masse to Tanzania to save its glaciers might not be the "ökologische Großtat" (247; great ecological achievement) that the politicians in the novel make it out to be. Rather, it is an act that, in tandem with numerous other human activities, has a deleterious impact on the planet's ecology and implicates the benefit runners in the disappearance of glaciers around the world.

The other key nonhuman presence in *Usambara* is the titular Usambaraveilchen, which suffers a similar fate to that of the glaciers: it too undergoes the sequence of "discovery," naming, colonial appropriation, commercial exploitation, and gradual disappearance. The violet, too, is made to function as the yearned-for, undiscovered object, the proverbial "blue flower" of the Romantic imagination in the eyes of its European "discoverer," Hagebucher: "Er wusste nicht, woher die vom ersten Moment an unerschütterliche Überzeugung kam, dass die Pflanze, die dort wuchs, noch unentdeckt war, dass sie noch kein europäisches Auge gesehen, dass sie auf ihn, Leonhard Hagebucher, gewartet hatte" (26; From the first moment he was gripped by an unshakeable conviction, the origin of which he did not know, that the flower that grew there was as yet undiscovered, that no European eye had yet beheld it, and that it had been waiting there for him, Leonhard Hagebucher). Hagebucher decides to christen the flower "Usambaraveilchen," or Usambara violet, after the mountain range where it grows. According to the story passed down to Fritz, he then loses the specimen during the 1888 uprising, when his vasculum is confiscated by the rebels. This incident serves to reinforce the link between the flower and the colonial occupation. It also explains why Hagebucher lost his claim to having discovered the violet.[67] Nevertheless, back in Germany, he would go on to become the first gardener to acquire the rights to cultivate the Usambaraveilchen commercially. The African violet became a great success that could soon be found "in vielen deutschen Wohnzimmern" (196; in many a German living room). The violet thus goes from being a singular object of desire

---

66 See Hamann and Honold, *Kilimandscharo*, 155–56.

67 This link is already part of the violet's history, as it was, in fact, discovered by Baron Walter von Saint Paul-Illaire (1860–1940), district commissioner of Tanga province at the time. The flower's scientific name, *Saintpaulia*, derives from his name.

to being a mass-produced commodity. Today, the violet is still a best-selling houseplant, generating an annual turnover of millions of euros in Germany alone.[68] At the same time, it is almost extinct in the wild owing to habitat destruction and has been described by scientists "as a sort of 'panda' of the plant world."[69]

The novel's consistent narrative focus on this "kleine, allerliebste Pflanze" (196; most precious little plant) and the Kilimanjaro glaciers constitutes a key scaling procedure. Having survived for thousands of years in East Africa, they have since all but vanished from their native habitat. These nonhuman figures stand synecdochally for a vast history of systematic colonial exploitation and environmental destruction, while also gesturing toward precolonial history and, indeed, prehuman deep time. Conversely, the novel employs synecdoche and repetition to scale up individual actions and gestures so that they become emblematic of the intertwined histories of colonialism and ecological violence. Thus, toward the end of the novel, Fritz evokes the German colonial imagination of the African continent as a mythical land of limitless wonders awaiting conquest and appropriation:

> Wir stellten uns den Regenwald als den verwilderten Garten Eden vor. Jede Hand, die da hineingriff … zog etwas erstaunliches heraus. Urgroßvaters Zuhörer wollten dahin. Sie wollten mit der Hand hineingreifen.
> Eine leere Hand hinein, eine gefüllte hinaus.
> Der Regenwald ein Glückssäckel.
> Mit einer leeren Hand hinein, mit einem Menschen fressenden Äthiopier hinaus.
> Mit einer leeren Hand hinein, mit einem Pygmäen hinaus.
> Mit einer leeren Hand hinein, mit einem Kongopfau hinaus.
> Mit einer leeren Hand hinein, mit einem Okapi hinaus. (211)

> [We imagined the jungle as an untamed Garden of Eden. Every hand that reached inside … emerged holding something astonishing. My great-grandfather's listeners wanted to go there. They wanted to reach their hands in too.
> An empty hand reaches in and comes out full.

68 See Hans-Christoph Behr and Richard Niehues, "Markt und Absatz," *Landbauforschung* 330 (2009): 69–98; Alain Chautems, Mathieu Perret, and David Aeschimann, *Von den Tropen in die Stube: Vielfalt der Gesneriengewächse* (Zurich: Botanischer Garten der Universität Zürich, 2016).

69 Charlotte Hsu, "Saving Saintpaulia, the African Violet," *UBNow*, last modified June 21, 2016, https://www.buffalo.edu/ubnow/working/announcements.host.html/content/shared/university/news/news-center-releases/2016/06/023.detail.html.

The jungle as a magic purse.
An empty hand reaches in and pulls out a man-eating Ethiopian.
An empty hand reaches in and pulls out a pygmy.
An empty hand reaches in and pulls out a Congo peafowl.
An empty hand reaches in and pulls out an okapi.]

This passage comes at the height of Fritz's altitude-induced delirium and is preceded by a series of references to historical figures, among them the famous zoologist Bernhard Grzimek and Walter von Saint Paul-Illaire, the actual discoverer of the Usambaraveilchen, two figures who bookend a century-long German political and ideological involvement in East Africa. These and other historical figures, as well as fictional ones such as Hagebucher himself, are introduced by a long series of classic fairy-tale *incipits* "Es war einmal" (once upon a time, 198–218) as if to underscore the role of cultural discourse in justifying and perpetuating the imperial narrative of Africa "als den verwilderten Garten Eden" (as an untamed Garden of Eden). Thus, the "we" in this passage encompasses not only colonizing subjects or beneficiaries but also implicated subjects in the aftermath of colonialism who either perpetuate or eagerly consume this imperialist narrative (such as Fritz and his mother before him). The litany of victimized peoples and endangered species that follows, anaphorically introduced through the phrase "an empty hand reaches in," condenses the large-scale practices of dehumanization and exploitation enabled by this (neo)colonial narrative. The list is potentially infinite and thus invites the reader to imagine a never-ending sequence of innumerable grasping hands reaching for Africa and extracting its riches. While each individual act of reaching may not have a measurable impact on the land, and may not be motivated by anything other than wonder and curiosity, on a larger temporal scale they add up to a devastating scale-effect of vast dimensions.

Usambara, as critics have noted, weaves together the memories of German colonialism and National Socialism, endorsing a tradition in postwar memory culture initiated by Arendt and Aimé Césaire that explores the historical and ideological links between these two histories.[70] It also gestures toward the endurance of colonial history in the ostensibly postcolonial present, revealing continuities between seemingly disparate times. But the novel does not stop here. By inviting its readers to adopt a large-scale, longue-durée perspective, it brings to light connections between colonialism and the present-day ecological crisis. More precisely, by zeroing in on the parallel stories of the glaciers and the African violet, *Usambara* exposes the workings and destructive effects of what Malcom Ferdinand calls "colonial inhabitation": a particular way of inhabiting the

---

70 See Göttsche, *Remembering Africa,* and Layne, "The Collective Responsibility."

earth that was implemented through European colonization and that is based upon the "commercial exploitation of the land" as well as of its human and nonhuman inhabitants "for the purposes of enrichment."[71]

The understanding that colonialism might have repercussions that are temporally delayed and geographically dispersed, such as species extinction and melting glaciers, is not made explicit at any point in the novel. Yet the text guides the readers to fill in the blanks and piece it all together by themselves, in contrast to the narrator, who stubbornly refuses to do so. The juxtapositional arrangement of different times, places, characters, and storylines establishes a material link between the foundational scenes of colonial appropriation featured in the text and the contemporary environmental destruction to which the melting glaciers of Kilimanjaro and the endangered Usambaraveilchen bear witness. Attending to these textual signals enables an expanded constellation of relationality that significantly broadens our understanding of the forms of complicity and implication addressed in the novel. Hagebucher and his great-grandson turn out to be implicated—albeit in different ways—not only in violent historical phenomena such as fascism and colonialism but also in a history of violence against nature that is "longer than the life span of any biological individual"[72] and that only becomes visible when readers consent to co-participate in *Usambara*'s scaling performance.

Conclusion: Against the Alibi of Nature

In this chapter we have explored the affordances of the Generationenroman for making visible the multidirectional links between different histories of violence and the transgenerational networks of complicity and implication that pertain to them. As a genre, the Generationenroman has been a crucial location for working through Germany's violent pasts and for coming to terms with the echoes and continuities of these pasts in the present. As such, the genre has also provided a space in which to reflect on and remember forgotten, repressed, and silenced aspects of German history; in particular, German colonialism. As the fierce and vitriolic debates in the German media surrounding the relationship between the history and memory of colonialism, on the one hand, and the Holocaust, on the other hand, have shown, however, the way in which these connections can and should be drawn remains an extremely fraught and sensitive issue.[73] It

---

71 Malcom Ferdinand, *A Decolonial Ecology: Thinking from the Caribbean World*, trans. Anthony Paul Smith (Cambridge: Polity, 2022), 28.

72 Dimock, "Low Epic," 5.

73 Zimmerer and Rothberg, "Enttabuisiert den Vergleich!"; Thomas Schmid, "Der Holocaust war kein Kolonialverbrechen," *Zeit Online*, April 11, 2021, https://www.zeit.de/2021/15/

may seem gratuitous or even perverse, therefore, to introduce yet another structure or scale of violence and implication into this already fraught arena. Yet as the example of *Usambara* illustrates, the contemporary Generationenroman is already negotiating the compounded position of implication and even complicity that one person may occupy in relation to all of these apparently disparate and incommensurable forms and histories of violence. Our aim in this chapter has been to develop an analytic framework that allows us to account for the way these novels establish connections and continuities across multiple scales.

Violence on a massive scale, be it genocidal, colonial, or ecological, poses fundamental representational challenges. The Generationenroman as a genre developed in part in response to these challenges, and so it provides a set of representational strategies and formal affordances that can accommodate and make visible long-term structures of violence. The genre gives us multiscalar access to the question of implication—multiplying it, complicating it, and differentiating it further, giving rise to productive contradictions and tensions. The ecological dimension of the contemporary Generationenroman is not always as prominent or explicit as it is in *Usambara*. Yet a remarkable number of these novels feature what one might call an "ecological unconscious" that comes to the fore at various moments but often remains unacknowledged in the text. The practice of scale reading that we have proposed in this chapter thus also often necessitates a reading of the text against itself in order to bring the background of ecological violence into the foreground. To be clear: reading at the third scale is not so much a question of reframing historical atrocities on a planetary, geological scale at which they would lose their historical and ethical significance, which would open the door to highly problematic relativizations of crimes against humanity. Rather, it is a question of what Clark calls "unframing"[74] the first two scales of interpretation in such a way that the parameters and implicit assumptions governing such readings are called productively into question.

Reading as responsible unframing, more specifically, can open up a space in which phenomena belonging to different scales, places, and temporalities are allowed to coexist, thus troubling our habits of interpreting, understanding, and remembering violence and the rigid "binaries between micro and macro, nature and culture, nonhuman and human"[75]

---

erinnerungskultur-holocaust-kolonialismus-menschheitsverbrechen-vergleich-barkeit-michael-rothberg-juergen-zimmerer; Friedländer et al., *Ein Verbrechen ohne Namen*.

74   Clark, *Ecocriticism on the Edge*, 104.

75   Karen Barad, "Troubling Time/s and Ecologies of Nothingness: Re-turning, Re-membering, and Facing the Incalculable," *New Formations* 92, no. 92 (August 2017): 56–86, here 56.

that sustain them. The messy multiscalar constellation produced in the process, as we have seen, reveals the links between the entangled histories of colonialism, fascism, and ecological violence. Such constellations, crucially, can only emerge if the reader refuses to treat the natural environment and the nonhuman world more generally as a mere backdrop to human endeavors or as a metaphorical or allegorical device for illuminating human concerns. The conception of nature as an untapped symbolic resource awaiting exploitation parallels the extractivist and colonialist logic that sees the world and its othered human and nonhuman inhabitants as raw materials. Ferdinand's notion of "colonial inhabitation" as a particular way of inhabiting the land, in this sense, can also be felt in a tradition of inhabiting, mastering, and interpreting the textual territory, whereby nature serves only as a passive object to be construed and assigned meaning by a rational human subject. Such readings implicitly appeal to and perpetuate what Louise Green calls the "alibi of nature," a conception of nature as outside history, politics, and culture, as "the perfect elsewhere."[76] Not only is such a conception of nature as an apolitical and ahistorical realm separate from human activity untenable in the age of the Anthropocene; it has also, crucially, furnished a justification for European imperialism and environmental devastation.[77]

Scaling complicity and implication in the act of reading, then, requires a stance of epistemological humility. Far from implying an Archimedean point from which "we" would be in a position to perceive the totality of all three scales together, a multiscalar reading entails a humbling realization that no such perspective is available, even when it comes to the familiar and well-established first and second scales. What these novels as scaling devices can help us to understand is that there can be no vantage point from which we are not ourselves implicated in the violence we observe. There can be no "elsewhere."

76   Louise Green, *Fragments from the History of Loss: The Nature Industry and the Postcolony* (University Park: Pennsylvania State University Press, 2020), 6–8.

77   See, for instance, Graham Huggan and Helen Tiffin, *Postcolonial Ecocriticism: Literature, Animals, Environment* (Abingdon, UK: Routledge, 2010); Jason W. Moore, *Capitalism in the Web of Life: Ecology and the Accumulation of Capital* (London: Verso, 2015); Amitav Ghosh, *The Great Derangement: Climate Change and the Unthinkable* (Chicago: University of Chicago Press, 2016).

4: German Engagement with Iraqi Conflict in Sherko Fatah's *Das dunkle Schiff* (2008; *The Dark Ship*, 2015) and *Der letzte Ort* (The Last Place, 2014)

Joanne Leal

Introduction

TOWARD THE END OF Sherko Fatah's 2014 novel *Der letzte Ort*, the German protagonist, Albert, who has been kidnapped by Iraqi militants, is led through a hostile crowd that pelts him with food waste. Offering an explanation for this behavior, one of his captors remarks to him in English, "'Sie mögen keine Fremde'" ("They don't like strangers"), to which Albert responds in German, "'Geht mir ähnlich'" ("Neither do I").[1] The fraught and only partially understood encounter (Albert's captors speak no German) between self and a potentially hostile other in the context of violent conflict is at the heart of all of Fatah's work, as is its counterpart, the search for security and (self-)understanding within a sympathetic community.

Born in 1964 in East Berlin to an Iraqi Kurd father and a German mother, Fatah spent time in Iraq as a child, and while he now lives in Berlin, his father and other family members still live in northern Iraq. His novels, from *Im Grenzland* (In the Border Land, 2001) to *Schwarzer September* (Black September, 2019), are concerned with the encounter between the Middle East and Europe, and in *Das dunkle Schiff* and *Der letzte Ort* this scenario is staged from complementary perspectives. In the former, an Iraqi Kurd, Kerim, leaves his homeland to seek asylum in Berlin after extricating himself from involvement with a group of self-proclaimed holy warriors. In the latter, Albert, who has grown up in the

---

1   Sherko Fatah, *Der letzte Ort* (Munich: btb, 2016), 166. Subsequent references appear as parenthetical page numbers in the text. English translations of quotations from this novel, as yet untranslated into English, and other German sources unless otherwise indicated, are by Mererid Puw Davies.

German Democratic Republic (GDR), travels after German unification to Iraq, where he is abducted by fundamentalists. Both works thus explore the relationship between Europe and the Middle East in the context of fundamentalist violence and with reference to the limit figure of the Islamic terrorist.

It can be argued that after 9/11, this figure has been constructed in most Western discursive contexts as marking the Western subject's most extreme other; and that this portrayal serves a political purpose. With reference to such politics of representation, Michael Frank has argued "that fictional depictions of terrorists do more than explore a general and abstract category of 'otherness.' They confront a very particular type of 'other,' one whose deeds pose a threat to the political status quo (and reveal cracks in the given world order), which is why the official discourse on terrorism is interested in imposing a particular interpretation on these deeds."[2] Frank seems to imply here that literature can offer alternatives to such official interpretations; but he and other commentators also draw attention to the limited range of literary responses to terrorism post-9/11. Frank himself notes that literary works have tended to "adopt the perspective of the people on the receiving end of the violence," seeking "to fathom the impact of the attacks without probing into their causes."[3] Richard Jackson concurs and argues further that "the current literature dealing with terrorism functions to reproduce (rather than challenge) the dominant cultural mythography of terrorism and maintain the taboo against engaging directly with the terrorist's subjectivity."[4]

2   Michael C. Frank, "'Why do they hate us?' Terrorists in American and British Fiction of the mid-2000s," in *Terrorism and Literature*, ed. Peter C. Herman (Cambridge: Cambridge University Press, 2018), 340–60, here 342.

3   Frank, "'Why do they hate us?,'" 340.

4   Richard Jackson, "Sympathy for the Devil: Evil, Taboo, and the Terrorist Figure in Literature," in *Terrorism and Literature*, ed. Peter C. Herman (Cambridge: Cambridge University Press, 2018), 377–94, here 377. Writing in 2011, Petra Fachinger suggests the Federal Republic's own history of left-wing terrorism has made German writers less cautious about engaging directly with the Islamic terrorist: "The recent literary and cinematic interest in leading Red Army Faction terrorists has thus also given German novelists and filmmakers the inspiration and the tools to portray terrorists of a different kind. Compared to the few American and British authors who have focused on the radical Islamist, a relatively large number of German writers and filmmakers have taken on the challenge of illuminating his motivation." Fachinger does, however, mention only two novels: Christoph Peters, *Zimmer im Haus des Krieges* (A Room in the House of War, 2006), and Fatah's *Das dunkle Schiff*; and two films, Elmar Fischer's *Fremder Freund* (Foreign Friend, 2003) and Benjamin Heisenberg's *Schläfer* (Sleeper, 2005). Petra Fachinger, "Fatal (In)Tolerance? The Portrayal of Radical Islamists in Recent German Literature and Film," *Seminar* 4, no. 5 (2011): 646–60, here 649.

Where there is a more direct engagement with the terrorist himself (the terrorist subject is almost invariably male) and where his motives are scrutinized, there is, Frank argues, a "taboo on acknowledging the political motivation"; and on this point too, Jackson agrees.[5] He sets out a range of ways in which the terrorist is depicted in contemporary fiction, including "as religiously fanatical and absolutist, in some cases as a result of negative (often sexual) formative experiences and individual maladjustment or the loss of a father-figure"; or "as motivated by a deep hatred of Americans and American society and culture borne out of fanatical religious devotion, rather than political grievances in relation to US foreign policy in the Middle East, for example"; or as more generally "suffering from a form of 'disintegration of the self' due to the destabilizing effects of neoliberal globalization and postmodernity," leading him to seek "identity and certainty of purpose from theological sources."[6] Jackson concludes that "whether [terrorists] are depicted as mentally deficient or enfeebled, fanatical and cruel, or sexually perverted, they are arguably dehumanized, demonized, and most importantly, depoliticized in the process," and insists that by representing them in this way, literature "has failed to challenge and destabilize the dominant cultural imaginary about terrorism, but has instead reproduced and amplified it."[7]

Jackson argues that this failure comes about despite the fact that "literature has the *potential* to illuminate our understanding of terrorism through the empathetic entrance of the writer into the life world and subjectivity of the 'terrorist' perpetrator."[8] In his *9/11 Fiction, Empathy, and Otherness*, Tim Gauthier considers why literature's empathetic potential should be harnessed in this way. The events of September 11, 2001, can be understood, he argues, as "the (ultimate?) intrusion of an other demanding to be recognized and acknowledged." Furthermore, we can read the terrorist attacks as "a symptom of an expanding and inevitable contemporary 'condition of togetherness' in which we live and from which there is no refuge."[9] In the light of this interpretation, we might need at least to consider what Gauthier describes as the "radical possibility" of our "'relationship' with the terrorist," arguing that "our negation of said relationship is only the most extreme indication of a general reluctance to acknowledge our connection with the multifarious others who populate the planet."[10]

5   Frank, "'Why do they hate us?,'" 342.
6   Jackson, "Sympathy for the Devil," 381.
7   Jackson, "Sympathy for the Devil," 382 and 384.
8   Jackson, "Sympathy for the Devil," 377.
9   Tim Gauthier, *9/11 Fiction, Empathy, and Otherness* (Lanham, MD: Lexington Books, 2015), 5.
10   Gauthier, *9/11 Fiction*, 6.

It is precisely this "radical possibility" of our "'relationship' with the terrorist" that Fatah's novels confront. In this formulation, Gauthier's use of "our" implies that he is addressing a reader who likely shares what he and other critics cited here have identified as a typically Western response to fundamentalist violence and its representation. My reading of Fatah's novels assumes that they address a similarly positioned reader, and I will reflect further on the interpretive consequences of this assumption below.

Before doing so, I propose to explore this "radical possibility" of our "'relationship' with the terrorist" by positioning *Das dunkle Schiff* and *Der letzte Ort* in relation to the statements above. I do so with a view to investigating whether their representation of post-9/11 terrorism and violent conflict in both the Middle East and Germany expands the range of literary engagements with this topic, including in regard to their depiction of the terrorist subject. I intend to approach the novels from two related angles.

First, I will investigate how Fatah represents the impact of violence, both physical and psychological, on the formation of self in relation to other; how it affects the way in which the individual constructs and engages with an idea of community; and its consequences for his division of a world into an "us" to which he belongs and a potentially hostile "them." This work will be done with reference to those who perpetrate terrorist violence and those who become its victims; to those who identify as German and to those for whom Germans are the enemy other. These subject positions are sometimes held at different times by one and the same individual. Terrorists are largely the focus of *Das dunkle Schiff*, while their victims are at the center of *Der letzte Ort*, although this perpetrator/victim binary is troubled in both texts.

Second, I will consider the potential of empathy in relation to narrative as it manifests in both novels, asking specifically whether storytelling can act to counter violence by enabling mutual understanding, even across the terrorist victim-perpetrator divide, and by making community possible at subnational, national, and supranational levels. In particular, I will consider the potential of narrative empathy for impacting German self-understanding in an era of transnational terrorist violence. Storytelling is understood here as encompassing both the narratives we construct about our own lives and communicate to ourselves and others; and literary narrative. I am interested in the way stories function for characters within the texts, as well as whether, on a meta level, they engage the reader in an empathetic encounter with the other in a way that opens up new possibilities for thinking about German identity in a post-9/11 context. I am going to explore these questions initially in relation to *Das dunkle Schiff*, then as they are illuminated by *Der letzte Ort*, before drawing some conclusions from the representation and narration of self and other in both novels.

Das dunkle Schiff

Das dunkle Schiff's main section opens with the words "Kerim erinnerte sich" (Kerim remembered). Thus, a third-person narrator, whose perspective rarely strays from the protagonist's, gives narrative voice and coherence to a story Kerim is actively discouraged from speaking and that has devastating consequences when he does. It begins in northern Iraq, where Kerim, an Alevi Kurd, was born sometime after the start of the Iran-Iraq war and where he spends a childhood so impacted by conflict that it affects his subject formation. The many occasions on which he is exposed to violence and its consequences culminate in his witnessing of the death of his father, a restaurant owner, who is run over in a senseless act of brutality by a member of Saddam Hussein's secret service whom he had challenged for not paying his bill.

The trauma of Kerim's father's death contributes to an already identifiable psychic fragility that sometimes manifests as fear, but often as an apparent lack of affect. It leaves Kerim susceptible to the influence of the Islamic fundamentalists by whom he is captured some time later and into whose community he allows himself to be integrated, under the influence of a charismatic imam who takes on the role of surrogate father. Given that Kerim will go on to participate in atrocities against both American soldiers and Iraqi civilians under the influence of the imam's teaching, it could be argued that he confirms Jackson's view that political motivations for terrorist acts are substituted for psychological ones in contemporary fiction.

The novel is careful, though, to show that the violence to which Kerim is initially exposed has political causes—the Iran-Iraq War, the Iraqi invasion of Kuwait, the first Gulf War, and Saddam Hussein's subsequent persecution of the Kurds. It shows too that the "Glaubenskrieger" (110; "holy warriors," 74) respond to political events, including the US invasion of Iraq and resulting civil war.[11] So, initially they take action against the Kurdish militia and politicians "die im Bunde waren mit dem amerikanischen Teufel" (116; "who were in league with the American devil," 78). Only after the American invasion do they also target Iraqi civilians who cooperate with the "Kreuzritter" (143; "Crusaders," 96). Moreover, the group's leaders reinforce the connection for Kerim and others between their own experience and political developments in Iraq and the Middle East more generally. Thus, the imam reminds Kerim that his father was killed by agents of a regime originally supported by the Americans, and when they come under US fire, he fortifies the resolve

---

11 Sherko Fatah, *Das dunkle Schiff* (Munich: btb, 2010). Subsequent references appear as parenthetical page numbers in the text. Translations are from Sherko Fatah, *The Dark Ship*, trans. Martin Chalmers (Kolkata: Seagull Books, 2015), also with parenthetical page numbers.

of his disciples with the cry "'Sagt mir nicht, Palästina sei kein Teil eurer Seele'" (149; "'Don't say to me that Palestine isn't part of your souls,'" 100). This representation shows the novel to be sensitive to the fact that in conditions of ongoing ethnic, religious, civil, or multinational conflict, personal and political motivations for participation in violence may be imbricated and the causes of any terrorist act overdetermined.

Kerim's father, as a nonpracticing Alevi Muslim, observed the religious rituals of his Shiite neighbors minimally and without enthusiasm, something Kerim experienced as alienating: "Es war das Gefühl, nirgends wirklich dazuzugehören" (18; "it was the feeling of not really belonging anywhere," 9).[12] Thus, his time with the holy warriors is his first real experience of religious community or, indeed, community of any sort. Kerim finds, as Warda El-Kaddouri puts it, "was er schon sein ganzes Leben sucht: soziale Zugehörigkeit und eine gerichtete Form für das Ausleben spiritueller Bedürfnisse" (what he has been searching for all his life: social belonging and a focused form in which to realize spiritual needs), and this experience marks him fundamentally.[13]

The maintenance of the community's identity relies almost exclusively on its ability to construct itself in relation to an antagonistic other. Islamic belonging is contrasted with Western individualism in ways that encourage the militants to erect an unbreachable divide between a virtuous but vulnerable "us," and a "them" so hostile that their annihilation is justified. While this community provides Kerim with a temporary home, the violence it uses to secure its identity increases his already marked self-alienation and stunts him emotionally. Thus, while he is with the holy warriors, he can align himself with their precepts sufficiently to worry only about the aesthetics of his camerawork while recording his friend detonating a suicide bomb in a local marketplace. Kerim's decision to

12   Hansjörg Bay points out that as Alevis, Kerim and his family are "nicht nur Teil einer von einem repressiven Regime diskriminierten und, wie der am Rande des Geschehens in den Blick gerückte Giftgasangriff auf Halabdscha deutlich macht, auch brutal verfolgten ethnischen Gruppe, sondern gehört auch in dieser Hinsicht noch einmal zu einer religiösen Minorität" (not only members of an ethnic group which is discriminated against by a repressive regime, and, as the chemical attack on Halabja, which is referenced in passing, shows, brutally persecuted; they belong in this sense also to a religious minority). "Migration, postheroisch: Zu Sherko Fatahs *Das dunkle Schiff*," in *Niemandsbuchten und Schutzbefohlene: Flucht-Räume und Flüchtlingsfiguren in der deutschsprachigen Gegenwartsliteratur*, ed. Thomas Hardtke, Johannes Klein, and Charlton Payne (Göttingen: V&R unipress, 2017), 3–37, here 25.

13   Warda El-Kaddouri, "'Gott, rette mich aus der Lehre!' Verlust, Religiosität und Radikalisierung in den Fluchtnarrativen von Abbas Khider und Sherko Fatah," in Hardtke, Klein, and Payne, *Niemandsbuchten und Schutzbefohlene*, 39–51, here 45.

escape their clutches comes only when his own forthcoming deployment on a suicide mission is destined to end his existence within the community. With his own life at risk, he flees first to his family's home and then, as the influence of fundamentalist groups in Iraq widens, to his father's brother, Tarik, in Berlin, where he seeks asylum immediately on arrival.

The success of Kerim's asylum application gives him the chance of a new start: "Alles werde ich anders machen, und nichts soll mich verbinden mit der Vergangenheit außer den Menschen, die ich wirklich liebe" (350; "I'm going to do everything differently and nothing is going to connect me to the past except the people I really love," 245–46). Given Kerim's evident psychic fragility, however, the ideological conditioning to which he has been exposed, and the traumatic nature of his experiences in Iraq, the failure of his attempt in the text's second half to find a substitute for the fundamentalist community in Germany comes as no surprise. It is unsuccessful in part because Kerim is unable to recalibrate his understanding of self and other sufficiently to identify with an alternative community, but also for two further reasons. The first is that Kerim's own "othering" of both the German and migrant communities in Berlin is mirrored by the ultimate failure of his German interlocutors to see in him anything other than an "other." The second is that he struggles to find a way to speak about his violent past that would allow him to create an empathetic connection to another, one that might provide him with support in confronting his trauma.

During his first months in Berlin, Kerim must live with other refugees in an asylum hostel. Despite potential parallels in their experiences, he fails to find in these men from "Ländern, deren Namen er nicht einmal kannte" (268; "countries whose names he didn't even know," 186) a community to replace the one he has lost. Life in the hostel is, in fact, structured around ethnic divisions, and Kerim's one close asylum-seeking acquaintance, the Albanian, Ervin, is anxious to have him onside in the formation of a "Gegenpol" ("counterweight") to the "Schwarzafrikaner" ("black Africans") whom he blames for inciting racist violence on the part of their German hosts, "da sie den Hass der deutschen Normalbürger förmlich auf sich zögen" (269; "since they literally attracted the hate of the average German," 187). Characterized as it is by suspicion, hostility, and exclusionary practices, Kerim finds hostel life a deeply alienating experience.

More hopefully, however, Kerim also develops relationships beyond the hostel as he works to establish a life for himself in Germany, and these connections provide him with three possible recipients for the traumatic story to which he wishes to give voice. His Uncle Tarik; his German girlfriend, Sonja; and his Palestinian-German friend, Amir, are the only people he encounters in Berlin "von denen er sich angeschaut fühlte, deren Wege nicht durch ihn hindurch, sondern zu ihm führten" (384; "by

whom he felt looked at, whose paths led not through him but to him,"
269). Each represents the potential of a different kind of community formation. Two can help him break from his radical past and anchor himself
in Germany; the other is associated with his failure to do just this.

Tarik stands for the possibility of maintaining contact to Kerim's
home culture. Kerim experiences the arrival at his uncle's apartment after
the dangerous journey from Iraq as a "Heimkehr'" (263; "homecoming,"
183)—but his is a migrant community made up mostly of older Turks and
Arabs who, with their families, represent the majority population in this
part of Berlin. Kerim, just like their own sons, has little in common with
them, and his uncle's hospitality, however warm, cannot open doors to
the kind of community he needs. Tarik is, moreover, unwilling to engage
with Kerim's past, counseling his nephew that "was immer du von dort
mitgebracht hast ..., du musst es jetzt vergessen und etwas Neues begin-
nen" (356; "whatever it is you brought from over there ... you now have
to forget it and begin something new," 250). With this advice, he reproduces the response to trauma already advocated by Kerim's father, who,
by encouraging him to suppress negative experiences, sets him up psychically to fail in the construction of a sustainable sense of self.

Sonja, whom Kerim meets in a symbolically loaded scene when she
rescues him after he falls through the ice of a skating pond, represents the
security of life within mainstream culture. She is confident of her place in
the social spaces she inhabits and asserts control over her life, including
her sexuality, inspiring in Kerim both desire and confusion. Despite the
affection that develops between them, however, neither is entirely able
to meet the other emotionally. Kerim struggles to communicate to Sonja
the fears and anxieties that imprison him in the past, and she is reluctant to hear them, not least because to her he remains "fremd" (385;
"strange," 270), too alienating in his otherness for her to want to break
down the barriers between them: "Ich weiß nicht, wer er ist. Ich weiß
nicht, was er tut" (386; "I don't know who he is, I don't know what
he does," 271). As a result, as Petra Fachinger argues, "rather than help
him to understand his new environment better, this relationship widens
the gulf between his world and hers, and he is pushed into isolation."[14]
It provides no release from trauma, leaving Kerim, when it ends, to sink
"schwer wie ein Stein, zurück in seine Erinnerungen" (389; "heavy as a
stone, back into his memories," 273).

Kerim's third relationship is with Amir, the estranged son of his
uncle's Palestinian friend. Amir represents an alternative community
made up of disenfranchised young men: the children of migrant parents,
who have failed to integrate into mainstream German society or to find
community through family networks. They create alternative forms of

14 Fachinger, "Fatal (In)Tolerance?," 653.

precarious belonging through gang culture and criminal acts, which leave them largely "ohne Ziel und ganz allein" (279; "without a goal and all alone," 194).

Some of Amir's experiences mirror Kerim's—he too has had a relationship and a child with a German woman, which has failed to ground him in family life—and, despite having grown up locally, his sense of belonging in Berlin is only a little less fragile than that of his new friend. An intimation of their shared alienation, and with it a sense of potential kinship, explains the two men's fascination with one another. It also accounts for Amir's readiness finally to become the recipient of Kerim's story, to which nobody else had wanted to listen. Not only is he unfazed by descriptions of horrific acts of violence, having already watched the like online; his own sense of deracination means that he is drawn in by Kerim's expression of the transformative experience of religious belonging, of the "Intimität einer Gemeinschaft, wie sie nur der Glaube stiften kann" (374; "intimacy which only belief can give a community," 262).

Kerim's failure to root himself in Berlin either through family ties or integration into mainstream German culture, his sense of leading instead "ein falsches Leben" (381; "a false life," 267), means that he is drawn back to the community of the faithful. His experience of alienation in Germany—"Hier aber lebten alle Menschen für sich" (313; "here, however, everyone lived for himself," 218), he claims—makes credible for him the anti-Western teachings of his imam and his message that "ihre Freiheit ist Einsamkeit" (383; "their freedom is loneliness," 269). Indeed, these teachings affect Kerim so much that after attending a university prayer meeting at which he feels among friends again at last, he is tempted to seek out a mosque—one that, he is assured, is "auch keine für normal Gläubige" (376; "not one for normal believers," 264). At the mosque he catches sight of his former spiritual teacher, the source of those fundamentalist beliefs that have taken hold of him again. As El-Kaddouri suggests, Karim's "Neurorientierung zu einem radikalen Islam in Deutschland ist die Folge einer gescheiterten Verortung in der neuen Heimat" (new orientation toward a radical form of Islam in Germany is the consequence of a failure to find his place in his new home).[15] It also underscores the sustained and pernicious influence of the kind of binary thinking he has learned during his time with the fundamentalists. In the final instance, Kerim is unable to move beyond an understanding of self as determined and sustained through the construction of a hostile other.

Kerim's turn back to such thinking also unsettles a binary worldview more common among his German hosts, one that assumes that "they," and the threat they represent, are over there, and "we" are here.

---

15   El-Kaddouri, "'Gott, rette mich,'" 51.

Germany is on heightened terrorist alert,[16] the holy warriors are at the local mosque, and on the novel's final pages Kerim is killed; not by one of his countrymen but by Amir, for whom hearing his story has been a significant step in a process of radicalization that began when he watched the kind of propaganda video made by Kerim during his time with the militants. With this unexpected and brutal twist in which one alienated young man radicalized in the West kills his counterpart, a man who has failed to find a refuge from radicalization in Germany, the novel ends its exploration of the causes and consequences of terrorist violence. It does so by suggesting that national communities that create others not only of those beyond their borders but also of those who seek refuge from violence within them, as well as of their own disenfranchised populations, represented here by Amir, risk bringing home the violence associated with foreign conflict.

Der letzte Ort

In *Der letzte Ort*, it is the Western subject who travels to Iraq, a locus of conflict, and is exposed to violence as a result. Set after the US invasion, probably late in 2004, it begins shortly after Albert's abduction by Shiite militants. Imprisoned alone, he tries to make sense of what is happening to him, reassuring himself with regard to his captors: "Sie sind nicht deine Feinde, sie wissen nur nichts von dir" (7; They aren't your enemies, they just don't know anything about you). This hopeful premise is one the novel sets out to examine: that is, it asks whether understanding the other, getting to know them in a meaningful way, can diffuse the violent conflict caused by ethnic, national, or religious tensions.

This question is explored from the perspective of Albert, with whom the narrator is initially aligned: a paradigmatic Western subject, for whom the Iraqis remain unremittingly other.[17] This otherness is embodied for

16 The presence of fundamentalists in Germany who are preparing a terrorist attack is explained in the novel by German secret service involvement in the capture of the Al-Qaeda number two. This circumstance, along with other contemporary points of conflict, the "Karikaturenstreit" (399; "quarrel about caricatures," 279) and the death of "den allmächtigen Diktator von Bagdad" (399; "the all-powerful dictator of Baghdad," 280), provides a political rationale for Amir's murder of Kerim as a traitor to the cause of the holy warriors. As the narrator notes in relation to Kerim: "Diesmal wirkten die weitentfernten Ereignisse direkt in sein Leben hinein" (399; "This time, the far-distant events had a direct effect on his life," 280).

17 The novel certainly suggests that Albert, in his attitude to the Iraqis as other, is prototypically Western. Equally, for his various captors he is an undifferentiated Westerner: they assume he must be American or British, speak to him in English, and rarely acknowledge that he is German, let alone note the distinction

him by the militants who have abducted him but also in more complex ways by his translator, Osama, captured in the same attack. Through this character, the inverse relationship between self and other is also investigated; that is, we are enabled to explore the (knowledgeable) Iraqi subject's view of the West. The narrative perspective shifts abruptly in the novel's second part to align itself with Osama and subsequently moves back and forth between the two protagonists. Thus the reader also experiences Osama as the self for whom the Western subject is strange. The reader can share, too, his shifting sense of familiarity with and distance from the militants who are his countrymen and coreligionists but for whom he is the enemy: a "verwestlichter, ein schlechter Gläubiger, der noch dazu für die Ausländer arbeitet" (53; Westernized, bad believer, and working for the foreigners to boot). As Osama reflects, "In den Augen dieser Leute, das wusste er, stand er tiefer als der Ausländer, denn aus für sie rätselhaften Gründen hatte er ihre Gemeinschaft verlassen und es gewagt, sich gegen den Glauben zu stellen" (91; In these people's eyes, he knew, he was something lower than the foreigner, because for reasons that were mysterious to them, he had left their community and dared to position himself in opposition to faith).

That Albert and Osama become targets for those radically opposed to a Western presence in Iraq is, ironically, the consequence of their own openness to otherness. Albert's reasons for coming to Iraq are complex. Having grown up in the GDR, his decision post-Wende to study journalism is an attempt both to follow in and to deviate from the footsteps of his globe-trotting, nomenklatura father. Albert's father is described as a "Geschichtenerzähler" (storyteller) who failed to grasp the transformative potential of storytelling, its ability to open the self to the other, returning instead from every foreign trip with a story that confirmed his worldview. Albert has come to Iraq to gather material for his master's dissertation but also, in his words, because he wants to help: "Ich wollte Gutes tun" (15; I wanted to do good). To this end, he takes a job in a museum cataloging plundered items.

---

between a GDR and an FRG heritage. When Albert is taken captive, he recognizes his captors' hate toward him as impersonal: "Dieser Mann ist mein Feind, dachte er, er kennt mich nicht, hatte bis zu jenem Mittag auf dem Markt nie etwas von mir gehört, außer vielleicht von seinen Auftraggebern—und doch will er mich vernichten" (15; This man is my enemy, he thought, he doesn't know me, hadn't heard anything about me until that noon at the market, except maybe from those who gave him this job—and yet he wants to destroy me). The exception is Abdul, who, on hearing of his GDR background, calls him a socialist, an ideology he dismisses as definitively as he does capitalism: "'Der Sozialismus,' sagte der Emir, 'war gottlos, schlimmer noch, er war ein Götzenkult'" (250; "Socialism," said the Emir, "was godless, worse than that, it was idolatry").

Osama comes from a liberal family and has learned German in the vague hope of going abroad, following the example of his mother, who studied in the GDR, a point of familiarity that attracts Albert to him: "Dieser ungewöhnliche Hintergrund schien sie in Alberts Augen miteinander zu verbinden" (58–59; This unusual background seemed, to Albert's eyes, to link them to one another). Osama's work as a translator positions him as somebody who is open to other cultures and in a position to mediate between them and his own. Also provoking his engagement with the West, though, is his attraction to the idea of a dollar-funded Western lifestyle, something that motivated him as a young man to engage in illegal trade with plundered artifacts stolen for the Western market.

Alone after his abduction, Albert thinks fondly of Osama, "der bis dahin nicht nur sein Ohr und seine Stimme in dieser Fremde gewesen war, sondern auch das vertraute, freundliche Gesicht des Landes" (13; who until now had been not only his ears and his voice in this strange country, but also its familiar, friendly face). A relationship that has functioned in this positive fashion in an everyday context comes under intense strain, however, in the exceptional circumstances of the men's captivity, just at the point when its dialogic development becomes crucial to their survival. This hinges on their ability to know one another, partly because their captors take ignorance of each other as confirmation of their identity as foreign agents. In addition, and more importantly, the trust that grows from mutual understanding, alongside a willingness to take responsibility for one another, is vital for these characters' coming together in solidarity to offer at least psychological resistance to captors who define them as an enemy other. Or, as Osama puts it: "Wir müssen zusammenhalten" (193; We have to stick together).

Mutual understanding requires of Albert and Osama a willingness to engage with each other as individuals, outside of the ready-made frameworks that guide their thinking about cultural, ethnic, religious, and national belonging. But it also demands an investigation of self, as self-knowledge underpins the successful encounter with the other. Storytelling is shown to be key to this twofold endeavor, as Osama and Albert both remember for themselves and communicate to each other aspects of their lives that have helped determine who they have become. For Albert, this process involves exploring his GDR past, particularly his relationship with an overbearing father and a psychologically damaged sister, and his less than successful transition to a postunification reality. For Osama, it is his abortive career as an antiquities thief, which ends in what he regards as a moment of shame when, in order to evade capture, he abandoned his friend, Abdul.

This sharing of stories does produce moments when Osama and Albert see beyond difference to perceive sameness in ways that trouble binary thinking. Thus Albert can refract Osama's criticism of aspects of the West through the lens of his father's condemnation of the decadence of the nonsocialist world and its illusory promise of freedom. And when Albert signals his ambivalence toward German unification with the claim that Osama cannot know "wie das ist, wenn dein Staat gerade untergegangen ist" (158; what it's like, when your state has just gone under), his translator tells him just to look out of the window. But the success of their attempt at mutual understanding is also limited by the fact that they succumb to the stresses of their situation physically as well as psychologically. For example, Albert falls asleep twice at key moments in Osama's story, excusing himself with a culturally dismissive barb: "Eure Geschichten sind immer windungsreich und lang" (190; Your stories are always convoluted and long). Under pressure, the two men find it difficult to abandon the binary modes of thinking that are key to their construction of self. When Albert complains that "Selbst eure Entführungen sind unkoordiniert und chaotisch" (193; Even your kidnappings are uncoordinated and chaotic), Osama reproves him for connecting him to the wrong collective: "Du sollst nicht 'eure' sagen. Wir gehören zusammen" (195; "You shouldn't say 'your.' We belong together"). But Osama equally casts Albert as an other, commenting of Western conceptions of freedom that "Jeder macht den Unsinn, der ihm gerade einfällt, und so werdet ihr alt. Und damit es hier genauso wird, schickt ihr eure Panzer her" (228; Everyone just does whatever nonsensical thing comes into their heads, and you grow old like that. And in order to make it just like that here, you send your tanks over).

This resort to damaging stereotype suggests that under conditions as extreme as those of their captivity, the men struggle to put self at risk in order to engage with the other. Instead, they shore it up with resort to narrowly defined conceptions of community belonging, something that informs Albert's behavior, in his self-understanding as a stranger in a foreign land, even more than it does Osama's. The more difficult the situation gets, the more Albert insists on difference, treating his translator with increasing suspicion. On occasion he aligns him with their captors as the enemy other, struggling to see him as an individual and not as part of a hostile collective. He does this despite the fact that after they have both managed to escape, and Albert is recaptured, Osama returns to find him, unable to forget Albert as easily as Albert does him: "Längst hatte er begonnen, nur für sich allein zu planen. Welche Szenarien auch immer er für seine Flucht entwarf … es gab darin keinen Platz für Osama" (127; He had long since begun to make plans just for himself. Whatever scenarios he dreamed up for his escape … there was no place in them for Osama). By contrast, Osama cannot put his own interests first, as he did when he abandoned his former friend, Abdul. This is not least because he perceives himself as a "host" to Albert in his own land: "Der Gedanke Albert zurückzulassen, war ihm unerträglich. Wieder und wieder sagte er sich, dass dieser ebenso gehandelt, ihn möglicherweise mit europäischer Sicherheit ohne Weiteres geopfert hätte. Aber es half ihm nicht" (130; The thought of leaving Albert behind was intolerable to him. He said to himself, again and again, that Albert would have done the same, would possibly, with European confidence, have sacrificed him with little ado. But it was no good).

In what is quite a plot twist, Abdul plays a significant role in the novel's final part. After his escape, Osama stumbles across the home of his childhood friend and finds him willing to help, despite Osama's youthful betrayal. Abdul is angered, however, by Osama's decision to return for Albert, outraged in particular by the fact that his friend behaves more generously toward the stranger than he had done toward his compatriot, something he regards as a perversion of the natural order: "Du willst sein wie sie und vergisst dabei, wer du selbst bist" (162; You want to be like them and along the way you forget who you are yourself).[18] When Osama is recaptured, he and Albert are handed on by their Shiite captors to a group of Sunni fundamentalists, led by none other than Abdul himself. This turn of events gives Osama momentary hope, until he realizes that Abdul regards his solidarity with the German, his prioritizing of a Western "them" over an Arab "us," as a second, unforgivable betrayal. He and Albert have in fact arrived at the "letzte Ort," the final place that gives the novel its title, a violent "elsewhere" in which neither can make a case for belonging and in which both risk falling victim to the bloody consequences of brutal othering.

Abdul is the novel's only terrorist to be represented in any detail. We are not offered the kind of insight into his motives provided for Kerim in *Das dunkle Schiff,* but we are privy to significant aspects of his life. His youthful dreams and his interactions with his parents, wife, and child humanize him to the extent that his own eventual vicious treatment of Osama is even more shocking than it might otherwise have been. Insofar as we can understand them, Abdul's motivations combine the personal (the failure of his early ambitions, including a Western-style accumulation of wealth) with the political (ethnic tensions and multinational conflict) in ways that align him with the terrorist subjects of *Das dunkle*

---

18 This notion that it is natural to prioritize the well-being of those who are similar to you over those who are different is also explored in *Das dunkle Schiff,* through Kerim's reflections on the people he perceives himself as having betrayed. Most telling in this respect is his interaction with Tony the "Schwarzafrikaner" (black African), who stows away on the ship that brings Kerim to Europe. Kerim betrays Tony to the sailors and eventually abandons him on a desert island; when Kerim himself is rescued at Tony's expense, this is explained by his racial difference: "Wir sind verschieden.... Schau auf meine Haut" (260; "We're different.... Look at my skin," 180).

Schiff. The implication in both novels is that terrorist action is causally overdetermined.

Significantly, given the concern in *Der letzte Ort* with the causes and consequences of constructions of self and other, in Abdul's world every other is construed as an enemy. These others include "die Kreuzfahrer, die Amerikaner und die Briten" (the Crusaders, the Americans, and the British), "im Norden die verwestlichten Kurden" (the Westernized Kurds in the North), "die Turkmenen" (the Turkmen), "Christen. Dann all jene, die mit den fremden Mächten zusammenarbeiten" (Christians. And then everyone who works with the foreign powers), and last but not least, "die gefährlichste Gruppe … die sich selbst Schiiten nennen" (261; the most dangerous group … who call themselves Shiites). Indeed, the terrorist attack that Abdul's men are planning is one against Shiite Muslims on Ashura, "der Härektiker barbarisches Fest des Blutes" (275; the heretics' barbaric blood festival), as one of the Sunni militants describes it. Given that Shiites and Sunnis are shown working together to realize the political and monetary value of their captives, this planned act of violent hostility implies that borders constructed between self and other are not natural but expedient, inasmuch as they allow for a construction of group belonging and purpose.

Almost at the novel's end, Osama manages to rescue himself from a gruesome death by engaging in conversation with the young terrorist who has been left to set light to the petrol-soaked cloth in which he has been wrapped. This demonstrates powerfully that dialogue can serve to humanize us in the eyes of another. Osama's encounter with Albert ends more ambivalently, however. Albert betrays Osama when he denies to Abdul that Osama prays, as part of an attempt to distance himself from his translator and realign himself with the terrorists to save his own skin, something that leads Osama to regret that he ever learned German, "diese fremde Sprache" (254; this foreign language). When the pair's ordeal is brought to an initial end by a US drone strike, Osama climbs the minaret of an abandoned mosque and watches a figure we can assume is Albert approaching the safety of a US armored vehicle. While the ending remains open, in all likelihood Albert will be able to save himself by demanding that the Americans recognize the sameness of his Western identity. By contrast, Osama knows that they will almost certainly identify him by his difference and assume he is a terrorist. And, despite the many hours Albert and Osama have spent in dialogue, the reader knows that Albert is unlikely to come to his interpreter's aid if it involves risk to himself. This circumstance suggests that the warning words of Osama's wife, that he chose not to heed, might contain some truth: "Die Leute aus dem Westen interessieren sich alle nur füreinander so sehr, dass sie uns gar nicht mehr sehen" (144; The people from the West are all only interested in one another, so much so that they don't see us at all).

Conclusion

I would argue that as post-9/11 texts that explore the causes and consequences of terrorism in relation to Iraqi and German subjects, Fatah's novels go some way toward countering Jackson's claim, quoted in my introduction, that literature has failed "to challenge and destabilize the dominant cultural imaginary about terrorism." While his list of the psychological motivations of literary terrorists does apply to Kerim, Amir, and Abdul, they are not, as we have seen, depoliticized subjects. Their lives are marked by both Iraqi politics, and the ethnic and religious tensions that shape them, as well as the consequences of Western interventions in the Middle East, both military and otherwise. These politics and the violence they have inspired shape their identities in ways that imply the difficulty of conceiving of a depoliticized subject in times of globalized conflict.

Importantly too, Fatah's representation of terrorist subjects is embedded within a broader analysis of the relationship between the Middle East and Europe that focuses on the way subjects from these regions see, or fail to see, each other. Responding to a political reality that shapes them and is shaped by them in turn, Fatah's terrorists commit to a community sustained only by an extreme form of binary thinking in which self is under constant threat from an other so hostile it must be annihilated. In constructing self and other in this way, they are shown to be practicing in extreme form ways of thinking that underpin Middle Eastern and European conceptions of self and other more generally. Albert and Osama are both open to difference but, under pressure, resort to a strategy of othering each other to protect selves that are at psychological and ultimately mortal risk. And, as *Das dunkle Schiff* shows, even in the environment of a major European metropolis, comparatively unthreatening for a majority of its inhabitants, there seems to be little appetite for undoing those binary ways of thinking that lead to the exclusion from mainstream society of asylum seekers and other new migrants as well as, potentially, any citizen with a migration background. The fates of Kerim and Amir suggest that this kind of setting can lead vulnerable individuals to embrace the extreme conceptions of a self at war with a hostile other that underpin Islamist violence. This outcome then raises the question of the responsibility for globalized violence not only of Western governments or other political agents but also of ordinary Westerners whose commitment to binary ways of thinking, the novels imply, has the potential to breed and sustain violent responses not only abroad but at home.

Both of Fatah's novels discussed here explore whether, in the context of conflict, storytelling as a way of sharing the self and learning about an other has any power to defuse violence by undercutting such binary modes of thinking. As we have seen, there is a glimmer of hope in *Der letzte Ort* when Osama saves his own life by engaging a young terrorist in conversation, challenging the boy's convictions. Osama achieves this outcome to the surprise of the terrorist leader, even if the latter finds a way to accommodate this turn of events to his own way of thinking: "Der Emir Abdul war überrascht, dass es Osama gelungen war, den Jungen zu überzeugen. Er wertete es als Gottesurteil" (277; the emir Abdul was surprised that Osama had succeeded in convincing the boy. He saw it as a divine judgment).

In general, however, the novels seem ambivalent about the power of stories in this regard. The sustained dialogue between Osama and Albert allows only one of them to move beyond self-interest when under threat, and this process stalls when it is not reciprocated: after his betrayal, Osama feels nothing but hatred "auf die verdammten Ausländer" (254; for the damned foreigners). The plural suggests that he reads Albert's behavior not as individually motivated but as symptomatically Western. In *Das dunkle Schiff*, Kerim fails to find an empathetic audience for the traumatic story in which he is "Opfer und Täter in einem" (victim and perpetrator in one)[19] in a way possibly too complex to accept for those who assume these terms' mutual exclusivity. This experience contributes to the psychic fragility that makes Kerim vulnerable to the continued appeal of the terrorist community and subsequently cuts him off from German society. Moreover, when he does finally speak to Amir about his violent past, his stories act to reinforce antagonistic ways of seeing the other, rather than undoing them.

Amir is not the only recipient of Kerim's story, however: we are too, just as we also continue to listen to Osama's tales after Albert falls asleep and, perhaps more significantly, to register nuances of Albert's GDR narrative that escape his translator. Stories that express the love he feels for his psychically damaged sister, for instance, are misinterpreted both by Osama and the terrorists, who assume they must share an incestuous relationship. When one of the men asks if Albert is going to marry his sister, he glosses his question for his friends with this insight into Western culture: "'Sie dürfen das dort,' behauptete der Mann lautstark. 'Sie dürfen Tiere heiraten, Hunde und Schweine'" (253; "They're allowed to do that over there," the man claimed loudly. "They're allowed to marry animals, dogs and pigs"). The German-speaking reader, by contrast, is likely to read the sister's story as one of failed accommodation to the demise of the GDR: "Man kann das Vergehen einer Epoche nicht genug bedauern, dachte Albert, auch wenn es sich in etwas Kleinem und Seltsamen wie dieser Geschichte verkörpert" (280; The end of an era can't be regretted enough, thought Albert, even if it's embodied in something small and strange, like this story). Indeed, the reader may also understand Albert's

19   Bay, "Migration, postheroisch," 25.

desire to travel to Iraq as a parallel to his sister's eating disorder and eventual disappearance. That is, it may be seen as a response to his failed post-unification integration into a Western world order in which, according to socialist critics like Albert's father, self always comes before community.[20] Commenting on what he finds objectionable in the behavior of Albert's generation, the father remarks, "Das alles nur, weil ihr die Gemeinschaft hasst. Freiheit ist nur Eigennutz und Selbstverliebtheit, eure ganze dumme Monadenhaftigkeit" (30; And all because you hate community. Freedom is just selfishness and narcissism, all your stupid monadism), using formulations that bring him "in verblüffende Nähe zur Kritik am Westen aus dem Mund der fundamentalistischen Entführer" (into baffling proximity with the criticism of the West that comes from the mouths of the fundamentalist kidnappers).[21] These refractions of the protagonists' experiences of both self and community formation through oppositional ideological lenses allows *Der letzte Ort* to be read, as Heide Reinhäckel writes of *Das dunkle Schiff*, as "ein Reise- und Migrationsroman im Zeitalter der ökonomischen Globalisierung, der mittels einer literaturimmanenten Ästhetik die Kontaktlinien, Fremdheitszonen und Zwischenräume zwischen der westlichen und arabischen Kulturen darstellt und damit einen nach dem 11. September immer wieder eingeforderten Dialog zwischen Orient und Okzident installiert" (a novel about travel and migration in the age of economic globalization that, by means of a literary aesthetic, delineates the lines of contact, foreign zones, and intermediate spaces between Western and Arabic cultures and thus sets up a dialogue between East and West of the kind that has been called for since September 11).[22]

A reading of Albert as the product of his GDR childhood, along with the suggestion that the memory of Soviet-era tensions between East and West might shed light on contemporary conflict between the West and the Muslim world, imply that the communication failures within the narrative might be offset by the response of the knowledgeable reader. That is, Reinhäckel's posited "Dialog zwischen Orient und Okzident" (dialogue between East and West) can take place beyond the text, even as it falters within the narrative itself. It is equally possible, however, that readers' familiarity with one context may highlight for them their lack of the

---

20 In his review of the novel, Stefan Weidner notes, "Es ist eine große deutsche Nachmauerfall-Orientierungslosigkeit, die Albert, den Sohn eines überzeugten Kommunisten, auf der Suche nach einer eigenen Geschichte in der Irak verschlägt" (Albert, son of a committed Communist, is driven to Iraq in search of a story of his own, by a large-scale German post-Wall disorientation). Stefan Weidner, "In der Hand von bewaffneten Kindern," *Frankfurter Allgemeine Zeitung*, October 1, 2014.

21 Weidner, "In der Hand."

22 Heide Reinhäckel, *Traumatische Texturen: Der 11. September in der deutschsprachigen Gegenliteratur* (Bielefeld: transcript, 2012), 193.

equivalent knowledge of other cultures that would allow them to read all characters in similarly nuanced ways. If that is the case, it puts the reader in a position that in many ways mirrors that of the protagonists.

This possibility raises the question whether there is anything that can mitigate the lack of knowledge that may limit readers' understanding of the protagonists and their stories. Unfamiliarity with different worlds is certainly a factor in Kerim's failure to bond with those who might help him escape his radical past and in Albert's and Osama's inability to remain united in the face of the threat of violence. But it is only one reason for their exposure to mortal danger and existential despair. Equally significant is these characters' failures to provoke an empathetic response to their narratives from their interlocutors: Kerim's stories contribute to the radicalization of the only person prepared to listen to them, and Albert's othering of Osama increases in the face of threat, despite the personal histories they share with one another. Only Osama, in the final lines of *Der letzte Ort*, provides some partial evidence that he can make a meaningful connection between self and other, putting himself in Albert's shoes as he watches the German approach his American rescuers: "Warum geht er so langsam, fragte sich Osama, als fürchtete er sich seine Rettung? Ich würde laufen, nichts würde mich zurückhalten, dachte er, ließ sich zu Boden sinken und lächelte" (284; Why is he going so slowly, Osama asked himself, as though he feared being rescued? I would be running, nothing would hold me back, he thought, and he let himself sink to the ground, smiling).

In this respect, I would argue, the reader's experience differs from that of the characters. Through the alignment of the narrative perspective almost entirely with Kerim in *Das dunkle Schiff* and fairly equally between Albert and Osama in *Der letzte Ort*,[23] through an intimate engagement with their experiences, a careful setting out of the worldviews that inform their engagement with others, and via an investigation of the factors that have determined their senses of self, the novels challenge readers to respond empathetically to characters fundamentally different from themselves. None of these figures, "taugt," as Hansjörg Bay notes of Kerim, "als positive Identifikationsfigur" (can be seen as a positive figure of identification).[24] The epithet "Nichthelden" (nonheroes),

---

23 Reinhäckel points out that toward the end of *Das dunkle Schiff* there is a shift to "Amirs Erzählperspektive, die seinen Veränderungsprozess vermittelt" (Amir's narrative perspective, which conveys the process of change he undergoes), reinforcing the idea that he is heir to the radicalization that destroys Kerim. Reinhäckel, *Traumatische Texturen*, 189.

24 Bay also remarks that the narrator makes Kerim's "Empfindungen und Motive in vielem nachvollziehbar und ermöglicht eine partielle Identifikation. In letzter Instanz aber bleibt Kerim dem Leser und auch sich selbst fremd" (makes Kerim's feelings and motives comprehensible in many respects and allows partial identification. In the final instance, though, Kerim remains a stranger to the reader

applied to Albert and Osama by Florian Kessler, seems entirely appropriate for them.[25] And these characters include those, like the terrorist, whose radical otherness challenges our capacity for understanding. If we are prepared to enter into the lifeworlds of these problematic characters, however, we have the opportunity to engage with, and possibly move beyond, what the novels identify as the failures of understanding that are a causal factor in repeated cycles of violence. That is, readers may actively work against the "reluctance to acknowledge our connection with the multifarious others who populate the planet" that Gauthier identifies behind our unwillingness to engage with the figure of the terrorist.

Literary explorations of that connection between self and repudiated other can be problematic and may make us uncomfortable, as acknowledged by Bay when he notes that some may feel that *Das dunkle Schiff* "allzu großes Verständnis aufbringt für einen Protagonisten, der sich an wirklich menschenverachtenden Verbrechen beteiligt, während er dessen Opfer nie richtig in den Blick bekommt" (offers far too much understanding of a protagonist who participates in truly inhuman crimes, while never really being able to see their victims).[26] Such reading experiences are also ever likely to bring only partial insight. As Fatah, commenting on *Der letzte Ort*, notes: "Es ist ja eigentlich die Geschichte eine Begegnung, einer zwangsweisen Begegnung. Es geht um Fremdheit und Nähe, es geht um DIE Fremde, DIE Fremdheit, etwas, was man einfach nicht in sein eigenes System ohne Weiteres hinein bekommt, etwas, womit man etwas tun muss, bevor es passt. Und wie man sich auch bemüht: Es fällt schwer. Und viele Dinge bleiben auch im Dunkeln. Die begreift man nicht" (Really, it's the story of an encounter, an enforced encounter. It's about being foreign, and close, *the* foreign, *the* strange, something you can't simply accommodate to your own system easily, something you have to do something with before it fits. And however hard you try, it's difficult. And many things remain obscure. You can't grasp them).[27] But however problematic and partial an insight we might gain, the empathetic engagement with the other through narrative has positive potential. In "The Word and the Bomb," Hanif Kureishi argues explicitly for storytelling's potential to combat religious fundamentalism: "In an age of propaganda, political simplicities and violence, our stories are crucial. Apart from the fact that the political has to be constantly interrogated, it is in

---

and also to himself). Bay, "Migration, postheroisch," 28. It could be argued that the fact that the reader shares Kerim's confusion about his own motivations only increases the likelihood of an empathetic response.

25 Florian Kessler, "Irakisches Endspiel," *Süddeutsche.de*, April 20, 2014.

26 Bay, "Migration, postheroisch," 36.

27 Quoted in Detlef Grumbach, "Entführungsgeschichte und zugleich Ideologiekriktik," December 12, 2014. https://www.deutschlandfunk.de/sherko-fatah-entfuehrungsgeschichte-und-zugleich-100.html.

such stories—which are conversations with ourselves—that we can speak of, include and generate more complex and difficult selves. It is when the talking and writing stops, when the attempt is to suppress human inconsistency by virtue, that evil takes place in the silence."[28]

Das dunkle Schiff and *Der letzte Ort* provide their German-speaking readers with the opportunity to engage with violence elsewhere through the medium of storytelling. The empathetic engagement with the novels' problematic characters that is likely to ensue, however partial, poses a challenge to the kind of binary conceptions of self and other that mark our imbrication in cycles of violence across the globe. It can also trouble the distinction between here and there, allowing us to acknowledge that in a globalized world, violent conflict is rarely only elsewhere but has causes and consequences that must be engaged with here. The achievement of such writing may be that it asks us to think imaginatively about the challenges of living with human inconsistency, with difference as well as sameness, with complex and difficult selves and the variously constructed worlds we inhabit, with the aim of working actively toward ending violent conflict.

28 Hanif Kureishi, *The Word and the Bomb* (London: Faber, 2005), 10.

5: Overview Effects: Violence and Planetarity in Durs Grünbein's *Cyrano oder Die Rückkehr vom Mond* (Cyrano; or, The Return from the Moon, 2014)

Nicola Thomas

THE ONGOING PLANETARY environmental crisis has prompted a reconceptualization of violence. The distribution of harms across time and space, the apparent decoupling of cause and effect, and the problem of how to allocate moral responsibility in complex systems are just some of the issues addressed by contemporary thinking about violence in the environmental humanities. Discussions of environmental violence in the context of our current predicament generally focus on the distinctive types of physical harm experienced by humans and nonhumans as a consequence of anthropogenic environmental change, as well as on the epistemic violence wrought by how that predicament is conceptualized. How we think about the earth as a whole planet, and human beings as a species, is important to both of these questions. Although it is self-evident that environmental harms transcend political, social, and cultural borders, and that the ongoing environmental crisis has the potential to affect the planet as a whole and all human beings, it remains unclear how, where, and whether one can speak of a planetary consciousness or culpability, of a unified humanity affected by—and with capacity to address—environmental crisis. Who, in other words, is perpetrating environmental violence, and against whom? Where is "here," and where is "elsewhere," and can the two be meaningfully separated in the era of anthropogenic climate collapse?

This chapter explores how Durs Grünbein's poetry collection *Cyrano oder die Rückkehr vom Mond* (Cyrano; or, The Return from the Moon) approaches these questions.[1] Grünbein's collection advocates

---

1   Durs Grünbein, *Cyrano oder Die Rückkehr vom Mond* (Berlin: Suhrkamp, 2014). Further references to *Cyrano* are given in-text, and translations are my own. I am grateful to Karen Leeder for her comments on these translations.

for the importance of poetic language in improving humankind's ability to imagine violence on a planetary scale. The poems, in their polysemy and subtlety, offer a space to reflect on the instability of positionality and comprehension, undermining subject/object binaries and the illusions of objectivity they generate. *Cyrano* provides a way of thinking about planetary consciousness—and thus also the causes and effects of violence at a planetary scale—that is rich and differentiated and that acknowledges that human beings can never reach the point of distant, critical observation (and therefore safety from violence) to which many aspire. Interestingly, it also does so without relinquishing a tradition that might be characterized as distinctively German, highlighting the tension between a (re) emerging planetary consciousness in the Anthropocene and the existing (national, cultural, disciplinary) perspectives through which we must make sense of it.

The collection addresses, across eighty-four poems divided into eight cycles of irregular length, what is framed as the "return" or retreat from extraterrestrial space that has taken place in the late twentieth and early twenty-first centuries. Dreams of human spaceflight that were so compelling between the 1950s and the 1980s appear, the collection suggests, to have evaporated and left humankind with a poorer sense of the meaning and importance of extraterrestrial space.

One of the collection's most striking features is its sustained engagement with the history of science and space exploration: Grünbein is known in the German context as a *poeta doctus*, an erudite or learned poet, and *Cyrano* conforms to this image. The poems are written in a loose terza rima, the interlocking three-line rhyme scheme invented by Dante; they encompass a wide range of historical and geographical settings, from ancient Rome to the *Challenger* disaster of 1986; and they contain many references to real and imagined historical figures. Each poem shares its name with a historical person after whom a moon crater has been named, generating an eclectic pantheon that includes Pythagoras and Abbas ibn Firnas, Jules Verne, and Neil Armstrong.

Grünbein's central figure is, as the title suggests, Cyrano de Bergerac (1619–55). Cyrano's *L'autre Monde ou les États et Empires de la Lune* (The Other World; or, The States and Empires of the Moon, 1657) counts as one of the earliest works of science fiction in the Western tradition. The work is a satire that tells the adventures of a flamboyant narrator, also called Cyrano, who travels to the moon and lives to tell the tale.[2] The text—together with another of Cyrano's works, *Les États et Empires du Soleil* (The States and Empires of the Sun, 1662) belongs to

2   In this chapter, I will use "Cyrano de Bergerac" to refer to the historical figure and "Cyrano" to refer to the character who appears in Grünbein's poems. *Cyrano* is the short title of the volume.

the early modern tradition of fantastical travel narratives, satirizing and commenting on contemporary intellectual movements, early modern science, and theology.

Grünbein's use of the figure of Cyrano locates his poem cycle in the context of ongoing debates about (alternatives to) Enlightenment humanism as a means of considering the Earth as a whole planet and humans as a unified species. Although the cycle's pessimistic engagement with the "return from the moon" speaks to the demise of a midcentury utopian vision of planetary wholeness, it also proposes some alternative ways of thinking about the planet as a whole that resonate with contemporary Anthropocene theory. This reimagining of planetary space takes place in dialogue with Cyrano de Bergerac, early modern philosophy, and the modern German tradition of negative anthropology, as well as in reflections on poetry as an art form. *Cyrano* provides—via the motif of "libration," an astronomical phenomenon that creates the illusion of planetary oscillation, indicative of a commitment to the polysemy inherent in the writing and reading of poetry—a model for thinking about planetary and species identity in the context of clashing epistemologies.

There is no doubt that ecological collapse and climate crisis are violent phenomena. The range of harms they cause is too large, and too diffuse, to catalog, but at a minimum one might note that irreversible changes to our environment in the form of toxins and pollutants affect human and animal health, bringing about individual illness, death, and the potential for mass extinction. Changes to the climate are also rendering larger and larger areas of land uninhabitable, causing suffering on a large scale. Rob Nixon offers an influential conceptualization of "slow violence" to describe these, and other, phenomena associated with environmental change, defining "a violence that occurs gradually and out of sight, a violence of delayed destruction that is dispersed across time and space, an attritional violence that is typically not viewed as violence at all."[3] Slow violence, for Nixon, is an unstable form of structural violence, which predominantly affects poor and marginalized people, "particularly (though not exclusively) across the so-called global South."[4]

The dispersion of violence across temporal scales that Nixon signals ("slow," "incremental and accretive") is no less important in his thinking than the dispersion of violence in geographical terms. For some, environmental violence is "elsewhere"; for others, it is terrifyingly close. Ecological violence is rendered invisible or elsewhere (to some) not just

---

3   Rob Nixon, *Slow Violence and the Environmentalism of the Poor* (Cambridge, MA: Harvard University Press, 2011), 2.

4   Nixon, *Slow Violence*, 4. On structural violence, see also 10; and Johan Galtung, "Violence, Peace, and Peace Research," *Journal of Peace Research* 6, no. 3 (1969): 167–91.

because it unfolds slowly but also because its effects can be (or feel) very remote from its causes. For example, the visibly harmful consequences of a flood caused by rising sea levels in Bangladesh are separated, temporally and spatially, from the carbon-emitting actions that can be said to have caused them, as well as from the various stages in the processes that brought them about.

Nixon's study is grounded in postcolonial theory, building on the work of Gayatri Chakravorty Spivak and others. For Spivak and Nixon, it is essential to avoid flattening the complex, discontinuous space(s) of the planet into a single abstract globe, the undifferentiated arena of capitalist globalization. Spivak, offering "planetarity" as an alternative to globalization, explains:

> Globalization is the imposition of the same system of exchange everywhere. In the gridwork of electronic capital, we achieve that abstract ball covered in latitudes and longitudes, cut by virtual lines, once the equator and the tropics and so on, now drawn by the requirements of Geographical Information Systems.... The globe is on our computers. No one lives there. It allows us to think that we can aim to control it. The planet is in the species of alterity, belonging to another system; and yet we inhabit it, on loan.[5]

Spivak's insistence on a particular view of Earth as a real planet—one that is fundamentally other, that does not belong to the same epistemological paradigm as the illusory globe—allows for the complex understanding of and engagement with alterity that is essential in postcolonial thought.[6]

But, as Dipesh Chakrabarty observes in his "The Climate of History: Four Theses," this intellectual move is at odds with how Earth systems scientists think about human beings and Earth in the context of the emerging configuration known as the Anthropocene, the proposed term for the current geological epoch in which human beings are leaving an indelible trace on the fabric of the planet:

5   Gayatri Chakravorty Spivak, *Death of a Discipline*, Wellek Library Lecture Series at the University of California, Irvine (New York: Columbia University Press, 2003), 72. In this chapter I employ the term "planetarity" according to Spivak's usage, and "planetary thinking" or "whole-earth thinking" to refer to ways of thinking about the earth as a whole planet other than Spivak's.

6   Spivak's definition of planetarity has proved influential in postcolonial studies and beyond, and there is an ongoing debate in the environmental humanities about contemporary planetary awareness, and the dialogue between human culture and Earth system sciences. See, for example, Cecilia Åsberg, "Portmanteau Planetarity," *Dialogues in Human Geography* 12, no. 3 (November 1, 2022): 476–80; Nigel Clark and Bronislaw Szerszynski, *Planetary Social Thought: The Anthropocene Challenge to the Social Sciences* (Cambridge: Polity Press, 2021).

> The word that [Earth systems scientists] use to designate life in the human form—and in other living forms—is *species*. They speak of the human being as a species and find that category useful in thinking about the nature of the current crisis. It is a word that will never occur in any standard history or political-economic analysis of globalization by scholars on the Left.... The task of placing, historically, the crisis of climate change thus requires us to bring together intellectual formations that are somewhat in tension with each other: the planetary and the global; deep and recorded histories; species thinking and critiques of capital.[7]

The problem of how to think about planetary space and species-being between the humanities and Earth systems sciences becomes a key intellectual issue in contemporary theory: the challenge is to acknowledge that environmental crisis is caused by and affects human beings *as a species*, and the planet *as a whole*, without "flattening" the necessary differentiation between people, places, and cultures that Spivak, Nixon, and others highlight as an ethical imperative in light of global inequality and injustice.

Although the twin questions of planetary unity and species-being have a long history in European intellectual traditions, two closely related Cold War technological developments have framed this discussion in and for the Anthropocene.[8] The advent of human spaceflight prompted reflection on the position of our planet within the universe, including the potential habitability of other planets. Iconic images of Earth from space, most notably 1972's "Earthrise," showed the beauty of planet Earth as an apparently borderless whole, seemingly reaffirming its unique value as the shared home of all human beings in a phenomenon known as the "overview effect."[9] At the same time, the development of the atom bomb, and the threat of planetary destruction it augured, served as a reminder of Earth's fragility and isolation. Mainstream responses to both the "Earthrise" moment and the nuclear threat entailed affirmations of unity and planetary wholeness, with the whole-Earth image rapidly becoming a

---

7   Dipesh Chakrabarty, "The Climate of History: Four Theses," *Critical Inquiry* 35, no. 2 (2009): 197–222, here 213.

8   *Gattungswesen*, the German term often translated as species-being or species-essence, is a salient concept for both Georg Wilhelm Friedrich Hegel and Karl Marx; Cartesian dualism implies human (species) uniqueness. (René Descartes famously designated animals as "bête-machines" [beast machines].) See Paul Santilli, "Marx on Species-Being and Social Essence," *Studies in Soviet Thought* 13, no. 1/2 (1973): 76–88; Peter Harrison, "Descartes on Animals," *Philosophical Quarterly* 42, no. 167 (1992): 219–27.

9   Frank White, *The Overview Effect: Space Exploration and Human Evolution* (Reston, VA: American Institute of Aeronautics and Astronautics, 1998).

symbol of ecological awareness and support for nuclear disarmament.[10] These issues still resonate in the early decades of the twenty-first century, but the tenor of the debate has changed. The fear that geopolitical tensions might exacerbate—or, with the same outcome, fail to stave off—an existential threat to the future of humanity remains live, insofar as both nuclear warfare and the climate crises are concerned. Space exploration continues apace, funded by governments and private corporations.

Space travel has long since ceased to inspire sentimental affirmations of unity, and it is this profound disenchantment that forms one of the key contexts to Grünbein's work. As the cover copy notes, it is half a century since the Apollo moon landings, and the cultural focus appears to have shifted away from celebrating those who "conquer" space toward an elegiac sense of Earth as an isolated, fragile planet.[11] "Heimkehr" (homecoming) and "Rückkehr" (return) are the collection's keywords, with the motif of the moon in particular playing a central role: what if, Grünbein's poems ask, the compulsion to explore the space beyond Earth was always connected with a need to return "home" and experience the comfort afforded by old perspectives?

This skepticism about the Cold War–era project of extraterrestrial adventure, with its overtones of colonization, should be read in the context of other responses to the Space Race in German intellectual tradition. While many Anglophone (and Soviet) thinkers and writers engaged with early landmarks in human spaceflight and exploration in a tone of celebration that reached a crescendo in US poet Archibald MacLeish's occasional poem marking the Apollo 8 lunar landings ("Presence among us … we have touched you!"), published on the front page of the *New York Times* the day after the historic event, some prominent thinkers originating from the German-speaking world were more circumspect.[12]

One notable contribution came from Hannah Arendt, who was asked in 1963 to respond to the question "Has man's conquest of space increased or diminished his stature?" Her response offers a poignant assessment of the conundrum faced by modern science, in which new discoveries and levels of abstraction proliferate without improving society's moral insight. Since man can never see himself from outside, he is, Arendt suggests, engaged in a perpetual search for an external perspective akin to that desired by Archimedes (who is said to have claimed that given a

10 Robert Poole, *Earthrise: How Man First Saw the Earth* (New Haven, CT: Yale University Press, 2008).

11 The cover copy to *Cyrano* positions the speaker(s) of Grünbein's collection precisely in the terms of species identity: "während hier unten eine Spezies in fragilen Elegien begreift, daß sie mutterseelenallein ist im All" (while down here a species grasps in fragile elegies that it is all alone in the universe).

12 Archibald MacLeish, "Voyage to the Moon," *New York Times*, July 21, 1969: 1.

stable enough point, he could create a lever to move the earth). Arendt criticizes man's search for this "Archimedean point" to which a lever of self-comprehension might be secured:

> The attempt to conquer space means that man hopes he will be able to journey to the Archimedean point which he anticipated by sheer force of abstraction and imagination. However, in doing so, he will necessarily lose his advantage. All he can find is the Archimedean point with respect to the earth, but once arrived there and having acquired this absolute power over his earthly habitat, he would need a new Archimedean point, and so on ad infinitum. In other words, man can only get lost in the immensity of the universe, for the only true Archimedean point would be the absolute void behind the universe.[13]

Arendt's pessimistic conclusion continues to resonate in the context of the Anthropocene predicament:

> Man, insofar as he is a scientist, does not care about his own stature in the universe or about his position on the evolutionary ladder of animal life; this "carelessness" is his pride and his glory. The simple fact that physicists split the atom without any hesitations the very moment they knew how to do it, although they realized full well the enormous destructive potentialities of their operation, demonstrates that the scientist qua scientist does not even care about the survival of the human race on earth or, for that matter, about the survival of the planet itself.[14]

It is no coincidence that Arendt's response to a question about "man's conquest of space" refers repeatedly to the development of nuclear fission, a technology with huge power to unleash violence on a planetary scale. Not only were these two era-defining developments clearly part of the same military-technological and scientific project that is also central to the history of the Anthropocene, as outlined above, but—as Arendt observes—all three speak to the same need to push boundaries and reach for new abstractions, regardless of the deadly and destructive consequences of doing so.

Günther Anders, Arendt's contemporary (and first husband), explores this connection across an oeuvre that grapples with the issue of moral responsibility for harm and violence in the age of nuclear technology and space exploration. The significance of space exploration for Anders lies

---

13 Hannah Arendt, "The Conquest of Space and the Stature of Man," *New Atlantis*, no. 18 (2007): 43–55, here 43.
14 Arendt, "The Conquest of Space," 51.

in the way it enables humanity to "encounter" itself; he frames the argument of his 1970 book *Der Blick vom Mond* (The View from the Moon) along these lines:

> Die Hauptthese [dieser Schrift ist], daß das entscheidende Ereignis der Raumflüge nicht in der Erreichung der fernen Regionen des Weltalls oder des fernen Mondgeländes besteht, sondern darin, daß die Erde zum ersten Mal die Chance hat, sich selbst zu begegnen, wie sich bisher nur der im Spiegel sich reflektierende Mensch hatte begegnen können.[15]

> [The central argument [of this text is] that the decisive experience of space travel consists not in reaching distant regions of the universe or the distant surface of the moon, but rather that Earth has the opportunity, for the first time, to encounter itself in the way that, until now, only the individual human looking in the mirror has been able to do.]

Anders's thought consistently emphasizes the agency of technology itself, especially its capacity to destroy: in a series of "Commandments in the Atomic Age," he exhorts mankind to "examine the secret voices, motives and maxims of your instruments ... look into your 'instrument hearts.'"[16] This interrogation of technology is necessary, he argues, because the complexity of the processes that underpin the harm caused by nuclear weapons exceeds the capacity of individual humans to conceptualize their own ethical responsibility for said harm. "Everyone [involved in the building, deployment, and detonation] of a nuclear weapon has a good conscience, because no conscience was required at any point."[17]

15 Günther Anders, *Der Blick vom Mond: Reflexionen über Weltraumflüge* (Munich: C. H. Beck, 1994), 12.

16 Günther Anders, "Commandments in the Atomic Age," in Claude Eatherly and Günther Anders, *Burning Conscience: The Case of the Hiroshima Pilot, Claude Eatherly, Told in His Letters to Gunther Anders* (New York: Monthly Review Press, 1962): 11–20, here 18–19. Anders's insights into the agency of technology itself anticipates Anthropocene critical theories in science and technology studies and object-oriented ontology. See Bruno Latour, *Reassembling the Social: An Introduction to Actor-Network-Theory*, Clarendon Lectures in Management Studies (Oxford: Oxford University Press, 2007); Graham Harman, *Object-Oriented Ontology: A New Theory of Everything* (London: Pelican, 2018).

17 Günther Anders, "Reflections on the H Bomb," *Dissent* 3, no. 2 (1956): 146–55, here 149. See also Christopher Müller, "Desert Ethics: Technology and the Question of Evil in Günther Anders and Jacques Derrida," *Parallax* 21, no. 1 (January 2, 2015): 42–57. The echoes of Arendt's "banality of evil" are striking, and, indeed, Anders's philosophy of technology is very clearly informed by ongoing debates in German philosophy, culture, and society about moral culpability

Anders's book *Die Antiquiertheit des Menschen* (The Antiquatedness of the Human Being) signals in the very title his belief, echoed by Arendt, that technological "progress" has the capacity to erode human moral agency entirely, because the power of technologies created by humans exceeds humans' capacity to imagine their power. In the "Commandments," he summarizes arguments he also makes elsewhere:

> For in the course of the technical age the classical relation between imagination and action has reversed itself. While our ancestors had considered it a truism that imagination exceeds and surpasses reality, to-day the capacity of our imagination (and that of our feeling and responsibility) cannot compete with that of our *praxis*.[18]

Both Anders and Arendt speak of "mankind" and "humanity" as a unified whole, in the voice of an undifferentiated "we." Anders defends the need for this gesture in terms that borrow from the German tradition of negative anthropology, on the basis that the nuclear threat creates, for the first time, a unified humanity under threat of extinction: "Nicht auf Grund einer gemeinsamen natürlichen Herkunft sind wir nun eine Menschheit, sondern auf Grund einer gemeinsamen, in Zukunftslosigkeit bestehenden Zukunft, auf Grund des uns gemeinsam bevorstehenden unnatürlichen Endes" (We are now one humanity not because of a common natural origin, but because of a common future without a future, because of the unnatural end that is approaching all of us together).[19]

It is perhaps ironic, in this context, that this chapter conforms to the approach Timothy Clark has characterized as "methodologically nationalist," guided as it is by the questions raised by the present volume as a whole about specifically German-language responses to violence

---

for the Shoah. In an exchange with one of the pilots involved in the mission that resulted in the nuclear destruction of Hiroshima, Claude Eatherly, Anders describes Eatherly—who could not come to terms with the small role he played in the mission that killed hundreds of thousands of people—as the "antipode" of Adolf Eichmann. Eatherly and Anders, *Burning Conscience*, 126.

18 Anders, "Commandments," 12.

19 Günther Anders, *Ketzereien* (Munich: C. H. Beck, 1996), 146. Quotation translated by Hannes Bajohr, "Anthropocene and Negative Anthropology," *Public Seminar*, July 29, 2019, https://publicseminar.org/essays/anthropocene-and-negative-anthropology/. See also Günther Anders, *Hiroshima ist überall* (Munich: C. H. Beck, 1995). Anders's notion of species-being extends across time: "For if the mankind of today is killed, then that which has been, dies with it; and the mankind to come too ... the door in front of us bears the inscription: 'Nothing will have been'; and from within 'Time was an episode,'" Anders, "Commandments," 11.

elsewhere.[20] Arendt, Anders, and Grünbein each have a complex, thorny affiliation to the overlapping, unstable traditions that might be described as "German": Arendt's essay was written (in English) during her tenure at the New School in New York City, after she left Germany for good; Anders was born in Breslau (now Wrocław, Poland) and died in Vienna; and Grünbein's German identity is inflected with the memory of the German Democratic Republic, the vanished state in which he was born. The extent to which a common grounding in German-language cultures and traditions of thought underpins their, or indeed any, approach to the topic of planetarity is an open question. It is clear, however, that habits of thought derived from place, language, and culture remain compelling even in the light of our "common future without a future," over and against the pull of the planetary.

Grünbein's collection is an extended exploration of hostility, isolation, decline, decay, and malcontent of the sort that Anders's and Arendt's works express. The violence it catalogs is overt and latent, contemporary and historical, physical and epistemic. Cyrano's return to Earth is described in the opening text, "Riccioli," in melancholy yet peaceful terms: "die Fallschirmseide [raschelt] / Im Herbstwind" (the parachute silk [rustles] / in the autumn wind, 11), but this image is almost immediately contrasted with the violent descent to Earth of the *Challenger* space shuttle, which experienced a technical malfunction shortly after takeoff in 1986, killing all seven crew members. The *Challenger* disaster seems, in *Cyrano*, to mark a turning point in human perceptions of extraterrestrial space, from a utopian optimism to fear and anxiety. The final communication from *Challenger* commander F. Richard Scobee is quoted in the volume's third text, "Euclides" (in English: "*Uh oh.*"), before the poem asks, "War der Mensch sein Versagen? Was zählte / Sein Schritt über alle Grenzen hinaus, alle Sinne?" (13; Was man his failure? To what did / His step beyond all limits, beyond all sense, amount?)—precisely the question Arendt and Anders raise. The violent spectacle of the 1986 disaster becomes an indictment of the senseless pursuit of transcendence via spaceflight regardless of the risks.

The next poem, "Cassini," picks up the dark tone, offering an uneasy vision of an Earth in the shadow of this hostile extraterrestriality:

> der Mond
> Hat Mumps seit gestern abend. Was ist los?
> Der alte Pfannekuchen strahlt so ungewohnt.
>
> Im Park die Hunde bellen lauter … (14)

---

20   Timothy Clark, *The Cambridge Introduction to Literature and the Environment* (Cambridge: Cambridge University Press, 2011), 131–32.

[the moon
Has had mumps since yesterday. What's wrong?
The old pancake shines so oddly.

In the park the dogs bark louder ...]

Here, the violence is much less immediate than in "Euclides": first, we learn that the moon "hat Mumps" (has mumps) and shines "ungewohnt" (oddly). Dogs are heard barking, in a reference to Cyrano's story, according to which the lingering scent of the moon on the traveler's clothing after his return to earth sends dogs far and wide into a frenzy. The displacement of the moon affects tides and oceans, causing tankers to sink and oceans to rage. An archipelago collapses into the sea "wie getroffen von Torpedos" (14; as though hit by torpedos). Migratory animals lose their way en masse, while human beings hide in dark cinema screening rooms, enjoying the spectacle: "Wo sonst zeigt sich die Elegie der Erde ungetrübt?" (14; Where else does the earth's elegy show itself, undimmed?)

Despite the poem's ambivalent ending—the final line asks if this could be "Ein gutes Omen?" (14; A good omen?)—one cannot help but read the events described by "Cassini" as portents, particularly in the context of the contemporary environmental crisis. The violent transformation of oceans, the derangement of nonhuman animals, and the obliviousness of humans who experience disaster as tragic spectacle all call to mind our current predicament. The type of violence Grünbein describes in "Cassini" is diffuse, latent, and—to the individual spectator—invisible. It echoes not only Nixon's "slow violence" but also the planetary destruction that Anders describes as "unseeable"—violence that is all the more dangerous because it appears to be taking place elsewhere.[21]

I share Jonas Nesselhauf's view that despite the fact that *Cyrano* is by no means a collection of eco-poems, the volume as a whole represents an attempt at "eine engagierte Lyrik im Zeitalter des Anthropozän" (an engaged poetry in the era of the Anthropocene), linking the varied contexts of twentieth- and twenty-first century planetary thinking with which this essay engages.[22] Nesselhauf observes that the poem "Taccini," which also appears on the book jacket as an apparently programmatic text for the volume, can also be read in this context—and yet another poem, "Hyginus," refers to the Fukushima earthquake and subsequent nuclear disaster: "Fern in Japan war die Erde aufgebrochen, brannten / Ein,

---

21 Nixon, *Slow Violence*, 2; Anders, "Commandments," 12.
22 Jonas Nesselhauf, "Zur Lyrischen Inszenierung 'natürlicher Heimat,'" *Kulturwissenschaftliche Zeitschrift* 5, no. 1 (October 1, 2020): 77–90, here 89.

zwei, drei Reaktorblöcke" (87; Far away, in Japan, the earth split open /
One, two, three reactors burned).

Cyrano, then, is interested in disaster and violence as spectacle, as in
the *Challenger* disaster, as well as in the "slow violence" of environmental
degradation, linked to the gradually unfolding catastrophe of technological modernity in general. The form of violence perhaps most central to
Cyrano, however, is epistemic violence: violence wrought by the conflict
between different ways of knowing the world, and in the suppression of
expression of knowledge.[23] Perhaps surprisingly, the primary engagement
with epistemic violence is not via direct engagement with the contemporary discourses of globalization and planetarity; rather, *Cyrano* goes back
in time to examine the *origins* of European humanist whole-Earth thinking, and the emergence of philosophies of species-being, at the transitional moment of early modernity. Cyrano, the central figure, serves as
a means of reflection on proto-Enlightenment engagements with rationality, the conflict between science and ethics (in the form of religious
morality), and attempts at transcendence through creativity.

In this context, as so often, epistemic violence is literalized in acts of
bodily, political violence. The poem "Pitiscus" finds Grünbein's Cyrano
in Toulouse:

> Ein Nest voller Inquisitoren, romgetreues Gewürm.
> Hier schrie Vanini im Feuer. Dies war die dunkle
> Seite der Erde. (20)

> [A nest full of inquisitors, papist vermin.
> Here Vanini screamed in the fire. This was the dark
> Side of the earth.]

Lucilio (Giulio Cesare) Vanini, a libertine philosopher whose work
influenced Cyrano de Bergerac's circle, was executed for blasphemy in
Toulouse in 1619. Like that of other thinkers referenced in the cycle,
including Cyrano himself, Vanini's work can be seen as an early part of
the Enlightenment transition to a humanist worldview, one that was
able to reconcile religious faith with scientific empiricism. The religious
violence Grünbein's poem portrays is a direct consequence of clashing
epistemologies in early modern Europe. It is notable that one of Vanini's
heresies was to contend that the heavens were part of the same material
sphere as the earth, rather than belonging to a separate (divine) realm—a
poignant reminder that extraterrestrial space has long been a conceptual

---

23 See Gayatri Chakravorty Spivak, "Can the Subaltern Speak?," in *Marxism
and the Interpretation of Culture* (Basingstoke, UK: Macmillan Education, 1988),
271–313.

battleground. Different ways of conceptualizing the planet as a whole are more than abstract intellectual exercises: they reflect closely-guarded religious and social principles and worldviews.

Another notable feature of the collection is its depiction of global space, and here the question of epistemic violence takes on a different resonance. As Spivak notes, "The clearest available example of … epistemic violence is the remotely orchestrated, far-flung, and heterogeneous project to constitute the colonial subject as Other. This project," she notes, "is also the asymmetrical obliteration of the trace of that Other in its precarious Subjectivity."[24] The geographic focus of the poems is very wide-ranging, and the lyric speaker(s) do(es) often appear to occupy precisely the transcendent, geographically free-floating, perspective that the "Earthrise" moment appeared to offer.

In excerpts quoted above, we have been shown Toulouse and the Kattegat (the sea between Denmark and Norway). A repeated stylistic feature of the texts is the listing of geographically disparate place names that evoke a sense of planetary "overview": "Rom / oder Riad, Brasilia" (Rome / or Riad, Brasilia; "Philolaos"); "[der] Weiße[] Nil, [der] Biwa-See" (The White Nile, Lake Biwa; "Orontius"); "Ätna, Krakatau, Hverfjall" (Etna, Krakatoa, Hverfjall; "Kant"); "Paris, Jerusalem und London" (Paris, Jerusalem and London; "Demonax"); "Ich … / Sah die Mauern von Helsingör und Borobudur / in der Morgendämmerung, Tokyo und Rom" (I … / Saw the walls of Helsingör und Borobudur / at sunrise, Tokyo and Rome; "Abenezra"). Individual poems take us to Egypt, Greece, Rome, and Japan, or explore the legacies of scientists from outside of Europe after whom moon craters are named. For instance, a poem entitled "Hirayama" starts:

> Am Sakurata-Tor ein Zwischenfall. Ein Weiser
> Stand dort und sah hinab vom Paß. Das klare Wasser
> Möge nach Osten fließen, Westen—sein Gebet. (58)

> [At the Sakurada Gate, an incident. A wise man
> Stood there and looked down from the pass. The clear water
> Would flow to the East, to the West—his prayer.]

The Hirayama crater is named for two Japanese scientists, Shin and Kiyotsugu Hirayama, and the "incident" described in the poem is likely the assassination at the Sakurada Gate in Tokyo in 1860 of an official of the Japanese military government who had signed a controversial treaty of trade cooperation with the United States. While this context to the poem suggests a nuanced engagement with the history of capitalist colonialism,

---

24 Spivak, "Can the Subaltern Speak?," 271.

the images of a "wise man" and the proverb-like final sentence invoke orientalist clichés that reflect the poem's positioning of the non-European culture as profoundly other.[25]

Since the title and intellectual framing of the collection remain very much grounded in European, proto-Enlightenment ontologies and epistemologies, the poems appear to play what Donna Haraway would call a "god trick," adopting a whole-Earth (and, by extension, whole-species) "conquering gaze from nowhere."[26] Indeed, the very names of the poems—the pantheon of global intellectuals and spaceflight pioneers who, Grünbein explains, have a somewhat arbitrary relationship to the poems they title—reflect this gesture of overview.[27] There is no doubt that the transcendent perspective is apt for the themes of planetary self-reflection the volume explores, but it could also run the risk of itself perpetuating epistemic violence, offering a false objectivity that denies its own positionality and its own grounding in a particular intellectual tradition.

This epistemologically violent gesture is replicated in the notion of the Anthropocene. As Zoe Todd and Heather Davis note, the notion of the Anthropocene enacts a form of epistemic violence on marginalized, and particularly Indigenous, populations.[28] The species-being implied by the idea of the *anthropos* elides cultural and power dynamics, Andreas Malm and Alf Hornborg explain: flattening humanity into an undifferentiated mass; implicating all of "us" equally in the Anthropocene predicament; and implying evenly distributed culpability for evenly distributed

---

25 Grünbein's collection makes little reference elsewhere to the early history of colonialism, despite the fact that this theme features prominently in Cyrano de Bergerac's narrative. The first attempt made by the protagonist of Cyrano de Bergerac's story to reach the moon fails, and he lands instead in the colonial territory of Nouvelle-France, where he is received as a curiosity. Ann T. Delehanty and Tyler Blakeney contend that "Cyrano's imaginative travels offer both a critique of any attempt to categorize the Other based on a pre-existing epistemological system, and a model for privileging an ethical, rather than definitional, approach to it." This part of *L'Autre Monde* recedes into the background in Grünbein's work and is only alluded to briefly in the accompanying essay. Ann T. Delehanty and Tyler Blakeney, "Textual Engagement with the Other in Cyrano de Bergerac's *L'Autre Monde*," *French Studies* 68, no. 3 (2014): 313–27, here 316.

26 Donna Haraway, "Situated Knowledges: The Science Question in Feminism and the Privilege of Partial Perspective," *Feminist Studies* 14, no. 3 (1988): 575–99, here 581.

27 Durs Grünbein, "Brief über Cyrano," *Suhrkamp Logbuch* (blog), accessed May 12, 2023, https://www.logbuch-suhrkamp.de/durs-gruenbein/brief-ueber-cyrano/.

28 Heather Davis and Zoe Todd, "On the Importance of a Date, or, Decolonizing the Anthropocene," *ACME: An International Journal for Critical Geographies* 16, no. 4 (December 20, 2017): 761–80.

suffering.[29] In reality, nothing could be further from the truth: as Nixon and Spivak's work highlights, both the causes and effects of climate change and environmental/ecosystem collapse are highly differentiated according to geography, race, class, gender, and other categories. Not only that, but the very conceptualizations of geological time and planetary space that the Anthropocene idea takes for granted are culturally specific, rather than universal, paradigms—the European/Western traditions of history and geography tend to dominate and overwrite other ways of thinking about time, the self, and environments. Here, again, we push up against the tension Chakraborty highlights, between a sense of planet and a sense of humanity, which are in some ways necessary or obvious in the age of potential planetary destruction and human extinction, and in other ways prove flawed or no longer intellectually sustainable when seen in the context of the same violent phenomena.

The elegiac tone of Grünbein's collection, I propose, is the product of a mourning for this lost, obsolete, or defunct aspiration toward an Enlightenment humanist planetary thinking. Spivak, Nixon, Malm, Hornborg, and Todd and Davis represent the emergence of a new, critical-postcolonial planetarity that rejects the tradition of Enlightenment humanist whole-earth thinking. *Cyrano*—in the vein of Anders and Arendt—mourns that same humanist tradition from within and asks whether any aspect of it can be salvaged.

The figure of Cyrano de Bergerac offers the ideal means by which to do so. This "Schriftsteller-Musketier" (120; author-musketeer)—as Grünbein's "Lyrische Libration" (Lyric Libration), an essay accompanying the collection, describes him—encapsulates the contradictions of Baroque Europe on the verge of the Enlightenment. Cyrano de Bergerac led a varied and adventurous life, by turns a soldier, scientist, poet, and philosopher. Although he is now best known for his satirical writings (and as a character in Edmund Rostand's eponymous play of 1897), these works are part of a wider project of antiauthoritarianism and intellectual radicalism that is based on scientific learning and scholarship.

Formally and tonally, Grünbein's Cyrano, like the historical figure on which he is based, is a poet—a flamboyant figure who belongs in the Baroque tradition—but this aspect of his persona is combined with a belief in scientific rationalism and philosophical materialism. As "Lyric Libration" explains, Cyrano de Bergerac was a pupil of Pierre Gassendi, a peer of René Descartes who was committed to the principles of classical (Epicurean) atomism, and who developed a theory of cognition revolving around the movement from sensory perception, to rational

29 Andreas Malm and Alf Hornborg, "The Geology of Mankind? A Critique of the Anthropocene Narrative," *Anthropocene Review* 1, no. 1 (April 1, 2014): 62–69.

understanding, to imagination, based on a belief in "effluxions" as the means by which visual images reached the eyes (and mind) from the material world. The theory of effluxions, at least according to Grünbein's summary, thus underpins Cyrano's poetic creations:

> Sie war das Herzstück aller Beschreibungskunst—das Fundament, auf das vor allem die Dichter, geborene Sensualisten, zu bauen hofften. Sie versprach, den Abstand vom Ich zur mannigfaltigen und doch konturenscharf verdichteten, in lauter herrlichen Formen ausgeprägten Materie zu überbrücken. (130)

> [It was the beating heart of all the arts of description—the foundation on which poets, above all, those born sensualists, hoped to build. It promised to bridge the gap from the "I" to the manifold and yet sharply contoured, concentrated, material of the world, shaped as it was into pure, wonderful forms.]

Gassendi's theory represents a significant intervention in the moral and religious philosophy of the early Enlightenment; his commitment to materialism is, in many ways, at odds with conventional understandings of divinity and spirituality. His philosophy attempted to make room for the divine because he rejected the idea of absolute knowledge, a stance that brought him into conflict with Descartes. As a pupil of Gassendi and as a poet, Cyrano's relationship to Cartesian principles—the principles that define and inaugurate Enlightenment humanism—is complex. Descartes appears, Grünbein explains (along with other ancient and early modern philosophers), as a character in one of Cyrano de Bergerac's sketches, in which "die cartesische Kognitionslehre, ein Kristall, löst sich in den Spiralnebeln auf" (131; the Cartesian theory of cognition, a crystal, dissolves into the spiral of mist).

There is, as this quotation demonstrates, a certain ambivalence in the figure of Cyrano, who appears in Grünbein's text, on the one hand, as an empiricist and rationalist, and, on the other, as a showman and storyteller; a disciple of the pious Gassendi, but himself an adventurer and associate of the early libertines. Rather than critiquing humanist planetary thinking from the perspective of its (post)colonial others, Grünbein uses the ambivalent Cyrano as a way of exploring its historical contingency and inherent contradictions—and the violence and harm these bring about—from within. Cyrano belongs to the intellectual milieu in which Cartesian principles were formed, but before they were solidified by centuries of philosophical habit. These same principles have been reopened for debate by postcolonial and postmodern theory—mind-body dualism and (crucially for our argument) the self-other, subject-object divide on which all humanist notions of the planet as whole, and of violence elsewhere, are predicated.

The way Grünbein's poems use the pronoun "er" (he) sheds light on the slipperiness of identity, selfhood, and otherness in *Cyrano*. This pronoun is the opening word of the collection:

> Er ist zurückgekehrt. Jemand hat ihn gesehen
> Hinter den Hangers, wo die Fallschirmseide
> Im Herbstwind raschelt, ein Ballon sich bauscht. ("Riccioli," 11)

> [He has returned. Someone has seen him
> Behind the hangars, where the parachute silk
> Rustles in the autumn wind, a balloon billows.]

We can read this pronoun in at least two ways. Perhaps the most self-evident interpretation is that the "he" simply refers to Cyrano, the collection's titular figure, whose "Heimkehr" (homecoming) is—again, as noted in Grünbein's accompanying essay—the moment at which his experience becomes public, narrativized as fable in Cyrano de Bergerac's satire.[30]

At least one reviewer of the collection offers an alternative explanation, however. In German, the masculine pronoun could refer to "der Mond," the moon itself: returned after a period of darkness, the new moon of the lunar cycle, peeping out from behind a building, rounding into a balloon.[31] Grünbein proposes further interpretations: "Unter dem voraussetzungslosen 'Er' machen sich mindestens drei Vertreter auf die Reise: die barocke Persona Cyrano de Bergerac, der weltraumeroberernde Mensch an sich—und der Poet" (At least three agents are on the move in the unqualified pronoun "he": the Baroque figure of Cyrano de Bergerac, space-conquering man per se, and the poet).[32] In light of this view, Grünbein explains, "schon die erste Zeile führt ja in eine Unbestimmtheitszone—und aus ihr folgt vieles weitere. Ein leichtes Schwindelgefühl ist von Anfang an im Spiel—so als würde man plötzlich von der Erde abheben ohne zu wissen warum. So hat das Subjekt der ersten Zeile sofort etwas Schillerndes" (the first line leads immediately into a zone of ambiguity—and things escalate from there. A mild vertigo is in play from the very beginning—as though one might suddenly

---

30 "[Er plante] den Aufstieg zum Mond in aller Stille ..., während er die Rückkehr an die große Glocke hängte als das wahre Spektakel" (123; [He planned] his ascent to the moon in silence ..., but shouted his return from the rooftops as the real spectacle).

31 Arno Widmann, "Der Er ist der Mond, auch wird er bewohnt," *Frankfurter Rundschau*, September 15, 2014, https://www.fr.de/kultur/literatur/mond-auch-wird-bewohnt-11647579.html.

32 Grünbein, "Brief über Cyrano."

take off from the Earth without knowing why. Thus the subject of the first line immediately has an iridescent quality).[33] The shimmering subject "er" destabilizes the subject/object binary as it relates to Cyrano and the reader, who may or may not identify as "der weltraumeroberne Mensch an sich" (space-conquering man per se), self and other, Earth and moon.

This shifting, overlapping, and unstable quality runs through the cycle in numerous ways, amounting to a metapoetic motif that Grünbein elaborates in "Lyrische Libration" and that offers some hints as to the role of poetry in addressing the ethical and conceptual challenge of violence at a planetary scale. Libration, in the context of astronomy, refers to a visual phenomenon whereby the surface of the moon closest to earth appears to slightly rotate when observed over a period of days and weeks. In part, it is an effect of the Earth's rotation, in essence a kind of optical illusion; but a very minor proportion of the effect is caused by actual movement of the moon as a consequence of tidal forces. It is a kind of interplanetary oscillation and is both real and illusory at the same time. For Grünbein, it replicates the "Schwindelgefühl" (vertigo) that his poems draw out of the polysemous pronoun "er," as well as the shifting quality of (poetic) language in general:

> Es war dies ein Taumeln, wie es einen ähnlich auch bei gewissen Worten erfassen konnte—festen, verläßlichen Größen wie Liebe, Einsamkeit oder Nacht.... Auch bei ihnen gab es dies Schwingen zwischen Nähe und Ferne—ihre *lyrische Libration*, wie man sie in Anlehnung an den Astronomenausdruck nennen konnte. Man sagt, im Gedicht seien die Wortbedeutungen schwankend, je nach dem Neigungswinkel des Lesers, seiner seelischen Inklination. (118–19)

> [It was a wobbling, like the one that can hit you when it comes to particular words—solid, dependable giants like love, loneliness, or night.... In these, too, there is an oscillation between proximity and distance—their *lyric libration*, as one might call it in reference to the astronomical expression. It is said that the meaning of poetic language varies according to the reader's angle, the inclination of his soul.]

Indeed, this suggestion is neatly reflected by the pun on "Schwindel," which can mean either dizziness or lightheadedness, as in "Schwindelgefühl"; or deception, as in the English word "swindle." Puns and double meanings evidently contribute to the semantic instability the collection celebrates.

The essay goes on to explore the relationship between the poetic imagination and the reality of space travel, positing that the reality of space

---

33 Grünbein, "Brief über Cyrano."

travel (that is, the seemingly objective planetary perspective it affords) effaces the complexity of this individual perspective that is drawn out (or better: restored?) in poetry. Even the word "moon" itself, Grünbein suggests, is deprived of its thickness of meaning by its straightforward scientific-technical application.[34]

The concept of "lyric libration" accounts for one of the collection's most striking qualities, its sustained metapoetic, programmatic engagement with poetry as a form and language per se. Aside from the fact that the cycle is densely intertextual, referencing works of moon art and poetry from Cyrano de Bergerac to Johannes Kepler's *Somnium* (1634), poems by Novalis, Johann Wolfgang von Goethe, and Friedrich von Schiller, among others, many poems explore the connections between language, rhythm, poetry, and meaning. In "Quetelet," modernist poetic rhythm—as influentially considered by Stéphane Mallarmé in his essay on poetics, "Crise de Vers" (1897), is celebrated:

> Vers-Krise war das Wort, mit dem die Wende kam.
> Das Ohr, befreit vom Metronom, lotet hinein
> Ins Auf und Ab der Silben in der losen Rede. (74)

> ["Crisis in poetry" was the word that brought the change.
> The ear, free of the metronome, took its soundings
> In the rise and fall of syllables in loosened speech.]

In "Mendeleev," the focus is on the interplay of word and image: "Denn Worte und Bilder / Kreisen fremd umeinander—Sputniks, Trabanten" (69; Since words and images / Circle one another strangely—sputniks, satellites). In "Zeno," the "er" is positioned as language lover:

> War er ein Kind des Überflusses, Narr der Parallelen
> Von All und Alphabet? ...

> Ein Glückatlas war ihm die Sprache (44)

> [Was he a child of surfeit, a fool of the parallel
> Between the All and the Alphabet? ...

> Language was his map of happiness]

34　Here we find another direct reference to the context of Anthropocene violence that informs this essay; the word *moon* is associated with "'Nacht, Romantik, Liebesweh, Melancholie ... usw.' Aber auch 'Ödnis, tote Materie, Kraterlandschaft, *Klimahölle, Atommülldeponie*'" ("night, romanticism, heartache, melancholy ... etc." But also "desolation, dead material, crater landscape, *climate hell, nuclear waste dump*," 138). Emphasis mine.

Perhaps the best examples of the collection's metapoetic reflexivity, however, are in the poem "Novalis,'" named for the crater named for the poet, in which (once again) it is the etymology and meaning of the moon's names that are at stake:

> Es war der weiße Glanz, ein Perlmuttschimmer
> Der ihm den Namen gab bei Juden und Etruskern,
> Lang vor den Mythenächten bis in unsern Tag.

> [It was the white shine, a mother-of-pearl shimmer
> Which gave it its name for the Jews and Etruscans
> Long before the mythological nights, until today.]

Even if the name itself is now "[i]m Dunst verblass[t]" (covered in mist), the poem goes on to imply, the moon itself still shimmers, albeit through a veil of irony. The shimmer of moon language (in poetry, in the imagination) functions as a mirror for Earth:

> Es scheint wie wir. Sein milchiges Trompe l'oeil
> Öffnet am Himmel Tunnel in den Meeresgrund,
> Auf dem die Sterne leuchten wie Medusen. (36)

> [It shines like us. Its milky trompe l'oeil
> Opens in the heavens a tunnel to the ocean floor
> On which the stars gleam like jellyfish.]

In addition to the programmatic metapoetic reflection—and the punning play on words like "scheint" (shines/seems) and "Medusen" (jellyfish/Medusas, in the sense of the ancient Gorgon)—two further qualities of this poem speak to the guiding concept of "lyric libration." These qualities can be seen, in the context of the volume as a whole, as part of Grünbein's attempt to work out a post-Enlightenment planetary poetics for the Anthropocene, one that can express the violent causes and consequences of overlapping planetary crises.

The first is the move from singular to plural (and vice versa), a kind of "splintering" of subject or object into multitudes, as in the final line of "Novalis," in which the singular presence of the moon refracts into the plural, starlike jellyfish. This move is repeated time and again throughout the collection and contributes to the vertiginous atmosphere Grünbein describes: in "Phocylides," "Jeder Apfel ist ein kleines Weltall für sich" (23; Every apple is a small universe of its own); in "Grimaldi," the "Vielheit der Welten" (multiplicity of worlds) is compared with the lice on the head of a beggar; "[es] wirbelte mehr als nur ein Volk um die Sonne" (18; more than one tribe whirled around the sun), we are told. In

"Copernicus," this pluralism is explicitly associated with the question of poetic *Neigungswinkeln* (angles of inclination) toward the moon:

> Nach all den Mysterien, fragt keiner: Was blieb
> Von den tausend Definitionen des Mondes?
> Die eine, sagt sie. Und auch er sagt: die eine. (34)

> [After all the mysteries, no one asks: what remained
> Of the thousand definitions of the moon?
> The one, she says. And he too says: the one.]

Of course, it will forever remain unknown—indeed, unknowable—whether and how the two speakers' definitions overlap. This plurality of perspectives must be seen as part of what Grünbein argues that poetry can accomplish: a kind of harmony in multiplicity, a productive poly-semy grounded in shared language and shared image, which feeds into a sense of planetary wholeness that is playful and subjective, rather than monolithic.

Second, we might also note the gesture of reflexivity per se, the mutuality of the relationship between self and other, Earth and moon, conveyed by the line "Es scheint wie wir" (It shines [or appears] like us). The figures of the circle, cycle, mirror, and orbit are everywhere in *Cyrano*, including in the title and opening line, reflecting the importance of "Selbstbegegnung" (self-encounter), as theorized by both Anders and Arendt, in the context of space-age thought.[35]

In light of these qualities of plurality and self-reflexivity, one could compare the intricate structure of the collection as a whole with its mul-tiple cycles and points of cross- and interreference, as well as the balanced forms of individual texts, to the movement of an orrery: a microcosm of a universe in balanced motion, moving not in perfect circles but, rather, in elliptical orbits. Grünbein's choice of tercets contributes to this effect: used freely (as can be seen in the examples above), they are formed and grouped into poems of different lengths, making prominent use of inter-nal and end-rhyme. Though the rhymes rarely adhere to a fixed pattern, there are clear echoes of a Dantean terza rima, the quintessential form for poetic explorations of the cosmos. In the final poem, "Möbius," the poem begins in terza rima but, as it works through a list of lunar metaphors ("treue[r] Hund der Erde / ... Ein Gong auch, lautlos, kor-rodierte Narrenschelle / ... ein grauer Riesenpilz," "Himmels Jo-Jo" (the Earth's faithful hound / ... A gong, too, silent, a corroded jester's bell / ... a giant grey mushroom," "heaven's yo-yo"), the rhymes begin to falter somewhat, moving from the *aba bcb* pattern of the terza rima to

---

35 See Anders, *Der Blick vom Mond*, 89–97.

cde dfe and finally ending on a half-rhyme ("Pharaonen / *Cyrano*" (pha-raohs / *Cyrano*). The italicized name that is the collection's final word—"Schreib einen Brief an den Mond. Schreib *Cyrano* ..." (Write a letter to the moon. Write *Cyrano* ...) opens up a range of possibilities: it could, perhaps, refer to the character or historical figure, or (as suggested by the italics) the title of a text, or, indeed, the very text we are reading—which would complete the collection's elliptical orbit.

Achille Mbembe, a thinker influenced by both Spivak and Michel Foucault, works to trace the "necropolitics" of planetary relations, a cor-relative of Foucault's "biopolitics" that illuminates the entanglement of death, violence, and war with questions of political and social power. Although explicitly framed by reference to coloniality, Mbembe's necrop-olitics also offers a framework for approaching other forms of violence in the Anthropocene: nuclear disaster, environmental crisis and catastro-phe, and space colonization. Crucially, Mbembe sees the violent impact of structural configurations at a planetary scale, describing contemporary necropolitics as a consequence of the attempt to "constitute a world out-side relation"—to exclude death, war, and violence from some contexts by directing them elsewhere. This attempt, Mbembe cautions, is destined to fail, since the subject-object relation on which it is predicated is inher-ently unstable:

> Owing to this structural proximity [between self and other], there is no longer any "outside" that might be opposed to an "inside," no "elsewhere" that might be opposed to a "here," no "closeness" that might be opposed to a "remoteness." One cannot "sanctuar-ize" one's own home by fomenting chaos and death far away, in the homes of others. Sooner or later, one will reap at home what one has sown abroad.[36]

I believe Mbembe's conclusion here mirrors the ideas mapped by Grünbein's *Cyrano*, albeit reached via an entirely different route. "Was ist innen, was Außen?" (53; What is inside, what outside?), the poem "Pythagoras" asks. This collapse of subject and object, inside and outside, is prompted by the twin crises of Cartesian dualism and subject-object relations that permeate both postcolonial theory and the intellectual tenor of *Cyrano*. The question asked by both writers is: What happens if there is no "other" against which to perpetrate violence and harm, and we (whomever "we" connotes) see ourselves as a fragmented, uneven whole, unable to reach an "Archimedean point" of self-knowledge and safety? Returning to the titular concept of the present volume, it becomes clear

---

36 Achille Mbembe, *Necropolitics* (Durham, NC: Duke University Press, 2019), 40.

that (in the context of colonialism, the nuclear threat, or environmental crisis—all questions and issues of the utmost significance in late-twenti- eth- and twenty-first-century societies) there is no violence elsewhere.[37] Violence at this scale affects humanity as a whole, requiring a differen- tiated and complex sense of species-being and planetary wholeness that can grasp the full scope and scale of the threat, while remaining alive to distinctions of class, gender, culture, and experience.

Cyrano belongs, I contend, to the same German tradition of "nega- tive anthropology" as Anders's thought, a tradition that, as Hannes Bajohr puts it, "holds on to [the human] as a variable that is impossible to solve, but that can't be canceled out from the equation, either"; this posi- tion overlaps with the approach taken by theorists of the Anthropocene and is distinct from "posthumanism," in which the human is consciously decentered.[38] Bajohr describes negative anthropology's chief intellectual gesture as "a turning back without returning," a description that could hardly be more fitting to describe the reprisal of proto-Enlightenment philosophy in Grünbein's *Cyrano*. Negative anthropology understands human species-being specifically as grounded in experiences of vio- lence and the possibility of annihilation, from its origins in Weimar and National Socialist Germany to Anders's emphasis on the nuclear threat in the twentieth century; these experiences continue to resonate in the con- text of overlapping existential threats facing humankind today.

Cyrano's way through this conceptual minefield is guided by the fig- ure of libration, particularly as a way of thinking about language and its function. The collection serves, in many ways, as an extended defense of poetry and the potential of polysemous lyric language to enable a differ- entiated planetary imaginary. That poetry, and the imagination, should be foregrounded again speaks to the relationship between Grünbein's work and the work of Arendt and Anders: "speech and everyday language" are one of the features of a common humanity that, Arendt postulates, would become invisible as a consequence of the extreme "view from outside" to which scientific thought appears to her to aspire—it "would indeed be no longer a meaningful utterance that transcends behavior even if it only expresses it, and it would much better be replaced by the extreme and in itself meaningless formalism of mathematical signs."[39] And for Anders, it is precisely human beings' lack of capacity to *imagine* the destructive consequences of rapidly developing technologies that must urgently be addressed in the interest of saving humanity from destroying itself: "Your task consists in bridging the gap between your two faculties: your faculty

---

37 See also Knittel and Forchieri's chapter in this volume.
38 Bajohr, "Anthropocene and Negative Anthropology."
39 Arendt, "The Conquest of Space," 64.

of *making* things and your faculty of *imagining* things ... *widen your moral fantasy.*"[40]

Restoring, or reshaping, this capacity is also *Cyrano*'s task: "Bis dahin hatte die Vorstellungskraft genügt: Sie war der natürliche Antrieb, Brennstoff der raumgreifende Psyche, die von der Erde abhob und wie immer nichts von sich wußte" (Up until this point imagination had been enough: it was the natural impulse, fuel of the space-conquering psyche, which took off from Earth and, as ever, knew nothing about itself, 141–42). Thinking through the planetary violence of the Anthropocene, which is in no sense "elsewhere," requires us to address, slow down, or perhaps even reverse the consequences of this shift from imagination to praxis, to "widen our moral fantasy"; poetry and poetic language are one means by which we may do so.

40 Anders, "Commandments," 13.

6: Violence "Elsewhere, within Here": Artistic Engagement in Armenian Remembrance at "Location Germany"

Lizzie Stewart

Violence "Elsewhere, within Here"

WHAT DOES IT MEAN to think of violence in relation to an elsewhere? What heavy lifting does the delicacy of this elliptical "else" obscure? If I translate it into German—*anderswo, woanders*—the etymology of otherness, which the English "else" tucks loftily under its light wings, rises more clearly to the surface. But still there is something deceptively playful in that willingness not to know where exactly an action, a moment, a specific instance of human activity takes place.

Perhaps the invocation of the "elsewhere" functions to make a "somewhere" "nowhere"—unknown, unknowable. With its lack of specificity, the invocation of an "elsewhere" suggests almost a nonspace: one so far removed from and unrelated to the "here" of the speaker that any further definition, any historicized and situated understanding of what lies there that may be held by another subject, is presented as not only unnecessary but impossible. As such the "elsewhere" can in many ways be considered akin to the mechanism of Orientalism. Historically "a Western style for dominating, restructuring and having authority over" Asia and the Middle East,[1] Orientalism famously functions by constructing these locations and their histories as empty, inarticulate, and feminized.[2] Although "elsewhere" is untied from one particular imaginary geography, its invocation removes "somewhere" from knowledge or representation, and from the existent holders of that knowledge, to then position it as outside of comprehension. And if the "elsewhere" is made, then it must be made by someone. There is an implicit agent, an implicit positioning at work in the "elsewhere"; a "here" against which the other is measured, compared, but to which it is also in some way connected. What looks like division is, in fact, entanglement, but one in which a particular positionality is given

---

1 Edward W. Said, *Orientalism*, rev. ed. (London: Penguin Books, 2003), 3.
2 Said, *Orientalism*, 56–57.

dominance. The "elsewhere" is thus a relational term and as such clues us into a relationship that cries out to be critically examined.

In the opening pages of her book *elsewhere, within here: immigration, refugeeism, and the boundary event* (2011), renowned feminist, postcolonial filmmaker, and theorist Trinh T. Minh-ha plays critically with the positioning that "the elsewhere" encapsulates in the post-9/11 world of the early twenty-first century. To do so she begins by retelling a short parable-like story from the teachings of Sufi musician, teacher, and mystic Hazrat Inayat Khan (1882–1927) about a "wall of mystery." This wall divides the known world from the unknown. In Inayat Khan's version of the story, the vision of what lies beyond the wall prompts those who are drawn to climb it to leave as soon as they encounter what lies beyond. Curious to know what lies beyond, but unwilling to climb the wall themselves, a group secures a wall-crosser midflight with chains and pulls him back in the hope of learning what he has seen. This wall-crosser, however, is only able to smile. Within Inayat Kahn's parable, what the wall-crosser has encountered in the moment of crossing—the experience of transcendence—is inexpressible in the language of "this" side.[3]

Reflecting on this short story as one of a "wide range of material and figural manifestations" of "the wall event,"[4] Minh-ha writes,

> The world one knows is the world one sees around oneself—whose limited and hierarchized access is protected with ever-higher and mightier walls. What lies beyond is often thought of as all fable. And although living in two dualistic worlds (here versus there) proves to be still acceptable to the rational mind, living in two and many non-opposing worlds—all located in the very same place as where one is—inevitably inscribes silence. Not from elsewhere, but more specifically, from an elsewhere within here.[5]

How does this "elsewhere, within here" relate to "the elsewhere" more broadly? Inayat Khan's story is located in a discourse on music and Sufiism. It addresses the impossibilities of sharing and articulating aesthetic and spiritual experience, or affect, in direct language. The story also emphasizes the delight to be had in embodied experiences of crossing that wall; even his thwarted wall-crosser remains smiling at the end. In Minh-ha's retelling or rendition, in contrast, the material barrier of the wall and a certain associated violence appear emphasized: the chains

3   Trinh T. Minh-ha, *elsewhere, within here: immigration, refugeeism, and the boundary event* (New York: Routledge, 2011), 2. Hazrat Inayat Khan, *The Mysticism of Sound and Music: The Sufi Teaching of Hazrat Inayat Khan*, rev. ed. (Boulder, CO: Shambhala, 2022), 329.

4   Minh-ha, *elsewhere*, 3.

5   Minh-ha, *elsewhere*, 2.

that those on "this side" of the wall use to bind the wall-crosser become more clearly carceral and punitive. The subsequent silence appears also traumatic. Minh-ha's framing of the story as part of a discussion of geo-political walls, such as the US-Mexico border, and between communities in Baghdad, entangles the impossibility of communicating an affective experience with another impossibility: the difficulties of articulating expe-riences of migration and multiplicity in a context that, often violently, demands stasis and duality.

Thinking through the implications of Minh-ha's "elsewhere, within here" for the work of "violence elsewhere," I wish to stick with the socio-political strand of her metaphor for a moment. Presenting us initially with a classic tale of the "self/other" relationship that dominates many hegemonic engagements with the world of migration, Minh-ha begins by comfortably interpolating the reader into the world of the "self" ("one knows"), which has authority to delineate the world it encounters into "here" and "there." The reality is, however, that these boundaries are not so simple. Whether moving from one supposedly bounded space to another, or whether building lives in one location with the resources and protections afforded by the movements of other people and objects, any *here* is more describable as a space of "many non-opposing worlds."[6]

Minh-ha's retelling effects this description, enacting communication. In the world of the story, however, silence, not narration, takes hold: there is no way for the chained figure within the story to articulate this multiplicity of knowledge within a framework that rejects such multiplic-ity as a way of knowing. This silent figure raises specters of the subal-tern who cannot speak, or speaks but is not heard.[7] Notably, though, in Minh-ha's fable of the wall, it is not "the elsewhere" itself, or its abstract representative "the other," which is held silently chained in the heart of the "here"—present, troubling, filled with potentiality. Rather, it is the disruption or refusal of the simple self/other, here/elsewhere state that the "elsewhere, within here" offers: the entanglement that migration reveals as constitutive of the contemporary bordered state. As Alyosxa Tudor suggests, "Studying migratism as a power relation includes analyz-ing the codification of a taken-for-granted 'elsewhere' as constitutive of the 'here.'"[8]

---

6   For a sociological perspective on this, see, for example, Arjun Appadurai, *Modernity at Large: Cultural Dimensions of Globalization* (Minneapolis: Univer-sity of Minnesota Press, 1996).

7   Gayatri Chakravorty Spivak, "Can the Subaltern Speak? Speculations on Widow-Sacrifice," *Wedge* 7/8 (1985): 120–30.

8   Alyosxa Tudor, "Cross-Fadings of Racialisation and Migratisation: The Postcolonial Turn in Western European Gender and Migration Studies," *Gender, Place and Culture* 25, no. 7 (2018): 1057–72.

Attention to what Minh-ha calls the "elsewhere, within here" is thus particularly significant, I would argue, in an inquiry into the notion of "violence elsewhere" in contemporary European contexts characterized by "super diversity."[9] Looking to the Federal Republic of Germany (FRG), one in four residents now have what the German state terms a "Migrationshintergrund" (background of migration), a term used in the FRG's statistical analyses for individuals born without German citizenship, or who have at least one parent born without German citizenship.[10] Discussing the term "Migrationshintergrund" critically, Tudor argues that

> the fixation of people and groups of people to an "elsewhere" is the precondition and the driving force of the idea of migratisation [the process of being discursively made migrant]. An "elsewhere" has to be imagined in order to mark the boundaries of the "here" and to regulate all border crossings (both on the level of national borders and on the level of the boundaries of privileged self-constructions).[11]

The multilayered entanglements of the "here" of Germany with realities considered to lie "elsewhere" is one that the German state's designator of people as "Menschen mit Migrationshintergrund" (people with a background of migration) arguably discursively obscures. Tudor thus "suggest[s] to think of migratisation (the ascription of migration) as performative practice that repeatedly re-stages a sending-off to an elsewhere and works in close interaction with racialisation."[12]

At the same time, the very statistics that the term "Migrationshintergrund" makes available raise the question, in the context of this volume, of how conceptions of and relationships to "violence elsewhere" from within Germany shift as the body politic of Germany transforms. Transnational family connections and lived experiences of migration, after all, mean that the hegemonic "elsewhere" of the German

9   This term initially referred to the dynamics of "an increased number of new, small and scattered, multiple-origin, transnationally connected, socio-economically differentiated and legally stratified immigrants"; Steven Vertovec, "Super-diversity and its implications," *Ethnic and Racial Studies* 30, no. 6 (2007): 1024–54.

10   "Bevölkerung mit Migrationshintergrund I," Bundeszentrale für politische Bildung (2019), accessed September 14, 2023, https://www.bpb.de/nachschlagen-und-fakten/soziale-situation-in-deutschland/61646/migrationshintergrund-i.

11   Alyosxa Tudor, "Queering Migration Discourse: Differentiating Racism and Migratism in Postcolonial Europe," *Lambda Nordica* 22 (2017): 21–40, here 30.

12   Tudor, "Cross-Fadings," 1057.

state can simultaneously be close to home, or home itself, for many of the Federal Republic's residents. This reality highlights a pressing need for a differentiated understanding of how different positionalities inform engagements with "violence elsewhere."

On a structural level, for example, denial of "violence elsewhere" enables divestment and disengagement with violence in ways that do harm. To give just one instance, this dynamic can be seen when the labeling of Tunisia, Algeria, and Morocco as "safe countries" by Germany in 2016 became a means for the German state to deny asylum claims from citizens of these countries.[13] Meanwhile, overinvestment in the idea of violence as existing primarily in other contexts can function as a convenient way of ignoring violence closer to home. Mark Terkessidis and Hito Steyerl, for example, highlight that in 2020 "der Tod von George Floyd in den USA mehr Personen auf die deutschen Straßen gebracht [hatte] als Anschläge oder gar Anschlagsserien, die quasi in der eigenen Nachbarschaft stattfanden" (the death of George Floyd in the USA had brought more people out onto German streets than attacks or series of attacks that took place effectively in their own neighborhood).[14] Here they refer to the right-wing murders of Ferhat Unvar, Gökhan Gültekin, Hamza Kurtović, Said Nesar Hashemi, Mercedes Kierpacz, Sedat Gürbüz, Kaloyan Velkov, Vili Viorel Păun, and Fatih Saraçoğlu in Hanau on February 19, 2020. An essentialist identification of particular geographies and cultures with violence also means that projections of "violence elsewhere" can come to rest on migratized bodies in Germany in ways that, in turn, enable or encourage violence. Thus, refugees fleeing violence in their home countries paradoxically become construed in public discourse as potential perpetrators of terrorist or sexual violence within Germany.[15] Far-right groups within the FRG then make use of this discursive twist to legitimize violent attacks against individuals they identify as migrant.[16]

13   Beverly Weber, "The German Refugee 'Crisis' after Cologne: The Race of Refugee Rights," *English Language Notes* 54, no 2 (2016): 77–92, here 77.

14   Mark Terkessidis and Hito Steyerl, "Rassismus in Deutschland: Die Wahrnehmungsschwelle," *Die Zeit*, no. 2/2021, January 6, 2021. See also the chapter by Marie Kolkenbrock in this volume. All translations from German are my own, unless otherwise stated.

15   Seth M. Holmes and Heide Castañeda, "Representing the 'European Refugee Crisis' in Germany and Beyond: Deservingness and Difference, Life and Death," *American Ethnologist* 43, no. 1 (2016): 12–24.

16   Sebastian Jäckle and Pascal D. König, "Threatening Events and Anti-Refugee Violence: An Empirical Analysis in the Wake of the Refugee Crisis during the Years 2015 and 2016 in Germany," *European Sociological Review* 34, no. 6 (2018): 728–43; Vanessa Plumly, "Refugee Assemblages, Cycles of Violence, and Body Politic(s) in Times of 'Celebratory Fear,'" *Women in German Yearbook* 32 (2016): 163–88, here 173; Weber, "The German Refugee Crisis."

Arguing that "Germany's history of extreme violence and war in the twentieth century" means that "imagining and depicting violence in post-war Germany has been fraught and challenging in distinctive, acute ways," Mererid Puw Davies and Clare Bielby suggest that "the elsewhere" "has offered a stage where violence could become imaginable and representable for what could loosely be termed the German imaginary."[17] The means, briefly outlined above, by which this imaginary can have harmful real-world consequences for migratized subjects in Germany are multiple. Indeed, Minh-ha's parable suggests that violence—initially symbolic but actualized in bordering practices—is already at work in encounters with the "elsewhere, within here." How then does attention to the complex opening of the "elsewhere, within here" reconfigure understandings of the mechanism at work in imaginaries of "violence elsewhere" from location Germany?

This chapter takes the multiplicity of postwar German imaginations seriously and thinks of "location Germany" as one of "many, non-opposing worlds."[18] It understands artistic interventions into the social imaginary, such as those both described and enacted by Minh-ha in the writing quoted above, as sites where the border work that seeks to obscure the "elsewhere, within here" can be brought to falter or fail.[19] Such artistic work helps bring the "elsewhere, within here" into view; a move that, this chapter will suggest, can draw other spaces, traces, and histories close, rather than using them as rationales for what Tudor terms "sending off."[20] As I will discuss in more detail in the following section, such discursive moves have both sociopolitical and epistemological implications.

17 Clare Bielby and Mererid Puw Davies, "Introduction," in *Violence Elsewhere 1: Imagining Distant Violence in Germany 1945–2001*, ed. Clare Bielby and Mererid Puw Davies (Rochester, NY: Camden House, 2024), 1–17, here 1. This language is also reminiscent of Said's discussion of "the Orient" as "the stage on which the whole East is confined." Said, *Orientalism*, 63.

18 I adopt the term "location Germany" from Randal Halle's work on shifts from film production within one nation-state to distributed transnational production processes. "The move from 'made for Germans' to 'made in Germany' results in products that evade apprehension by national-orientated approaches" (252). The discursive emphasis of this materialist reframing on Germany as one location among others also has an epistemological effect, provoking a "transnational decentring whereby ethnocentrism is replaced with intersubjective openness" (258–59). Randall Halle, "German Film, European Film: Transnational Production, Distribution and Reception," *Screen* 47, no. 2 (2006): 251–59.

19 Minh-ha's writing challenges the orthodoxies of academic writing and thus Western knowledge production by disrupting the boundary between an aesthetic and an informational style.

20 Tudor, "Cross-Fadings," 1057.

The performance, installation work, and digital art of Berlin-based, Argentinian-born, Armenian artist Silvina Der Meguerditchian, for example, often responds to the histories of violence that connect Turkey, Germany, Argentina, and the Armenian diaspora.[21] Her installation and performance piece *Verstrickungen* (*Entanglements*)[22] deals with this entanglement quite literally, using spoken word, movement, and a crochet-based installation to address the legacies of the Armenian genocide against the background of the interconnecting political, economic, educational, and institutional relationships between the German and Ottoman Empires in the period leading up to World War I. This piece was performed at the Maxim Gorki Theater, a key institution in the Berlin theater scene, in 2014 and 2015, while an earlier version of the installation appeared under the title *Freundschaft* (*Friendship*) in the theater's 2013 event *Berliner Herbstsalon* (Berlin Autumn Salon).[23] As such, *Verstrickungen* has formed part of that theater's broader engagement with global histories of violence from "location Germany" since artistic director Shermin Langhoff took the helm in 2013.[24] Langhoff herself moved to Germany from Turkey as a child, and one particular focus within this engagement has been on the legacies of violence in the former Ottoman Empire and the Republic of Turkey.[25]

Verstrickungen thus emerges from within a location of production, Berlin, which lies at a significant geographical distance from the violent events that necessitate the memory work the project undertakes.[26] Distance

21   Der Meguerditchian's surname is also sometimes presented with a hyphen. Here I follow her preferred spelling.

22   The title is translated as "Entanglements" on the website of the Maxim Gorki Theater, Berlin, but as "Entwinements" in *Fruitful Threads*, ed. Silvina Der Meguerditchian (Vienna: Verlag für moderne Kunst, 2021). Here I use the translation under which the piece was marketed.

23   The title is a play on the *Erster Deutscher Herbstsalon* (First German Autumn Salon), held in Berlin in 1913, and thus signals a continuation between early twentieth century avant-garde experimentation and the Gorki's program under Shermin Langhoff's leadership.

24   For discussion of another such example, see Brangwen Stone, "Migration and Theater in Berlin: The Maxim Gorki Theater and the Komische Oper Berlin," in *Theater and Internationalization: Perspectives from Australia, Germany, and Beyond*, ed. Ulrike Garde and John R. Severn (London: Routledge, 2021), 199–214. Langhoff's leadership came into public disrepute in 2021. At the time of writing, she remains artistic director but shares the leadership with a broader team.

25   As of May 2022, the Turkish government has requested to be officially referred to as the Republic of Türkiye in English. As the period of time to which this chapter refers predates this change, I retain the spelling "Turkey" here.

26   Berlin is understood here as part of "location Germany" but, despite its symbolic power as the capital city, does not simply stand for that location in its

is not equivalent with separation or division here, though. As engagement with Der Meguerditchian's work will show, this distance is also an outcome of the violence in question. Indeed, through this work, which will be discussed in more detail in subsequent sections, "location Germany" more broadly is shown to also be intimately and materially connected to these acts of violence.[27] Taking my cue from the title of *Verstrickungen*, as well as from Minh-ha's parable, in this chapter I will use the language of "entanglement" to support a discussion of artistic engagement from "location Germany" with this violence and to address the relationship between "violence elsewhere" and the "elsewhere, within here."

German, Turkish, Armenian Entanglements

German, Armenian, and Turkish history are entangled on many levels, particularly around the genocide that began in 1915. This is a violence that the FRG as a political entity selectively recognizes. Germany has long deployed reference to it in debates over Turkey joining the European Union (EU), where Turkey's failure to acknowledge the violence that took place against Armenian populations in the late Ottoman Empire as genocide forms a stumbling block to EU accession. At the same time, the FRG itself only named the violence against Armenians as genocide in 2016, following renewed attention to the matter in the anniversary year of 2015. This recognition also marked formal acknowledgment of the role that the German Empire, allied with the Ottoman Empire, had to play in enabling this violence. Historians in this field highlight, for example, the active involvement of German officers in some military actions, including deportations, against Armenians, the documentation by German officers of deadly camp conditions, and the passive inaction of the German Foreign Office in response to information.[28] Others trace the effects that discussions of the Armenian genocide in the German press had on "justifications" for genocide entering public and political discourse back in the

---

entirety; as will be discussed further on, the particular dynamics of support available for cultural production there are significant, while access to live performance and installation art produced there requires residence or travel to the city.

27 See also Benjamin Nienass, "Transnational Memories, National Memory Regimes: Commemorating the Armenian Genocide in Germany," *German Studies Review* 43, no. 1 (2020): 127–47, here 130. Discussing the Lepsiushaus and Berlin's Gedenkstätte für Genozidopfer im Osmanischen Reich, he notes, "drawing the 'elsewhere' close means filtering and thus relocating it" (128); thus "the 'elsewhere' is filtered by 'older debates'" (142–43).

28 See, for example, Jürgen Gottschlich, *Beihilfe zum Völkermord: Deutschlands Rolle bei der Vernichtung der Armenier* (Bonn: bpb, 2015); Donald Bloxham, *The Great Game of Genocide: Imperialism, Nationalism, and the Destruction of the Ottoman Armenians* (Oxford: Oxford University Press, 2005), 115–33.

Weimar Republic.[29] Berlin-based activist Vahé Tachjian thus argues that "of course, it is also German heritage, the genocide."[30]

This entanglement is continued via the bilateral recruitment agreements struck between the FRG and Turkey in 1961. Anthropologist Alice von Bieberstein, whose work engages deeply with Armenian politics of remembrance in the FRG, summarizes:

> Armenians, mainly from rural parts of eastern Turkey, but also from Istanbul, seized the chance that the guest worker agreement offered to escape enduring persecution from the 1960s onwards. Once in Germany, community associations were slowly set up, providing a setting where literature on Armenian and Turkish history, to a large degree inaccessible in Turkey, could be read and experiences of persecution and survival shared.[31]

The narrativization of this violence as "elsewhere" on a state level is therefore further complicated by the long-standing presence of Armenian communities within Germany. Armenian and German histories become entangled not only through the interactions of historical actors on a state level, but also through ongoing processes of migration, which carry these histories to "location Germany."

Von Bieberstein's anthropological work on strategies used by Armenian community and advocacy groups in Germany to gain public recognition of the genocide in and by the FRG argues that the politics of memory work in the Federal Republic has strongly shaped the ways in which the Armenian community there articulate demands for recognition. Discussing the public commemoration of the Armenian genocide

29 See Stefan Ihrig, "Transnational and Entangled Histories of National Socialism? The Turkish Dimension of German Interwar History," *Plural* 4, no. 2 (2016): 27–45.

30 Vahé Tachjian, in correspondence with and cited in Gönül Bozoğlu and Susannah Eckersley, "Difficult Heritage in Europe: Paradoxical Dimensions of Time, Place and Memory," in *Dimensions of Heritage and Memory: Multiple Europes and the Politics of Crisis*, ed. Christopher Whitehead et al. (London: Routledge, 2019), 143–70, here 162. Tachjian is co-lead of the Houshamadyan project, for which Der Meguerditchian serves as artistic director, and which will be discussed in more detail later in the chapter. Bozoğlu and Eckersley emphasize a European rather than national frame in discussing historical violence against the Armenians under the Ottoman Empire as "a heritage which is both beyond and within Europe physically and metaphysically." They also discuss Houshamadyan in more detail.

31 Alice von Bieberstein, "Not a German Past to be Reckoned With: Negotiating Migrant Subjectivities between *Vergangenheitsbewältigung* and the Nationalization of History," *Journal of the Royal Anthropological Institute* 22, no. 4 (2016): 902–19, here 908.

at a ceremony on April 24, 2008, in Berlin, von Bieberstein notes the role of memory studies academics of Armenian descent in "shaping the expression of political demands by reconciling them with particular German sensibilities arising from the established genre of genocide commemoration."[32] This adoption of aspects of German memory culture related to the Holocaust has, she argues, a disciplinary function insofar as it demands particular behaviors, modes of remembrance, and scripts of citizenship.[33] In this respect, it has also influenced the ways in which non-Armenian Turkish-Germans position themselves in relation to such demands.[34]

Focusing more on the field of literature than community activism, Kader Konuk also highlights the role that residence in Germany has had on engagements by artists of Turkish origin with the historical violence against Armenians: "Für ein Land wie die Türkei, in der die Aufarbeitung der armenischen, griechischen und jüdischen Geschichte durch Zensur, Anklagen wegen Verleumdung des Türkentums und Morddrohungen behindert wird, leistet die Literatur der türkischen Diaspora in Deutschland ein bedeutsames Stück an Erinnerungsarbeit" (For a country like Turkey, in which the working through of Armenian, Greek, and Jewish history is hindered through censorship, charges of denigrating Turkishness, and death threats, the literature of the Turkish diaspora in Germany performs a significant amount of memory work).[35] Further examples of this diasporic or postmigratory[36] engagement with

32 Von Bieberstein, "Not a German Past," 906.

33 As I add the final corrections to this chapter in early March 2024, these demands have been brought to public attention very visibly in the German state's response to the violence being enacted by the state of Israel against civilian populations in Gaza, following the massacre and kidnappings by Hamas in October 2023. For trenchant public critique of the demands that residents of Germany conform to a model of Holocaust remembrance that disallows criticism of Israel's military actions, see, for example, the "Open Letter from Jewish Intellectuals" published on 22 October, 2023, in the *taz* newspaper, https://taz.de/Offener-Brief-juedischer-Intellektueller/!5965154/.

34 Von Bieberstein, "Not a German Past," 903.

35 Kader Konuk, "Genozid als transnationales historisches Erbe? Literatur im Kontext türkischer und deutscher Geschichte," in *Gegenwart schreiben: Zur deutschsprachigen Literatur 2000–2015*, ed. Corina Caduff und Ulrike Vedder (Paderborn: Wilhelm Fink, 2017), 165–75, here 165–66.

36 The term "postmigrantisch" or "postmigratory" came into popular usage in Germany primarily following its adoption by theater practitioners and curators at the Ballhaus Naunynstraße theater, Berlin; a theater with which Akın, Polat, and Der Meguerditchian have all worked. This act of self-labeling aims to counter the exclusionary terminology of the German state, to highlight the multiple inheritances and knowledges that come with migration as centrally important to society, and to draw attention to parallels with postcolonial power relations in a

the history of the Armenian genocide in other media include films such as the fictional epic *The Cut* (2014) by Fatih Akın, and the documentary film *Ötekiler* (The Others, 2016) by Ayşe Polat, as well as the installation and performance work I discuss below.

Encarnación Gutiérrez Rodríguez highlights that "*histoire croisée*," or "entangled history," as a "methodological approach … goes beyond mere comparative studies as it is interested in how history is a product of interlaces between places, people, and practices."[37] Given the focus in this volume on cultural engagements in Germany with "violence elsewhere," I have so far outlined some of the ways in which legacies of the historical violence against Armenians under the Ottoman Empire connect to Germany today. Doing so draws to some extent on the approach of "*histoire croisée*," but an emphasis on Germany runs the risk of leaving intact a sense of distinct national historiographies simply meeting. With Gutiérrez Rodríguez's words in mind, it is important to highlight that discourses and practices around memory and commemoration of violence against minority groups in contemporary Turkey have also been influenced by the German "memory model." The role of that model in the self-fashioning of the EU as a postwar democratic entity where the crimes of the Holocaust must be remembered to avoid their repetition is also significant here. Esra Özyürek, for example, highlights "the emergence of a critical mass of intellectuals in Turkey who believed that admitting to the genocidal crimes of the late Ottoman empire was important" in the early 1990s; intellectuals for whom "Germany was perceived as a positive role model" in this regard.[38] And as Eray Çaylı discusses in his recent work on architecture and the spatial politics of commemorative practices in Turkey, the 2000s subsequently saw a "proliferation" of "discourses and practices of 'confronting the past' (*geçmişle yüzleşme*)" in Turkey that involved both independent activists and state actors.[39] While the practices in question differed from those at work in Germany, the language in use here bears a strong resemblance in its phrasing to the

---

context where migration and racialization interact. In contrast to the "diasporic," which emphasizes a singular ethnicity and former homeland, the "postmigratory" emphasizes the relationship with residence in Germany and has been used to create space there for solidarity across different migrant positionalities.

37   Encarnación Gutiérrez Rodríguez, "Entangled Migrations: The Coloniality of Migration and Creolizing Conviviality," *Mecila Working Paper Series* 35 (2021): 1–25, here 18.

38   Esra Özyürek, *Subcontractors of Guilt: Holocaust Memory and Muslim Belonging in Postwar Germany* (Stanford, CA: Stanford University Press 2023), ix.

39   Eray Çaylı, *Victims of Commemoration: The Architecture and Violence of Confronting the Past in Turkey* (Syracuse, NY: Syracuse University Press, 2023), 11.

language of "Vergangenheitsbewältigung" (mastering the past). Indeed, von Bieberstein and Ayhan Kaya argue that a direct line of influence is traceable both in the engagement of Turkish or Turkish-origin intellectuals with discourses emerging from the German context, and in the activities of organizations such as the Goethe Institute, the Heinrich Böll Foundation, and the Friedrich Ebert Foundation in Turkey in the 2000s.[40]

Turkey has also seen a restriction of civil society spaces for such "confrontation" or engagement, however, with key incidents including the murder of Armenian journalist and activist Hrant Dink in 2007, the violent police response to the Gezi park protests of 2013, and the state-led persecution of academics who signed the "Academics for Peace" petition in support of Kurdish rights in 2016.[41] Çaylı engages in close analysis of practices and discourses between 2011 and 2013 surrounding the commemoration of violence against minority groups in Turkey—a period that, as the events noted above show, also included new incidents of violence. His work on this paradoxical period leads him to warn that "commemoration's power-laden effects entangle it in the very violence it commemorates."[42] He argues that "students of commemoration must avoid taking it for granted as indexing the aftermath of violence and focus instead on how it might operate as violence's medium."[43] This emphasis on how remembering one instance of violence can also be entangled in enacting another will be important to consider in looking at artistic performance that enacts commemorative work below. This is particularly the case given von Bieberstein's argument that there is a disciplinary dimension to the ways in which Holocaust memory shapes articulations of other histories of violence within "location Germany."

Çaylı's focus is on entanglements of practices related to violence across temporal planes, rather than across national borders. As I move from the historical context to the specific instance of artistic engagement with "violence elsewhere" at the heart of this chapter, Çaylı's "spatial ethnography," rooted in his background in architecture, also serves as an example of the ways in which the term "entanglement" itself weaves and warps its way across a range of disciplines. Gutiérrez Rodríguez

---

40 Alice von Bieberstein, "Memorial Miracle: Inspiring *Vergangenheitsbewältigung* between Berlin and Istanbul," in *Replicating Atonement: Foreign Models in the Commemoration of Atrocities,* ed. Mischa Gabowitsch (Cham, Switzerland: Palgrave Macmillan, 2017), 237–66; Ayhan Kaya, "Turkish *Vergangenheitsbewältigung*: The Unbearable Burden of the Past," in Gabowitsch, *Replicating Atonement,* 99–130.

41 For details on the petition, see the website of the Academics for Peace, accessed September 15, 2023, https://barisicinakademisyenler.net/node/63.

42 Çaylı, *Victims,* 19.

43 Çaylı, *Victims,* 11.

explains that thinking through the lens of "entanglement" in the context of critical migration studies, for example, "focuses on the movements, circuits, and interdependencies within multiple times and geographical scales brought into connection through migratory movements, policies and discourses."[44] Drawing together multiple ways in which the term "entanglement" shifts foci and agency in history, sociology, and philosophy, she outlines how a turn to entangled histories and historiographies connects with reassessments of human and nonhuman relationality on an epistemological level. In particular she highlights the feminist materialist thought arising from science and technology studies, in which new understandings of entanglement at the quantum level and in the area of biology have fundamentally undone notions of "bounded individualism."[45]

Such studies have traced the material properties and histories of atoms, rays of light, and interspecies relations to reveal the ways in which "neither biology nor philosophy any longer supports the notion of independent organisms in environments."[46] Scholars such as Donna Haraway and Karen Barad thus suggest, in the words of Barad, that "existence is not an individual affair. Individuals do not pre-exist their interactions; rather, individuals emerge through and as part of their entangled intra-relating."[47] Both explicitly draw on work by Minh-ha,[48] with Barad in particular folding in Minh-ha's language of "elsewhere, within here" to argue that "each bit of matter, each moment of time, each position in space is a multiplicity, a superposition/entanglement of (seemingly) disparate parts. Not a blending of separate parts or a blurring of boundaries, but in the thick web of its specificities, what is at issue is its unique material historialities and how they come to matter. Elsewhere, within here."[49]

Despite the language of specificity, Barad herself does not engage in depth with sociopolitical events and contexts in the article from which the

---

44   Gutiérrez Rodríguez, "Entangled," 1.

45   Donna Haraway, *Staying with the Trouble: Making Kin in the Chthulucene* (Durham, NC: Duke University Press, 2016), 5, 33. See also Francesca Lewis's chapter in this volume.

46   Haraway, *Staying with the Trouble*, 33.

47   Karen Barad, *Meeting the Universe Halfway: Quantum Physics and the Entanglement of Matter and Meaning* (Durham, NC: Duke University Press, 2007), 439; cited in Gutiérrez Rodríguez, "Entangled," 4.

48   Donna Haraway, "The Promises of Monsters: A Regenerative Politics for Inappropriate/d Others," in *Cultural Studies*, ed. Lawrence Grossberg, Cary Nelson, and Paula A. Treichler (New York: Routledge, 1992), 295–337, here 300. Cited in Karen Barad, "Diffracting Diffraction: Cutting Together-Apart," *Parallax* 20, no. 3 (2014): 168–87, here 172. Barad also cites Minh-ha on pages 169–70, 175, and 182–84.

49   Barad, "Diffracting," 176.

above quotation is taken, focusing instead on the interplay between physics, understanding of diffraction, and feminist theorizing of difference. As Gutiérrez Rodríguez and others highlight, the approach developed by Barad and others in science and technology studies has also been criticized as depoliticizing, as "it disregards the historically sedimented relations of domination and power within the intra-active configuration."[50] Indeed, as Gutiérrez Rodríguez's development of entanglement thinking in the sociological sphere makes clear, particularly in the context of a discussion of migration, one cannot afford to remain either abstractly or concretely at the quantum level: "The spatial relational perspective needs to be put into relation with a historical materialist analysis of social configurations and relations."[51] Similarly, thinking particularly in relation to violence, Yael Navaro et al. argue that "the turn to the non-human in the human sciences has arguably been mobilised by a washing away of violence, its histories, and its traces."[52] In the following I will trace how thinking through the entanglements that migration "surfaces" in the arts[53] allows for attention to the material connections of violence "elsewhere" with the "here" of "location Germany" in different spaces and registers than those provided by historical studies or formal commemorations. This attention to materiality, migration, and the arts also highlights the ways in which artistic material itself circulates and connects with a range of environments. Both of these interventions have significance for how cultural engagements with "violence elsewhere" can be conceptualized.

Verstrickungen (2014), *Freundschaft* (2013): As Installation

If the term "entangled history" suggests histories and historiographies that "kreuzen, überkreuzen, sich gegenseitig verschränken, verflechten und verweben" (cross, intersect, mutually interlace, intertwine, and interweave),[54] such entanglement is made literal and thus visible in the work of the key artist with whose work this chapter engages, Silvina Der Meguerditchian. In her 2014 performance *Verstrickungen*, Der

---

50   Gutiérrez Rodríguez, "Entangled," 4.

51   Gutiérrez Rodríguez, "Entangled," 4.

52   Yael Navaro et al., "Introduction: Reverberations of Violence across Time and Space," in *Reverberations: Violence across Time and Space*, ed. Yael Navaro et al. (Philadelphia: University of Pennsylvania Press, 2021), 1–29, here 6.

53   Gutiérrez Rodríguez talks of migration "surfacing" dimensions of coloniality: "Entangled," 8.

54   Michael Werner and Bénédicte Zimmermann, "Vergleich, Transfer, Verflechtung: Der Ansatz der Histoire croisée und die Herausforderung des Transnationalen," *Geschichte und Gesellschaft* 28, no. 4 (2002): 607–36, here 618.

Meguerditchian crocheted together photographs of Armenian families preserved primarily by relatives in the diaspora,[55] while seated in front of her earlier installation (*Freundschaft*): a bold red woolen constellation of laminated photographs that archive German imperial interests in the late Ottoman Empire and vice versa (see Fig. 6.1).[56]

The description provided on the artist's website and in the Gorki's publicity material positions the work as follows: "As if mending a spider's web connected by red thread, Silvina Der Meguerditchian shows in her installation, supported by a live performance, the catastrophic consequences of the alliance between Wilhelmine Germany and the late Ottoman Empire for the people of the falling empire and tells, [*sic*] how the threads of their stories can [be] followed to [*sic*] today."[57] The project engaged traditional craft skills, with the first row of the installation having been crocheted in collaboration with a group of women in Armenia during one of Der Meguerditchian's visits there.[58] The aesthetics and methods used have much in common with other crocheted memory "carpets" by the artist, such as *Fluchtteppich* (*Flight Carpet*) and *Made in Turkey II*, both shown at the Martin Gropius Bau, Berlin, in 2005, and *Familien II* (*Families II*) from 2013. Binding together images of Armenian life preserved in diaspora, these works help bring materials of memory from the private sphere, although not exclusively from Der Meguerditchian's own family, into the public sphere.[59]

The discourse of "mending" and the constitution of an otherwise dispersed photographic archive might, at first glance, suggest that these projects are primarily engaged in a form of restorative memory in response

---

55   These images were also used in her installation *Familien II* (2013), which is documented in *Fruitful Threads*, 34–35.

56   The photographs' subject matter includes individuals, such as Colmar von der Goltz, who built military links with and served in the Ottoman Empire prior to and during World War I; materials relating to German companies with financial interests in the Ottoman Empire; objects, e.g., a pocket watch gifted to Abdul Hamid II by Wilhelm II; and places or events, e.g., the Treaty of Sèvres. A selection of the images chosen are documented in the sixteen-page booklet that accompanied the installation in its first iteration, *Freundschaft*, accessed on March 2, 2024, https://issuu.com/silvina.der.meguerditchian/docs/freundschaft_edited_last_1_. There the image sources are listed as the internet and Manfred Pohl's *Von Stambul nach Bagdad: Die Geschichte einer berühmten Eisenbahn* (Munich: Piper, 1999).

57   "Verstrickungen," Publicity Material (in English) on the website of Silvina Der Meguerditchian, accessed on September 14, 2023, https://www.silvina-der-meguerditchian.de/works/verstrickungen-2013/.

58   Information provided by the artist.

59   See Çağlar Ilk and Silvana Der Meguerditchian, "In Conversation Part 1," in Der Meguerditchian, *Fruitful Threads*, 57–59.

Figure 6.1. *Freundschaft* (*Friendship*), rehung in the foyer of the Maxim
Gorki Theater, Berlin, as part of Silvina Der Meguerditchian's performance
Verstrickungen (*Entanglements*). Image © Silvina Der Meguerditchian.
Reproduced with permission from the artist.

to the violent destruction of Armenian lives and communities in 1915.
In the case of *Familien II*, for example, images from which are reused
in the performance of *Verstrickungen*, the crochet stiches that connect
the photographs could be seen to restore the integrity of a collection of
images originally produced in one location—the Ottoman Empire—and
then dispersed following political violence. In its quotidian usage, however, crochet as a technique is more often used in creating new textiles
or attaching separately existing pieces into a (potentially ever-expanding)
whole than in repair work. Each loop created by the turn of the crochet
needle and the pulling through of the thread becomes both a new point
of connection and encloses a new space or gap.

This technique speaks to how the connective work of *Verstrickungen*
and *Freundschaft* can be understood. As Marianne Hirsch, who has
worked with Der Meguerditchian, among other artists and academics,
within a multiyear project titled "Women Mobilizing Memory," explains
in a piece written for Der Meguerditchian's recent artist book: "After
now four generations of official denial, Armenian memory is often mobilized in the interest of reconstruction and restitution, its mobility tethered
by nostalgia. In her multi-media work, however, Der Meguerditchian
rejects identitarian politics and aesthetics, ethno-nationalism and its

monumentality."[60] That is to say, her artistic work makes use of the materials of memory and heritage but does not seek to respond to the historical violence of genocide by reinforcing the borders of ethnicity and kin relations.[61] Indeed, the crotchet stars created for *Freundschaft/ Verstrickungen*, which here surround the German and Ottoman materials alike, are reminiscent of the cells in a neural network or of astral constellations—pathways are built on both the intimate material level and in the imagination of the viewer.[62]

The ethos and aesthetics at work here can be further understood by turning to Der Meguerditchian's work as artistic director for the Houshamadyan project, a digital project that aims "to reconstruct Ottoman Armenian town and village life,"[63] and that itself takes an approach influenced by Hirsch's earlier scholarship on memory.[64] Established in 2010, the Houshamadyan project has an institutional base in Berlin, where it is headed by Elke Hartmann, from the Freie Universität Berlin, and Vahé Tachjian. The website is also supported by the Houshamadyan educational association, which is based in the USA. The editorial team is based across Berlin, Brussels, Beirut, and the USA, and the digital archive it aims to produce is held in the transnational space of the internet server. Material is presented in English, Armenian, and Turkish. While there is a material connection to "location Germany," then, the project exceeds this location not only in the scope of the material it archives and the audiences it addresses but also in its points of inspiration and organizational structure.

The project has engaged in extensive archival work, for which photographs, maps, letters, and documents of Ottoman Armenian life prior

60 Marianne Hirsch, "Flying Carpets," in Der Meguerditchin, *Fruitful Threads*, 23–26, here 23.

61 This approach is also taken by some Armenian activist groups within Turkey; see Eray Çaylı, "Inheriting Dispossession, Mobilizing Vulnerability: Heritage amid Protest in Contemporary Turkey," *International Journal of Islamic Architecture* 5, no. 2 (2016): 359–78.

62 For the new installation of *Freundschaft* as part of the *Verstrickungen* performance, the piece moved from being hung against the wall to being viewable from all sides. The originally single-sided laminated photographs were cut out and replaced by a double-sided version. This further highlights the artist's emphasis on animation and activation over monumentality.

63 "Introduction," Houshamadyan, accessed September 14, 2023, https://www.houshamadyan.org/introduction.html. On Houshamadyan, see also Bozoğlu and Eckersley, "Difficult heritage," 143–70.

64 Jose Luis Rubio Tamayo et al., "Use of an AR Technology and Media Environments for Reconstruction of Historical Sites in West Armenia: An Approach to Educational Applications," poster presentation at XIX Congreso Internacional de Tecnologías para la Educación y el Conocimiento, July 2014.

to the genocide are digitized and, in some cases, retouched. These documents are uploaded alongside contextualizing text to the Houshamadyan website under the headings of particular village names or under themes such as economy, religion, and local characteristics. Quite unusually, the emphasis in digitizing these is not on preserving a documentary authenticity that might connect to the monumentality Hirsch notes above. Rather, there is a focus on creating digital artifacts that engage the contemporary imagination. As the website explains,

> Unfortunately many of these pictures are obviously not of the best quality.... This circumstance has driven our editorial staff to carry out work on the majority of the pictures that are presented to the public on our website—to improve their colours, brightness and quality, with the aim of creating images that are equal to the high expectations of our contemporary visual age.[65]

As artistic director, Der Meguerditchian plays a key role here; she has worked with the artifacts as well as designing the branding of the website.[66] The images of landscapes and songbirds that decorate the Houshamadyan web pages speak to the locations and relations in which Armenian lives were lived under Ottoman rule but also refuse to reproduce these faithfully or fully.

The illustration method drawn on here and in the work on some other artifacts on the website is that of punching holes in paper along the lines of an image using a Japanese bookbinding tool. The use of these holes is described by Der Meguerditchian as follows:

> This is my attempt to depict the absence of these spaces. A positive shadow is cast on the wall through the holes, a shadow of light. From a distance they look like dots, and these dots resemble templates when painting by numbers.... In order to reconstruct Armenian history, we have only drawn dots, traces, in the form of objects, books, or stories. We have to imagine the lines, entanglements, and connections between them.[67]

The holes punched might be suggestive of a violence done to the source image, one that replicates the violence done to Armenian bodies and culture. Der Meguerditchian, however, characterizes the light these holes let in as pinpointing the absences created by actual historical violence and as illuminating new means of remembrance.

---

65 "Visual Materials," Houshamadyan, accessed September 14, 2023, https://www.houshamadyan.org/en/introduction/visual-materials.html.
66 See Ilk and Der Meguerditchian, "In Conversation."
67 Ilk and Der Meguerditchian, "In Conversation," 58.

Der Meguerditchian's approach here connects consciously to the artistic techniques associated with what Hirsch has termed "postmemory." This term is used to describe the complex relationship to the memory of the Holocaust for those "who grow up dominated by narratives that preceded their birth," which they access not through experience but through "imaginative investment."[68] While Hirsch's concept of postmemory was initially developed specifically in relation to Holocaust remembrance, she has subsequently argued both that the structure of postmemory applies in other contexts and that it can extend beyond the familial context in which the concept was developed, positioning it as a "connective art."[69] Hirsch herself comments on video animations created for Houshamadyan in her contribution to *Fruitful Threads*, a recently released artist's book showcasing Der Meguerditchian's oeuvre.[70]

As noted earlier, both women have been in sustained dialogue as members of "Women mobilizing memory": a "multiyear feminist collaboration," which held workshops in Chile (2013), Turkey (2014), and New York (2015). The aim of that collaboration was "to consider how the memories of violent histories ... could be mobilized for more progressive and hopeful futures."[71] For Hirsch, then, the red wool employed by Der Meguerditchian in installation works such as *Freundschaft* and *Verstrickungen* can be understood as not only a *roter Faden* (red thread), or connecting thought "evoking the blood of genocidal murder," but also as "threads of open-ended potential histories yet to be written, about the Armenian genocide, about its memory, about exile and diaspora—histories in which cycles of violence might be interrupted and in which teleologies leading to disaster might be redirected. That work is left up to us as active and engaged visitors responding to an urgent invitation."[72] In her discussion of works by Der Meguerditchian exhibited at the Depo Gallery in Istanbul in 2014 that similarly use crochet to connect together photographs, Hirsch nonetheless focuses on a logic of return over futurity, highlighting "the depth of history and memory they were bringing back to the

---

68 Marianne Hirsch, "Past Lives: Postmemories in Exile," *Poetics Today* 17, no. 4 (1996): 659–86, here 659.

69 Marianne Hirsch, "Connective Arts of Postmemory," *Analecta Politica* 9, no. 16 (2019): 171–76, here 172–73.

70 Hirsch, "Flying," 25.

71 Marianne Hirsch, "Introduction: Practicing Feminism, Practicing Memory," in *Women Mobilizing Memory*, ed. Ayşe Gül Altınay et al. (New York: Columbia University Press, 2019), 1–23, here 1. A detail from *Freundschaft* appears on the front cover of this volume, and the acknowledgments note that it "illustrates the delicate and fragile web of connections in which this volume engages, as well as its critical feminist exposure and reframing of national and transnational histories of power, violence, and repair" (xi).

72 Hirsch, "Flying," 26.

very site of eviction and destruction."[73] This dimension of the work is of great significance. The location in which much of Der Meguerditchian's work is created, however, and thus one important node in the spaces she stitches together, is left out of Hirsch's considerations of her work. The material dimension of the location of production is a "red thread" that itself could be followed further.[74] The exhibition at Depo in Istanbul, for example, was also partially supported by a German political organization, the Friedrich Ebert Foundation, a foundation promoting social democracy associated with the SPD (Social Democratic Party of Germany), and one that von Bieberstein noted as promoting German memory models in Turkey.[75] Der Meguerditchian has also discussed the influence of East and West Germany's divided past on her consideration of Ottoman Armenian histories.[76] What is labeled as Armenian diaspora work when displayed in Turkey and New York is simultaneously rooted in "location Germany" and can usefully also be contextualized in relation to approaches to memory and commemoration developed in the German context.

Notably, installed in the foyer of the Gorki Theater Berlin, as it was in 2014 and 2015, and performed in the German language, *Verstrickungen* does not address primarily an Armenian community. Nor does it return a photographic archive to contemporary Turkey. The Maxim Gorki Theater is a state-subsidized theater with significant symbolic capital in Germany's cultural landscape. In 2013/14 Langhoff had just taken over the role of artistic director there and, together with her co-artistic director Jens Hillje, framed its work as "new German theater."[77] The Gorki provided *Verstrickungen* with a space, financial support via funding from the Kulturstiftung des Bundes (German Federal Cultural Foundation), and an audience, initially as part of a large-scale workshop and artistic program revisiting the legacies of World War I titled *Europe 14–14*.[78] In doing so, it positioned commemoration of Armenian lives and deaths as

73 Hirsch, "Flying," 23.

74 See also Nienass, 141–42.

75 See the exhibition catalogue: *Hafızayı Harekete Geçirmek: Kadinlarin Tanikliği/Mobilizing Memory: Women Witnessing,"* ed. Ayşe Gül Altınay and Işın Önol (Istanbul: Depo, 2014), https://www.depoistanbul.net/wp-content/uploads/2018/08/Mobilizing-Memory-Women-Witnessing-Catalogue-.pdf. On FES in Turkey, see von Bieberstein, "Memorial," 250.

76 See Ilk and Der Meguerditchian, "In Conversation," 57.

77 "Shermin Langhoff im Interview: Her mit einem neuen deutschen Theater!," *Berliner Zeitung*, March 29, 2019, https://www.berliner-zeitung.de/kultur-vergnuegen/shermin-langhoff-im-interview-her-mit-einem-neuen-deutschen-theater-li.14697.

78 Maxim Gorki Theater, *Europe 14|14* (Berlin: Maxim Gorki Theater, 2014). Program. Available at https://issuu.com/maximgorkitheater/docs/gorki_europe1414_final.

part of European memory culture and as being of significance to contemporary realities in "location Germany." It thereby addressed not only the four hundred young people from across Europe who took part in *Europe 14–14* but, as a prominent space led by a curator of Turkish origin, also made a symbolic intervention in Turkish diasporic memory. This was also the case when *Verstrickungen* was reprised at the Gorki in spring 2015 as part of a program titled *Es schneit im April—eine Passion und ein Osterfest: Zum 100 Jahrestag des Völkermords an den Armeniern/It Snows in April—A Passion and an Easter Celebration: 100 Years after the Mass Murder of the Armenians*. Running for over a month (March 7 to April 25, 2015), the extensive program drew together filmic work, public talks, lecture-performances, performance art, installations, dance, concerts, staged readings, and plays, all of which engaged with the genocide and its legacies.[79]

Within *Verstrickungen* itself, the red yarn knots and loops together the materials of memory. At the same time, the holes through which the yarn moves, the space in which the works hang, and the movement of the bodies and gazes of audience members also imbricate and implicate the contemporary viewer and the spaces of "location Germany" in the work's connective web. Wherever it hangs, space and air that were "elsewhere" or other to the textile are now also enclosed within it—the holes are part of what gives a crocheted textile its warmth. The surrounding air and location can be understood as not separate or unrelated but as part of what gives the textile its material qualities. Creating a web of relation, rather than a linear inheritance of trauma, the installation at the heart of *Verstrickungen* both draws in and itself perforates the context of its production and display. In doing so, it not only enacts commemoration, engaging a range of individuals and audiences in memory work but also embodies the complex ways in which one location, and the violence that takes place there, can be understood as materially entangled with another.

Verstrickungen: As Performance Text(ile)

In her engagement with Der Meguerditchian's artistic works, Hirsch joins a number of thinkers who have found textile work, and crochet in particular, useful in thinking through questions of entanglement, especially questions of connection, relationality, and responsibility, through

79 Maxim Gorki Theater, *Es schneit im April—eine Passion und ein Osterfest: Zum 100 Jahrestag des Völkermords an der Armeniern/It Snows in April—A Passion and an Easter Celebration: 100 Years after the Mass Murder of the Armenians; Sonderheft* (Berlin: Maxim Gorki Theater, 2015). Program. English title as published in the bilingual program.

both a metaphorical and a materialist lens.[80] Influential theorist Haraway engages extensively with what she calls "string figures," which include practices like cat's cradle but also crochet.[81] She invokes the metaphor of following a thread as a means of tracing material histories of relationships between species in which "who lives and who dies and how might become clearer for the cultivating of multispecies justice."[82] In Haraway's theorization, this move not only brings ethical-political subject matter into view; her method of thinking with "string figures" also aims to enact an ethico-political approach:

> Playing games of string figures is about giving and receiving patterns, dropping threads and failing but sometimes finding something that works, something consequential and maybe even beautiful, that wasn't there before, of relaying connections that matter, of telling stories in hand upon hand, digit upon digit, attachment site upon attachment site.... Scholarship and politics are like that too—passing on in twists and skeins.[83]

While coming from very different fields and lines of intellectual development, Hirsch's and Haraway's thought seem to converge briefly around Hirsch's engagement with Der Meguerditchian's crochet work. Both theorists emphasize expanded inheritances and give license to the transformative potential of the artistic intervention. Here, remembrance is positioned as an iterative process that refuses to locate an act of historical violence, its effects, and the responsibility toward it as simply "here" or "elsewhere."

This moment of convergence in contemporary feminist theorization about relationality and entanglement also speaks to what appear to be multiple lines of influence on or convergence with Der Meguerditchian's installation and performance work. These convergences become particularly clear during Der Meguerditchian's performances, where the performer's own actions and words add further layers of meaning and effect to the installation. Here, the photographs and their subjects are not the only objects that move between and connect Germany, Turkey, and Argentina. In the first half of the performance, Der Meguerditchian sits on a high stool in front of the installation, her face covered with her hair, and crochets together a further set of photographs (see Fig. 6.2).

80 See Birgit Haehnel and Sascha Reichstein, "On Nomadic Textile Forms— The Aesthetic of Nomadic Textiles," in *Handbook of Art and Global Migration: Theories, Practices, and Challenges*, ed. Burcu Dogramaci and Birgit Mersmann (Berlin: De Gruyter, 2019), 145–57.

81 Haraway, *Trouble*, 76–81.

82 Haraway, *Trouble*, 3.

83 Haraway, *Trouble*, 10.

Later I realized that I had gone
because there was a knot to undo.

Figure 6.2. Silvina Der Meguerditchian crochets further photographs
together as part of her performance *Verstrickungen* (*Entanglements*), Maxim
Gorki Theater, Berlin. Still from video recording with caption showing
her narration in English translation. Image © Silvina Der Meguerditchian.
Reproduced with permission from the artist.

As she does so, a recording narrates the following memories from Der
Meguerditchian's childhood:

> In diesem Garten [in Buenos Aires] gab es keinen Wein. Aber dort
> stand eine riesige Linde. Sie schenkte uns Duft und Schatten....
> Diese Linde wurde zu unserer Weinrebe. Wenn man sehr daran
> glaubte, konnte man sich vorstellen, dass diese Blätter Weinblätter
> waren. Meine Schwester und ich saßen stundenlang unter der Linde
> [und] spielten.... Und so unter der Linde drehten wir gefüllte
> Weinblätter aus Lindenblättern für unsere Puppen. Vielleicht ging
> mir deswegen der Geruch der Linden bis ins Herz, als ich in den
> Sommern der 90er Jahre mit dem Fahrrad durch den Tiergarten zur
> Humboldt-Universität fuhr. Diese Lindenblätter, meine Weinblätter,
> haben mich jeden Tag den Kaiserdamm entlang bis Unter den
> Linden Nummer 6 willkommen geheißen.[84]
>
> [In this garden [in Buenos Aires] there was no [grape]vine. But a
> giant linden tree did stand there. It gifted us scent and shade.... This
> linden became our grapevine. If you really believed in it, you could

---

84   Silvina Der Meguerditchian, *Verstrickungen* (performance), my transcription from video recording. My thanks to the artist for access to this.

imagine that these leaves were vine leaves. My sister and I sat for hours under the linden [and] played.... And so under the linden we rolled stuffed vine leaves for our dolls. Perhaps that is why the smell of the linden trees went to my heart when I cycled through the Tiergarten park to the Humboldt University in the summers of the 1990s. Every day, [as I went] along the Kaiserdamm until I reached Unter den Linden number 6, these linden leaves, my vine leaves, bade me welcome.]

The stitching together of photographs, the recounting of a family history, also set memories of linden leaves and vine leaves in motion. These are vegetal materials that do not physically leave their own contexts but become substitutes or proxies for one another in the life of the granddaughter of Armenians who fled the genocide in Turkey for Paris, then later, Buenos Aires.

The narration that Der Meguerditchian performs allows her to trace moments of connection on a personal level between the contexts her installation brings together. The linden tree has a significant role to play in German literary and cultural history, while its presence as nonnative vegetation lining the streets of Buenos Aires remains a living legacy of city-planning norms imported from European metropoles in a "colonial approach" to landscape design.[85] Curiously, the species of linden tree most commonly found in Buenos Aires appears to be the *Tilia moltkei*,[86] a species named after Helmuth von Moltke,[87] a high-ranking officer of the Prussian army. Von Moltke's photograph is one of those crocheted into the installation at the heart of the *Verstrickungen* performance, as he served from 1836 to 1839 in the Ottoman Empire, advising on the modernization of the Ottoman army. The presence of these trees in both Berlin and Buenos Aires thus points to further historical entanglements, colonizations, and migrations that also structure the Argentinian space of the artist's childhood. At the same time, the linden tree reference reminds

85   See Ana Faggi and Maria Ignatieva, "Urban Green Spaces in Buenos Aires and Christchurch," *Proceedings of the Institution of Civil Engineers—Municipal Engineer* 162 no. 4 (2009): 241–50. Faggi and Ignatieva observe that the city's "landscape design can be defined as the united 'colonial approach,' which gave settlers confidence and a sense of wellbeing ..., setting against the local landscape and native vegetation to create green spaces that mirrored European approaches of the 17th, eighteenth and nineteenth centuries" (247).

86   Cristina L. de Bugatti, "Diferentes especies de tilo," *La Nacion*, December 18, 2020, https://www.lanacion.com.ar/propiedades/diferentes-especies-de-tilo-nid1334201/. See also Faggi and Ignatieva, "Urban," 249.

87   Owen Johnson and Julian Sutton, "Tilia americana" (2020), *Trees and Shrubs Online*, online encyclopaedia of the International Dendrology Society, https://www.treesandshrubsonline.org/articles/tilia/tilia-americana/#15135./

the listener of the arbitrary nature of the national lines drawn around these locations—the natural world and its arboreal representatives ultimately exceed, connect, and are at home in both locations. This "naturalizes" the performer's own transnational belonging, while the presence of the linden trees and her lack of access to vine leaves simultaneously points to the presences and absences created through histories of violence.

Several minutes later, the linden leaves, and the connections they provoke, are returned to in the context of a question about Der Meguerditchian's place in Germany:

> Früher dachte ich, ich bin gekommen, weil ich gehen musste. Später wurde mir klar, dass ich gegangen bin, weil es einen Knoten zu lösen gab. Eigentlich lag dieser Knoten in der Türkei. Da ich mich aber niemals dorthin getraut hätte, bin ich nach Deutschland gekommen. Was hat Deutschland mit der Türkei zu tun? Und überhaupt mit dem Knoten, den ich zu lösen hatte? Und diese Linden, die mich an unseren Garten in Claypole erinnerten. Sie katapultierten mich von Anatolien über Süd-Amerika nach Deutschland.[88]

> [I used to think, I came because I had to leave. Later it became clear to me that I left because there was a knot to unpick. Actually this knot lay in Turkey. But as I would never have dared to go there, I came to Germany. What does Germany have to do with Turkey? And what at all with the knot I had to unpick? And these linden trees, which reminded me of our garden in Claypole. They catapulted me from Anatolia, via South America, to Germany.]

Just as the vine leaves of Turkey haunt the childhood games described, Turkey as a third untrodden point in the narrator's trajectory haunts her time in Berlin. No direct answer is given by the recorded voiceover to this question of how Germany might relate to the narrator's family history in what is today Turkey. Der Meguerditchian's own actions as she crochets create further knots rather than undoing existing ones.

In the second half of the performance Der Meguerditchian places the ends of red threads hanging from particular images in the installation around the wrists of audience members in the front row. In several instances the audience member is also given a slip of paper to read aloud. These are the texts of missing-person notices from an Istanbul newspaper from 1915 to 1917, used by Armenians at that time to search for missing relatives. In others, the thread is simply wrapped around the audience member's wrist as Der Meguerditchian announces, "Unbekannt" (Unknown). Each audience member is then cut loose from the installation by Der Meguerditchian with a small pair of scissors, as she places a

---

88   Der Meguerditchian, *Verstrickungen* (performance), my transcription.

kiss on their cheek. Although the kiss releases them gently and lovingly, a section of the red thread remains tied around their wrist, a material trace of their moment of physical entanglement with the installation and with the evidence of violence it carries. The Berlin-based audience, whether initially connected through their own family histories or not to the historical violence to which *Verstrickingen* responds, thus also become marked by or entangled in it. As moving parts then released from their momentary physical connection into the installation piece, these audience members carry a degree of knowledge of this violence with them into their lives beyond the theatrical space. While not positioned as inheritors of the traumatic legacies of this violence in the same sense as Der Meguerditchian, this moment of material, bodily connection has significant affective power.

The performer's own body as connective node is further present in the monologue when Der Meguerditchian turns to ask the German forest to allow her to become its "humus." Verbally she creates an image that suggests both nourishment and fertilization as well as rotting and decay: "Lass mich dein Wurm, dein Moos, dein verdorbener Apfel, dein zermürbter Aprikosenkern, dein verschimmelter Ostfriesentee, dein übelriechender Fliegenpilz, dein zerkauter Knochen [sein]" (Let me [be] your worm, your moss, your rotten apple, your worn-down apricot stone, your mildewed East Frisian Tea, your stinking fly agaric, your gnawed-up bone).[89] The desire to become "humus" or compost, and the domesticity of some of the foods listed, functions as an assertion of the narrator as constitutive part of the environment in which she lives. As such, it also seems to speak intertextually to Haraway's assertion that "Human as humus has potential": a phrase by which Haraway communicates her desire to move beyond a focus on the human as central to the universe, without lapsing into the potentially alienating language of posthumanism.[90] If historically the "German forest" has been connected to ideas of a singular German "Volk,"[91] here the turn to the creaturely and to the language of fertilization denaturalizes a connection between place and ethnicity or even species. The notion of inheritance and responsibility in the face of violence thus expands, in line with Haraway's thought, beyond that of the bounded individual's relationship to a bounded community or even, momentarily, species.

89 Der Meguerditchian, *Verstrickungen*.

90 Haraway, *Trouble*, 32. Der Meguerditchian's references to spiderwebs in her publicity material can be understood as a further intertextual link to Haraway's thought.

91 See Johannes Zechner, *Der deutsche Wald: Eine Ideengeschichte zwischen Poesie und Ideologie; 1800–1945* (Darmstadt: Philipp von Zabern, 2016).

At the same time, the language of decay and the slow mournful move-ments of the performer create a somewhat abject affect; one that leaves behind the more celebratory style that Haraway herself adopts.[92] Indeed, in the final minutes of the performance, Der Meguerditchian herself lies down horizontally, facing upward, under the installation. The red threads are gathered in and allowed to dangle down onto her still body, integrat-ing the performer bodily into the web of images. This creates a tableau both peaceful and disturbing. Navaro et al. suggest that in new materialist or posthumanist thought such as Haraway's, a focus on "vitalism" rather than "death and suffering" is positioned as "politically and ethically nec-essary in order to move into a future of possibilities. As a consequence, violence, suffering, and death are rendered invisible."[93] This critique raises questions about the extent to which new materialist approaches that decenter the human individual allow space for discussion of the very material histories of violence. In contrast, in Der Meguerditchian's per-formance, the language of decay and affect of abjection bring death to the fore, rendering the (bio)politics of memory culture visible. Rather than offering up images of historical deaths, however, notably it is the imag-ined decay of the performer's body—that is to say, a contemporary reen-actment of extinguishment—that becomes the mode of entry into the "German forest." A degree of violence might then be said to accompany, or become the vehicle for, the positions the grandchildren of Armenian genocide survivors may need to adopt to find space within the German memory landscape.[94] If Der Meguerditchian herself becomes part of the rich soil of the German forest, these German contexts thus also become part of the "humus" that fertilizes her approach.

Red Threads of Violence Elsewhere

Tracing red threads that entwine artistic work produced in "location Germany" with the memory and experience of violence in the former Ottoman Empire has involved attempting to attend to the simultaneously disruptive and connective potentiality of the "elsewhere, within here." Violence figures here both as the historical act that triggers a need for

---

92 Here I am also influenced by recent critiques of Haraway's work in rela-tion to race. Dixa Ramírez-D'Oleo argues that "the ludic language … costumes a violent relationship to 'the black(ened) position.'" She argues that in Haraway's discussions of humus or compost, "blackness … continues performing the func-tion it has had in Western epistemes as that which must be destroyed so that it can give life to other life-forms." Dixa Ramírez-D'Oleo, *This Will Not Be Generative* (Cambridge: Cambridge University Press, 2023), 2–3.

93 Navaro et al., "Introduction," 8.

94 Cf. Çaylı, *Victims*, 11, and von Bieberstein, "Not."

commemoration and as an ongoing threat or potentiality that accompanies, shapes, and is reflected on in artistic-activist work that performs that commemoration outwith the usual spaces of community or national remembrance. The ambivalences that appear in Der Meguerditchian's own engagements with entanglement, relationality, and inheritance of responsibility thus raise important questions both about how the Armenian genocide can be memorialized in itself and about the forms of sociopolitical positioning at work in postmigratory artistic engagements with violent historical acts in Turkey from "location Germany." There is arguably a tension between the webby aesthetic that performs a transnationally legible mode of entangled remembrance and the insistence on detail, specificity, and the effect of mourning that the performance activates.

The textility of Der Meguerditchian's work uses stitching and crochet to model a form of simultaneous mending and perforation that complicates dualities of past and present, history and memory, and "here" or "elsewhere." Following Der Meguerditchian's red threads joins materials, contexts, and audiences across and beyond "location Germany" with an investment in remembering violence against the Ottoman Armenians. Set against a context in which migratization "as performative practice ... repeatedly re-stages a sending-off to an elsewhere,"[95] Der Meguerditchian's *Verstrickungen*, in contrast, brings into view and draws close the complexities of historical and contemporary violence, "not from elsewhere, but more specifically, from an elsewhere within here."[96]

95 Tudor, "Cross-Fadings," 1057.
96 Minh-ha, *elsewhere*, 2.

7: Encountering Violence Elsewhere at Home in Clemens Meyer's Short-Story Collection *Die stillen Trabanten* (2017; *Dark Satellites*, 2020)

Frauke Matthes

Writing the World Locally

Aᴄᴄᴏʀᴅɪɴɢ ᴛᴏ ʟɪᴛᴇʀᴀʀʏ sᴄʜᴏʟᴀʀ Rebecca L. Walkowitz, we live, or, rather, write and read, in "an age of world literature."[1] Walkowitz's study, which is concerned with the effect of translation on contemporary Anglophone literature, is one of a number of leading publications that have responded to a renaissance of "world literature" in literary studies since the early 2000s, with David Damrosch's *What Is World Literature?* (2003) paving the way for the revival of the term.[2] Famously coined by Johann Wolfgang von Goethe in 1827 in his conversations with Johann Peter Eckermann,[3] the term *Weltliteratur* (world literature) has gained notable popularity among scholars to describe the way local and national literatures have been produced, distributed, and consumed in relation to and in interaction with the global.[4] This is certainly not a surprising development in literary scholarship, considering the more recent

---

1   Rebecca L. Walkowitz, *Born Translated: The Contemporary Novel in an Age of World Literature* (New York: Columbia University Press, 2017).

2   David Damrosch, *What Is World Literature?* (Princeton, NJ: Princeton University Press, 2003).

3   Damrosch, *What Is World Literature?*, 1. See also the rest of the introduction to Damrosch's book, "Goethe Coins a Phrase," 1–36.

4   See, for example, titles such as Thomas Oliver Beebee, *German Literature as World Literature* (New York: Bloomsbury, 2014). See also Frauke Matthes, "'Weltliteratur aus der Uckermark': Regionalism and Transnationalism in Saša Stanišić's *Vor dem Fest*," in *German in the World: The Transnational and Global Contexts of German Studies*, ed. James Hodkinson and Benedict Schofield (Rochester, NY: Camden House, 2020), 91–108.

transnational movements of people, goods, and ideas that produce ever-widening global networks, including those of literature.[5]

What I am interested in in this chapter, however, is the way in which local-global interactions are perceived from a local's perspective in contemporary German-language writing itself, when encounters between the local and the global may be subtle and less immediate and their impact on the local individual not blatantly obvious. Such a focus will allow me to tease out in this chapter how a contemporary author, Clemens Meyer, explores in his short-story writing the interaction between "here" (the directly experienced local) and "elsewhere" (the often nebulous global) and the role that different forms of violence—across time and space, elsewhere and at home—play in this interaction. Emily Jeremiah reminds us that encounters between the local and the global are crucial in contemporary societies, "where global and local stand in a relationship of 'mutual interconnection and interdependence.'"[6] As this chapter will highlight, literature and its capacity to let readers into the worlds of those "other" to them can explore these interconnections from multiple perspectives, not least from that of the local.

If we follow Jeremiah's argument, then we should not be surprised by the centrality of the entanglement between the local and the global in Meyer's work, a writer with a particularly strong sense for the local. At first glance, Meyer's emphasis on the local in his work appears to stand in contrast to his consciously outward-looking perception of literature, which entails a reassessment of "world literature."[7] Meyer's view is that "du kannst jedes kleine Dorf zu Weltliteratur machen, indem du die Geschichten der Leute erzählst und sie zur selben Zeit groß machst durch Sprache, durch Konflikte, eben alles, was Literatur ausmacht" (you can turn every small village into world literature by telling people's stories and by amplifying them with language and conflict—simply everything that constitutes literature—at the same time).[8] In much of Meyer's work, but especially in his short

---

5   Rebecca Braun has written extensively about this phenomenon in German studies in relation to world authorship. See, for example, "Introduction: The Rise of the World Author from the Death of World Literature," in *World Authorship and German Literature*, ed. Rebecca Braun and Andrew Piper, special issue, *Seminar* 51, no. 2 (2015): 81–99.

6   Emily Jeremiah, *Nomadic Ethics in Contemporary Women's Writing in German: Strange Subjects* (Rochester, NY: Camden House, 2012), 12. Jeremiah is quoting Alexandra Kogl, *Strange Places: The Political Potentials and Perils of Everyday Spaces* (Lanham, MD: Lexington Books, 2008), 8.

7   Frauke Matthes, "'A Saxon Who's Learnt a Lot from the Americans': Clemens Meyer in a Transnational Literary Context," *Comparative Critical Studies* 15, no. 1 (2018): 25–45.

8   Clemens Meyer, in Matthias Schmidt, "Aus Anger-Crottendorf in die Welt: Angekommen in der 'Scheiß-Literatur'—Clemens Meyer wird 40," *MDR*

stories, conflict can take on different forms: quite often conflict is caused by an encounter between two characters across cultural borders, social spheres, or even times, yet sometimes violent conflict is also indirectly brought into those local spaces from elsewhere and shapes the story in different ways.

Thus, as I will argue in this chapter, Meyer does evaluate the impact of the global on the local by telling local, apparently parochial stories and by infusing them with transnational issues shaped by violence; above all, flight and migration and war.[9] Drawing on his short-story collection *Die stillen Trabanten* (The Silent Satellites, 2017; in English as *Dark Satellites*, 2020),[10] I will demonstrate that it is precisely Meyer's focus on the local that, somewhat paradoxically, enables him to engage with the global as he explores how transnational issues, such as violent conflict outwith Germany's borders, impact local concerns.[11] By focusing on the lives of those who do not physically move but who are nonetheless indirectly impacted by the transnational movements of those who, for instance, flee violent conflict and seek refuge in Germany, he gives a literary voice to those perceived as being peripheral to world events and can thereby contribute to his own perception of world literature.[12]

In order to unpack this specific dynamic between the local and the global, I will focus on one of Meyer's stories from the collection; namely, "Glasscherben im Objekt 95" ("Broken Glass in Unit 95"). This story explores the interaction between violence elsewhere and violence against

---

Kultur, August 17, 2017, https://www.mdr.de/kultur/literatur/clemens-meyer-geburtstag-vierzig-jahre-leipzig-100.html [URL no longer available]; my transcription. Unless otherwise stated, translations in this chapter are mine. I have explored Meyer's view of world literature in more detail in "'A Saxon Who's Learnt a Lot,'" esp. 29–31 and 38–39.

9   I have explored the interaction between the local and the global with a particular focus on marginalized East German masculinities in transnational contexts in Meyer's novels *Als wir träumten* (*While We Were Dreaming*) and *Im Stein* (*Bricks and Mortar*) in the chapter "Men without Women: Clemens Meyer," in Frauke Matthes, *New Masculinities in Contemporary German Literature: From "Native" to Transnational* (Cham, Switzerland: Palgrave Macmillan, 2023), 29–63.

10   Clemens Meyer, *Die stillen Trabanten: Erzählungen* (Frankfurt am Main: S. Fischer, 2017). Page references to *Die stillen Trabanten* will appear in the text. Translations are taken from *Dark Satellites*, trans. Katy Derbyshire (London: Fitzcarraldo Editions, 2020). Page references to *Dark Satellites* refer to the e-book version (page numbers may vary) and will also appear in the text.

11   Compare Matthes, "'Weltliteratur aus der Uckermark,'" 93.

12   Compare my analysis of local working-class masculinities in Feridun Zaimoglu's novel *Ruß* (Soot, 2011) in *New Masculinities*, 173–84. In particular, I comment, "Globalization is nothing that happens elsewhere anymore and this has dire consequences for those who suddenly find themselves at the social margins of society" (175).

those perceived as other at a local level particularly effectively. I will also probe how the short-story form allows Meyer to pursue his interest in the local and the peripheral and in the ordinariness and everydayness of the lives of his characters, and the impact of conflict—violence elsewhere—on those lives.

Thus, my main question in this chapter on "encountering violence elsewhere at home" is: How does violence elsewhere in Meyer's stories shed a new light on local, even "peripheral," lives in a supposedly affluent, stable, and secure Germany? Further: How do various expressions of violence interact in those stories? What do they reveal about "elsewhere" as something that is supposedly far removed? What do we learn, then, about the relationship between elsewhere and at home, here and there, but also between past and present, if we consider how the memory of past events sometimes impacts the current situation of Meyer's characters? And going one step further: How do Meyer's stories reconsider the local-global nexus? I will argue that Meyer's choice of the short-story form, with its roots in Anglophone storytelling traditions and its focus on "the lonely voice," to quote the title of Frank O'Connor's seminal work,[13] not only lends itself particularly well to capturing the way in which violence elsewhere influences local lives. It also reveals to us the global, transnational issues, not as an opposite to the local but, rather, as an integral part of his work.

The Short Story and the Everyday: Clemens Meyer

Meyer was born in 1977 in Halle an der Saale and grew up in Leipzig, where he still lives and where, in his own words, he can "write the world."[14] Meyer is well known for his empathetic look at those who are not well off or who are, for whatever reason, socially ostracized.[15] These figures include, for instance, the young delinquents who are figuring out who they are in Leipzig around the time of the *Wende* (the political

---

13 Frank O'Connor, *The Lonely Voice: A Study of the Short Story* (Cleveland: World, 1963).

14 Meyer, in Schmidt, "Aus Anger-Crottendorf in die Welt."

15 On "Meyer's reputation as a spokesman for marginal figures," see Gillian Pye, "The Liminal Space of the Short Story: Clemens Meyer's *Die Nacht, die Lichter* and *Die stillen Trabanten*," in *The Short Story in German in the Twenty-First Century*, ed. Lyn Marven, Andrew Plowman, and Kate Roy (Rochester, NY: Camden House, 2020), 118–36, here 128. See also Frauke Matthes, "Clemens Meyer, *Als wir träumten*: Fighting 'Like a Man' in Leipzig's East," in *Emerging German-Language Novelists of the Twenty-First Century*, ed. Lyn Marven and Stuart Taberner (Rochester, NY: Camden House, 2011), 89–104, here 89–90 and 101; Matthes, "'A Saxon Who's Learnt a Lot,'" esp. 26; and Matthes, *New Masculinities*, 30–32.

turning point of 1989/90) in Meyer's debut novel, *Als wir träumten* (2006; *While We Were Dreaming*, 2023);[16] the characters best described as loners in his short-story collection *Die Nacht, die Lichter* (The Night, the Lights, 2008; in English as *All the Lights*, 2011);[17] or the sex workers and pimps whose voices shape the narrative of his novel *Im Stein* (In the Stone, 2013; in English as *Bricks and Mortar*, 2017).[18]

In Meyer's work, violence, as something directly experienced, is frequently a driving force behind his characters' actions or development. Yet violence that is outwith the characters' control can also determine their positions in the respective narratives. This factor is most noticeable in *Gewalten: Ein Tagebuch* (Forces or Acts of Violence: A Diary, 2010),[19] a collection of short-story-like pieces that zoom in on episodes from the narrator's personal life, often in relation to contemporary events; violence at home as well as elsewhere holds the pieces together. Meyer's subsequent short-story collection, *Die stillen Trabanten*—the focus of this chapter—may not use violence (elsewhere) as a leitmotif in as obvious a way as *Gewalten*; instead, it offers snapshots of the lives of characters whose existence at the peripheries—of city life as well as of global developments—does not automatically equate to ignorance of the global circumstances that impact them. More recently, Meyer's 2020 story *Nacht im Bioskop* (Night at the Bioscope) addresses the massacre in Novi Sad in January 1942 when the town, located in the Bačka district of northern Serbia, then under Hungarian occupation, was cut off from the rest of the country, and Hungarian soldiers murdered five hundred Serbs and eight hundred Jews.[20] Violence elsewhere, in terms of geography but also history, is more obviously central here.[21] In Meyer's story collection *Stäube* (Dusts, 2021), the author draws the reader's attention to what occurs underneath the surfaces of Germany's social and political

---

16   Clemens Meyer, *Als wir träumten: Roman* (Frankfurt am Main: S. Fischer, 2006); *While We Were Dreaming*, , trans. Katy Derbyshire (London: Fitzcarraldo Editions, 2023).

17   Clemens Meyer, *Die Nacht, die Lichter: Stories* (Frankfurt am Main: S. Fischer, 2008); in English as *All the Lights*, trans. Katy Derbyshire, introduced by Stuart Evers (High Wycombe, UK: And Other Stories, 2011).

18   Clemens Meyer, *Im Stein: Roman* (Frankfurt am Main: S. Fischer, 2013); in English as *Bricks and Mortar*, trans. Katy Derbyshire (London: Fitzcarraldo Editions, 2016).

19   Clemens Meyer, *Gewalten: Ein Tagebuch* (Frankfurt am Main: S. Fischer, 2010).

20   Yad Vashem website, "This Month in Holocaust History: January: Hungarian policemen and soldiers standing over murdered Jews in Novi-Sad, Yugoslavia, 23 January 1942," accessed February 21, 2023, https://www.yadvashem.org/holocaust/this-month/january/1942-3.html.

21   Clemens Meyer, *Nacht im Bioskop* (Leipzig: Faber & Faber, 2020).

landscapes—to loss, disappearance, and social change—by setting them near Saxony's former ore and brown-coal mines, whose miners literally went underground to extract mineral deposits.[22] Reflecting on times past and memory are also central in Meyer's most recent publication at the time of writing: his inner dialogue with arguably one of the most influential East German writers, Christa Wolf, in *Clemens Meyer über Christa Wolf* (Clemens Meyer on Christa Wolf, 2023).[23] Here Meyer explores the significance of literature both in the GDR and for himself; that is, for the writer he is today.

Meyer's interest in the local in geographical terms—many of the primarily urban spaces in his work can be located in East Germany, specifically Leipzig—is interlinked with his focus on the ordinariness and everydayness of his characters' lives.[24] As I explained above, conflict is at the heart of Meyer's perception of literature and thus at the heart of his stories, because conflict, as a consequence both of local, personal matters and of global social and political issues, or as an intertwining of the two, disrupts the everyday and interferes with the ordinariness of his characters' lives. So, while Meyer may be telling "small" or local stories, he not only gives them significance with the help of the literary tools that he has available as a writer but also places these stories into a broader, more global context by doing so. This move then not only ties in with his view of world literature quoted above but also gives him the opportunity to remind his readers that the local is always part of the global.

Meyer's focus on the everyday experiences of his characters suits his choice of the short-story form very well.[25] Although at the time of writing, Meyer has published two novels,[26] he has embraced the short-story form even within those novels: the novels appear to be composed of short stories—each chapter could be read on its own—and thereby seem to defy the notion of a "grand narrative."[27] Meyer's favored novel structure echoes Paul March-Russell's observation of an "increasing tendency towards episodism in the contemporary novel"; that is, "the boundaries

---

22 Clemens Meyer, *Stäube: Drei Erzählungen und ein Nachsatz* (Leipzig: Faber & Faber, 2021).

23 Clemens Meyer, *Clemens Meyer über Christa Wolf* (Cologne: Kiepenheuer & Witsch, 2023).

24 See Matthes, *New Masculinities*, 32.

25 See Matthes, "'A Saxon Who's Learnt a Lot,'" 27.

26 Meyer is due to publish a new novel in August 2024: *Die Projektoren: Roman* (Frankfurt am Main: S. Fischer).

27 I have briefly commented on the influence of the short-story form on Meyer's novels in *New Masculinities*, 50–51. See also Matthes, "'A Saxon Who's Learnt a Lot,'" 32.

between the novel and the short story cycle are dissolved."[28] Meyer's writing style too is suggestive of his creative proximity to the short-story form, as he recognizes himself in his acknowledgment of the significant influence on his work of, for instance, US American short-story writers such as Ernest Hemingway.[29] In many ways, Meyer's preference for the short-story form in his literary writing ties in with the reemergence of the short story "in the German-speaking world as a vibrant literary genre" since the 1990s.[30] Meyer does not, however, seem to perceive a revival of the genre in contemporary German-language writing, instead lamenting its demise as he explains in his essay "Wozu Literatur" (Why Literature), which was published alongside the three short stories in *Stäube*:

> Woran ist … der Niedergang dieser Gattung, also der Kurzgeschichte, festzumachen, sollte sie nicht gerade heute, in der Zeit der Shortcuts, der Clips, des Schnell-Konsumierbaren in voller Blüte stehen? Kann sie, also die Shortstory, nicht am ehesten und auch am schnellsten eingreifen *in unsere Zeit*, getreu dem Titel des ersten Shortstory-Bandes von Hemingway *In our time*?[31]

> [How do you … explain the demise of this genre, that is, the short story, because should it not be in full bloom especially today, in these times of short cuts, clips, and the quickly consumable? Can it, that is, the short story, not intervene *in our time* most easily and quickly, true to the title of Hemingway's first volume of short stories, *In Our Time*?]

While I disagree with Meyer's pessimistic view of the state of the short story in German today,[32] the close link between the short-story genre and the notion of contemporaneity is evident in recent German-language short-story writing, including Meyer's, and perhaps also explains the revival of the genre in German since the late twentieth century. Lyn

---

28 Paul March-Russell, *The Short Story: An Introduction* (Edinburgh: Edinburgh University Press, 2009), 105.

29 Matthes, "'A Saxon Who's Learnt a Lot,'" 26–27. See also Matthes, *New Masculinities*, 51.

30 Lyn Marven, Andrew Plowman, and Kate Roy, "Introduction to the Contemporary Short Story in German," in Marven, Plowman, and Roy, *The Short Story in German*, 1–16, here 1.

31 Meyer, "Wozu Literatur," in *Stäube*, 97–128, here 122; Meyer's emphasis.

32 Even a quick look through Marven, Plowman, and Roy's *The Short Story in German in the Twenty-First Century* draws the reader's attention to the wealth of short stories or short-story collections published in German over the past thirty years or so, which led the editors to initiate the publication of their volume in the first place.

Marven, Andrew Plowman, and Kate Roy highlight "the open-endedness and multiple possibilities of the genre."[33] It seems that the flexibility of the short-story form can capture the diversity of experiences in our time particularly well. Marven, Plowman, and Roy explain: "The inherent characteristics of the short-story genre lend themselves to the concerns of our contemporary age—liminality, open-endedness, ambiguity, intensified subjectivity, and the need to perform identity within or against a sociocultural backdrop."[34] I would like to add a noticeable awareness of the presence of the global in the local in many short stories in German, something at which Marven also hints with reference to Catalin Dorian Florescu's collection *Der Nabel der Welt* (The Navel of the World, 2017).[35]

The presence of the local in the global, or more precisely, the peripheral in the global network of events, ties in with the short story's own perceived "marginalization" or "peripherality" as a genre.[36] Viorica Patea explains that the short story has come to be regarded as "a form at the margins" largely owing to "its long-standing theoretical neglect."[37] Looking into themes and topics addressed in short stories, Mary Louise Pratt argues that "the short story is often the genre used to introduce new (and possibly stigmatized) subject matters into the literary arena," and this includes writing about marginalized societies or geographically "marginal [spaces] with respect to some metropolis."[38] It seems that the genre's "peripherality" as outlined by both Patea and Pratt offers a particularly suitable space for Meyer to draw attention to those on the "periphery" of many readers' experiences. Meyer's characters are marginalized or

33 Marven, Plowman, and Roy, "Introduction to the Contemporary Short Story in German," 3.

34 Marven, Plowman, and Roy, "Introduction to the Contemporary Short Story in German," 12.

35 Lyn Marven, "Trends and Issues in the Contemporary German-Language Short Story," in Marven, Plowman, and Roy, *The Short Story in German*, 272–90, here 286.

36 Cf. Marven, Plowman, and Roy, "Introduction to the Contemporary Short Story," 2. The authors speak here of "the relative marginalization of short-story collections in the literary arena compared with the more prominent and culturally prestigious form of the novel."

37 Viorica Patea, "The Short Story: An Overview of the History and Evolution of the Genre," in *Short Story Theories: A Twenty-First-Century Perspective*, ed. Viorica Patea (Amsterdam: Rodopi, 2012), 1–24, here 7. Patea refers to Clare Hanson's introduction to *Re-reading the Short Story*, ed. Clare Hanson (New York: St. Martin's, 1989), 1–9, here 3.

38 Mary Louise Pratt, "The Short Story: The Long and the Short of It," in *The New Short Story Theories*, ed. Charles E. May (Athens: Ohio University Press, 1994), 91–113, here 104 and 105. Pratt also points out that "the novel is, and has been for some time, the more powerful and prestigious of the two genres" (96).

peripheral not only in terms of geography but also in terms of their position in relation to global events. On the surface, nothing much happens in Meyer's characters' worlds. And yet Meyer's choice of the genre of the short story with its American influence complicates his characters' positions.[39] Not only does the short story make the peripheral experience of its characters a central concern and thereby draw his readers' attention to the fact that the peripheral is part of a wider globality and, indeed, stands in a reciprocal relationship with it; it also enables Meyer to "intervene in our time," as he says, and to give his characters the attention on the world literary stage that they deserve.

The significance of the local in Meyer's work also needs to be considered in a larger context, because Meyer's writing ties in with, yet also differs from, a noticeable interest in the local or in regional identities in recent German-language writing. This argument holds especially true for what Anja Brockert has termed "d[as] mittlerweile etwas strapazierte[] Genre des ostdeutschen Dorfromans" (the by now somewhat strained genre of the East German village novel).[40] Despite some German-language writers' engagement with the local in their work, a fear of parochialism has been part of literary production in Germany since the 1990s.[41] More recently, Stuart Taberner has identified an "anxiety about provinciality [that] once again intimates nonminority Germans' sense of their exceptionalism, linked first and foremost to the Nazi past."[42] Taberner argues

---

39   Charles E. May writes, "Most critics and literary historians agree that short fiction underwent a change in the mid-nineteenth century, especially in America.… Certainly, short narratives existed before the period between 1820 and 1860, during which Washington Irving, Nathaniel Hawthorne, Edgar Allan Poe, and Herman Melville irrevocably transformed the short story." Charles E. May, *The Short Story: The Reality of Artifice* (New York: Twayne, 1995), 21.

40   Anja Brockert, "Buchkritik: Angelika Klüssendorf—Vierunddreißigster September," *SWR2*, Literatur, August 31, 2021, https://www.swr.de/swr2/literatur/angelika-kluessendorf-vierunddreissigster-september-100.html. See also Ursula März, "Heimatromane: Auf einmal Heimat," *Die Zeit*, no. 44 (2017); available at *Zeit Online*, October 25, 2017, updated October 31, 2017, http://www.zeit.de/2017/44/heimatromane-dorf-renaissance-literatur. I have also commented on "a noticeable revival in an interest in regional identities in German literature" in "'Weltliteratur aus der Uckermark,'" 93. Here, see also my brief discussion of März's categorization of the "village novel."

41   See Stuart Taberner's comments on the *Literaturstreit* in the 1990s, in "Introduction: German Literature in the Age of Globalization," in *German Literature in the Age of Globalization*, ed. Stuart Taberner (Birmingham: University of Birmingham Press, 2004), 1–24, here 14–15. See also Matthes, "'A Saxon Who's Learnt a Lot,'" 28.

42   Stuart Taberner, *Transnationalism and German-Language Literature in the Twenty-First Century* (Cham, Switzerland: Palgrave Macmillan, 2017), 76; see also 77–78.

that a number of those authors believe that "German culture—and German writing—might seem to be a peripheral phenomenon that can only achieve globality by passing through dominant languages, sites of production and reception, and articulations of 'international style.'"[43]

As far as I am aware, Meyer has never expressed such a concern, yet the combination of local subject matter and American-style short-story form complicates local-global interactions in his work. Marven deploys the widely-used term "glocal" to capture the interconnection between the global and the local in German-language novels since the turn of the millennium that can help us unpack the complexity of this issue in Meyer's stories. While Marven links the global outlook of contemporary novels to their "cosmopolitan plots and content ..., as well as their language," she also acknowledges their "engage[ment] with local concerns."[44] One could certainly argue that the short-story form facilitates Meyer's "international style" and thereby tackles any potential parochialism upfront. Through this style, combined with his largely local (if, unlike in the afore-mentioned "village novel," urban) subject matter, Meyer creates a different "glocality" than the one Marven describes. This is because, despite the apparent focus on the local, the "glocality" of his stories is not dependent on cosmopolitan plots or content but it is shaped by a more subtle, or local, engagement with global concerns and thereby reassesses the local-global relationship, as will become clear in the next section of this chapter.

Die stillen Trabanten: Violence Elsewhere and the Peripheral

Meyer's stories are not only local: they are often set at the "peripheries" of society. As Gillian Pye highlights, however, these "peripheries" are highly "complex" and various.[45] She reads those peripheral spaces as "in-between" locations or liminal spaces and writes, "Meyer's work illuminates the everyday world of those who have not profited from neoliberal capitalism; a space between East and West, past and present, local and global."[46] Pye's comment directs us toward space, or location, and the liminality of some of these quantities as a crucial factor

---

43 Taberner, *Transnationalism*, 77. See also Matthes, *New Masculinities*, 169–70.

44 Lyn Marven, "Introduction: New German-Language Writing since the Turn of the Millennium," in *Emerging German-Language Novelists of the Twenty-First Century*, ed. Lyn Marven and Stuart Taberner (Rochester, NY: Camden House, 2011), 1–16, here 2.

45 Pye, "The Liminal Space," 127.

46 Pye, "The Liminal Space," 121.

in Meyer's stories, in the way they are constructed and where conflict is set. Rather than speaking of "in-between" spaces, like Pye, however, I suggest that "here" and "there" merge in those spaces. Their merging not only reflects violence in the presence of the people that fled it elsewhere but also generates violence at a local level, as that presence of "others" is unwanted by some.

The title *Die stillen Trabanten* already makes readers aware of these and other social tensions, the term *Trabanten* (satellites) referring to the satellite towns on the periphery of, as one of the characters says, "der richtigen Stadt" (13; "the town proper," 15), where lives appear marginal or peripheral to global developments. These satellite towns are, in Pye's words, "neither part of, nor separated from, the contemporary metropolis."[47] They are anything but the flourishing city centers where the glamorous side of transnational movement—leisurely travel or moving to another country by choice, and the movement of capital and products, including cultural ones—has taken hold. Instead, these satellite towns are home to spaces where the underside of transnational movement, often caused by violent conflict, is noticed the most by the socially and economically less privileged. These spaces include the "Ausländerwohnheime" (literally "hostels for foreigners"; that is, for non-Germans, who are clearly set apart from German citizens, as they are not seen to belong to the nation, or, in Katy Derbyshire's translation, "refugees' reception centre[s]"[48]) where people fleeing war and persecution find temporary abode but are also often subject to racist attacks (in "Glasscherben im Objekt 95"). They are also the tower blocks, "Plattenbauten," where working-class people live side by side with so-called foreigners, here Muslims (in the title story). The underside of transnational movement also manifests itself in places of largely physical work such as train stations (in "Späte Ankunft"/"Late Arrival"; "Die Entfernung"/"The Distance"). Several of Meyer's stories in this collection refer to the "Ausländerviertel" (literally translated as "foreigners' neighborhoods," a term that again emphasizes a presumed clear separation between Germans—the "native" population—and non-Germans, who do not belong to the nation) of the city that some of the characters are trying to avoid—or sometimes are specifically seeking out. It tends to be in such marginalized areas of the city that those who experienced violence outside Germany's borders find a place of abode. It is, furthermore, in these parts of German society that

---

47 Pye, "The Liminal Space," 124.

48 Here, Derbyshire has decided to specify "Ausländer" in her translation. Derbyshire also translates "Ausländer" as "asylum-seekers" in this story. An "Ausländerwohnheim" can accommodate immigrants in general, not only refugees and asylum seekers, though the latter are very likely to make up the majority of residents.

cannot profit from the prosperity that many associate with Germany that violence elsewhere has its greatest impact on the local experience; and violence at a local level can also be part of the everyday experience of its inhabitants.

In the following, I would like to work through some of my ideas regarding peripherality and the impact of the global as elements closely connected to violence elsewhere in *Die stillen Trabanten* by taking a closer look at the story "Glasscherben im Objekt 95." In several of the stories collected in *Die stillen Trabanten*, violence elsewhere plays specific roles: it can, for instance, lead to new job opportunities (in "Unterm Eis"/"Under the Ice," in which the narrator's work involves rebuilding the railway tracks in the Balkan region after the wars of the 1990s); or it returns to the local in the form of trauma (in "Der Spalt"/"The Crack," in which the protagonist by chance enters the flat of an old woman who mistakes him for her grandson, a presumably dead soldier, who was deployed in what was, according to her, a "schreckliche[n] Land" [112; "terrible country," 157]). Likewise, in "Glasscherben im Objekt 95," the narrator does not directly experience violence elsewhere, and while that violence does not immediately shape the direction of his life, it still influences the life of one man in a remarkable way. The story's peripheral setting also appears to be a flashpoint for violence and demonstrates how violence elsewhere can be intertwined with local forms of violence.

The story, set circa 2015, revolves around an unnamed narrator, a security guard who works night shifts at the "Objekt 95" mentioned in the title. The Objekt 95 is situated at the periphery of a satellite town (the periphery of the periphery). It is "ein Rechteck aus zehnstöckigen Plattenbauten, ein großer Innenhof zwischen den Blöcken, und ein Stück außerhalb das AW [abbreviation used by the security guards for the "Ausländerwohnheim"; F.M.]; eine Immobilienfirma hatte all das vor Jahren gekauft und saniert, und jetzt musste jemand drauf aufpassen" (11; "a square of ten-storey concrete blocks, a large courtyard between the blocks, and the RC [abbreviation used by the security guards for the "Reception Centre"; F.M.] a bit further outside the square; a property company had bought it all and done it up years ago, and now someone had to look after it," 13). Patrolling on his own at night, the narrator represents quite clearly O'Connor's "lonely voice." He does not even have a name, which suggests that he could be any one of those people whose work makes them invisible to wider society.

The narrator recalls seeing a young woman, a resident of the hostel in the recent past, whose image triggered his memory of a brief romance with another woman from the former Soviet Union, Marika, also a resident of the hostel, twenty years prior in the mid-1990s. He had first seen her through, and then met her at, the fence that separated the Objekt 95 and the abandoned Russian barracks, which had not been demolished at that point and which were also part of his patrol, from the hostel. The story ends with the narrator's memory of the more recent past of watching residents of the hostel, presumably including the young woman who reminded him of Marika, boarding a bus to be moved to a different place following a xenophobic attack on the hostel.

Pye has already analyzed carefully "Meyer's preference for anachronic narrative, in which the memories of an autodiegetic narrator or focalizer are interwoven with action in the present of the narration, underlining the point that nothing—and yet everything—is present."[49] Time and space are constantly shifting; or, rather, past and present, here and there are merging, something that is also hinted at literally in this story. The narrator's comment that "[das Funkgerät] sprach mit uns durch Zeiten und Räume" (12; "[the radio] spoke to us through time and space," 15) early on in the story already indicates that it is often not clear whether the narrator's memories of the young woman and their encounter relate to the mid-1990s or the more recent past, thus thwarting coherence in the narrative.[50] Readers thereby get a sense of the narrator's fragmented memories and the way in which they blur into each other. In many ways this lack of unity on the narrative level could also be read as a stylistic comment on the "fragmented society" in which the narrator found himself after the end of the Cold War,[51] and the social and political consequences it had for him and East German society as a whole.

The shifts in time and space in "Glasscherben im Objekt 95" are also linked to the mundanity of the narrator's work, and they transport a sense of loneliness (he patrols on his own) as well as "stasis and restriction."[52] In his memory, every working night followed the same pattern; they were interchangeable. Or so readers are led to believe initially because as early as in the first paragraph, we learn, as Pye puts it, about the "political [and social] developments [that] are reflected primarily in the harsh working conditions of the security guards."[53] The narrator tells us, "Ich kannte die Wohnheime, die wir manchmal 'Kanacken-Burgen' nannten, in denen die Ausländer lebten, keiner hatte dort je gern Dienst gemacht, und jetzt wurde alles noch schlimmer" (10; "I knew the hostels the other guys sometimes called 'roach motels,' where the asylum-seekers lived, no

49   Pye, "The Liminal Space," 133.

50   Pye, "The Liminal Space," 133. Pye also links this lack of coherence to "the experience of disconnection and disorientation ... communicated by frequent, sometimes severe disruptions to logical relationships or chronological sequencing, and in which boundaries of identity become blurred" (130).

51   Referring to "Frank O'Connor and other short story writers and critics," Charles E. May states that "the short story seems to thrive best in a fragmented society." May, *The Short Story*, 13.

52   Pye, "The Liminal Space," 125.

53   Pye, "The Liminal Space," 134.

one had ever liked working shifts there, and now it was all getting even worse," 12).[54]

The narrator does not specifically tell us what was getting worse, but readers may certainly be reminded of the racist, xenophobic, and fatal attacks on such hostels that frequently made the news in the 1990s, such as the one in Rostock-Lichtenhagen in August 1992, and that seem to flare up again here. The 1990s were a time when state borders had disappeared or were disappearing (18), a phenomenon that went hand in hand with migration movements. Borders or boundaries, such as the fence at which the narrator met the woman in the mid-1990s, but also, as already hinted at earlier, the blurring of boundaries between time and space—past and present, here and there—play a crucial role in the story.[55]

The shifting of physical borders is also reflected in the setting of the story, the Objekt 95 itself. Right behind the Object 95, as well as the hostel, were "Plattentürme und Planquadrate aus der Zeit des Sozialismus" (14; "slab constructions and grid squares from the days of socialism," 18); in the 1990s, abandoned Russian barracks were part of the area. In Pye's words, "the physical remnants of communism coexist with spaces of post-Wende capitalism [speculative development projects; F.M.] and [and this is what is of particular interest in this chapter; F.M.] of global population shifts."[56] East Germany's Communist past meets its capitalist as well as its postmigrant present in these spaces. This encounter is particularly reflected in the people who used to inhabit the spaces and those who now either profit from them or—and again this is more relevant in the context of this chapter—seek refuge in them. The narrator thus comments, "'Die Russen [in East Germany] gingen, die Kanacken kamen,' sagten die Kollegen" (19; "'The Russians left, the Yugos[57] came,' the guys at work said," 24).

The global population shifts of the 1990s included "Russlanddeutsche, die aus dem zerfallenen Riesenreich zu uns kamen, aber die landeten

---

54 The "K-word" is a pejorative term used to refer to presumed "foreigners," or their children, of primarily Turkish or Middle Eastern backgrounds. The term was reappropriated in the 1990s by authors such as Feridun Zaimoglu and the antiracist network "Kanak Attak." I have explored the use of this term and its reappropriation in *Writing and Muslim Identity: Representations of Islam in German and English Transcultural Literature, 1990–2006* (London: igrs books, 2011), 134–36. As I am quoting from Meyer's story, I leave it (in its pejorative, nonreappropriated meaning) here.

55 Pye points out the "repeated images in which figures look inwards and outwards across boundaries"; "The Liminal Space," 126.

56 Pye, "The Liminal Space," 134.

57 Derbyshire's translation reduces this term to people from the Balkans, when, in fact, it is usually used to refer to people of wider backgrounds; above all, of Turkish or Middle Eastern backgrounds.

meistens nicht in den Ausländerwohnheimen" (16; "Russian Germans who came to us from the gigantic collapsing empire, but most of them [*sic*] didn't end up in the hostels," 21). Other migrants are not specified; we are only told that, unlike the so-called Russian Germans, they looked "different" (see 16). This nonspecificity or noninterest in differentiating the asylum seekers or refugees is interesting in itself; they remain in a vague elsewhere for the story's German characters.

Yet the migration of people caused by war triggers the encounter that is at the core of the story in the first place. The woman whom the narrator met in the 1990s is called Marika (or so the narrator believes), and the narrative does not specify her background. From their conversation, however—Marika initially mistakes the narrator in his uniform for an officer—we do learn certain things about her:

> "Du bist aus Russland," sagte ich, "aus der großen Sowjetunion."
> "Nicht Russland," sagte sie, "kleines Land, ganz weit. Und Berge. Unser Dorf ... vor den Bergen." (23)

> ["You're from Russia," I said, "From the big Soviet Union."
> "Not Russia," she said, "small country, very far. And mountains. Our village ... near the mountains."] (30)

Throughout the story the "kleines Land, ganz weit" remains unspecified. Marika's comment later on—"Als die Sowjets bei uns weg, begann Krieg" (31; "When the Soviets go from us, war began," 41)—points us to one of the various conflicts following the collapse of the Soviet Union. It could be the war in Chechnya, for instance. By not specifying this country, Meyer keeps it far away from his narrator as well as from his readers: in many ways it is the ultimate "elsewhere" that adds to the extraordinariness that interrupted for a moment the ordinariness of the life of the narrator. This unspecified "elsewhere" simultaneously highlights the end of the Cold War as a global phenomenon, which triggered violent conflict and subsequent migration of people from the former Eastern bloc to Western Europe, and thus appears as one of the ways that the story binds here and there, that is, local, peripheral space and elsewhere together. Yet it is not only migration, fleeing violence, that ties the narrator to Marika but also the historical context and their experiences of having grown up under Communist regimes: as someone socialized in the GDR, the narrator conveys to the reader how he tried to make sense of Marika's background by, for instance, trying to remember Russian words or phrases he had once learned at school, so that he could communicate with her.

I mentioned earlier that "Glasscherben im Objekt 95" also engages with other forms of violence against "others"; namely, those who were fleeing their homes to escape violence. In his everyday life, the narrator was also witness to racism, prejudice, or certain assumptions about people, that, one could argue, were really brought to light in the 1990s. Meyer subtly intertwines these (here less direct or physical, yet nonetheless noticeable) forms of violence with what still makes Marika so outstanding to the narrator:

> Sie hatte rotbraune, halblange Haare, und ihr Gesicht war sehr hell, auch die Haut ihrer Hände war fast weiß, und kurz dachte ich, dass sie vielleicht im AW arbeitete, denn sie sah nicht aus wie eine der dunklen Fremden, die die Kollegen manchmal "Kanacken" nannten, auch ich benutzte dieses Wort hin und wieder, wenn wir einen Kaffee tranken, bevor meine Schicht endete und die Schicht der Ablöse begann, wie man manchmal eben so redet, um nicht schwach zu wirken, obwohl ich kein Problem mit den Kanacken hatte. (19)

> [She had red-brown, medium-length hair and her face was very pale, the skin on her hands was almost white too, and for a moment I thought maybe she worked in the RC; she didn't look like one of the dark asylum-seekers in the "roach motel." I used the word now and then too, when we were having coffee, before my shift finished and the next guy's shift began, just the way you talk sometimes so you don't look weak, even though I never had a problem with the asylum-seekers.] (24–25)

In sentences like the ones in this quotation, the "intensity" of the short form comes to the fore particularly well: several aspects are raised here and complete the scene, the situation, the mood, and the atmosphere that the story tries to capture in condensed form.[58] Starting with Marika's appearance (especially her red-brown hair that marks her as different from the "others" and that reappears toward the end of the story), the narrator comments on the lumping together of so-called foreigners based on their appearance and the racist assumptions that go with it. The narrator's thoughts also give readers an insight into the narrator's perception of his masculinity and the wish to avoid coming across as weak that triggered a certain form of behavior, something that goes hand in hand with the narrator's difference, at least in the way he sees himself: he repeatedly says that his colleagues used racist language and presumably acted on it, not him.

Yet there is also a "vulnerability" about the narrator, especially in the face of such verbal and psychological violence.[59] Unwilling or unable to confront his colleagues' violence, he seemed to wish to compensate for it by comforting, or even by trying to protect, Marika, who was clearly

58 Marven, Plowman, and Roy, "Introduction to the Contemporary Short Story in German," 7. The authors refer to Patea, "The Short Story," 3.
59 Pye, "The Liminal Space," 125.

traumatized. For instance, she never responded to the narrator's questions about her parents (32–33). The following two parallel examples from the story illustrate this point particularly well:

> "Hund tot," flüsterte sie, als sie sich an mich lehnte. Ich legte meinen Arm um sie und sagte: "Alles ... alles gut."
> "Nein," sagte sie, "nix gut."
> "Ja," sagte ich, "vielleicht. Aber jetzt, du ... du bist ..."
> "Ja," sagte sie, "jetzt bin ich hier. Du gut." (26)

> ["Dog dead," she whispered as she leaned against me.
> I put my arm around her and said, "Everything ... everything's fine."
> "No," she said, "nothing fine."
> "Yes," I said, "maybe. But now, you ... you're ..."
> "Yes," she said, "now I'm here. You good."] (33–34)

> "Du auf mich aufpassen, kleiner Offizier, nein?"
> "Du ... du musst keine Angst mehr haben, Marika."
> "Ich habe gewartet, ich ..."
> "Jetzt bin ich wieder da."
> "Das ist gut." (29)

> ["You have to look after me, little officer, no?"
> "You ... you don't need to be scared any more, Marika."
> "I waited, I ..."
> "I'm here again now."
> "That's good."] (38–39)

Nothing is good, however, for two reasons: the blurring of space (here and elsewhere) and, above all, time (past and present), that is, the narrator's blurring of his memories of the short time spent with Marika in the mid-1990s and those of the other woman twenty years later,[60] bring to the fore the idea that that history is repeating itself, and it does not matter where in the world violence is happening. The result is the same: people flee and try to find safety in another country, away from violence.

In a way, the story's "elsewhere," only left vague as somewhere in the former Soviet Union, becomes an "everywhere," that is, a somewhat generic place where violence is happening and that people want or need to leave.[61] Thus the narrator comments, "Nichts hatte sich verändert.

---

60 See also Pye, "The Liminal Space," 132.

61 Lizzie Stewart commented during a September 2021 symposium on the topic of violence elsewhere that "elsewhere" could also be read as "everywhere"

Irgendwo war wieder ein Krieg, der sie zu mir zurückgebracht hatte"
(34; "Nothing had changed. Somewhere there was a war again, which
had brought her back to me," 46). Despite the safety that the narrator,
and Germany, hope to offer, we learn that Germany is not the safe haven
that those fleeing war might imagine, because racist attacks are part of
the reality of the residents of the hostel. They are also part of the narrator's life, if for different reasons, not least because his memory of seeing residents of the hostel, including the other woman who reminded
him of Marika, boarding a coach that would bring them to a different
place and to safety leads the narrator to recount his time with Marika
(30 and 36). What remains is the memory of the red-brown hair that, as
a sort of pars pro toto representing Marika, stands out in both the darkness and the narrator's loneliness. The broken glass of the title is partly a
reference to the end of the Cold War (the abandoned Russian barracks in
the 1990s) but also, importantly, to what has come after it; namely, the
violence and destruction caused by those racist attacks. The latter may
also remind readers of the Nazi pogroms, which are commonly associated
with this trope of broken glass. It is a reminder that violence against those
perceived as "other" are not only part of Germany's brutal past but that it
has become a part of Germany's present again.

We can thus conclude that violence is never really elsewhere—neither
temporally nor spatially—for Meyer's characters in *Die stillen Trabanten*.
It follows them in many ways; conflict is never resolved, and there cannot
be any closure. Perhaps we can read this insight as the narrator's epiphany
or realization at the end. Yet instead of changing his life,[62] this moment
only enabled the narrator to stand by passively, symbolically picking
up and then discarding one of the shards of glass of a window that was
smashed during an attack on the hostel or watching on as the migrants
were leaving.

Conclusion

The question remains as to how my reading of Meyer's story relates to
the alleged provincialism of German literature, and its simultaneous orientation toward world literature, with which I opened my chapter. This is
a particularly intriguing question considering my emphasis on the peripheral setting of Meyer's story and the outspokenly local position of his

---

in some of the contributions. Although Stewart made this comment more generally, rather than with specific reference to Meyer's story, her observation chimes
with my reading of it here.

62   Compare with Pratt's comment on the "moment-of-truth" in some short
stories, in "The Short Story," 99. See also May, *The Short Story*, 19.

characters. How does violence elsewhere come in here and disrupt this peripherality?

We can find an answer to this question in Meyer's thoughts on contemporary German literature, its aspirations and wider-reaching value, and his own relation to it. He writes, "Die Idee, gesellschaftliche Brüche als einen ganz normalen Steinbruch für eine (deutsche) Literatur zu sehen, ist anscheinend abhanden gekommen, biografisch/persönliches Klein-Klein, dazu banale Histörchen, biederes Erzählen, keine Reisen mehr ans Ende der Nacht oder meinetwegen an ihren Anfang!" (The idea of regarding the cracks in society as quite a normal quarry for a [German] literature has obviously been lost, biographical/personal insignificant stuff, plus banal little histories, tame storytelling, no more journeys to the end of the night or to its beginning, for all I care).[63] Meyer's presumed allusion to Louis-Ferdinand Céline's 1932 novel *Voyage au Bout de la Nuit* (*Journey to the End of the Night*, 1934) here allows him to criticize and to distance himself from his peers' writing that, according to the author, ignores, in terms of content as well as style and form, the social frictions and fractures in contemporary society as they are often played out at the social and geographical peripheries. Instead, as my analysis of "Glasscherben im Objekt 95" has demonstrated, it is through the formal possibilities of the short-story genre—which Meyer refers to as "Verknappung und zeitnahe Realitätsverdichtung" (tightening and timely compression of reality)[64]—that the author can draw our attention to those "gesellschaftliche Brüche," including those caused by violence elsewhere, that Meyer regards as the source for a literature that really matters and that is of concern to a wider social context.

Although readers do not explicitly read about violence elsewhere in "Glasscherben im Objekt 95," violence as a theme not only shapes the narrative, the encounter between the characters, and the setting on a formal level. It also enables Meyer to expose violent structures that have (re)emerged as a racist reaction of some against the unwanted presence of "others." And he can then dig deeper into the "normal quarry for a (German) literature" and expand the German literary canon with stories that go beyond the themes and "banal" narrative styles of which Meyer is so critical.

Furthermore, in the conscious interconnection between form and content in his stories, Meyer can respond effectively to the global concerns of our time from a local perspective and introduce his characters as globalized local subjectivities. Although his characters (apart from the refugees and a few others) may never or rarely leave their satellite towns, and so find themselves stuck in their local environs, they are not, as my

63   Meyer, "Wozu Literatur," 101.
64   Meyer, "Wozu Literatur," 109.

reading of "Glasscherben im Objekt 95" has shown, detached from or untouched by global developments and conflicts.[65] Returning to Meyer's assessment of world literature quoted earlier in this chapter, Meyer shows his readers how social peripheries become the center in his writing; how he gives them significance through conflict, including violence elsewhere; and how the short story as a form originating from "elsewhere" contributes to his endeavor to lend significance to his local characters with their specific experiences well beyond the German literary canon. Put differently, in his work Meyer demonstrates how, to lean on Djelal Kadir's words, "world literature has always had a translocal, supranational significance. That is, it has always reflected a particular view of the world."[66]

In his short-story writing Meyer comes across as one of those "writers who are aware of their roots, but who are also conscious of being part of a globalized world."[67] His authorial position goes hand in hand with that of his work because it reflects the entanglement of the locals who are at the center of his writing with the global, and this entanglement is mirrored in the literary form of the short story that dominates his writing. Thus, in his stories the global *is* very much in the local and vice versa. The peripheral spaces in Meyer's stories remind us that different forms of violence are entangled: violence may be removed from us—geographically, socially, politically—and thus be perceived to be elsewhere, but it is simultaneously very much here;[68] it may be in the past, but it has returned to the present. In that way, as I have demonstrated in this chapter, violence elsewhere becomes part of, disrupts, and, at least to an extent, reevaluates Meyer's stories' local worlds.

65   Compare again with my reading of the male characters in Zaimoglu's *Ruß* in *New Masculinities*, in which I make a connection between "being 'stuck'" and class (178).

66   Djelal Kadir, "World Literature: The Allophone, the Differential, and the Common," *Modern Language Quarterly* 74, no. 2 (June 2013): 293–306, here 294.

67   Mads Rosendahl Thomsen, *Mapping World Literature: International Canonization and Transnational Literatures* (London: Continuum, 2010), 54.

68   Lizzie Stewart, in her contribution to this volume, similarly questions the boundaries between "here" and "there." Drawing on Trinh T. Minh-ha's book *elsewhere, within here: immigration, refugeeism, and the boundary event* (New York: Routledge, 2011), Stewart speaks of "entanglement" of "here" and "elsewhere": "What looks like division is, in fact, entanglement, but one in which a particular positionality is given dominance. The 'elsewhere' is thus a relational term." Stewart, "Violence 'Elsewhere, within Here': Artistic Engagement in Armenian Remembrance at 'Location Germany.'"

8: The Entangled Mess of the Embodied Elsewhere in Luca Guadagnino's *Suspiria* (2018)

Francesca Lewis

> In these troubling times, the urgency to trouble time, to shake it to its core, and to produce collective imaginaries that undo pervasive conceptions of temporality that take progress as inevitable and the past as something that has passed and is no longer with us, is something so tangible, so visceral that there is a sense in which it can be felt in our individual and collective bodies.[1]

IN THIS QUOTATION from a 2017 article, feminist new materialist Karen Barad asks us to "produce collective imaginaries" that present embodied, collective, nonlinear experiences of time. The past, Barad assures us, is not simply "passed," as in gone, no longer with us. Neither is future progress inevitable. These notions have important resonance with what Clare Bielby and Mererid Puw Davies have conceptualized as "violence elsewhere," since the notion of elsewhere is so often also elsewhen.[2] Responses to calls for political change are often "that was in the past," when colonial histories are raised; or "that won't happen for many years," when the urgency of climate crisis is invoked. Toward a better understanding of the kind of nonlinear and embodied temporality Barad asks us to imagine, I will here consider Luca Guadagnino's 2018 film *Suspiria*, a remake of Dario Argento's 1977 cult horror film of the same name.[3]

I will argue that *Suspiria* produces "collective imaginaries that undo pervasive conceptions of temporality" by making Germany's complex history of violence, guilt, perpetration, and trauma tangible, visceral, felt, and

---

1   Karen Barad, "Troubling time/s and ecologies of nothingness: re-turning, re-membering, and facing the incalculable," *New Formations: A Journal of Culture/Theory/Politics* 92 (2018): 56–86, here 57.

2   Clare Bielby and Mererid Puw Davies, "Introduction," in *Violence Elsewhere 1: Imagining Distant Violence in Germany 1945–2001*, ed. Clare Bielby and Mererid Puw Davies (Rochester, NY: Camden House, 2024), 1–17.

3   *Suspiria*, directed by Dario Argento (20th Century Fox, 1977); *Suspiria*, directed by Luca Guadagnino (Amazon Studios, 2018).

embodied. I begin by outlining this chapter's diffractive approach, arguing that this feminist new materialist methodology is particularly suited to speculative genres like supernatural horror and explicitly interested in both the deconstruction and the reimagining of elsewheres. I discuss the critical reception of Guadagnino's film and argue that critics' accusations of messiness and lack of political clarity in the film's invocations of Germany's history of violence miss the messy entanglement of affects and agencies that Barad calls for us to understand. I next outline the plots of both Argento's original 1977 film and Guadagnino's 2018 remake, highlighting where the latter deviates from genre conventions in its attribution of violent and morally complex, rather than heroic and morally pure, agency to its female protagonist. I then analyze key scenes of the film to highlight how they give us insight into the way collective affects and agencies can be both messily entangled and violent. Throughout this discussion I focus on how *Suspiria* (2018) troubles linear temporality through these embodiments, creating space for mapping and questioning the ways history, agency, and responsibility intersect.

This reading argues that Guadagnino's use of dance, magic, and dreams articulates how violence operates in collective space, queering ideas of bounded individuality and the very notions of then/now, here/there, inside/outside. Within *Suspiria*, individual responsibility and blame become difficult to assign, and we are left disoriented. I argue that this very disorientation can in itself be productive of an agency that emerges from the encounter, from the in-between, rather than from personal will. Finally, I explore this kind of agency through the character of Josef Klemperer, who plays the role of witness in the film, as a character who sits outside the main action, as a psychotherapist, and as an old man who has lived through the many violent upheavals of twentieth-century Berlin. Ultimately, this chapter argues that Guadagnino's *Suspiria* offers a meaningful text to think and feel through and with toward an understanding of violence as never elsewhere, or elsewhen, but always here—always embodied, always collective, and always bound up with others.

Diffraction, Intra-action, and The Speculative Elsewhere

Diffraction as a feminist methodology was first proposed by feminist new materialist philosopher Donna Haraway in her 1992 essay "The Promises of Monsters: A Regenerative Politics for Inappropriate/d Others."[4] In

---

4   Donna Haraway, "The Promises of Monsters: A Regenerative Politics for Inappropriate/d Others," in *Cultural Studies*, ed. Lawrence Grossberg, Cary Nelson, and Paula A. Treichler (New York: Routledge, Taylor & Francis, 1992), 295–336.

classical physics, diffraction is a phenomenon that occurs when light waves are interrupted by an obstacle and make a patterning of light and shadow. Haraway took this definition and imagined diffraction as "a mapping of interference, not of replication, reflection, or reproduction" that "does not map where differences appear, but rather maps where the effects of difference appear."[5] Diffraction became a method of attending to processes and their impact on human and nonhuman, social and material bodies. As an alternative to the binary logic of reflection, Haraway wanted diffraction to orient us in the hostile territory of a world that taxonomizes people according to supposed inherent difference. Diffraction can trouble taken-for-granted binary distinctions, allowing the copresence of the scientific and speculative, fictional and factual. This makes it especially applicable to a film like *Suspiria*, where historical events and supernatural powers are not opposed but intertwined.

The "optical features" of Haraway's diffraction "are set to produce not effects of distance, but effects of connection, of embodiment, and of responsibility for an imagined elsewhere that we may yet learn to see and build here."[6] Instead of vision, or imagination as a kind of vision, taking us further away from what we see, as in the classical idea of objectivity, looking brings us closer, so close that we are caught up in it. Haraway's use of diffraction is an example of figuration. Similar to a metaphor, figuration is an articulatory practice that emphasizes the mapping of action, processes, and movement over the reflection of identity or essence. "Figurations," Haraway writes, "are performative images that can be inhabited. Verbal or visual, figurations can be condensed maps of contestable worlds."[7]

In their 2007 book *Meeting the Universe Halfway*,[8] and in numerous publications since, Barad has built upon Haraway's diffractive proposition, in their case drawing from a background in quantum physics, to propose the method of diffractive reading:

---

5   Haraway, "The Promises of Monsters," 300.

6   Haraway, "The Promises of Monsters," 300. In her hugely influential essay "Situated Knowledges," Haraway describes a feminist way of working that rethinks "objectivity" as embodied and embedded positionality, against the idea of the scientific "gaze from nowhere" and toward greater responsibility and accountability in academic work. Donna Haraway, "Situated Knowledges: The Science Question in Feminism and the Privilege of Partial Perspective," *Feminist Studies* 14, no. 3 (Autumn 1988): 575–99, here 581.

7   Donna Haraway, *Modest_Witness@Second_Millennium: FemaleMan_Meets_OncoMouse; Feminism and Technoscience* (London: Routledge, 1997), 11.

8   Karen Barad, *Meeting the Universe Halfway: Quantum Physics and the Entanglement of Meaning and Matter* (London: Duke University Press, 2007).

Diffraction, understood using quantum physics, is not just a matter of interference, but of entanglement, an ethico-onto-epistemological matter.... Instead of there being a separation of subject and object, there is an entanglement of subject and object, which is called the "phenomenon." Objectivity, instead of being about offering an undistorted mirror image of the world, is about accountability to marks on bodies, and responsibility to the entanglement of which we are a part.[9]

Barad calls this diffractive entanglement "intra-action": the way that objects, bodies, and agents are always already entangled; not separate and discrete entities interacting but part of the interwoven processes from which emergent phenomena are produced. Both events and agencies have no fixed properties but emerge from encounters as always contingent phenomena. Diffractive reading reads events, experiences, and theories through each other, making what Haraway might call "a map of tensions and resonances."[10]

This chapter attempts to produce such a map of the tensions and resonances between the concept of violence elsewhere and Guadagnino's film. Haraway wanted diffraction "to orient, to provide the roughest sketch for travel" through the territory of representation and mastery to "a science fictional, speculative factual, SF place called, simply, elsewhere."[11] From the beginning, then, diffraction and the elsewhere are linked. Diffraction can disrupt the common-sense binary of fact versus fiction and, as Haraway writes, provide a map for finding that imagined elsewhere. This elsewhere is not a projection or a distancing trick; quite the opposite. Haraway wanted diffraction to produce connection, embodiment, and responsibility, which for Haraway is always "response-ability," the capacity to respond. I take these principles both as modus operandi and as concepts to think with in my exploration of *Suspiria* and violence elsewhere.

The horror genre is, like all speculative genres (such as science fiction and fantasy), its own kind of elsewhere. It can produce work that is deeply interested in difference, in the Other, in what has been considered abject. In supernatural horror, these themes are explored through the introduction of unreality, a world where the impossible is possible, where irrational fears come to life. Sometimes, supernatural horror film can operate as an imagined elsewhere, showing us a world that, though it may share features with our own, seems fundamentally unreal. Though

---

9   Karen Barad, "Interview with Karen Barad," in *New Materialism: Interviews & Cartographies*, ed. Rick Dolphijn and Iris van der Tuin (Ann Arbor, MI: Open Humanities Press, 2012), 48–70, here 52.

10   Haraway, "Situated Knowledges," 588.

11   Haraway, "The Promises of Monsters," 295.

these films often leave much space for political readings, they rarely feature explicit depictions of real-life history and politics. Instead, the violence is projected onto an abject elsewhere—a creature or place that does not exist—and any real-world political resonances operate purely at the level of metaphor. This, I will argue, is what Argento's 1977 *Suspiria* does. Alternatively, horror film can produce a different kind of elsewhere, one where rational fears are figured through images of the unreal, diffractively mapping the entangled and intra-active nature of history and violence, the processes and phenomena at work. This kind of elsewhere, I will argue, is what Guadagnino produces with his reimagining of *Suspiria*, allowing for a more collective, less individualized idea of horror and a queering of the many taken-for-granted distinctions that underpin our ideas of then and now, here and there, me and you, hero and villain, victim and monster. As such, the film demands responsiveness, openness, willingness to see meaning as "an ongoing performance of the world in its differential dance of intelligibility and unintelligibility."[12]

The "Differential Dance of Intelligibility and Unintelligibility": *Suspiria*'s Entangled Mess

The critical and audience reception of Guadagnino's *Suspiria* was extremely polarized. This highly stylized film about a young woman dancer becoming caught up in witchcraft features graphic and disturbing scenes of violence. This alone would not surprise critics, as in the horror genre such scenes are not unusual. What seems to have invited the heavy dose of critique the film received is, rather, the film's setting of 1970s West Berlin and its invocation of serious real-world politics. Richard Brody of *The New Yorker* felt that *Suspiria* "has nothing to say about women's history, feminist politics, civil violence, the Holocaust, the Cold War, or German culture. Instead, Guadagnino thrusts some thusly labelled trinkets at viewers and suggests that they try to assemble them."[13] Many other reviews, whether positive or negative, included words like "messy," "muddled," and "confounding." These critical responses reveal the way that we tend to view art and cinema as representational, expecting it to reflect a fixed preexisting reality. These critics expected the film to work as a mirror, missing the ways in which—as I argue in this chapter—it can be understood as a map. Film and literature scholar Luke Lewin Davies argues that Guadagnino, through a "mistaken belief" in the power of

12   Haraway, "The Promises of Monsters," 295.

13   Richard Brody, "Luca Guadagnino's 'Suspiria' Is the Cinematic Equivalent of a Designer Che T-Shirt," *New Yorker*, October 30, 2018, https://www.newyorker.com/culture/the-front-row/review-luca-guadagninos-suspiria-is-the-cinematic-equivalent-of-a-designer-che-t-shirt.

the abject feminine, "ensures that rather than harnessing the seductive and terrifying power of horror, powerless remnants of abjectness instead *undermine and confuse the film's intended message*" (my italics).[14] Davies speaks here of an intended message and of confusion, again suggesting an expectation of clarity and an unwillingness to think with messiness.

All of the ways in which the film references historic and contemporary violence and conflict, both explicit and implicit, raise questions about how appropriate it is to engage with such complex and difficult topics in a piece of entertainment. The messiness of the film makes for a disorienting experience, and the audience can be left feeling that there are uncomfortable implications to some of what unfolds on-screen. *Suspiria* features much accurate and clearly researched period detail alongside pulp horror tropes, a juxtaposition that in itself might strike some viewers as troubling. The inclusion of fact blended with fiction, and the ambiguity of many characters' motivations and actions, can furthermore seem to absolve real-life perpetrators. I do not want to refute these responses but to ask that we do not allow them to shut down any interest in engaging critically with this unique text. If we treat *Suspiria* as a film about West German terrorism or the legacy of National Socialism or even recent contemporary violence and discourse, we reduce it to a mere representation of past events, to a "message" about the past.

Thinking with Barad and their focus on phenomena over identities, I contend that it is important to consider not what the film says but what it does. Rather than seeing Guadagnino's *Suspiria* as a metaphor for a particular conflict or expecting it to didactically deliver a political or cultural statement, I am interested in how the film might be understood as an articulation rather than a representation. A representation, according to philosophers Gilles Deleuze and Félix Guattari, is a tracing of an object it attempts to copy. Rather than tracing, Deleuze and Guattari recommend mapping, which can focus on the processes involved, on what is between objects, on movement. Articulation is such a mapping of a process.[15] Haraway writes that "articulation must remain open, its densities accessible to action and intervention. When the system of connections closes in on itself, when symbolic action becomes perfect, the world is frozen in a dance of death."[16] When we expect metaphor from a text, reading each object as standing in for another analogous one, we may be missing the way parts of the text function as figurations, as ways of exploring process

14 Luke Lewin Davies, "Appropriating the Abject: Witchcraft in Dario Argento and Daria Nicolodi's *Suspiria* (1977) and David Kajganich and Luca Guadagnino's 2018 Remake," *New Cinemas* 18, no 1–2 (2020): 43–59, here 56.

15 Gilles Deleuze and Félix Guattari, *A Thousand Plateaus*, trans. Brian Massumi (London: Bloomsbury, 2013).

16 Haraway, "The Promises of Monsters," 327.

and phenomena. *Suspiria* can help us understand historical violence and our own present entanglements and agencies, articulating how they operate and asking us to consider what may become possible, what futures we are opening up with our collective, embodied intra-actions.

From Representation to Articulation: Supernatural Horror Meets Political History

Argento, an Italian filmmaker, set his *Suspiria* in Germany, with an international cast speaking in their own languages, dubbed into English (a common practice in Italian cinema of the period). It was released in 1977, and though no reference is made to the time period, it can be assumed from period details (clothing, cars, and so on) that it is intended to be set in 1977. The film tells the story of Suzy Bannion, a young ballet dancer from the US who comes to Freiburg, West Germany, to join a dance school. After one of the dancers is brutally murdered, Suzy experiences a series of bizarre occurrences at the school, such as hearing strange breathing in the night and maggots falling from the ceiling. She forms an alliance with another dancer, Sara, who has also noticed that something odd seems to be going on. When Sara goes missing, Suzy consults an occult expert, Professor Milius, who tells her that the school is run by a coven of witches who derive their power from their leader, Helena Markos, whom Suzy has never seen. Back at the dance school, Suzy attempts to investigate the coven, following clues she obtained from Sara, and eventually finds Markos sleeping in the basement, her heavy breathing dominating the sound mix. When Suzy accidentally breaks an ornamental peacock, Markos awakens, and Suzy sees her gray and unnatural, corpse-like face for the first time. The two struggle; Suzy triumphs, killing Markos with the broken ornament. As Suzy flees into the rainy night, the building begins to collapse and is consumed in flames. The plot of Argento's film is typical of supernatural horror, where fairy tales often directly or indirectly inspire the events and characters, and is not what gained the film its cult-classic status. Rather, it is Argento's use of unusual and arresting sound and visuals that create a dreamlike atmosphere for this dark, violent, at times absurd fairytale.

Guadagnino, also Italian and best known for his 2017 adaptation of queer coming-of-age romance *Call Me by Your Name*, reimagines *Suspiria*. Though his adaptation shares roughly the same plot, setting, characters, and language (though not dubbed) as Argento's, Guadagnino made many choices in style and content to differentiate his adaptation from the source text. Where Argento's film is a lavishly colorful and dreamlike gothic horror movie, full of stylized violence and very little dance for a film set at a dance school, Guadagnino's *Suspiria* uses stark desaturated visuals and body horror and makes the dancing integral to the story and themes. These changes make the film's extensive modern dance scenes—which are also the scenes in which violence happens—visceral and disturbing. Though both films are set in the year 1977, Guadagnino relocates the setting to West Berlin, placing the dance school, where most of the action occurs, right next to the Berlin Wall, so that the wall itself becomes a constant presence in the film.

Guadagnino's film begins with a title card that reads, "Amazon Studios and K Period Media Present Six Acts and an Epilogue Set in Divided Berlin" in text stylized to evoke the look of Soviet-era poster art. This explicit reference to six acts and an epilogue is unconventional. Drawing attention to the constructed nature of the film, it evokes Brechtian theater and suggests that this will be a more serious viewing experience than horror audiences may be used to. Being specific about "divided" Berlin, rather than simply saying the film is set in Berlin, sets up the idea from the start that the picture is aware of and interested in sociopolitical locatedness, as well as other connotations of division: conflict, binaries.

Suspiria's opening moments further emphasize that this will not be a typical supernatural horror film, where any real-world resonance is purely metaphorical. The setting of West Berlin in 1977 is no mere backdrop. We see the smoke-filled streets of Berlin and hear the sounds of just-off-camera protests ringing out. We see a girl running with a backpack as she passes riot police and protesters with signs and flags. The camera does not follow the protest; it is elsewhere. We continue to follow the young girl, Patricia Hingle. We will learn later that she is a member of a local world-famous dance company, led by the charismatic Madame Blanc. Patricia runs into a building to bang on the door of her psychotherapist, Klemperer, who is not expecting her visit. Patricia is agitated, paranoid, singing a song she cannot get out of her head. She speaks of being groomed by a group of witches, of them giving her "perfect balance, perfect sleep" in the beginning, then later taking her hair, her urine, watching her through her own eyes. She speaks of a Mother Markos: "She wants to get inside of me." Klemperer makes notes about delusions and panic. At the end of the session, Patricia flees into the night, and the audience does not see her again until the film's climactic final scenes.

We are now introduced to our protagonist, Susie, a naive dancer from a strict religious background who leaves her Mennonite family in Ohio to pursue her dreams of dancing in Madame Blanc's company.[17] We follow her from the train station to the dance company's imposing building. The word "Tanz" (dance) is stenciled in black block spray-painted letters

---

17 Argento and Guadagnino spell their protagonists' names Suzy and Susie, respectively.

above its monumental entrance, which directly faces the Berlin Wall. The camera, slowly panning until now, is still as Susie stops on the threshold, looking up at the giant building, tiny and fragile in comparison. We might think at this point that the violence outside the school will be contrasted with the feminine world of the dance company, suggesting the binaries of the masculine world of violence and politics against the feminine world of dance and the arts, or of dangerous exterior/safe interior. As the film goes on, however, these binary distinctions, and many more, become meaningfully complicated and messy.

Susie auditions for Madame Blanc and impresses with her strange, animalistic dancing. Though she has no formal dance training, Susie quickly rises up the ranks of the company. She also begins another, more subtle and supernatural, transformation into a powerful witch. When one of the dancers, Olga, accuses the leaders of the company of being involved with Patricia's disappearance, she is brutally beaten by an unseen force as Susie dances. It is hard to tell who, if anyone, is responsible for this violence, and I will return to this scene in more depth later. The witches telepathically vote the as-yet-unseen Markos as their formal leader and conspire to use Susie as a vessel for her spirit, since her ancient body is dying. Susie becomes the star of the company, taking the lead role in their dance performance *Volk*, choreographed by Blanc.

Klemperer, having noticed Patricia's disappearance, attempts to investigate what is happening at the dance school. After trying to involve the authorities, he eventually joins forces with Sara, another dancer who has become suspicious of the disappearing dancers and strange events at the school. He explains to Sara that the dance school is run by women who consider themselves witches. Though he does not believe they have supernatural power, he does believe that they are a dangerous organization:

> Klemperer: You can give someone your delusion, Sara. That's religion. That is the Reich. The Reich had these things: insignia, esoteric ritual. These mothers, they could be code names for founding members with metaphorical histories. I don't know. But I do know you are living with dangerous people.

Klemperer is referring here to the "Third Reich." Having lived through the Second World War, and having studied psychology, Klemperer does not underestimate the women of the dance school. In their tactics and rhetoric he sees hallmarks of manipulation and control. He tells Sara that from what he has learned from Patricia, the witches worship three mothers: Mother Tenebrarum (Mother of Darkness), Mother Lachrymarum (Mother of Tears), and Mother Suspiriorum (Mother of Sighs).

Both Sara and Klemperer are punished by the witches for their interference. They find Sara snooping in the basement during a dance event and break her leg, magically fix it, then put her into a trance that forces her to dance in the performance taking place upstairs. They send Klemperer a vision of his long-lost wife, Anke, who has been missing, presumed dead, since the war. It now seems that Anke has returned, alive and well, and she and Klemperer have a romantic walk in the snow before she disappears, revealing her to be a witch's trick. The witches kidnap the devastated Klemperer, taunting him—"You had years to get your wife out of Berlin before the arrests began!"—and force him to take part in their final ritual as a witness, as they put it.

In the film's bloody climax, Susie is brought in to be sacrificed, looking strangely at peace with the bizarre display in front of her. The witches, naked and chanting, dance as they disembowel the half-dead and entranced Patricia, Olga, and Sara. In a surprising turn, Susie reveals that she will not become a vessel for Markos, who finally appears, her ancient and decrepit form waiting eagerly to be reborn. We learn that Susie herself is in fact Mother Suspiriorum. The audience is given no indication of how long this has been the case, or how long Susie has known this. Susie summons a shadowy ghoul to kill Markos and her followers. Klemperer is released into the night, dazed and confused. In the epilogue, Susie/Mother Suspiriorum visits Klemperer, apologizes for what was done to him by the witches, and offers him the truth as a consolation: his wife was killed in the Holocaust. Much is left ambiguous: What do the witches represent, is Susie good or evil, are Klemperer and his wife Jewish? I will return in the final sections of this chapter to that last question, but first, shifting my thinking from representation to figuration, I want to address what exactly the witches might articulate.

Suspiria is set during the so-called German Autumn of 1977, during which far-left militant organizations, most prominently the Red Army Faction (RAF), carried out a series of terrorist actions. These included the RAF kidnapping of businessman and former SS member Hanns Martin Schleyer and the hijacking of Lufthansa Flight 181 by the Popular Front for the Liberation of Palestine (PFLP). The political unrest of this period is ever-present, though never directly seen in the film. We hear protests and explosions taking place just off camera, and radio news reports often play diegetically in the background or are played nondiegetically over transitional scenes and montages that figure the passage of time. The characters discuss the situation, but we never see any of these real historical events depicted onscreen. Yet the political unrest outside is much more than a backdrop. The political events of the day are at first implicitly framed as taking place "elsewhere," by the way the camera in the opening sequence follows Patricia and not the protest. We are soon told, however, that certain dancers in the company sympathize with the cause of the RAF, particularly Patricia, whom the witches suggest left to join the group. This initially seems like a lie to cover up the witches' crimes, but we later see that Patricia's journal, which she left behind at Klemperer's office, is full of scribbles about the RAF and about the witches, side by side.

Sara, too, directly expresses sympathy for and potential involvement in some of the radical action happening outside. Early in the film, after being accepted by the dance company, Susie gathers her belongings in her hotel room. Sara arrives to help her move to the dance studio, where the dancers also live. As the two talk, they hear a loud bang outside. Sara rushes to the window and throws it open, in an ambiguous state of agitation or excitement, leaning out into the pouring rain. "It's a bomb," she says, "I can smell it." Revolution is in the air, and Sara wants Susie to understand what is happening. Referring to the imprisoned RAF members and the PFLP members calling for their freedom, Sara says, "The hijackers are negotiating a release for the Stammheim prisoners tonight. There are riots. The RAF? Baader-Meinhof?" Susie admits sheepishly that she does not know who the group is. "They kidnapped an executive. During the war he was Nazi SS. An officer. Now he runs the German Employer's Association. [Sara pauses] You don't get how awful that is, do you?"

In this same scene, when we are primed by Sara's interest in the RAF to think about terrorism and the appeal that joining a terrorist group might have for a young person (excitement, agency, perhaps the attention of a charismatic leader), Sara speaks reverently of the dance company's choreographer, describing Madame Blanc's energy as "addictive." Blanc is a leader whom the dancers admire, one who inspires a strong affective response. A thread begins here that runs through the whole of *Suspiria*, bringing the world of dance and witches into conversation with the world of politics and radical action. This relationship is not one of mirroring, which those who saw the film's messiness as a failing had expected to see. *Suspiria* troubles time, as Barad called us to do, and does not use the witches to represent the terrorism of 1970s Germany or the fascism of the Nazis or even present-day neofascism on the rise in the West, but to articulate how the violence of all of these contexts is entangled, embodied, messy.

The "Lively Dance of Mattering":[18]
Suspiria's Entangled (Dis)orientations

We take shape through our orientations. The things around us work as "orientation devices," situating us in space and in ourselves.[19] "Disorientation as a bodily feeling," writes feminist philosopher and affect theorist Sara Ahmed, "can be unsettling, and it can shatter one's sense of confidence in the ground or one's belief that the ground on which we reside can support the actions that make a life feel livable."[20] When disoriented, we are unsure of our surroundings and of ourselves. As phenomenologist Maurice Merleau-Ponty writes, disorientation "produces not only the intellectual experience of disorder, but the vital experience of giddiness and nausea, which is the awareness of our own contingency and the horror with which it fills us."[21] When disoriented, we become horrified by the realization that without an orientation device, we are not only nowhere but nothing.

Dance, magic, and dreams in *Suspiria* are, crucially, all *collective* acts. They are things the witches do together, sharing their bodies and psyches. As Patricia tells us in her therapy session with Klemperer, at first she was given gifts by the witches, including "perfect balance"—presumably for dancing, but perhaps also for a feeling of equilibrium. As well as an early hint at the seductiveness of being singled out for greatness by charismatic leadership, this scene also highlights an important aspect of the embodied experience that unfolds onscreen in *Suspiria*. Balance is pivotal in dance and is, of course, a faculty that relies on orientation; we can balance because we know which way is up and which is down. For Patricia, then, the witches are orientational. They granted her the boon of being able to understand her orientation in time and space, which is to say, her place in the world, where she belongs, and what is possible for her in that space. Patricia may have her perfect balance, but it means relying on the witches to keep her on her feet.

---

18   Barad, *Meeting the Universe Halfway*, 37. Barad uses this phrase to describe the interwoven "material differences, relationalities, and entanglements" of their book. I use it here in part because it is one of two instances in which Barad uses the concept of dance in reference to entangled agencies, something Haraway also does—and these other instances appear in some of the subheadings of this chapter. The figuration of dance as one of implicitly and explicitly negotiated and affect-laden agencies is threaded through this chapter.

19   Sara Ahmed, *Queer Phenomenology: Orientations, Objects, Others* (London: Duke University Press, 2006).

20   Ahmed, *Queer Phenomenology*, 157.

21   Maurice Merleau-Ponty, *Phenomenology of Perception*, trans. Colin Smith (London: Routledge, 2002), 296.

In Klemperer's office, Patricia behaves as if the witches can see her, and the film's use of sound and camera movement suggest that she is not delusional in this belief. The camera lingers on photographs in the room as if the witches are present in or through them, watching. It seems the dancers are never alone, deeply intertwined with the witches, and, through them, with each other. The witches can communicate telepathically, one witch's voice materializing inside the body of another, and when the dancers sleep, they share dreams. Madame Blanc tells Susie, "When you dance the dance of another ... You empty yourself so that her work can live within you." Orientation as possession. In the context of a horror film about witches, it is easy to read this transgressing of bodily or ontological boundaries as merely an evocation of the supernatural horror trope of body horror, part of the inescapable power of the witches as movie monsters. If we hold these ideas more lightly, there is room here for thinking with Barad's intra-action, reminding us that agents and actors are always already bound up with each other. We balance each other, we need each other. We are each other's orientation devices. And sometimes, as for Patricia, that *feels* horrific.

As a text, *Suspiria* moves beyond merely depicting or representing disorientation, in two ways. First, it uses figurations like dance, dreams, and magic to articulate how disorientation operates, how it affects us. Second, it extends the sense of intersubjectivity it articulates beyond the screen, so that what emerges between the dancers resonates on an affective level for the viewer. Watching *Suspiria*, we too are disoriented. Dance theorist Deidre Sklar proposes an embodied engagement with dance performance, which she calls "empathic kinaesthetic perception."[22] As a more affectively attuned way of looking, or witnessing, "a combination of mimesis and empathy," empathic kinaesthetic perception involves shifting away from objective visual perception from a distance to a more connected and embodied experience, akin to Haraway's diffractive approach. "This kind of 'connected knowing,'" argues Sklar, "produces a very intimate kind of knowledge, a taste of those ineffable movement experiences that can't be easily put into words." This experience "produces not a blurry merger but an articulated perception of differences."[23] Again like Haraway, Sklar here considers connected knowing to be integral to articulating or mapping difference—or as Haraway would put it, articulating where the effects of difference appear. For the viewer of *Suspiria*, a

---

22 Deidre Sklar, "Five Premises for a Culturally Sensitive Approach to Dance," in *Moving History/Dancing Cultures: A Dance History Reader*, ed. Ann Cooper Albright and Ann Dils (Middletown, CT: Wesleyan University Press, 2001), 30–32.

23 Sklar, "Five Premises," 32.

felt experience of disorientation may allow them to more deeply perceive what is felt when violence is enacted within the collective.

Of course, dancing, dreaming, and casting spells could have been used to stand in for violence, without ever including any actual depictions of violent acts within the film. These embodiments of affect, particularly the long and hypnotic scenes of dancing, work very well to suggest the seductiveness of power—whether that is the power to manipulate others, or the power of belonging. Interestingly, for this to be a supernatural horror film, for this to chill and thrill, there need be no direct physical violence. Guadagnino could have used choreography alone as an "else-where," a place to project discomfort upon, a place where the abject is kept at arm's length. *Suspiria*, however, does not keep violence at arm's length, and this dancing is no mere metaphor. Here dance does not *represent* violence, it *articulates* what violence *does*, how it *operates*.

In the first scene that shows how dance and violence work together in this way, Susie replaces Olga to become the new star of the company. Olga is angry at the witches' complacency at (or complicity in) the disappearance of Patricia, who has not been seen since she fled Klemperer's office in distress. Olga storms out of the dance studio, and Susie volunteers to take her place as the protagonist of the dance they are rehearsing. She is asked to run through the performance alone, to show Blanc that she is capable and knows the choreography, as the rest of the company looks on. Susie dances a strange, animal, and otherworldly dance that seems effortless for her. As she dances, Olga flees to the basement and finds herself trapped in a mirrored room. Already upset, she frantically tries to escape the room and is thrown around by an unseen force, her limbs contorting and her bones breaking. The editing, which makes use of cross-cutting to switch back and forth between Susie's dance and Olga's brutalization, seems to suggest that Susie's movements are inflicting this horrifying violence on Olga's body. Susie's expression makes it very difficult to discern whether she is aware of or even somehow causing what is happening to Olga, and the meaningful looks exchanged by the witches suggest that they could be responsible, though the overall effect is of confounding ambiguity. There is something deliberate about Susie's movements, a sense of intent, of imbuing the dance with something more than its technical steps. Despite this sense of intentionality, it is unclear what Susie knows or sees, how aware she is of inflicting violence on Olga.

We might even ask if she *is* inflicting violence. The film makes use of our expectation that cross-cutting creates a relationship between two events. We might read this as Guadagnino using filmic language to communicate that Susie is causing Olga's pain. Or we might read this as a metacinematic gesture, one that says "the editing is telling you that Susie is hurting Olga, but is she?" It is undeniable that with every forceful movement of Susie's body, Olga responds as if pushed by an unseen force.

Yet how much we can say Susie is the cause of Olga's injuries is ambiguous. This is further complicated by a very subtle special effect, visible for only a moment before Susie begins to dance. Blanc touches Susie's hands and feet and we glimpse what looks like a trace of light or energy seeping into Susie. This very easy to miss moment seems to suggest that Blanc has put some kind of spell on or power in Susie (even the difference between these two possibilities has very different implications for Susie's level of agency here), but the audience has no idea what intent, if any, is behind this little glimmer of light, gone in an instant. The unseen forces of magic are very hard to track. Different members of the company seem to have different levels of awareness of the magic that is manifesting, differing levels of guilt or enjoyment of the violence, and the room ripples with myriad affects as Susie dances. Based on the consequences of her actions, we might say that Susie is oriented toward Olga here, because her every action is mirrored by some new injury inflicted on Olga's body. As the dance comes to a frantic and unexpected end, however, and Susie loses balance, falling down, Madame Blanc tells her, "It'll pass. You're not the only dancer who lost the room." Did Susie become lost in a collective wave of affect that was also a collective act of violence?

The viewer is left wondering if our innocent protagonist is, in fact, a villain. This scene shows how doing violence, witnessing evil, and experiencing trauma are messily entangled, frustratingly and horrifyingly so. The violence is present and yet invisible, far away and yet reverberating in the air. Through the cross-cutting, we as viewers are disoriented—impressed by Susie's dance talent, horrified by Olga's brutalization, intrigued by the power we cannot quite pinpoint. Are the witches doing this? Is Susie? Are they using her energy somehow, or influencing her, or did they imbue her with power and these actions are her own? Who is responsible for this, who is the perpetrator? Should we be concerned for Susie or afraid of what she might do next?

These questions articulate the real dilemmas that face us when violence is perpetrated within a community. Our intersubjectivity makes ascertaining who is to blame, who is the real perpetrator, almost impossible. Political theorist Ashley Biser describes how difficult it is to orientate ourselves in violent times. Our "inner compass," as Hannah Arendt called it, becomes confused.[24] "As political actors," says Biser, "we are continually acting into (and thus located within) a swiftly changing world that

---

24 Hannah Arendt, "Understanding and Politics," in *Essays in Understanding: 1930–1954*, ed. Jerome Kohn (New York: Harcourt Brace, 1994), 307–27, here 323.

makes it difficult to find our sense of direction."[25] We "take our bearings" from the world around us, and that world includes other people.

Issues of agency, action, and morality are intrinsically linked to (dis)orientation. *Suspiria* demonstrates how interdependent we often are, especially in times of great upheaval when we may be even more likely to look for the stabilizing support of the collective. When this support produces instead a feeling of disorientation, or a paradoxical feeling of both balancing and falling, moral agency can be disrupted or confused. It is important to remember, however, as Ami Harbin argues, that though disorientation is usually understood as "a threat" to moral agency, "experiences of bodily disorientation can strengthen the moral agency of individuals" because they "allow for shifts in attention that cultivate morally productive reflection."[26] Like any affective experience, disorientation is not inherently good or bad. A bodily sensation of fear, felt as heightened awareness and coursing adrenaline, might lead a person to lash out at perceived dangers or to make more empathetic decisions. When we become disoriented, by shifting ground or uncertain times, "the point," as Ahmed writes, "is what we do with such moments of disorientation."[27]

The horrors of intersubjectivity are not the only embodied and ambiguous disorientations in *Suspiria*. The film's title means "sighs" in Latin, and Argento's film features a memorable scene in which the dance students sleep, while the impossibly loud and otherworldly heavy breathing of Mother Markos can be heard from below. In Guadagnino's film, the motif of audible breath is ever-present. His *Suspiria* begins with Susie's mother's labored wheezing as she lies on her deathbed—the situation Susie has left behind to pursue her dancing destiny in Berlin. This early scene sets up an audio motif of breath sounds, with either nondiegetic breathing serving to soundtrack certain scenes, or the diegetic breath of dancers accentuated in the sound mixing. The process of breathing brings the outside inside and takes the inside outside, as we inhale air from our environment, transform its composition within our bodies, then exhale it back to the environment, changed by the process of our breathing. The witches' magic, though it may result in impossibly shared dreams and telepathic communications, requires very tangible and embodied rituals involving movement, breath, hair, and urine to achieve these incorporeal connections. These articulations of what Stacy Alaimo calls "trans-corporeality" challenge inside/outside, me/you, body/nature, mind/matter

25   Ashley Biser, "Calibrating Our 'Inner Compass': Arendt on Thinking and the Dangers of Disorientation," *Political Theory* 42, no. 5 (2014): 519–42, here 522.

26   Ami Harbin, "Bodily Disorientation and Moral Change," *Hypatia* 27, no. 2 (Spring 2012): 261–80, here 262, 263, 265.

27   Ahmed, *Queer Phenomenology*, 158.

boundaries.[28] The figuration of the breath, a phenomenon both invisible and entirely material that, much like the dancing, dreaming, and magical practices in the film, connotes both the ineffable/spiritual and the limits of the body, troubles the division between corporeal and incorporeal.

The dancers being so trans-corporeally entangled means that it is not always clear how they are affected, how they are moved, what it is that drives them. As Ahmed writes, "in moving this way rather than that, and moving in this way again and again, the surfaces of bodies in turn acquire their shape. Bodies are 'directed' and they take the shape of this direction."[29] Olga's body, for example, appears to literally take shape through the movement and direction of Susie's body. Susie's orientation to an unclear location seems anything but intentional in the colloquial sense, that is, on purpose, with conscious effort; and absolutely intentional in the phenomenological sense, that is, oriented toward something, even if that something is nothing or herself.

Suspiria helps to articulate how what and whom we are oriented toward, and how we are trans-corporeally linked with each other and with our environments, create the conditions for the things we do. Whether we are alone or with others, we are always bound up with the world and with people who matter to us. Our phenomenological intentionality (the ways we are oriented toward things and shaped by them) and our everyday conscious intentions (the things we mean to do, the choices we make) are entangled. Embodied affects queer our sense of cause and effect, space and time. In all this mess, who is response-able?

The "Ongoing Dance of Agency": *Suspiria*'s Entangled Elsewhen

Suspiria's Klemperer, Patricia's psychoanalyst, is drawn into the strange events surrounding the witches. Viewers may recognize the character's surname as a reference to Victor Klemperer (1881–1960), German scholar and diarist. The historic Klemperer lived through the Nazi regime as a Jewish man and documented what he saw and experienced in diaries published in Germany in 1995 as *Tagebücher* and in the UK in three volumes: *I Shall Bear Witness* (1998), *To the Bitter End* (2000), and *The Lesser Evil* (2003).[30] Klemperer's 1957 book *The Language of the Third*

---

28 Stacy Alaimo, *Bodily Natures: Science, Environment, and the Material Self* (Bloomington: Indiana University Press, 2010), 2.

29 Ahmed, *Queer Phenomenology*, 15–16.

30 Victor Klemperer, *Tagebücher* (Berlin: Aufbau, 1995), *I Shall Bear Witness* (London: Weidenfeld & Nicolson, 1998), *To the Bitter End* (London: Weidenfeld & Nicolson, 2000), *The Language of the Third Reich* (London: Athlone Press, 2000), *The Lesser Evil* (London: Weidenfeld & Nicolson, 2003).

Reich has been cited by Guadagnino as "a source of study and work and inspiration" during the process of making *Suspiria*.[31] Knowing about the real-life Klemperer makes audience interpretation of *Suspiria*'s fictional Klemperer quite difficult. The real Klemperer was Jewish, while his wife, Eva, was not; but the events of *Suspiria* suggest that the fictional Klemperer's wife, given her arrest by the Nazis, may have been Jewish. The film does not make it clear whether Klemperer himself is Jewish, making the repeated suggestion that he may be complicit in Anke's death difficult to understand. If the witches are taunting him with the truth, and he did fail or even refuse to help his wife get out of harm's way, whether he (or she, for that matter) is Jewish becomes an important factor in how we might regard his actions.

Throughout the film, Klemperer is depicted as a kind and thoughtful man who nonetheless can be dismissive of his female patients' pain and is over-reliant on rationality. He does not believe Patricia when she comes to him for help. In fact, the witches imply, when they taunt him for his actions regarding his wife, that his dismissal of Patricia's fears is typical: "When women tell you the truth, you don't pity them. You tell them they have delusions!" This may suggest that he also read his wife's fears about the very real dangers of the Nazi regime as delusional, perhaps explaining why the witches consider him responsible for her death. Yet if Klemperer was Jewish too, he would not have been able to travel freely and so would have had little power to help his wife. Either way, it could be seen as problematic to assign blame to Klemperer when those whose actions directly caused her death (members of the Nazi regime who gave orders and those who followed them in imprisoning her and leaving her out in the cold to freeze to death) are rarely explicitly mentioned in the film. This ambiguity can be very frustrating, and here Guadagnino comes closest to deserving those accusations of messiness and of having nothing meaningful to say about the real events and politics he invokes. The audience does not know how much to empathize with Klemperer or how much to be critical of his actions, and it certainly has no idea where the film lands on these thorny questions. Yet on the other hand, fostering this conversation about all the differential variables that might change levels of responsibility prompts us to contemplate how agencies might intersect here, how matters of gender and race might complicate power dynamics. This thinking is indeed productive, and remains so regardless of whether the filmmakers intended to provoke it. The inarticulate mess

31 Hannah Lack, "From Witches to Freud: Six Books that Inspired Luca Guadagnino's Suspiria," *AnOther*, November 16, 2018, https://www. anothermag.com/design-living/11297/from-witches-to-freud-six-books-that-inspired-luca-guadagninos-suspiria.

of articulations here is meaningful to think with in a way that straightforward, clear-cut representations would not be.

The witches humiliate and torture Klemperer. Having been kidnapped by the witches to witness their bloody ritual, the climactic scene of Susie's vengeful rebirth, he lies on the altar naked, crying out, "Ich bin nicht schuldig! Ich bin unschuldig! Ich kann mich an alles erinnern!" (I am not guilty! I am innocent! I can remember everything!). This scene is supposed to be the culmination of all the witches' machinations; the moment when Markos will enter Susie's body, supposed by now to be a hollow vessel. Unfortunately for them, Susie has imagined other possibilities, has opened up another future, and has fully come into her powers as Mother Suspiriorum. As a man in his eighties who has lived through numerous violent periods of German history, Klemperer, named for a real-life witness, functions in some ways as the ultimate bystander. Well before the witches claim him as a "witness," saying that this is an old custom, and force him to watch their murderous ritual, his function in the film is as a background presence, aware of events but not really involved in them, only able to stand on the sidelines and interpret what he sees. Yet this assumption of passivity on Klemperer's part is not entirely fair, as Klemperer does attempt to act, to intervene, by contacting the police and by approaching Sara. He may be a witness, but he is not entirely passive.

Intra-actions, writes Barad, can reconfigure "what will be" as well as "what will be *possible*" (my italics). They can create the conditions for the future, not through fixed and predetermined choices but through the "ongoing dance of agency."[32] David Kajganich, who wrote the screenplay for Guadagnino's *Suspiria* and who, like me, does not see Susie as a passive victim, argues that the main character in most horror films "is just the *object* [my italics] of the violence of the film, of the threat of the film," stating further that he and Guadagnino wanted Susie to be, "certainly by the end," the *subject* of the film's horror.[33] In this shift from object to subject, Susie also shifts from innocent to complicit. According to Kajganich, to be a subject, unlike objecthood, is to be imbued with the horror of agency. For Barad, however, agency is not located within subjects or objects but emergent in the dance between the two, a phenomenon that arises in the encounter. In setting the film in 1977 Berlin, Kajganich and Guadagnino wanted to "open up this continuum of being politically passive, being a witness, [versus] being politically active and politically revolutionary." As Kajganich describes,

---

32 Barad, *Meeting the Universe Halfway*, 246.

33 David Kajganich, interviewed by Jamie Righetti, "'Suspiria' Screenwriter Explains That Wild Ending and Why Dakota Johnson Is a New Kind of Final Girl," *IndieWire*, November 7, 2018, https://www.indiewire.com/2018/11/suspiria-screenwriter-explains-wild-ending-spoilers-ideas-for-sequel-1202018427/.

All the characters exist somewhere on that continuum, for different reasons. And to me, [the film] is very much about becoming politically active. The way that Susie [becomes politically active] is a big surprise, and the way that Klemperer doesn't is a big tragedy. To me, the film is full of everyone making choices about how to react to some very difficult and dangerous political situations.[34]

In my view, Klemperer's tragedy does not lie in simply being a passive witness, as a fixed representation of this rather simplistic trope. It lies in his shift from the part of the continuum where, though he has little power, he uses what he has to attempt to foster collective agencies with others (the police, Sara), to where he actively rejects both collective action and witnessing. He and Sara had worked to learn what the witches are up to, bonding over their concern for the missing Patricia. But when Sara goes missing too, Klemperer loses heart and decides not to act against the witches, throwing Patricia's notebooks full of evidence against them in the river. Without Sara, Klemperer is disoriented, loses his bearings, and ceases to be a politically active witness, becoming entangled in the work of the witches instead, as their passive symbolic and powerless witness.

In the scene that establishes Klemperer as a psychoanalyst, the camera lingers over books on his desk, including *Die Psychologie der Übertragung* (The Psychology of Transference) by Carl Gustav Jung.[35] Jung was a protégé of Sigmund Freud's, but where Freud saw psychological problems as deriving from individual pathology, Jung became increasingly interested in the possibility of shared and collective experiences that might operate in a more spiritual and intangible manner than Freud's strictly ordered psyche. The film's credits list the actor playing Klemperer as Lutz Ebersdorf, but a closer look reveals that he is, in fact, played by Tilda Swinton in heavy old-age makeup—an actor playing an actor playing a character. There is no obvious reason, either given or easily gleaned, for the invention of Ebersdorf, which the actors and filmmakers turned into an elaborate ruse, giving him an Internet Movie Database (IMDb) page and talking about him in promotional interviews. Though the reason for inventing the actor is unclear, the choice to have Swinton play Klemperer serves an important purpose. Swinton playing Madame Blanc and Klemperer, as well as the malevolent ancient witch Mother Markos, makes her the single face behind a highly symbolic triad: the witness (Klemperer), the manipulator (Blanc), and the perpetrator (Markos). One is tragic, one is powerful, one is ridiculous. But their connection troubles

34 Katie Rife, "Jessica Harper and screenwriter David Kajganich on the politics of *Suspiria*," A.V. Club, November 5, 2018, https://www.avclub.com/jessica-harper-and-screenwriter-david-kajganich-on-the-1830191488.

35 C. G. Jung, *Die Psychologie der Übertragung* (Zurich: Rascher, 1946).

the notion that these roles are distinct, leading the viewer to wonder if Markos is a little tragic, Blanc is a little ridiculous, Klemperer a little powerful. This meta-association with Blanc also helps us see that Klemperer does indeed have some power as a man and as a doctor because he is capable of fostering collective agencies with someone like Sara and of keeping his records as a form of resistance, as the real-life Klemperer did. Swinton's three characters' intra-acting lives and selves also span across time: Markos is ancient, Klemperer an old man, Blanc much younger. All have lived through different hardships: the Nazi regime, the misogynistic expectations put on women during the war, atrocities layering over atrocities.[36] "The self," says Barad, "is itself a multiplicity, a superposition of beings, becomings, here and there's, now and then's. Superpositions, not oppositions."[37] These characters are not three distinct and opposing forces but three (of many) intertwining forces, three phenomena that unfold together in the social and in the personal, in history and right now. What are the differences here to be mapped, what processes have to unfold to produce witnessing, manipulation, perpetration? What possibilities and agencies?

Klemperer, Blanc, and Markos rarely interact, seemingly unaware of each other's struggles. This is in contrast to Susie in her final form as Mother Suspiriorum, the avenging angel with the power of life and death, who seems to know all. Guadagnino has described the three characters played by Swinton as "the three aspects of the human psyche in the terms of Freudian psychoanalysis: the id, the ego and the superego."[38] By this logic, Susie may function as everything left over, everything that escapes Freud's representational framework. As the Mother of Sighs, of breath, of instinctive movement, a dancer with no formal training, a witch with innate power, Susie embodies affect and animality, as well as the queer. Perhaps Susie is the elsewhere, Haraway's elsewhere—not a convenient scapegoat or easy projection but a "spacetimemattering" of the unspeakable and inexpressible effects, and affects, left over by violence.[39]

---

36 Sara says of Blanc, "She kept the company alive through the war—think about that—when the Reich just wanted women to shut off their minds and keep their uteruses open, there was Blanc."

37 Karen Barad, "Diffracting Diffraction: Cutting Together-Apart," *Parallax* 20, no. 3 (2014): 168–87, here 176.

38 Guadagnino, interviewed by Jen Yamato, "'Suspiria' in the time of Trump: Luca Guadagnino warns, 'Let's have a look back into where we come from,'" *LA Times*, October 29, 2018, https://www.latimes.com/entertainment/movies/la-et-mn-suspiria-tilda-swinton-dakota-johnson-20181029-story.html.

39 According to Barad, "Phenomena are not located in space and time; rather, phenomena are material entanglements enfolded and threaded through the spacetimemattering of the universe." The events of history are not singular, fixed, or ordered in a linear fashion, nor can they be attributed to simplistic

In the film's epilogue, which follows Susie's blood-soaked rebirth, Klemperer lies in bed resting after his ordeal. He mournfully looks over his yellowing "Aryan papers" and those of his missing wife, Kajganich and Guadagnino refusing yet again to provide clarity as to Klemperer and Anke's Jewishness. Susie arrives, and the two have a strangely intimate talk, despite having never spoken before. The epilogue is titled "A Sliced-Up Pear," a reference to the pear that Klemperer's maid brings him to eat just as Susie arrives. The pun here is quite telling—a sliced-up pair, Klemperer and Susie, both deeply wounded by recent events, but here together. Or perhaps the slicing denotes the ways in which they are diffractively intra-acting; what Barad calls "cutting-together-apart."[40] Susie tells Klemperer that she regrets what the witches, her "daughters" as she calls them, did to him. He deserves to hear the truth, she says, and begins telling him the story of his wife's death at Theresienstadt, a story naive Susie from Ohio should have no way of knowing. It is now Susie's turn to be the witness, her impossible knowing seeming to come from her affinity with the elsewhere, her access to collective trauma and memory. Susie uses her magic to make Klemperer forget everything he witnessed: the deaths of the dancers he tried to help and presumably, therefore, his own abandonment of his initial acts of resistance; the death of his wife; the witches ("the women of your undoing," as Susie calls them). "Wir brauchen Schuld, Doktor," she tells him in German, "und Scham. Aber nicht deine" (We need guilt, doctor, and shame. But not yours).

Kajganich's comment that setting the film in 1970s West Berlin opens up "this continuum of being politically passive, being a witness" and "being politically active and politically revolutionary" is a useful way of highlighting the role of politics in the film. But this description is somewhat reductive in how it creates a false binary between passive and active, witness and revolutionary. I argue that the film articulates how difficult to categorize these different roles often are. To witness, to hold space for atrocity, for what many want to forget, can be deeply political, deeply radical. If we do this and refuse to act on the agencies we are collectively response-able for, however, what kind of action does our inaction become caught up in? Ultimately, the film is, as Kajganich says, "full of everyone making choices about how to react to some very difficult and dangerous

---

cause-and-effect/subject-meets-object logics. Rather, they are diffractive phenomena, iterative reworkings and repatternings: spacetimematterings. They are intra-active, lively, and dynamic, always both new and ancient, like Susie. Karen Barad, "Quantum Entanglements and Hauntological Relations of Inheritance: Dis/continuities, SpaceTime Enfoldings, and Justice-to-Come," *Derrida Today* 3, no. 2 (2010): 240–68, here 261.

40   "Entanglements are not unities. They do not erase differences; on the contrary, entanglings entail differentiatings, differentiatings entail entanglings. One move—cutting together-apart." Barad, "Diffracting Diffraction," 176.

political situations."[41] In Susie we have a character who embodies the place where all of these choices intersect: the active and the passive, the victim and the perpetrator, the witness and the revolutionary.

"Why Is Everyone So Ready to Think the Worst Is Over?": *Suspiria* as Intra-Active Map of Entangled Histories

Suspiria is an articulate mess. It is a film that does not use simple analogy and metaphor to articulate the messiness of our entangled bodies, orientations, traumas, and memories but, rather, articulates itself through figurations that show how intersubjectivity, transcorporeality, and intra-active agency operate. The film raises many questions and answers few, at times touching on very sensitive ground without providing the clarity needed to avoid some quite damning interpretations. Yet it is these very open and unresolved spaces that make it such a productive text to think with in the context of violence elsewhere. Confronted by the felt sense of these aporia in the film, these spaces in which the intentions, agencies, and responsibilities behind violence are ambiguous, we are left to grapple with the uncertainty of collective experience. Guadagnino manages to evoke the horror of agency and the disorientation that often accompanies violence but also to imagine possibilities of resistance and of revolutionary action. Within these evocations, victim and perpetrator, active and passive are shown to be reductive binaries that do not begin to account for the interconnected nature of our intra-actions. *Suspiria* is a film interested in elsewheres and elsewhens, troubling not only our idea of inside and outside, us and them, but also of then and now. In the quotation at the start of this article Barad called for "collective imaginaries that undo pervasive conceptions of temporality." These linear views of time and progress, where the past is considered passed, obscure the felt embodied sense that this is not how temporal experience works and not how accountable and responsible action happens. *Suspiria* makes space for an urgently needed troubling of temporality and agency and for an exploration of affective and trans-corporeal aspects of Germany's complex history of violence. In Susie's embodiment of histories and affects, and in the dancing affects of collective agencies, the film makes a case that what we deem to be elsewhere or elsewhen is often always here, always present, always felt. In this openness to the ways that past, present, and future diffract through our collective experiences, *Suspiria* creates an embodied experience of the tensions between disorientation and agency and resonates with the horrifying and vital effects of response-ability.

41   Rife, "Jessica Harper and screenwriter David Kajganich."

9: Utopias of Restorative Justice: Speculative Fiction, Gender, and Violence in Sharon Dodua Otoo's *Adas Raum* (2021; *Ada's Realm*, 2023)

Priscilla Layne

Introduction

IN THE GRAPHIC NOVEL *Becoming Unbecoming* (2015), white British author Una explores her experience with sexual assault in girlhood and adulthood, the lasting trauma, and how her individual biography intersects with the local history of the Yorkshire Ripper murders (1975–80) and the tradition of misogyny and rape culture that normalized the Ripper's killing of "disposable" women.[1] On one iconostatic page, Una draws a globe with empty speech bubbles emerging from all sides as she imagines all the oppressed women who have been unable to speak about, and speak out against, sexual assault. In a world where violence against women has been labeled "the shadow pandemic" by UN Women, women everywhere find it important to unite, strategize, and organize globally.[2] The world of fiction has often been a space for women to imagine a world or a future where women no longer feel vulnerable and unsafe because of their gender.

Throughout the tradition of feminist speculative and science fiction (SF) in particular,[3] authors have found unique solutions to solving the problem of violence in a future society. Particularly among white, female SF authors, the solution to the problem of violence tends to involve

---

1 Una, *Becoming Unbecoming* (Vancouver: Arsenal Pulp Press, 2016).

2 Kate Fitz-Gibbon and Sandra Walklate, "Cause of death: femicide," *Mortality* 28, no. 2 (2023): 236–49, here 236.

3 "Speculative fiction is a cover term for a diverse range of genres, linked by their utilization of nonrealist narrative strategies." Esther L. Jones, "Speculative Fiction," Oxford Bibliographies, last modified June 28, 2016, https://www.oxfordbibliographies.com/display/document/obo-9780190280024/obo-9780190280024-0030.xml.

segregating men and women. Two examples of this approach can be seen in the novels *Herland* (1915), by Charlotte Perkins Gilman, and *The Gate to Women's Country* (1988), by Sherri S. Tepper.[4] In *Herland*, an all-female society develops naturally, after the men of a particular civilization die off and the women develop parthenogenesis: the ability to conceive without a male. When three men happen upon this civilization, the women attempt to integrate them into their society and even marry them. But an act of male violence—attempted marital rape—results in all three men being banished. In *The Gate to Women's Country*, men and women have decided to largely live separately. The women live within the towns and the men, who are warriors, live outside of the towns in garrisons. They only meet twice a year, at carnival, for the purpose of sexual relations and conception. Some men do live within the towns, but they do so voluntarily as servants, accepting the women's and girls' authority. Thus, in both texts, women only manage to live in peace because men have either been completely removed from society and are no longer needed; or exist on the margins, their interactions with women limited to necessity.

Within the tradition of Black feminist writing, Black women have not taken the same separatist approach to the question of violence and gender as in the tradition represented by Perkins and Tepper. Historically, Black feminists have argued that Black men are also oppressed within a patriarchal, white supremacist society and that working for the liberation of Black women means working for liberation of *all* people, regardless of gender.[5] Furthermore, Black feminist politics has long been a part of Black women's SF, as can be seen in the work of authors like Octavia Butler, Nalo Hopkinson, and Nnedi Okorafor. These authors frequently center strong female protagonists, and in the novel *Dawn* (1987), Butler even imagines alien civilizations where gender and sexuality are not understood in the same binary terms as on Earth.[6]

Butler's, Hopkinson's, and Okorafor's writing is frequently described as Afrofuturist, or African Futurist in Okorafor's case.[7] Afrofuturism combines appreciation for the past with speculative thinking about how best to

4   Charlotte Perkins Gilman, *Herland and Selected Stories* (New York: Penguin, 2014); Sheri S. Tepper, *The Gate to Women's Country* (New York: Bantam, 1989).

5   Keeanga-Yamahtta Taylor, *How We Get Free: Black Feminism and the Combahee River Collective* (Chicago: Haymarket Books, 2017), 11.

6   Octavia Butler, *Dawn: Xenogenesis* (New York: Warner Books, 1987).

7   Nigerian American Okorafor calls her work African Futurism on the grounds that Afrofuturism has largely stemmed from the US, with its authors concerned with inventing an African past to counter white American beliefs in Black inferiority. For an author like Okorafor, SF is a vehicle for engaging with modern-day African issues, rather than viewing Africa as an empty cipher that can have meaning projected onto it. See Nnedi's Wahala Zone Blog: African

design the future to provide hope for Black people. This appreciation for the past is important, because it involves countering racist understandings of Black culture that would posit Black people as outside of human history and incapable of invention. While science fiction may imagine new technologies and themes like aliens and space travel to make us contemplate how such things might impact our society, Afrofuturist authors frequently eschew such tropes. For African American author Pauline Hopkins, it was more important to invent a past, an ancient Ethiopian civilization, to prove Black people's humanity. Thus, at its core, Afrofuturism is about countering white supremacy and challenging Eurocentric thinking.[8]

This does not mean that Afrofuturism has not had its own gender problem. Earlier Afrofuturist texts, from George Schuyler's *Black No More* (1931) to John Coney's *Space Is the Place* (1974), perpetuated all kinds of sexist stereotypes about Black women.[9] In Schuyler's narrative about a Black scientist who invents a potion to turn Black people white, dark-skinned Black women are portrayed as ugly and undesirable, while light-skinned Black women are portrayed as materialistic and superficial. *Space Is the Place* is greatly influenced by contemporary Blaxploitation films.[10] Black women are displayed as sexual objects, even if Sun Ra's character hopes to save them from Earth's oppressive conditions by taking them into outer space. Despite these harrowing beginnings, Afrofuturism has developed along a critical attitude toward gender that originated during the "new wave" of science fiction (of the 1960s and 1970s) when female authors like Butler rejected the "supermen" of the golden age of science fiction (1938–46) and instead wrote narratives creating "new conceptions of manhood" and promoting "interests in community and equality that are historically identified as feminine."[11]

When one observes the phenomenon of Black German Afrofuturism, one sees a continued effort to unite concerns about the future with gender equality and liberation for people of all genders and sexualities. In my forthcoming book, *Out of this World: Afro-German Afrofuturism*, I argue that what is unique about Black German Afrofuturism lies in the

---

Futurism Defined, October 19, 2019, http://nnedi.blogspot.com/2019/10/africanfuturism-defined.html.

8   Pauline Hopkins, *Of One Blood, or the Hidden Self* (1902; New York: Washington Square Press, 2004).

9   George Schuyler, *Black No More* (1931; New York: Modern Library, 1999); *Space Is the Place*, directed by John Coney (North American Star System, 1974).

10   Female characters are frequently sexually objectified in these exploitative films, even when they are major characters; for example, Pam Grier's character in *Foxy Brown* (1974).

11   Michael Pitts, *Alternative Masculinities in Feminist Speculative Fiction: A New Man* (London: Rowman and Littlefield, 2021), 4.

way it embraces children as a symbol of futurity but without prescribing heteronormativity. In the artworks I examine, Black men and women are portrayed as actively wanting to throw off the oppressive chains of heteronormativity and embrace a certain fluidity that allows men to be vulnerable and emotional and women to be strong and capable. And in these Afrofuturist texts, Black German women want to live together *with* Black men, rather than exile them—a reflection of the kind of cooperation to be found throughout the activist work of the Black German community.[12]

Motherhood plays an important role in Black diasporic texts about futurity and Black survival, because it is one of the many identities that were stolen from the enslaved during the transatlantic slave trade.[13] Black feminist scholars like Hortense Spillers and Saidiya Hartman have argued that part of the brutality of slavery for Black women was turning them into flesh.[14] This means Black women were not only racialized but stripped of their gender and right to kinship. They could not be seen as women, because femininity was solely associated with whiteness. Therefore, they most certainly couldn't be seen as mothers. Spillers argues that as "flesh," Black women were without gender, without a need for respect, and without agency. Thus, they could be sexually assaulted, murdered, and their children could be taken from them without consequence.

In this essay, I explore how Black German Afrofuturism approaches the problem of violence in society by looking at how Sharon Dodua Otoo's speculative novel, *Adas Raum* (2021; *Ada's Realm*, 2023),[15] depicts the vicious circle of violence between races and ethnicities and both toward and by women. I argue that because Black feminists insist on building a society with men rather than without them, as authors, they reject a simplified approach to gender and violence that associates men with violence and women with nonviolence as seen in the tradition represented by Gilman and Tepper. Although Afrofuturist texts acknowledge the historical damage done by racist and patriarchal violence, they also recognize not only that women are capable of violence but that violence is not necessarily a

---

12 Tiffany Florvil, *Mobilizing Black Germany: Afro-German Women and the Making of a Transnational Movement* (Urbana: University of Illinois Press, 2020), 95.

13 In *Black Feminist Thought*, Patricia Hills Collins describes how Black women have historically had to reconceive of motherhood and rely on so-called other mothers to assist in childcare. Patricia Hills Collins, *Black Feminist Thought* (New York: Routledge, 2000), 178.

14 Hortense Spillers, "Mama's Baby, Papa's Maybe: An American Grammar Book," *Diacritics* 17, no. 2 (Summer 1987): 64–81, here 67.

15 Sharon Dodua Otoo, *Adas Raum: Roman* (Frankfurt am Main: S. Fischer, 2021). English translations of quotations are taken from Sharon Dodua Otoo, *Ada's Realm*, trans. Jon Cho-Polizzi (New York: Riverhead Books, 2023). Page references to both versions follow in the text.

hindrance to a utopian society. Such an attitude toward violence seems particularly necessary for Black diasporic communities, who have historically had to first free themselves from racist oppression, often by using violence, to start building a better future. Instead of focusing on whether we can rid society of violence, Otoo is interested in creating a system of restorative justice so that moving on after violence is possible. And a key part of moving on is the important network of care Black women establish for each other and each other's children, which is why motherhood is an important theme in the novel. As noted previously, in German Afrofuturist texts, neither children nor motherhood are used as a tool to reinforce cisheteronormative norms. Rather, for Otoo and other Afrofuturist authors, biological kinship isn't necessary for raising a child.

Adas Raum is a three-hundred-page work of speculative fiction that spans five centuries and two continents.[16] The novel follows the stories of four women named Ada, who each exist in a different time and space. There is fifteenth-century Ada, who lives in Totope, a West African village in what is today Ghana. Then there is Ada Lovelace, the nineteenth-century British mathematician whose important work on computation helped make modern-day computers possible. There is Polish Ada, a prisoner in the concentration camp Dora, a subcamp of Buchenwald, in 1945, whom the Nazis have compelled to do sexual forced labor. And finally, there is Ada of 2020, a pregnant Ghanaian British woman who is attempting to start a new life in Berlin and desperately searching for a room to rent. In each of their timelines, all four Adas have a fateful encounter with a man named William. For the first three Adas, this violent confrontation causes their deaths. For the final Ada, this encounter is life-changing but not fatal. The book is organized in four main sections: "The First Orbits," "Between the Orbits," "The Next Orbits," and an "Epilogue," and each section includes subchapters.

What links each Ada is a being—an inanimate spirit that can embody objects but is never born. During each of Ada's orbits on earth, this being exists in her surroundings and serves as a witness to violence. In the fifteenth century, it is a broom; in the nineteenth century, a doorknocker; then a room in 1945; and a passport in 2020. An additional important object at the center of the novel is a fertility bracelet that was originally stolen from fifteenth-century Ada by Portuguese colonizer Guilherme

16   The novel can be understood as an extended version of the short story that gained Otoo mainstream success in German literature, "Herr Gröttrupp setzt sich hin" (Mr. Gröttrup Sits Down), with which she won the prestigious Ingeborg Bachmann German literary prize in 2016. In her analysis, Sarah Colvin argues that Otoo uses speculative fiction to comment on sexism, racism, and how they intersect in German society. Sarah Colvin, "Talking Back: Sharon Dodua Otoo's *Herr Gröttrup setzt sich hin* and the Epistemology of Resistance," *German Life and Letters* 73, no. 4 (2020): 659–79.

Fernandes Zarco. Guilherme violently kills Ada for the bracelet, setting off a chain of reactions that lead to Ada's next two incarnations also dying at the hands of violent men who are in close proximity to the bracelet. But the novel's ultimate goal is not to reunite Ada with the bracelet. Rather, it is to help present-day Ada remember her past lives, so that she can recognize her strength and status as a mother, whether or not she has a child—in her community, being a mother can be understood in less narrow terms than biological ones: being a mother means caring for others and trying to protect them from violence. The section "Between the Orbits" stands out as unique, because it is in this section that we hear from the being and God about what happens in the afterlife, before each Ada returns to earth. By the end, the book comes full circle: after beginning with a West African Ada who doubts whether she can ever become a mother, it ends with a West African Ada who not only successfully gives birth but realizes that she was already prepared for motherhood long before then.

Throughout the novel, inanimate beings are not just witness to violence; they also help narrate the story from their perspective as varying objects over time, though sometimes the narrating "I" is Ada herself "in any one of her four incarnations."[17] By imbuing objects with the ability to narrate, Otoo participates in object-oriented ontology ("Triple O"): the practice of not viewing objects as simply "inhuman or utterly inanimate … [rather, object] means anything that has a surplus beyond its constituent pieces and beneath its sum total of effects on the world."[18] Triple O means, rather than differentiating between humans and nonhumans, humans and animals, or humans and things, all of these combined can be viewed as objects. One could read this in the vein of Afrofuturism, particularly because there are ways in which Otoo's narrative invokes West African belief systems. Throughout the novel, spiritual terms from the Ga, an ethnic group from Ghana, are used not only by the West African Adas but also by God.

Object-oriented ontology is also interesting to a Black speculative writer like Otoo, because of how Black people have historically been excluded from the category of human. During the transatlantic slave trade, it was convenient to argue that slavery was justifiable because Black people were not fully human. While Black people worldwide have since been legally afforded this right, arguably since the UN Declaration of Human Rights of 1948, protest movements like Black Lives Matter demonstrate that around the world, Black people are still not always viewed

---

17 Sarah Colvin, "Freedom Time: Temporal Insurrections in Olivia Wenzel's *1000 Serpentinen Angst* and Sharon Dodua Otoo's *Adas Raum*," *German Life and Letters* 75, no. 1 (2022): 138–65, here 139.

18 Graham Harman, *Object-Oriented Ontology: A New Theory of Everything* (London: Penguin, 2018), 50.

as if they have a right to humane treatment. This is why Afrofuturist artists frequently experiment with the questions, What does it mean to be human and to what extent are Black people excluded? These questions are at the center of canonical Afrofuturist works, including Sun Ra's jazz albums, the funk band Parliament's album *Mothership Connection* (1975), and John Sayle's film *Brother from Another Planet* (1984). By imagining inanimate objects that are sentient and have agency, Otoo encourages us to decenter our human perspective and imagine a scenario where all the nonhuman phenomena we take for granted are just as sentient as human beings.

One of the critiques Otoo has faced from critics of the novel is whether or not she, as a British Ghanaian woman, can accurately portray even a fictional account of Nazi Germany.[19] But Otoo's perspective as a non-German is part of what makes the novel's message so powerful. First, by telling the stories of several different women across centuries and national borders, Otoo demonstrates that one does not need to have an intimate understanding of a particular violent event to empathize with its victims. Second, by examining the way violence impacts the lives of women from very different socioeconomic and cultural backgrounds and leads to their premature deaths—or their mother's premature death in Berlin Ada's case—Otoo emphasizes that "femicide is a product of a social structure of power relations embedded in the global political economy ... [influenced by] relations of production, exchange, investment, labour, and migration that produce and allocate value across borders."[20] Third, through creating sentient inanimate objects that bear witness to these violent events, Otoo offers us an Afrofuturist depiction of Nazi Germany (among other violent eras), which clearly differentiates her novel from previous German authors' attempts to depict this time. Furthermore, by using inanimate objects to link her four protagonists across space and time, Otoo resists Germany's narrative of the Holocaust as a singular event, instead emphasizing what makes oppressed and oppressive subjects across history more similar than different.

By the novel's end, Ada's ultimate life lessons are, first, recognizing her strength; second, recognizing her capability to mother; and, third, embracing reconciliation with past perpetrators. All these lessons are

19 See for example, Shirin Sojitrawalla's review, which suggests that Otoo bit off more than she could chew by trying to cover such different female subjects across time and place. Shirin Sojitrawalla, "Ausweitung der Erzählzone," Deutschlandfunk, February 21, 2021, https://www.deutschlandfunk.de/sharon-dodua-otoo-adas-raum-ausweitung-der-erzaehlzone-100.html.

20 Allison Brysk and Vitória Moreira, "Femicide and the Global Political Economy," in *The Routledge International Handbook on Femicide and Feminicide*, ed. Myrna Dawson and Saide Mobayed Vega (London: Routledge, 2023), 29–39, here 29–30.

important for how violence figures in the novel. In the following sections, I discuss how violence is depicted in the first three eras of the novel before considering the importance of the *inanimate being's* mediation of this violence and how this all leads to a happy ending.

Colonial Violence in Africa

We first meet West African Ada in March 1459, in Totope, right after her newborn baby has died. As we soon learn, she has had two infants die and is plagued with insecurity because she does not understand why. Ada has decided to tie a bracelet around her newborn before she places his body in the river. This bracelet is tied to a violent event from Ada's past. She received it from her biological mother when she was a child, shortly before her first village, Kuntanase, was invaded by warriors and she fled to Totope. During this invasion, Ada and her brother Damfo hid among trees, from where they heard violence being perpetrated on the women of the village. These African warriors subsequently enslaved Ada and Damfo, but she was able to hide the bracelet in her vagina. Ada's traumatic memories give us insight into the formative experiences that shaped her life, alerting us also to the fact that she has always lived with violence, even before the white colonizers arrive.

Because Ada refuses to bury her baby in a grave, she also faces violence from the female elders of her village, whom Ada refers to as "die Zahnlosen" ("the toothless ones"), who beat her to make her conform to their traditions. An elder, Mami Ashitey, punishes Ada for continuing to mourn the infant by beating her with a broom, but the "beating" is not very effective because the broom actively resists hitting her. This is one of the unique narrative techniques of Otoo's novel, where objects can act with intention and, in several cases, try to protect Ada from harm. Mama Ashitey's attempted beating of Ada is the first instance in the novel where Otoo demonstrates women's, and in particular Black women's, capacity for violence. But rather than encouraging us to castigate Mami Ashitey for it, the narrating broom offers us a perspective from within the community that allows us to see her actions in a different light. We are told: "Die Frauen Totopes kümmerten sich um Ada, als hätte Mami Ashitey sie aus den eigenen Lenden gepresst. In deren Augen war ihre Prügelstrafe der glühenden Beweis dafür" (33; "The women of Totope treated Ada as though she had emerged from Mami Ashitey's own loins. In their eyes, her daily floggings were glowing proof of familiarity and love," 26). Thus, regardless of the narrator's own view of this violence, its remarks convey that for the women in Ada's village, Mama Ashitey's actions are a loving act, rather than something negative. The narrator thereby encourages us to understand this violence within its cultural and historical context. Mami Ashitey is likely worried about Ada's mental and physical well-being. Not wanting Ada to dwell on the death of a second newborn baby, she thinks the best way to help her move on is to physically chastise her to force her to conform to tradition. For without following tradition, Ada likely faces negative consequences from her community.

It is also significant that this interpersonal violence is soon after contrasted with another, completely different kind of violence; namely, colonial violence. By contrasting these forms of violence, Otoo does not suggest that in the absence of colonialism Africa would be free of violence. Rather, she encourages us to ponder both the ever-present nature of violence and how interpersonal and colonial violence affect communities differently. As Ada attempts her baby's water burial, she encounters Guilherme, the white Portuguese explorer recently arrived on the continent. As we learn from the broom, Guilherme was a businessman who had gone bankrupt two years previously and therefore, like many other Europeans in a similar financial situation at this time, sought his fortunes abroad. In addition, Guilherme had also lost any money he had left a few days earlier, owing to a failed bet. Thus, when we encounter him, he is desperate and eager to get his footing in this new, unfamiliar environment. As the narrator explains, what has brought him and the sailors to Africa was the promise "dass sie mit mehr Gold beladen zurückkehren würden, als sie sich jemals hätten vorstellen können" (36; "that they would return with unimaginable quantities of gold," 29). With that, Otoo invokes the centuries of colonial violence and exploitation that continue to plague the African continent.

Violence in Nineteenth-Century England

The second Ada, based on the historical Ada Lovelace, is the novel's first white female character, and through her Otoo presents us with the interconnections between racism, colonialism, and sexism. Descriptions of blackface troupes performing in the streets of London, and Englishmen referring to Ada's "Zofe" ("lady's maid"), Lizzie, as "dreckige Irin" (63; "manky Irish," 58) provide hints of Britain's racist past. We eventually learn that having taken the bracelet off the baby's corpse and killed fifteenth-century Ada when she tried to retrieve it, Guilherme took the bracelet to France, where he sold it—an example of femicide being part of the global political economy. Nineteenth-century Ada is given the bracelet, which at this time would be a costly colonial artifact, by her husband, Lord William King, a man with conservative monarchist political beliefs who had received it from his mother. And when we meet this Ada, she has given the bracelet to Lizzie to hide, in case she needs to sell it to escape her husband.

As we learn through the minor character Lizzie, this is a time of considerable political upheaval in London. Lizzie and her brother, Alfie, have fled to England because of the Irish potato famine, leaving behind their parents, who subsequently died in a poorhouse. Now in England, they have become involved in revolutionary movements. But Lizzie feels torn between loyalty to her brother and class and loyalty to Ada.

This second Ada would appear to have an easy life. She is white, aristocratic, and educated. But not only is she unhappily married; her husband is violent toward her. The narrator informs us that at this time, white men were becoming paranoid about losing their privileged role in society, which made them even more aggressive. The *being*, this time a doorknocker, informs us: "Männer, die sich eigentlich für die 'Guten' hielten, doch—zwischen den Schwarzen auf der einen Seite und den Frauen auf der anderen—nicht mehr wussten, woher die nächste Anfechtung ihrer gottgegebenen Autorität kommen würde und deswegen vorauseilen an allen Fronten kämpften" (20; "Men who actually considered themselves to be the 'good ones' and yet—between the Africans on one side and the women on the other—never knew where to expect the next challenge to their God-given authority and therefore fought preemptively on every front at once," 11). Considering the connections between violence, capitalism, and colonialism at this time, it is no wonder that Ada and Lord King are also connected to slavery. The *being* describes their street, Battersea Road, as "eine unschuldige Straße" (96; "a perfectly innocent street," 96), in contrast to the people who live there:

> Sie [die Herren] trugen mit Stolz ihre makellosen Westen, obwohl ihnen bewusst war, dass die Baumwolle, aus der diese gefertigt waren, von unfreien Händen geerntet wurde. Glücklich waren diejenigen, die Handelsbeziehungen quer durch das britische Empire pflegten. *Am glücklichsten* waren allerdings diejenigen, die die menschlichen Kosten anderer durch erhebliche Gewinne, selbstverständlich nur für sich ausgleichen konnten. (96–97)

> [They [the Lords] wore their immaculate vests with pride although they knew that the cotton they had been made from was harvested by unfree hands. Those whose business relations stretched from one end of the vast British Empire to the other considered themselves lucky. The *luckiest* of all were those who could write off the human cost against their own enormous profit margins.] (96)

It is arguably because of Otoo's positionality as a Black British woman that she includes this history of British racism in a story largely concerning German racism. By entangling these two histories, Otoo demonstrates that no national legacy of racism in Europe exists in a vacuum and that Black Europeans are contending with multiple legacies of oppression simultaneously.

Despite British Ada's close proximity to this oppression, she does not use her experience with sexism as an impetus to become more politically active. As the *being* informs us:

> Es bestand kein Zweifel daran, dass Ada um die Knollenfäule, die Irland befallen hatte, wusste. Die Berichte waren allgegenwärtig, die armseligen Neuankömmlinge auch. Es wäre für Ada am allereinfachsten gewesen, die gesamte Misere nicht wahrzunehmen. Wie ihre Claras, Lucys und Henriettas hätte auch Ada von Salon zu Salon schweben, ihre Tage mit Klavierspielen, Briefeschreiben oder Blümchensticken verbringen können, ohne sich Sorgen zu machen über Dinge, die sie nie am eigenen Leibe erleben würde. (60–61)

> [There could be no doubt that Ada knew about the potato blight afflicting Ireland. The reports were as omnipresent as the wretched new arrivals flooding London's streets … It would have been quite easy for Ada to ignore the misery altogether. Like her Claras, Lucys, and Henriettas, Ada, too, could easily have drifted from salon to salon, spending her days playing piano, writing letters, or embroidering tiny flowers without taking notice or worrying about things that would never affect her.] (56)

Ada cannot escape her worries through leisurely activities, not because she worries about politics and oppression but, rather, because of the affair she is having with Charles Dickens. But she doesn't know that the violence committed by white men in power, violence normally directed against those poorer and Blacker than she is, will soon be directed toward her. One of Lizzie's jobs is to warn her mistress if her husband returns while she is with her lover. And because Lizzie fails to do so, after her brother convinces her to go to a political meeting instead of waiting outside the house, Lizzie misses Lord King's premature return, and Ada pays with her life.

That Ada's husband and men like him saw themselves as the "good ones" recalls that even the era's abolitionists did not necessarily see Black people as equals. Thus, the narrator seems to be suggesting, it did not take much to count oneself as one of the "good [white] ones" during this time, and those who did were not necessarily to be trusted. Lord King had gone to France because he was advising King Louis Philippe I on how to put down the February 1849 revolution. His political views are part of what makes Lord King an unsympathetic character. He doesn't agree with workers fighting for their rights in France or in England, believing that they should be happy with what they have. And Ada isn't able to find a true ally in Charles, who doesn't believe in her academic skills because she's a woman.

When Lord King returns from France and sees his wife's lover leaving his home, the *being* describes him as "fingering" (37; "streicheln," 44) the pistol in his pocket—a description that sexualizes the action, as if the lord views the pistol as an extension of his manhood, making it apt that he will use it to overcome what he experiences as the shame of his wife's affair. Lord King has reached a new level of frustration with the affair; he is no longer willing to just speak with Charles, because Charles and Ada have flaunted their liaison so brazenly: "Für so eine zivilisierte Lösung war es aber eindeutig zu spät. Er hatte den Schwindler mit eigenen Augen *gesehen*" (44; "It was clearly too late for a civilized solution. Now he had *seen* the rascal with his own eyes," 38).

Despite Ada's apolitical stance and ignorance about Lizzie's economic and social problems, the *being* does not condemn her for her shortsightedness. It informs us that Ada didn't intentionally ignore Lizzie's private life but would approach every problem as if it were mathematical and could be solved with a rational equation. In fact, there is even an intimate moment, where Ada breaks down in front of Lizzie over the stress of her affair, and the closeness between the two suggests that they could become allies:

> Einmal hatte sie deswegen vor Lizzie weinen müssen. Sicherlich, sehr unangenehm. Aber hätte sie nur einen weiteren Moment ausgehalten, und innegehalten, wäre es auch Ada klar geworden, dass Lizzies Leid unermesslich größer als ihr eigeneswar. Ein langer Weg stand Ada bevor. (61–62)

> [It had even once brought her [Ada] to tears in front of Lizzie. Quite bothersome, indeed! And yet, had she paused for even a single moment longer and held her peace, it would have been clear, even to Ada, that Lizzie's suffering was immeasurably greater than her own. Ada still had a long journey ahead of her.] (57)

As the narrator implies, if Ada had shown Lizzie the same care and empathy that Lizzie had shown her, she would have asked what was troubling her and could have better understood Lizzie's political turmoil. But because Ada doesn't do so, class remains a wedge between them. Ultimately, Lizzie will choose class allegiance over Ada, sealing Ada's fate to be murdered at her husband's hands. The *being*'s comment, "Ein langer Weg stand Ada bevor," could be understood as a comment about the metanarrative. Though Ada Lovelace won't ever learn the important lesson of intersectional allyship, Ada in 2020 Berlin will. In a foreshadowing, London Ada reflects on how she dreamed of freeing herself: "Dass ich mich nach einem ganz anderen Ort sehnte, irgendwo, wo ich mich entfalten konnte. Ein Zimmer für mich allein. Denn mir wurde jeden Tag klarer, dass das Versprechen 'bis dass der Tod uns scheidet' von William in aller Konsequenz Ernst gemeint war" (153; "That I longed for a different place entirely, a realm where I could just be. A room of my own. For each day it grew clearer to me that William regarded the promise 'till death do us part' with deadly earnestness," 155). Ironically, the next Ada does get a room of her own—this time embodied by the *being*. But it is a room in which she is imprisoned as a sexual forced laborer at a concentration camp. Thus, the cycle of violence has not yet been broken.

Violence during Nazi Germany

Polish Ada is interned during World War II in a concentration camp, where she is forced to do sexual labor and happens to be pregnant. But her understanding of the pregnancy is unfamiliar, because she has disassociated herself from her body. She remarks, "Ich weiß also nicht mehr, wie sich Schmerz anfühlt" (27; "I no longer know what pain is anymore," 19) because "das alles würde darauf hindeuten, dass mein Körper mir gehörte. Aber was für ein seltsames Konzept! … Das Zeichen, dass ich ein Leben zur Welt bringen könnte, ist weg" (27; "All that would suggest this body still belonged to me. What a strange notion! … All the signs that I could bring life into this world are gone," 19). So with this third incarnation of Ada, instead of a woman who is sure she must become a mother, we have a woman who could never imagine becoming one, because her body no longer feels like her own. Like West African Ada, she has lost her bracelet, but in this case it was taken from her by the Nazis. "Reichsbesitz. Wie ich es bin. Mir gehört gar nichts mehr" (27; "Property of the German Reich. Like me. Nothing belongs to me anymore," 19), she asserts.

Ada's particular experience of forced sexual labor, as opposed to forced nonsexual labor, separates her from even the male prisoners in the concentration camp. She reflects: "So viel Opfer kannst du nicht sein, wenn dir noch dein Pimmel gehört. Und da ich keinen Besitz habe, kann ich nicht einmal recht oder unrecht haben" (29; "*You can't be that much of a victim if your weiner still belongs to you.* And since I don't have any possessions, I can't really have an opinion," 22). This experience dehumanizes Ada; she goes from woman to flesh in the sense of Giorgio Agamben's "Muselmann" (Muslim) or Spillers's description of enslaved Black women.[21] The *being* remarks of the female prisoners, "Bei ihrer Ankunft hatten sie—noch waren sie Frauen—jede eine sechsstellige Zahl zugeteilt bekommen" (48; "When they had arrived—they had still been women then—each had been allocated a six-digit number," 42). Thus, they were still women before their experience of living at the camp, where

21 Giorgio Agamben, *Remnants of Auschwitz: The Witness and the Archive* (New York: Zone Books, 2000), 41–86.

they are dehumanized to the point that gender no longer signifies in the same way.

Another example of Ada's dehumanization at Dora is when the narrating room, the *being*, refers to the female inmates as "die weiblichen Sechsstelligen" (50; "the six-digits," 45), referring to the tattoos on their arms. (The gendered qualifier is dropped in the English translation.) The women have been told that they should be grateful to be there, compared to the alternative, which would be death. We also learn that Ada had already given birth to a baby, who was subsequently murdered; a traumatic experience she witnessed that is recalled when she sees an officer who resembles the murderer.

In the camp, Ada's only friend is Friederike Lindauer, whom she calls Linde or Bärchen. It is Linde who inadvertently reunites Ada with the bracelet and unintentionally causes her death. In order to survive, Linde has made a deal with a Kapo named Walde, a prisoner with special privileges, in exchange for his protection. And it is Walde who gives Linde the bracelet as a gift. The introduction of Walde further complicates how violence is treated in the novel. A victim and prisoner himself, he is faced with the choice of either collaborating with the Nazis for special treatment so as to possibly preserve his life, or refusing to collaborate, which could mean an earlier death.

Walde is guilty for not acting when an SS officer, Helmut Wilhelm, finds Ada and Linde with the bracelet. After Walde gives Linde the bracelet, she carefully hides it in her and Ada's room. But when Ada happens to see a prisoner hiding outside their window, she screams, causing Linde to drop the bracelet. When Wilhelm comes to inquire about the scream, he finds the bracelet. Seeing Ada and Linde led away with the bracelet in the officer's hand, Walde knows that this is their death sentence but chooses to save himself, rather than intervene, and the third Ada's death follows. But instead of going quietly to her execution, she breaks free and tries to run to the electric fence, where she is shot.

Thingness and Violence

It is not until the section "Between the Orbits" that we learn how and why these three women are connected and what this *being without a body* has to do with their stories. The *being* tells us that by Ada's fourth orbit on earth, in Berlin in 2020, "die Zeit war jedenfalls gekommen, um Ada daran zu erinnern, dass alle Wesen—vergangene, gegenwärtige und zukünftige—in Verbindung miteinander sind, dass wir es immer waren und immer sein werden" (127; "the time had come to remind Ada that all beings—past, present, and future—are connected to one another. That we always were and always will be," 130). Although this *being* wishes to serve a protective function for Ada, it is not the case that it is always with her. Rather, each time Ada dies, it must find her, but only "nachdem sie sich gänzlich im Weißen aufgelöst hatte" (128; "[after] she [has] had time to dissolve herself completely into white," 130).

As the *being* explains, its creation, as a kind of protector for Ada, relates to how souls are distributed before people are brought into the world. Paraphrasing God—who is gendered feminine in the novel, can take on countless forms, and has several conversations with the *being*—the *being* compares the distribution of souls to how sausage is produced. God takes a mass, which she presses through a machine, creating a soul; the *being* is the bits of that soul still left in the machine. After this process, this *being* searches for Ada and embodies different objects to remain in proximity to her. Thus, what makes *Adas Raum* speculative fiction is both the granting of agency and subjectivity to inanimate objects and the inclusion of a narrative of what happens in the afterlife.

After we finally understand who or what the *being* is, we meet the fourth, final Ada: the pregnant Ghanaian immigrant living in Berlin in 2020. And this time, God has granted the *being* the opportunity to choose the object it becomes: her British passport. With the passport functioning as the ultimate symbol of agency, Otoo comments not only on the privilege that comes with certain passports today; she also remarks on the potential significance of freedom of mobility for a woman in a desperate situation. The *being* informs us that if only it had been a passport for nineteenth-century Ada, then she would have never found herself in such a life-threatening situation with her husband. She would have left him, or "Sie hätte ihn gar nicht erst geheiratet" (223; "She would never have married him in the first place," 231).

By introducing the fantastical element of this shapeshifting *being*, Otoo asks how might interpersonal violence between humans change when objects can intervene on behalf of what's right? The answer is: objects, when allied with the victimized, can disrupt and delay violence, allowing for hopeful outcomes that may not otherwise be possible. The *being* remarks on this point: "Immerhin—immerhin habe ich es geschafft, *eine* von den Demütigungen in Adas zahlreichen Leben ein wenig abzumildern. Also war meine Hoffnung groß, dass ich noch eine Chance bekommen könnte. Geboren zu werden war die größte Sehnsucht meines Daseins" (178; "And in any case—in any case, I had managed to lessen just *one* of the many humiliations and abasements in Ada's many lives. And so, I had great hope that I could be given another chance. To be born was the greatest aspiration of my being," 184). But although these objects—the broom, door knocker, and room—watch over Ada and pass judgment on the people in her life, they cannot influence what has already taken place. Their job is to ensure that certain things happen to achieve a necessary outcome in the future: this is why, although the three Adas in the past all meet a violent end, this is necessary and cannot be avoided, according to the logic of the text, because the past cannot be changed. When Ada and Guilherme first meet in Totope, the broom remarks, "Wurde auch Zeit ... Es war wichtig, dass Ada und Guilherme sich kennenlernten" (39; "About time! I thought. It was important that Ada and Guilherme met," 31). Thus, the narrative voice implies a sense of inevitability and necessity about the violence that the first three Adas experience.

This notion that some historical events have to happen, even if they are brutal, violent, and unjust, recalls African American SF author Butler's speculative neoslave narrative *Kindred* (1979).[22] In *Kindred*, African American woman protagonist Dana, whose contemporary moment is California in the 1970s, experiences multiple instances of being ripped back in time to the days of slavery in nineteenth-century Maryland. At first, Dana cannot understand why this is happening; on each trip back in time, she encounters a white boy, and eventually a white man, named Rufus—the same person at different stages of his life. Each time, she is ripped back to the past at a key moment that allows her to save his life. Eventually, Dana learns that Rufus, a white slaveowner, is a distant relative, and keeping him alive and ensuring that he rape her great-great-grandmother is necessary in order to ensure her own existence. Dana is finally able to break whatever spell causes her time travel and leave her ancestors in the past, but not without losing an arm, which Rufus was holding onto as he tried to keep her with him. Butler's argument appears to be that the history of slavery is an integral part of African Americans' history that continues to leave scars on future generations. Furthermore, Dana returning to the present with a limb difference, and as a result being permanently disabled, demonstrates how, as Jasbir K. Paur argues in *The Right to Maim*, power is made visible on the body. Paur writes that certain populations are "slated for death or slated for debilitation"; either way, "both are forms of the racialization of individuals and populations."[23] Dana's disability is a permanent, visual reminder of white supremacy's debilitating, deadly impact on Black people's lives.

But while Butler's ending is ambivalent and not necessarily hopeful, Otoo seems to suggest that these violent past events are not only necessary but can eventually lead to a desired peaceful outcome/future. Otoo's speculative take is less about the trauma of slavery and more about the West African belief in ancestral worship. Ada in 2020 is only able to successfully deliver a healthy baby because she can finally recall all the struggles of her predecessors and recognize their antagonists in Herr Wilhelm, the now elderly son of SS officer Helmut Wilhelm. And upon recognizing this, when Herr Wilhelm is having a heart attack in 2020, she still chooses

---

22 Octavia Butler, *Kindred* (Boston: Beacon Press, 2013).

23 Jasbir K. Paur, *The Right to Maim: Debility, Capacity, Disability* (Durham, NC: Duke University Press, 2017), x.

to help him. Therefore, she chooses reconciliation over revenge. By saving Wilhelm's life—by calling an ambulance and accompanying him to the hospital—she gets there in time to have her baby.

But to reach this happy ending, all of the violence that happens to Ada during her previous trips to earth *has* to happen; hence the role of Otoo's inanimate objects being to ensure that a series of events happen rather than having the power to change those events. As a room in a concentration camp, the entity states, "Ich war verdammt, alles zu bezeugen, aber nichts verhindern zu können. Alles zu verschleiern, aber nichts je vollständig tilgen zu können" (51; "I was condemned to witness everything and yet remain unable to hinder anything. To conceal everything and yet erase nothing," 46). The inanimate objects are also important as witnesses to history; they are the ones who narrate the story. The room reflects, "Meine Wände waren so dünn, jeder Schrei, jedes Stöhnen ging durch mich hindurch.... Da gefiel mir meine kurze Tätigkeit als Türklopfer eindeutig besser. Jedoch mussten Fakten geschaffen werden: Die Übergabe des Armbands war, möglichst noch vor dem Sturm, dringend zu sichern" (51; "My walls were so thin that every cry, every moan resonated through me corporeally.... My short tenure as a door knocker struck me then as infinitely preferable. And yet I needed to get on with things. If at all possible, the transfer of the bracelet was to be achieved before the storm!," 46). Otoo seems to be arguing that while we can't change the colonial, sexist, and racist violence of our past, we can turn the lessons learned from that violence into something positive through reconciliation.

Restorative Justice in Berlin

Berlin Ada, born in England and with British citizenship, is introduced in the section "Zwischen den Schleifen" ("The Next Orbits"). Her Ghanaian father, we learn, had immigrated to England, where he had married her mother; but her mother had died while Ada was young, and she was sent to Ghana to be raised by his sisters. Ada's father returned to Ghana in 2003, when she was seven, and she learns that while he was away, he had moved to Germany and had a second daughter, Elle, with a white German woman. We first encounter the two sisters looking for a room for Ada to rent. Since meeting, Ada and Elle have tried to build a relationship, but there are moments when they clearly don't see eye to eye owing to cultural differences. For example, Elle is disappointed that Ada is heavily pregnant and sleeping on her couch because she has split up with her boyfriend, Cash.

Ada is nervous about becoming a mother because of personal and political problems. Boris Johnson has just been elected prime minister of the UK, and Brexit is underway, so she is not certain how long her British passport will be helpful to her in Germany.[24] Furthermore, she doubts whether she's qualified to be a mother, because she never knew her biological mother; she only has fragments of her in her mind. Ada also knows that Elle judges her for getting pregnant without the means to care for herself and the baby. What ultimately empowers Ada to become a mother is, in part, meeting two elderly Ghanaian (Igbo) women with a room for rent who tell her about her mother and her culture.

Theirs is the apartment Elle and Ada view before Ada looks at Herr Wilhelm's spare room. Their conversation with the elderly women turns to mothers and daughters, which leads to the old women revealing that they knew Ada's mother, Ijemma, *and* that she had died in a fire during a racist arsonist attack of which the perpetrators were never found. Thus, although Ada in 2020 has not experienced direct violence herself, her life is still impacted by the racist violence that took her mother.

It is also from these two old women that Ada hears about the bracelet and its origins. During a previous apartment viewing, she had met a white German man who was interested in colonial history and had a catalog of a museum exhibit containing several West African artifacts. Ada sees a photo of the bracelet and is drawn to it. She takes the catalog with her and shows the bracelet to the two Igbo women, one of whom proclaims that she's not going to pay to see her own belongings. Ada asks,

> "Das Armband gehört Ihnen?"
> "Nicht mir, uns. Dir und mir. Und meinen Schwestern. Und Müttern. Und Vormüttern." Inzwischen hatte sich die Frau, die am schlechtesten hörte, zu ihnen gestellt und sah sich auch die Katalogseite an. "Wusstet ihr," sagte sie, "dass das Armband ursprünglich aus Kuntanase kommt?" (257)

> ["The bracelet belongs to you?"
> "Not to me, *us*. To you and me. And to my sisters. And mothers. And their mothers before them." The woman whose hearing was poorest had shuffled over to them and was now examining the page as well. "Do you know," she said, "that this bracelet originally came from Kuntanase?"] (267)

Kuntanase is the place where Totope Ada was born; the place from which she had to flee when it was raided by warriors. It is significant that the old woman refers to the bracelet as belonging to *all* the women of their tribe and to all the mothers, plural. That a person can have more than one

---

24   On June 23, 2016, citizens of the UK voted to leave the European Union, a move that took effect in 2020, when UK citizens who previously could have resided in other EU countries without a visa suddenly were faced with new travel and residency restrictions.

mother, not just a biological one, is a cultural difference that separates those raised on the African continent, like Ada and the old women, from those raised in the diaspora, like Elle. For example, Elle doesn't understand Ada's frequent references to the paternal aunts who raised her as her mothers. Ada explains, "'Aber das sind die Frauen, die mich erzogen haben. Wie soll ich sie sonst nennen?'" (271; "'But those are the women who raised me. What else should I call them?,'" 282). The *being* informs us, "Die Schwestern ihres Vaters waren ihre Mütter" (271; "The sisters of her father were her mothers," 282).

When God and the *being* finally find Ada before her fourth orbit and explain to her who she is, she reads the cards that she's been dealt—allegedly the story of how her life will play out—and discovers that she's supposed to become a mother in this life. But she asks, How is she going to be a mother when she's never had one? The *being* responds that there are more ways to be a mother than just biologically.

It is in Herr Wilhelm's apartment that the timelines converge. As we learn, Herr Wilhelm's father, the SS officer responsible for Polish Ada's death, had a seamless transition to ordinary citizen after the war, demonstrating how easily racist violence gets buried in Germany. During the war, officer Wilhelm gave the bracelet to his wife, and after his death, his son found it in a box of his belongings. The *being* describes Herr Wilhelm as a perfectly ordinary white German man who has had a very easy life as part of the majority, particularly compared to Ada, a pregnant Black immigrant desperately in search of shelter for herself and her child. But he likely doesn't view his life as being "blessed," even though he has far more privilege than Ada.

During her viewing of Herr Wilhelm's spare room, Ada puts down the museum catalog she has been carrying, and he happens to see the photo of the bracelet. A chain reaction is triggered. Herr Wilhelm falls in slow motion and suddenly becomes connected to all of the male perpetrators who committed violence against the Adas across centuries: Guilherme, William, and his own father, SS officer Wilhelm. Berlin Ada doesn't understand what is happening, attempts to show him her documents to secure the room for rent, and when he falls, thinks he's having a heart attack:

> "Hier mein Pass ... und meine Kontoauszüge.... Was habe ich vergessen?" Er antwortete nicht. Ada schaute ihn an. Die Broschüre lag aufgeschlagen neben ihrer Tasche. Er blickte wortlos das Bild des Armbandes an und schien nicht mehr zu wissen, dass sie mitten in einem Gespräch gewesen waren. Als Ada seinen Namen ein drittes Mal sagte, schaute er nur zögerlich zurück auf sie. Augenblicklich verschwand die ganze Farbe aus dem Gesicht. Er fiel ... wie in Zeitlupe....

"Herr Wilhelm!"
Zum Glück landete er nicht auf Ada. (291)

["Here's my passport ... and my bank statements.... Now, what am
I forgetting?" He did not answer. Ada looked up at him. The exhibition catalog lay open beside her bag. He stared wordlessly at the
picture of the bracelet as if he no longer realized that he had been
mid-conversation. It was not until Ada had repeated his name for
the third time that he slowly returned his gaze to her. All the color
drained from his face. He fell ... as if in slow motion.
    "Herr William!"
He did not land directly on Ada.] (304)

A series of conversations follows, which at first appear to be between Herr
Wilhelm and Ada in 2020, but it soon becomes clear that Wilhelm's and
Ada's subjectivities are blending with their past iterations. When Wilhelm
nearly lands on the pregnant Ada, and she asks him to be careful, he
murmurs, "'Ich war doch immer vorsichtig'" (290; "'I've always been
careful,'" 305). And while this statement may make sense in the present
context, the subsequent dialogue suddenly shifts the context to another
time and place:

"Ich war doch immer vorsichtig," murmelte er.
    "Was?"
    "Er rannte!"
    "Was erzählen Sie?" (291)

["I've always been careful," he murmured.
    "What's that?"
    "He ran!"
    "What did you say?"] (305)

"Er rannte!" could be a reference to Guilherme running away after mur-
dering fifteenth-century Ada in Totope, or to Lord William King running
away after killing nineteenth-century Ada in London, or to the prisoner
whom Ada sees spying on her and Linde outside their window at camp
Dora in 1945. And as these points in time blend, Wilhelm doesn't seem
to understand what is happening to either himself or Ada. Nevertheless,
Ada continues to interrogate him. The context shifts from Dora to
Totope, and Guilherme tries to justify killing Ada just because he wanted
to take the bracelet. He didn't have enough respect for her or her culture
to allow her to explain why she had sent the baby off down the river with
her bracelet. In his mind, she was an ignorant woman doing something
senseless with a valuable object. As I argue, the function of this scene, in
which the subjectivities and timelines of all four Adas and "Williams" are

intertwined, is reconciliation. The "Williams" get an opportunity to make amends for the violence they committed. Guilherme apologizes for killing Totope Ada, but he also stands in for William and Wilhelm. And in the final exchange, Berlin Ada's words merge with those of the "toothless" women:

> "Wir wollen das Armband zurück," sagte sie schließlich. Ihre Stimme war ruhig, ihre Hände streichelten ihren Bauch.
> "Bekommt ihr nicht. Das gehört jetzt uns."
> "Aber Sie wissen, wir werden das Armband zurückbekommen. Es dauert nicht mehr lange."
> "Bekommt ihr nicht. Ich habe keine Angst vor euch. Ihr seid zahnlos."
> "Wir sind vieles," erwiderte sie. "Aber niemals zahnlos. Niemals."
> (296)

> ["We want the bracelet," she said at last. Her voice was calm, her hands rubbing her belly.
> "You can't have it. It's ours now."
> "But you know we'll get it back. It won't take long now."
> "You will not. I'm not afraid of any of you. You have no teeth."
> "We are many things," she countered. "But we are never toothless. Never."] (310)

In this final declaration of "wir" (we), it's unclear whether the toothless maternal women of the village are meant or all the Adas together as a collective. And their declaration, "we are never toothless," should be understood figuratively, rather than literally. These female ancestors may be so old that they lack any teeth, but they are not powerless.

The novel's final chapter shows what happens after Herr Wilhelm's and Ada's consciousnesses have intertwined with their various past counterparts. Herr Wilhelm has had a heart attack, and Ada accompanies him to the hospital, where Cash comes to meet her, thinking she has gone into labor. Slightly embarrassed, she tries to explain to Cash why she was with Herr Wilhelm and why she feels responsible for this strange old man, whom she barely knows:

> "Er hat sich am Kopf verletzt. Jetzt redet er nur noch wirres Zeug."
> "Wirres Zeug?"
> "Er erzählte von Banketten und ertrunkenen Babys und … Ich weiß nicht. Ich habe Angst bekommen." (302)

> ["He hurt his head, and now he's talking nonsense."
> "Nonsense?"

> "He told me about some banquets and drowned babies and ... I
> don't even know. I got scared."] (316)

Things become even more confusing when a nurse informs Ada that Herr
Wilhelm called her his daughter. When Herr Wilhelm finally regains consciousness, and Ada questions him, he immediately speaks of the bracelet,
which he had given to the museum, and promises it to her. Ada is happy
at the prospect of returning the bracelet to the descendants of its original owners. After he is discharged, Ada and Herr Wilhelm set off for the
museum, but her water breaks in front of the hospital, so they immediately return.

In the epilogue directly thereafter, entitled "Mir. Wir" (Me. We), we
hear from Berlin Ada about her daughter's birth.[25] Not only has her child
been born safely, but she has managed to break the tragic cycle of the
Adas before her, because she can finally remember her pasts. And it is giving birth to a daughter that enables her to remember, which Ada is able
to articulate at the very end of the book. Holding her baby and seeing
her sister, Elle, asleep in her room, she states, "Denn endlich hatte ich
verstanden, wer ich bin.... ich [drehte] den Kopf und richtete meinen
Blick auf unseren Schatz" (317; "For I finally understood who I was.... I
turned my head and focused my eyes on our treasure," 331). Their treasure was the next generation; not the bracelet. And the baby girl is not
just Ada's treasure, she is *their* treasure. She belongs to Elle and all the
other mothers of their community.

Conclusion

In treating violence as something unavoidable, *Adas Raum* is arguably
about the inevitability of colonial violence, in the sense that these past
events have happened, and we cannot undo them—a common fantasy
in Afrofuturism. Instead of using time travel to undo the violent past,
Otoo's narrative encourages us to think about not just the past but all the
violent aftershocks of colonialism and to ponder how we can best move
toward reconciliation. Ada is ultimately a soul who needs to be made
whole again. Her murder at the hands of Guilherme can't be stopped; all
the *being* can do is accompany her in different forms and try to help her
remember. Part of the *being*'s task is to make different forms of violence
apparent to those around it; not just violence between races and ethnicities, but violence between men and women too. When it laments to God
that as a door knocker it couldn't save Ada from William's violence, it
could only alert her to William's presence, it exasperatedly asks, "Was soll
dann weiter gewesen sein? Ada hat William hineingelassen. Obwohl sie

---

25   This is possibly a reference to Mohammad Ali's poem "Me We" (1975).

das lieber nicht gemacht hätte" (229; "What else was there supposed to be? Ada let William in. Although it would have been better for her if she had not," 237). God's response is that of course, Ada couldn't escape William's violence, because as his wife in the sociohistorical context, "Selbstverständlich hatte er freien Zugang zu ihr!" (229; "Of course, he had open access to her!," 238).

In making these forms of violence evident, one can only hope another iteration of Ada will remember and be capable of better understanding her positionality in society, as well as having the capability of forgiving the perpetrators. It is because Ada not only remembers "William's" violence but also holds him accountable and forgives him that the novel is able to come to a positive ending. If Berlin Ada hadn't taken Herr Wilhelm to the hospital, not only would he have likely died, but her unborn daughter could have, too. Thus, there are several lessons we learn about violence by the end of the novel. First, violence motivated by race and gender has not just been a threat historically across time and space; it continues to be a threat, and it is a global problem. Second, the novel contends, white Germans frequently would rather discuss past violence (that is to say, the Holocaust) rather than contemporary violence, because discussing the past allows them to claim that it has been overcome (*bewältigt*), but past and present structural violence are always interlinked. Finally, in the vision of *Adas Raum*, Germans must recognize the continuation of violence and violent trends in order to achieve some form of reconciliation between perpetrators, victims, and descendants.

Selected Bibliography

Agamben, Giorgio. *Remnants of Auschwitz: The Witness and the Archive.* New York: Zone Books, 2000.

Ahmed, Sara. *The Cultural Politics of Emotion.* Edinburgh: Edinburgh University Press, 2014. First published 2004.

———. *Queer Phenomenology: Orientations, Objects, Others.* London: Duke University Press, 2006.

Alaimo, Stacy. *Bodily Natures: Science, Environment, and the Material Self.* Bloomington: Indiana University Press, 2010.

Anders, Günther. *Der Blick vom Mond: Reflexionen über Weltraumflüge.* Munich: C. H. Beck, 1994.

———. "Commandments in the Atomic Age." In Eatherly and Anders, *Burning Conscience,* 11–20.

———. *Hiroshima ist überall.* Munich: C. H. Beck, 1995.

———. *Ketzereien.* Munich: C. H. Beck, 1996.

———. "Reflections on the H Bomb." *Dissent* 3, no. 2 (1956): 146–55.

Aras, Maryam. "68, ein deutsches Unschuldsmoment." *Collateral: Online Journal for Cross-Cultural Close Reading* 70 (June 2021). http://collateral-journal.com/index.php?collision=70&fbclid=IwAR2k7Yr3fWmzlnxIl8mkztxbHxk9d3Keur5NUPZ1IUCt9IXNLpd8_g9zfyg.

Arendt, Hannah. "The Conquest of Space and the Stature of Man." *The New Atlantis,* no. 18 (2007): 43–55.

———. *On Revolution.* London: Penguin, 1963.

Åsberg, Cecilia. "Portmanteau Planetarity." *Dialogues in Human Geography* 12, no. 3 (November 1, 2022): 476–80. https://doi.org/10.1177/20438206221077151.

Austin, Jonathan Luke. "Posthumanism and Perpetrators." In *The Routledge International Handbook of Perpetrator Studies,* edited by Susanne C. Knittel and Zachary J. Goldberg, 169–80. London: Routledge, 2020.

Bajohr, Hannes. "Anthropocene and Negative Anthropology." *Public Seminar,* July 29, 2019. https://publicseminar.org/essays/anthropocene-and-negative-anthropology/.

Barad, Karen. "Diffracting Diffraction: Cutting Together-Apart." *Parallax* 20, no. 3 (2014): 168–87.

———. "Interview with Karen Barad." In *New Materialism: Interviews & Cartographies,* edited by Rick Dolphijn and Iris van der Tuin, 48–70. Ann Arbor, MI: Open Humanities Press, 2012.

———. *Meeting the Universe Halfway: Quantum Physics and the Entanglement of Meaning and Matter.* London: Duke University Press, 2007.

———. "Troubling time/s and ecologies of nothingness: re-turning, re-membering, and facing the incalculable." *New Formations: A Journal of Culture/Theory/Politics* 92, no. 92 (August 2018): 56–86.

Bartosch, Roman. "Scale, Climate Change, and the Pedagogic Potential of Literature: Scaling (in) the Work of Barbara Kingsolver and T. C. Boyle." *Open Library of Humanities* 4, no. 2 (2018): 1–21.

Baumann, Marc, Mauritius Much, Bastian Obermayer, and Franziska Storz, eds. *Feldpost: Briefe Deutscher Soldaten aus Afghanistan*. Reinbek: Rowohlt, 2011.

Bay, Hansjörg. "Migration, postheroisch: Zu Sherko Fatahs *Das dunkle Schiff*." In *Niemandsbuchten und Schutzbefohlene: Flucht-Räume und Flüchtlingsfiguren in der deutschsprachigen Gegenwartsliteratur*, edited by Thomas Hardtke, Johannes Klein, and Charlton Payne, 3–37. Göttingen: V&R unipress, 2017.

Beste, Ralf, Petra Bornhöft, Ulrich Deupmann, Horand Knaup, Hartmut Palmer, Gerhard Spörl, and Alexander Szandar. "Abmarsch in die Realität." *Der Spiegel*, November 11, 2001. https://www.spiegel.de/politik/abmarsch-in-die-realitaet-a-605b894c-0002-0001-0000-000020660098.

Bielby, Clare. "Gendering the Perpetrator; Gendering Perpetrator Studies." In *The Routledge International Handbook of Perpetrator Studies*, edited by Susanne C. Knittel and Zachary J. Goldberg, 155–68. London: Routledge, 2020.

———. "Narrating Violent Agency Elsewhere in Inge Viett's *Nie war ich furchtloser* (Never Was I More Fearless)." In Bielby and Davies, *Violence Elsewhere 1*, 149–73.

Bielby, Clare, and Mererid Puw Davies, eds. *Violence Elsewhere 1: Imagining Distant Violence in Germany 1945–2001*. Rochester, NY: Camden House, 2024.

Biser, Ashley. "Calibrating Our 'Inner Compass': Arendt on Thinking and the Dangers of Disorientation." *Political Theory* 42, no. 5 (2014): 519–42.

Bloom, Paul. *Against Empathy: The Case for Rational Compassion*. London: Penguin, 2016.

Bloxham, Donald. *The Great Game of Genocide: Imperialism, Nationalism, and the Destruction of the Ottoman Armenians*. Oxford: Oxford University Press, 2005.

Boltanski, Luc. *Distant Suffering: Morality, Media and Politics*, translated by Graham Burchell. Cambridge: Cambridge University Press, 1999.

Borchert, Semjon, and Martin Wengeler. "Friedensmission, kriegsähnliche Zustände oder Krieg? Öffentliche Sprachreflexion im Zusammenhang mit dem Einsatz der Bundeswehr in Afghanistan." In *Sprachvariation und Sprachreflexion in interkulturellen Kontexten*, edited by Corinna Peschel and Kerstin Runschke, 263–82. Frankfurt am Main: Peter Lang, 2015.

Braun, Rebecca. "Introduction: The Rise of the World Author from the Death of World Literature." In *World Authorship and German Literature*, edited by Rebecca Braun and Andrew Piper, special issue, *Seminar* 51, no. 2 (2015): 81–99.

Brockert, Anja. "Buchkritik: Angelika Klüssendorf—Vierunddreißigster September." *SWR2*, Literatur, August 31, 2021. https://www.swr.de/swr2/literatur/angelika-kluessendorf-vierunddreissigster-september-100.html.

Brody, Richard. "Luca Guadagnino's 'Suspiria' Is the Cinematic Equivalent of a Designer Che T-Shirt." *New Yorker*, October 30, 2018. https://www.newyorker.com/culture/the-front-row/review-luca-guadagninos-suspiria-is-the-cinematic-equivalent-of-a-designer-che-t-shirt.

Brummer, Klaus, and Stefan Fröhlich. "Einleitung: Zehn Jahre Deutschland in Afghanistan," edited by Klaus Brummer and Stefan Fröhlich. *Sonderheft der Zeitschrift für Außen- und Sicherheitspolitik: Zehn Jahre Deutschland in Afghanistan*, no. 3 (2011): 3–30.

Butler, Judith. *The Force of Nonviolence: An Ethico-Political Bind*. London: Verso, 2020.

Butler, Octavia. *Dawn: Xenogenesis*. New York: Warner Books, 1987.

———. *Kindred*. Boston: Beacon Press, 2013.

Çaylı, Eray. *Victims of Commemoration: The Architecture and Violence of Confronting the Past in Turkey*. Syracuse, NY: Syracuse University Press, 2023.

Clair, Johannes. *Vier Tage im November: Mein Kampfeinsatz in Afghanistan*. Berlin: Ullstein, 2012.

Clark, Nigel, and Bronislaw Szerszynski. *Planetary Social Thought: The Anthropocene Challenge to the Social Sciences*. Cambridge: Polity Press, 2021.

Clark, Timothy. *The Cambridge Introduction to Literature and the Environment*. Cambridge: Cambridge University Press, 2011.

———. *Ecocriticism on the Edge: The Anthropocene as a Threshold Concept*. London: Bloomsbury Academic, 2015.

Clarke, Michael Tavel, and David Wittenberg, eds. *Scale in Literature and Culture*. Cham, Switzerland: Palgrave Macmillan, 2017.

Clifford Mann, Robert. "German Warriors." In *Deutschland in Afghanistan*, edited by Michael Daxner, 139–53. Oldenburg: BIS-Verlag, 2014.

Collins, Patricia Hill. *Black Feminist Thought*. New York: Routledge, 2000.

Colvin, Sarah. "Freedom Time: Temporal Insurrections in Olivia Wenzel's *1000 Serpentinen Angst* and Sharon Dodua Otoo's *Adas Raum*." *German Life and Letters* 75, no. 1 (2022): 138–65.

———. "Talking Back: Sharon Dodua Otoo's *Herr Gröttrup setzt sich hin* and the Epistemology of Resistance." *German Life and Letters* 73, no. 4 (2020): 659–79.

Damrosch, David. *What Is World Literature?* Princeton, NJ: Princeton University Press, 2003.

Davies, Luke Lewin. "Appropriating the Abject: Witchcraft in Dario Argento and Daria Nicolodi's *Suspiria* (1977) and David Kajganich and Luca Guadagnino's 2018 Remake." *New Cinemas* 18, no 1–2 (2020): 43–59.

Davis, Heather, and Zoe Todd. "On the Importance of a Date, or, Decolonizing the Anthropocene." *ACME: An International Journal for Critical Geographies* 16, no. 4 (December 20, 2017): 761–80.

Daxner, Michael. "Heimatdiskurs—ein deutsches Problem?" In *Heimatdiskurs: Wie die Auslandseinsätze der Bundeswehr Deutschland verändern*, edited by Michael Daxner and Hannah Neumann, 15–68. Bielefeld: transcript, 2012.

Delehanty, Ann T., and Tyler Blakeney. "Textual Engagement with the Other in Cyrano de Bergerac's *L'Autre Monde*." *French Studies* 68, no. 3 (2014): 313–27.

Deleuze, Gilles, and Félix Guattari. *A Thousand Plateaus*, translated by Brian Massumi. London: Bloomsbury, 2013.

Demmer, Ulrike, Markus Feldenkirchen, Ullrich Fichtner, et al. "Ein deutsches Verbrechen." *Der Spiegel* (October 6, 2016). https://www.spiegel.de/spiegel/kunduz-bombardement-ein-deutsches-verbrechen-a-1115445.html.

Der Meguerditchian, Silvina, ed. *Silvina Der Meguerditchian: Fruitful Threads*. Vienna: Verlag für moderne Kunst, 2020.

Deutscher Bundestag. "Der Afghanistan-Einsatz 2001–2021: Eine sicherheitspolitische Chronologie." Wissenschaftliche Dienste, January 20, 2022. https://www.bundestag.de/resource/blob/881198/27fd4f597e1d4ee43350aafffc6f9d8c/WD-2-062-21-pdf-data.pdf.

———. "Plenarprotokoll 14/210," December 22, 2001. https://dserver.bundestag.de/btp/14/14210.pdf.

Dimock, Wai Chee. "Low Epic." *Critical Inquiry* 39, no. 3 (2013): 614–31.

Eatherly, Claude, and Günther Anders. *Burning Conscience: The Case of the Hiroshima Pilot, Claude Eatherly, Told in His Letters to Gunther Anders*. New York: Monthly Review Press, 1962.

Ebert, Jens. "Ein Gefallen für die Bundeswehr." In *Attitudes to War: Literatur und Film von Shakespeare bis Afghanistan*, edited by Claudia Glunz and Thomas F. Schneider, 139–42. Göttingen: V&R unipress, 2012.

Eigler, Friederike. *Gedächtnis und Geschichte in Generationenromanen seit der Wende*. Berlin: Erich Schmidt, 2005.

El-Kaddouri, Warda. "'Gott, rette mich aus der Lehre!' Verlust, Religiosität und Radikalisierung in den Fluchtnarrativen von Abbas Khider und Sherko Fatah." In *Niemandsbuchten und Schutzbefohlene: Flucht-Räume und Flüchtlingsfiguren in der deutschsprachigen Gegenwartsliteratur*, edited by Thomas Hardtke, Johannes Klein, and Charlton Payne, 39–51. Göttingen: V&R unipress, 2017.

Fachinger, Petra. "Fatal (In)Tolerance?: The Portrayal of Radical Islamists in Recent German Literature and Film." *Seminar: A Journal of Germanic Studies* 4, no. 5 (2011): 646–60.

Fatah, Sherko. *Das dunkle Schiff*. Munich: btb, 2010. First published 2008. Translated by Martin Chalmers as *The Dark Ship*. Kolkata: Seagull Books, 2015.

———. *Der letzte Ort*. Munich: btb, 2016.

Ferdinand, Malcom. *A Decolonial Ecology: Thinking from the Caribbean World*, translated by Anthony Paul Smith. Cambridge: Polity Press, 2022.

Florvil, Tiffany. *Mobilizing Black Germany: Afro-German Women and the Making of a Transnational Movement*. Urbana: University of Illinois Press, 2020.

Frank, Michael C. "'Why do they hate us?' Terrorists in American and British Fiction of the Mid-2000." In *Terrorism and Literature*, edited by Peter C. Herman, 340–60. Cambridge: Cambridge University Press, 2018.

Galtung, Johan. "Violence, Peace, and Peace Research." *Journal of Peace Research* 6, no. 3 (1969): 167–91.

Gauthier Tim. *9/11 Fiction, Empathy, and Otherness*. Lanham, MD: Lexington Books, 2015.

Gilman, Charlotte Perkins. *Herland and Selected Stories*. New York: Penguin, 2014.

Gordon, Philip H. "Berlin's Difficulties: The Normalization of German Foreign Policy." *Orbis* 38, no. 2 (1994): 225–42.

Göttsche, Dirk. *Remembering Africa: The Rediscovery of Colonialism in Contemporary German Literature*. Rochester, NY: Camden House, 2013.

Gottschlich, Jürgen. *Beihilfe zum Völkermord: Deutschlands Rolle bei der Vernichtung der Armenier*. Bonn: bpb, 2015.

Green, Louise. *Fragments from the History of Loss: The Nature Industry and the Postcolony*. University Park: Pennsylvania State University Press, 2020.

Grünbein, Durs. "Brief über Cyrano." *Suhrkamp Logbuch* (blog). https://www.logbuch-suhrkamp.de/durs-gruenbein/brief-ueber-cyrano/.

———. *Cyrano oder Die Rückkehr vom Mond*. Berlin: Suhrkamp, 2014.

Gül Altınay, Ayşe, et al., eds. *Women Mobilizing Memory*. New York: Columbia University Press, 2019.

Gutiérrez Rodríguez, Encarnación. "Entangled Migrations: The Coloniality of Migration and Creolizing Conviviality." *Mecila Working Paper Series* 35 (2021): 1–25.

Hamann, Christof. *Usambara*. Göttingen: Steidl, 2007.

Hamann, Christof, and Alexander Honold. *Kilimandscharo: Die deutsche Geschichte eines afrikanischen Berges*. Berlin: Wagenbach, 2011.

Haraway, Donna. *Modest_Witness@Second_Millennium: FemaleMan_Meets_OncoMouse; Feminism and Technoscience*. London: Routledge, 1997.

———. "The Promises of Monsters: A Regenerative Politics for Inappropriate/d Others." In *Cultural Studies*, edited by Lawrence Grossberg, Cary Nelson, and Paula A. Treichler, 295–336. New York: Routledge, Taylor & Francis, 1992.

———. "Situated Knowledges: The Science Question in Feminism and the Privilege of Partial Perspective." *Feminist Studies* 14, no. 3 (1988): 575–99.

———. *Staying with the Trouble: Making Kin in the Chthulucene*. London: Duke University Press, 2016.

Harbin, Ami. "Bodily Disorientation and Moral Change." *Hypatia* 27, no. 2 (Spring 2012): 261–80.

Harman, Graham. *Object-Oriented Ontology: A New Theory of Everything.* London: Pelican, 2018.

Harrison, Peter. "Descartes on Animals." *Philosophical Quarterly* 42, no. 167 (1992): 219–27.

Hilal, Moshtari, and Sinthujan Varatharajah. "Gespräch über Nazierbe," Instagram Live: https://www.instagram.com/tv/CLU2dZiqvMG/?igshid =YmMyMTA2M2Y%3D.

Hopkins, Pauline. *Of One Blood, or the Hidden Self.* New York: Washington Square Press, 2004. First published 1902.

Jackson, Richard. "Sympathy for the Devil: Evil, Taboo, and the Terrorist Figure in Literature." In *Terrorism and Literature,* edited by Peter C. Herman, 377–94. Cambridge: Cambridge University Press, 2018.

Jacobi, Daniel, Gunther Hellmann, and Sebastian Nieke. "Deutschlands Verteidigung am Hindukusch: Ein Fall misslingender Sicherheitskommunikation." *Sonderheft der Zeitschrift für Außen- und Sicherheitspolitik: Zehn Jahre Deutschland in Afghanistan,* no. 3 (2011): 171–96.

Jeremiah, Emily. *Nomadic Ethics in Contemporary Women's Writing in German: Strange Subjects.* Rochester, NY: Camden House, 2012.

Kadir, Djelal. "World Literature: The Allophone, the Differential, and the Common." *Modern Language Quarterly* 74, no. 2 (June 2013): 293–306.

Kajganich, David. "'Suspiria' Screenwriter Explains That Wild Ending and Why Dakota Johnson Is a New Kind of Final Girl." *IndieWire,* November 7, 2018. https://www.indiewire.com/2018/11/suspiria-screenwriter-explains-wild-ending-spoilers-ideas-for-sequel-1202018427/.

Karcher, Katharina, and Evelien Geerts. "Problematizing Political Violence in the Federal Republic of Germany: A Hauntological Analysis of the NSU Terror and a Hyper-Exceptionalized '9/11.'" In Bielby and Davies, *Violence Elsewhere 1,* 174–95.

Kaya, Ayhan. "Turkish *Vergangenheitsbewältigung:* The Unbearable Burden of the Past." In *Replicating Atonement: Foreign Models in the Commemoration of Atrocities,* edited by Mischa Gabowitsch, 99–130. Cham, Switzerland: Palgrave Macmillan, 2017.

Kiedaisch, Petra, ed. *Lyrik nach Auschwitz? Adorno und die Dichter.* Stuttgart: Reclam, 1995.

Knelangen, Wilhelm. "Die deutsche Reaktion auf 9/11: Eine 'neue' Politik der Terrorismusbekämpfung?" In *Zeitenwende 9/11? Eine transatlantische Bilanz,* edited by Till Karmann, Simon Wendt, Tobias Endler, and Martin Thunert, 87–114. Opladen: Verlag Barbara Budrich, 2016.

Konuk, Kader. "Genozid als transnationales historisches Erbe? Literatur im Kontext türkischer und deutscher Geschichte." In *Gegenwart schreiben: Zur deutschsprachigen Literatur 2000–2015,* edited by Corina Caduff and Ulrike Vedder, 165–75. Paderborn: Wilhelm Fink, 2017.

Latour, Bruno. "Agency at the Time of the Anthropocene." *New Literary History* 45, no. 1 (2014): 1–18.

————. *Reassembling the Social: An Introduction to Actor-Network-Theory.* Clarendon Lectures in Management Studies. Oxford: Oxford University Press, 2007.

MacLeish, Archibald. "Voyage to the Moon." *New York Times,* July 21, 1969.

Malm, Andreas, and Alf Hornborg. "The Geology of Mankind? A Critique of the Anthropocene Narrative." *Anthropocene Review* 1, no. 1 (April 1, 2014): 62–69.

March-Russell, Paul. *The Short Story: An Introduction.* Edinburgh: Edinburgh University Press, 2009.

Marven, Lyn. "Introduction: New German-Language Writing since the Turn of the Millennium." In Marven and Taberner, *Emerging German-Language Novelists of the Twenty-First Century,* 1–16.

————. "Trends and Issues in the Contemporary German-Language Short Story." In Marven, Plowman, and Roy, *The Short Story in German in the Twenty-First Century,* 272–90.

Marven, Lyn, Andrew Plowman, and Kate Roy, eds. *The Short Story in German in the Twenty-First Century.* Rochester, NY: Camden House, 2020.

————. "Introduction to the Contemporary Short Story in German." In Marven, Plowman, and Roy, *The Short Story in German in the Twenty-First Century,* 1–16.

Marven, Lyn, and Stuart Taberner, eds. *Emerging German-Language Novelists of the Twenty-First Century.* Rochester, NY: Camden House, 2011.

März, Ursula. "Heimatromane: Auf einmal Heimat." *Die Zeit,* no. 44 (2017). Available at *Zeit Online,* October 25, 2017, updated October 31, 2017. http://www.zeit.de/2017/44/heimatromane-dorf-renaissance-literatur.

Matthes, Frauke. "Clemens Meyer, *Als wir träumten*: Fighting 'Like a Man' in Leipzig's East." In Marven and Taberner, *Emerging German-Language Novelists of the Twenty-First Century,* 89–104.

————. *New Masculinities in Contemporary German Literature: From "Native" to Transnational.* Cham, Switzerland: Palgrave Macmillan, 2023.

————. "'A Saxon Who's Learnt a Lot from the Americans': Clemens Meyer in a Transnational Literary Context." *Comparative Critical Studies* 15, no. 1 (2018): 25–45.

————. "'Weltliteratur aus der Uckermark': Regionalism and Transnationalism in Saša Stanišić's *Vor dem Fest.*" In *German in the World: The Transnational and Global Contexts of German Studies,* edited by James Hodkinson and Benedict Schofield, 91–108. Rochester, NY: Camden House, 2020.

————. *Writing and Muslim Identity: Representations of Islam in German and English Transcultural Literature, 1990–2006.* London: Institute of Germanic & Romance Studies, 2011.

May, Charles E. *The Short Story: The Reality of Artifice.* New York: Twayne, 1995.

Mbembe, Achille. *Necropolitics.* Durham, NC: Duke University Press, 2019.

McGurl, Mark. "Critical Response II—'Neither Indeed Could I Forebear Smiling at My Self': A Reply to Wai Chee Dimock," *Critical Inquiry* 39, no. 3 (2013): 632–38.

Meyer, Clemens. *Als wir träumten: Roman*. Frankfurt am Main: S. Fischer, 2006. Translated by Katy Derbyshire as *While We Were Dreaming*. London: Fitzcarraldo Editions, 2023.

———. *Gewalten: Ein Tagebuch*. Frankfurt am Main: S. Fischer, 2010.

———. *Im Stein: Roman*. Frankfurt am Main: S. Fischer, 2013. Translated by Katy Derbyshire as *Bricks and Mortar*. London: Fitzcarraldo Editions, 2016.

———. *Die Nacht, die Lichter: Stories*. Frankfurt am Main: S. Fischer, 2008. Translated by Katy Derbyshire as *All the Lights*. Introduced by Stuart Evers. High Wycombe, UK: And Other Stories, 2011.

———. *Nacht im Bioskop*. Leipzig: Faber & Faber, 2020.

———. *Stäube: Drei Erzählungen und ein Nachsatz*. Leipzig: Faber & Faber, 2021.

———. *Die stillen Trabanten: Erzählungen*. Frankfurt am Main: S. Fischer, 2017. Translated by Katy Derbyshire as *Dark Satellites*. London: Fitzcarraldo Editions, 2020.

———. *Die Projektoren: Roman*. Frankfurt am Main: S. Fischer, forthcoming 2024.

Minh-ha, Trinh T. *elsewhere, within here: immigration, refugeeism, and the boundary event*. New York: Routledge, 2011.

Müller, Christopher. "Desert Ethics: Technology and the Question of Evil in Günther Anders and Jacques Derrida." *Parallax* 21, no. 1 (January 2, 2015): 42–57. https://doi.org/10.1080/13534645.2014.988910.

Navaro, Yael, et al., eds. *Reverberations: Violence across Time and Space*. Philadelphia: University of Pennsylvania Press, 2021.

Nesselhauf, Jonas. "Zur Lyrischen Inszenierung 'natürlicher Heimat.'" *Kulturwissenschaftliche Zeitschrift* 5, no. 1 (October 1, 2020): 77–90.

Nixon, Rob. *Slow Violence and the Environmentalism of the Poor*. Cambridge, MA: Harvard University Press, 2011.

Noetzel, Timo. "The German Politics of War: Kunduz and the War in Afghanistan." *International Affairs* 87, no. 2 (2011): 397–417.

Nussbaum, Martha. *Political Emotions: Why Love Matters for Justice*. Cambridge, MA: Belknap Press of Harvard University Press, 2013.

O'Connor, Frank. *The Lonely Voice: A Study of the Short Story*. Cleveland: World, 1963.

Oppermann, Kai. "Der 11. September 2001 und die Normalisierung der deutschen Außenpolitik." In *Zeitenwende 9/11? Eine transatlantische Bilanz*, edited by Till Karmann, Simon Wendt, Tobias Endler, and Martin Thunert, 115–42. Opladen: Verlag Barbara Budrich, 2016.

Otoo, Sharon Dodua. *Adas Raum: Ein Roman*. Frankfurt am Main: S. Fischer, 2021. Translated by Jon Cho-Polizzi as *Ada's Realm*. New York: Riverhead Books, 2023.

Patea, Viorica. "The Short Story: An Overview of the History and Evolution of the Genre." In *Short Story Theories: A Twenty-First-Century Perspective*, edited by Viorica Patea, 1–24. Amsterdam: Rodopi, 2012.

Pitts, Michael. *Alternative Masculinities in Feminist Speculative Fiction: A New Man*. London: Rowman and Littlefield, 2021.

Plowman, Andrew. "Afghanistan, Soldiers' Experiences and Literary Invention in Dirk Kurbjuweit's *Kriegsbraut* (2011) and Norbert Scheuer's *Die Sprache Der Vögel* (2015)." *Oxford German Studies* 47, no. 4 (2018): 523–40.

———. "The Return of the Military Memoir: The Bundeswehr Deployment to Afghanistan and the Re-Emergence of a Literary Form." *Modern Languages Open* 1 (2020): 1–19.

Poole, Robert. *Earthrise: How Man First Saw the Earth*. New Haven, CT: Yale University Press, 2008.

Pratt, Mary Louise. "The Short Story: The Long and the Short of It." In *The New Short Story Theories*, edited by Charles E. May, 91–113. Athens: Ohio University Press, 1994.

Pye, Gillian. "The Liminal Space of the Short Story: Clemens Meyer's *Die Nacht, die Lichter* and *Die stillen Trabanten*." In Marven, Plowman, and Roy, *The Short Story in German in the Twenty-First Century*, 118–36.

Reinecke, Stefan. "Krieg ohne Hitler." *taz*, November 8, 2001. https://taz.de/!1142096/.

Reinhäckel, Heide. *Traumatische Texturen: Der 11. September in der deutschsprachigen Gegenwartsliteratur*. Bielefeld: transcript, 2012.

Reiter, Margit. "'Uneingeschränkte Solidarität'? Wahrnehmungen und Deutungen des 11. September in Deutschland." In *Europa und der 11. September 2001*, edited by Margit Reiter and Helga Embacher, 43–75. Vienna: Böhlau, 2011.

Remarque, Erich Maria. *Im Westen nichts Neues*. Cologne: Kiepenheuer & Witsch, 1997. First published 1929. Translated by Brian Murdoch as *All Quiet on the Western Front*. London: Vintage, 2005.

Rife, Katie. "Jessica Harper and screenwriter David Kajganich on the politics of *Suspiria*." *The A.V. Club*, November 5, 2018. https://www.avclub.com/jessica-harper-and-screenwriter-david-kajganich-on-the-1830191488.

Rothberg, Michael. *The Implicated Subject: Beyond Victims and Perpetrators*. Stanford, CA: Stanford University Press, 2019.

———. *Multidirectional Memory: Remembering the Holocaust in the Age of Decolonization*. Stanford, CA: Stanford University Press, 2009.

Sanders, Mark. *Complicities: The Intellectual and Apartheid*. Durham, NC: Duke University Press, 2002.

Santilli, Paul. "Marx on Species-Being and Social Essence." *Studies in Soviet Thought* 13, no. 1/2 (1973): 76–88.

Sanyal, Debarati. *Memory and Complicity: Migrations of Holocaust Remembrance*. New York: Fordham University Press, 2015.

Scheuer, Norbert. *Die Sprache der Vögel*. Munich: Fischer Taschenbuch, 2016. Translated by Stephen Brown as *The Language of Birds*. London: Haus, 2018.

Schmidt, Matthias. "Aus Anger-Crottendorf in die Welt: Angekommen in der 'Scheiß-Literatur'—Clemens Meyer wird 40." *MDR Kultur*, August 17, 2017. https://www.mdr.de/kultur/literatur/clemens-meyer-geburtstag-vierzig-jahre-leipzig-100.html (URL no longer available).

Schuyler, George. *Black No More*. New York: Modern Library, 1999. First published 1931.

Skiveren, Tobias. "Fictionality in New Materialism: (Re)Inventing Matter." *Theory, Culture & Society* 39, no. 3 (2022): 187–202.

Slobodian, Quinn. *Foreign Front: Third World Politics in Sixties West Germany*. Durham, NC: Duke University Press, 2012.

Slote, Michael. *The Ethics of Care and Empathy*. Oxford: Routledge, 2007.

Sontag, Susan. *Regarding the Pain of Others*. London: Penguin, 2003.

Spillers, Hortense. "Mama's Baby, Papa's Maybe: An American Grammar Book." *Diacritics* 17, no. 2 (Summer 1987): 64–81.

Spivak, Gayatri Chakravorty. "Can the Subaltern Speak?" In *Marxism and the Interpretation of Culture*, 271–313. Basingstoke, UK: Macmillan Education, 1988.

———. *Death of a Discipline*. Wellek Library Lecture Series at the University of California, Irvine. New York: Columbia University Press, 2003.

Stone, Katherine. "Projecting Violence Elsewhere: Remembering Conflict-Related Sexual Violence in Cold War Germany." In Bielby and Davies, *Violence Elsewhere 1*, 18–37.

Taylor, Keeanga-Yamahtta. *How We Get Free: Black Feminism and the Combahee River Collective*. Chicago: Haymarket Books, 2017.

Tepper, Sheri S. *The Gate to Women's Country*. New York: Bantam, 1989.

Thomsen, Mads Rosendahl. *Mapping World Literature: International Canonization and Transnational Literatures*. London: Continuum 2010. First published 2008.

Tudor, Alyosxa. "Cross-Fadings of Racialisation and Migratisation: The Postcolonial Turn in Western European Gender and Migration Studies." *Gender, Place and Culture* 25, no. 7 (2018): 1057–72.

Utlu, Deniz. "Empathische Solidarität: Gegenwartsbewältigung als Emanzipation." *Jalta: Positionen zur jüdischen Gegenwart* 4, no. 2 (2018): 65–72.

Von Bieberstein, Alice. "Not a German Past to be Reckoned With: Negotiating Migrant Subjectivities between *Vergangenheitsbewältigung* and the Nationalization of History." *Journal of the Royal Anthropological Institute* 22, no. 4 (2016): 902–19.

Walkowitz, Rebecca L. *Born Translated: The Contemporary Novel in an Age of World Literature*. Columbia University Press: New York, 2017. First published 2015.

Weigel, Sigrid. *Genea-Logik: Generation, Tradition und Evolution zwischen Kultur- und Naturwissenschaften*. München: W. Fink, 2006.

White, Frank. *The Overview Effect: Space Exploration and Human Evolution.* Reston, VA: American Institute of Aeronautics and Astronautics, 1998.

Widmann, Arno. "Der Er ist der Mond, auch wird er bewohnt." *Frankfurter Rundschau,* September 15, 2014. https://www.fr.de/kultur/literatur/mond-auch-wird-bewohnt-11647579.html.

Wiegold, Thomas. "Der Bundeswehreinsatz in Afghanistan." Bundeszentrale für politische Bildung. https://www.bpb.de/themen/militaer/deutsche-verteidigungspolitik/238332/der-bundeswehreinsatz-in-afghanistan/.

Willeke, Stephanie. *Grenzfall Krieg: Zur Darstellung der neuen Kriege nach 9/11 in der deutschsprachigen Gegenwartsliteratur.* Bielefeld: transcript, 2018.

Wolting, Monika. *Der neue Kriegsroman: Repräsentationen des Afghanistankriegs in der deutschen Gegenwartsliteratur.* Heidelberg: Universitätsverlag Winter, 2019.

Zehfuss, Maja. *Wounds of Memory: The Politics of War in Germany.* Cambridge: Cambridge University Press, 2007.

Zylinska, Joanna. *Minimal Ethics for the Anthropocene.* Ann Arbor, MI: Open Humanities Press, 2014.

Contributors

CLARE BIELBY is senior lecturer in the Centre for Women's Studies, University of York. She has published widely on the subject of gender, violence, and (self-)representation with a focus on the postwar culture of the Federal Republic of Germany. With Mererid Puw Davies, Clare coedited a companion to this volume, *Violence Elsewhere 1: Imagining Distant Violence in Germany 1945–2001* (Rochester, NY: Camden House, 2024). Clare is the author of *Violent Women in Print: Representations in the West German Media of the 1960s and 1970s* (Rochester, NY: Camden House, 2012) and coeditor (with Jeffrey Murer) of *Perpetrating Selves: Doing Violence, Performing Identity* (London: Palgrave, 2018), and (with Anna Richards) *Women and Death 3: Women's Representations of Death in German Culture since 1500* (Rochester, NY: Camden House, 2010). Together with Davies, she was principal investigator on the research project "Violence Elsewhere: Imagining Violence outside Germany since 1945," which was funded by the German Academic Exchange Service and out of which the present volume emerged.

MERERID PUW DAVIES is professor of German studies at University College London. She has published widely on modern German-language literature, film, and culture, and with Clare Bielby, coedited a companion to this volume, *Violence Elsewhere 1: Imagining Distant Violence in Germany, 1945–2001* (Rochester, NY: Camden House, 2024). She has also coedited two further volumes of scholarly essays and is the author of three monographs, among other publications. Her interests include fairy tales, the culture and literature of the 1960s protest movements and their aftermaths in West Germany, and comparative studies. Together with Clare Bielby, she was principal investigator on the research project "Violence Elsewhere: Imagining Violence outside Germany since 1945," which was funded by the German Academic Exchange Service and out of which the present volume emerged.

SOFÍA FORCHIERI is a PhD candidate at Radboud University Nijmegen, the Netherlands. She obtained her degrees in comparative literature from Goethe University Frankfurt (BA, 2017) and Utrecht University (MA, 2020). Sofía's PhD project explores how contemporary Latin American women writers are opening up new ways of remembering and understanding feminicide, the killing of women because of their gender. Her areas of interest include cultural memory studies, complicity studies, and decolonial feminisms, with particular interest in the relation between aesthetics, affects, and politics. Her work has appeared in *Memory Studies, Frame: Journal of Literary Studies, Journal of Perpetrator Research*, and the edited volume *Afectos y violencias en la cultura latinoamericana* (Madrid: Iberoamericana, 2022). Sofía's doctoral research has involved research stays at the University of California, Los Angeles; Universidad de Alcalá (Spain); and Universidad de Buenos Aires (Argentina).

SUSANNE C. KNITTEL is associate professor of comparative literature at Utrecht University in the Netherlands. In her research, she explores how societies remember atrocities, specifically how they deal with questions of guilt, complicity, and responsibility. Her current ERC consolidator project, "Ecologies of Violence: Crimes against Nature in the Contemporary Cultural Imagination," explores the intersections of colonialism, genocide, and ecocide. She is the author of *The Historical Uncanny: Disability, Ethnicity, and the Politics of Holocaust Memory* (New York: Fordham University Press, 2015) and the editor, with Zachary Goldberg, of *The Routledge International Handbook of Perpetrator Studies* (London: Routledge, 2020). She is the founder of the Perpetrator Studies Network and editor in chief of *JPR: The Journal of Perpetrator Research*.

MARIE KOLKENBROCK holds a PhD from the University of Cambridge (2014) and is a Branco Weiss Fellow in the Department of Languages, Literatures and Cultures at King's College London. Her monograph *Stereotype and Destiny in Arthur Schnitzler's Prose* was published with Bloomsbury (London) in 2018. She coedited the volume *The Politics and Poetics of Refusal: Towards a Theory of Primary Rejection*, a special issue of *German Life and Letters* (2021), with Andreas Gehrlach. Marie's current project is concerned with ideals of cultivated interpersonal and emotional distance in conceptualizations of the public sphere of the twentieth and twenty-first centuries. Her research has always been informed by an interest in the ways psyche, society, and culture are inextricably linked and mutually constitutive to one another. More recently, this interest has led Marie to explore these themes also from a clinical perspective: she is currently undergoing training as an integrative psychotherapist at the Minster Centre in London.

PRISCILLA LAYNE is professor of German and director of the Center for European Studies at the University of North Carolina at Chapel Hill. She is also adjunct associate professor of African diaspora studies. Her book, *White Rebels in Black: German Appropriation of Black Popular Culture*, was published in 2018 by the University of Michigan Press. Priscilla has also published essays on Turkish German culture, translation, punk, and film. In addition to her research and teaching, she is a published translator. She has translated Olivia Wenzel's debut novel, *1000 Coils of Fear* (New York: Catapult, 2022), and Sam Meffire's autobiography, *Sam: The German, the Officer, the Man* (London: Dialogue Books, 2023). She translated Birgit Weyhe's graphic novel, based on Layne's life, *Rude Girl* (Berlin: Avant-Verlag, 2022). Priscilla is currently finishing a manuscript on Afro-German Afrofuturism and a critical guide to Rainer Werner Fassbinder's film *The Marriage of Maria Braun* (1979).

JOANNE LEAL is professor of German studies at Birkbeck, University of London. She undertakes research primarily in the area of twentieth- and twenty-first-century German literature and film. Joanne works on gender and sexuality in film and literature and on the representation of social issues in the contemporary German novel, including migration and social exclusion. She is also interested in constructions of the family in literature, film, and other visual media. Publications include the volumes *Wim Wenders and Peter Handke: Collaboration, Adaptation, Recomposition* (Amsterdam: Rodopi, 2011), with Martin Brady, and *Picturing the Family: Media, Narrative, Memory* (London: Bloomsbury, 2018), coedited with Silke Arnold-de Simine.

FRANCESCA LEWIS is lecturer in women's studies at the University of York, where she obtained her PhD. Her doctoral work explores borderline onto-epistemology from a feminist neuroqueer materialist perspective. She is cofounder (with Veronica Heney) of the Mad Feeling Collective, an interdisciplinary research collective that brings lived experience and affect-led approaches to explorations of madness on TV. She was research project coordinator on the "Violence Elsewhere" research project. Her writing has appeared in the *Journal of Psychosocial Studies* special issue on borderline personality disorder, and her work on film/TV will appear in forthcoming edited collections published by Bloomsbury Academic and Routledge.

FRAUKE MATTHES is senior lecturer in German at the University of Edinburgh. Her research focuses on contemporary German-language writing, transnational and world literature, and masculinity studies. Publications include the monographs *Writing and Muslim Identity: Representations of Islam in German and English Transcultural Literature, 1990–2006* (London: igrs books, 2011) and *New Masculinities in Contemporary German Literature: From "Native" to Transnational* (Cham, Switzerland: Palgrave Macmillan, 2023); and *Ethical Approaches in Contemporary German-Language Literature and Culture*, Edinburgh German Yearbook, vol. 7 (Rochester, NY: Camden House, 2013), coedited with Emily Jeremiah; *Emine Sevgi Özdamar at 70, Oxford German Studies* special issue (2016), coedited with Lizzie Stewart; and *Politics and Culture in Germany and Austria Today*, Edinburgh German Yearbook, vol. 14 (Rochester, NY: Camden House, 2021), coedited with Dora Osborne, Katya Krylova, and Myrto Aspioti.

Lizzie Stewart is senior lecturer in modern languages, culture, and society at King's College London. Her research attends to cultural production in contexts of migration, with a focus on political theater and performance. She was a member of the Core Group of scholars on the "Violence Elsewhere" research project. Further work by Lizzie that connects to the ideas of "violence elsewhere" includes the conclusion of her first book, *Performing New German Realities: Turkish-German Scripts of Postmigration* (Cham, Switzerland: Palgrave Macmillan, 2021), as well as her contributions to *Die Filme Fatih Akins* (Paderborn: Wilhelm Fink, 2021), *Gegenwartsliteratur: Ein germanistisches Jahrbuch* (2018), and the *Journal of Aesthetics & Culture* (2017).

Nicola Thomas is lecturer in German studies at Lancaster University. Her research focuses on twentieth-century and contemporary poetry and theory, and she is interested in place and time across geographical and linguistic boundaries, including the multiple meanings of extraterrestrial space in the context of environmental crisis. She is the author of *Space, Place and Poetry in English and German 1960–1975* (Cham, Switzerland: Palgrave Macmillan, 2018). She is currently leading two British Academy-funded projects that address questions of time and temporality in the Anthropocene in comparative contexts.

Kathrin Wunderlich completed her PhD in German studies at the University of Cambridge in 2022. Her thesis, from which this chapter is excerpted, focuses on German literary representations of the wars in Kosovo, Afghanistan, and Iraq and the 9/11 terrorist attacks; and considers the impact of violence elsewhere on Germany's processes of "normalization" after unification. Kathrin is particularly interested in the various ways in which "normalizations" articulate themselves in and shape politics, society, and culture; and how discourses on memory and violence correlate with and alter one another. From 2019 until 2021 she served as research project coordinator on the "Violence Elsewhere" research project.

Index

Printed and bound by CPI Group (UK) Ltd, Croydon, CR0 4YY

29/10/2024

14582699-0001